CRITICAL ISSUES IN INFORMATION SYSTEMS RESEARCH

John Wiley
INFORMATION SYSTEMS SERIES

Editors

Richard Boland
University of Illinois at Urbana-Champaign

Rudy Hirschheim
Oxford University

CRITICAL ISSUES IN INFORMATION SYSTEMS RESEARCH

Edited by

R. J. Boland, Jr.

Department of Accountancy,
University of Illinois at Urbana-Champaign

R. A. Hirschheim

Templeton College,
Oxford University

 *John Wiley*
INFORMATION SYSTEMS SERIES

JOHN WILEY & SONS
Chichester · New York · Brisbane · Toronto · Singapore

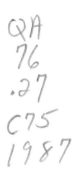

Library of Congress Cataloging in Publication Data:

Main entry under title:

Critical issues in information systems research.

  (John Wiley information systems series)
  I. Boland, Richard J.   II. Hirschheim, R. A. (Rudy A.)
  III. Series.
  QA76.27.C75   1987   004'.072   86–19049

ISBN 0 471 91281 6

British Library Cataloguing in Publication Data:

Critical issues in information systems research—
  (John Wiley information systems series)
  1. Electronic data processing—Research
  I. Boland, R. J.   II. Hirschheim, R. A.
  001.5'072   QA76.27

ISBN 0 471 91281 6

Phototypeset by Dobbie Typesetting Service, Plymouth, Devon.
Printed in Great Britain by Bath Press, Avon.

To

Nora and Sally

Series Foreword

In order for all types of organizations to succeed, they need to be able to process data and use information effectively. This has become especially true in today's rapidly changing environment. In conducting their day-to-day operations, organizations use information for functions such as planning, controlling, organizing, and decision making. Information, therefore, is unquestionably a critical resource in the operation of all organizations. Any means, mechanical or otherwise, which can help organizations process and manage information presents an opportunity they can ill afford to ignore.

The arrival of the computer and its use in data processing has been one of the most important organizational innovations in the past thirty years. The advent of computer-based data processing and information systems has led to organizations being able to cope with the vast quantities of information which they need to process and manage to survive. The field which has emerged to study this development is *information systems* (IS). It is a combination of two primary fields: computer science and management, with a host of supporting disciplines, e.g. psychology, sociology, statistics, political science, economics, philosophy, and mathematics. IS is concerned not only with the development of new information technologies but also with questions such as: how they can best be applied, how they should be managed, and what their wider implications are.

Partly because of the dynamic world in which we live (and the concomitant need to process more information), and partly because of the dramatic recent developments in information technology, e.g. personal computers, fourth-generation languages, relational databases, knowledge-based systems, and office automation, the relevance and importance of the field of information systems has become apparent. End users, who previously had little potential of becoming seriously involved and knowledgeable in information technology and systems, are now much more aware of and interested in the new technology. Individuals working in today's and tomorrow's organizations will be expected to have some understanding of and the ability to use the rapidly developing information technologies and systems. The dramatic increase in the availability and use of information technology, however, raises fundamental questions on the guiding of technological innovation, measuring organizational and managerial productivity, augmenting human intelligence, ensuring data integrity, and establishing strategic advantage. The expanded use of information systems also raises major challenges to the traditional forms of administration and authority, the right to privacy, the nature and form of work, and the limits of calculative rationality in modern organizations and society.

The Wiley Series on Information Systems has emerged to address these questions and challenges. It hopes to stimulate thought and discussion on the key role information systems play in the functioning of organizations and society, and how their role is likely to change in the future. This historical or evolutionary theme of the Series is important because considerable insight can be gained by attempting to understand the past. The Series will attempt to integrate both description—what has been done—with prescription—how best to develop and implement information systems.

The descriptive and historical aspect is considered vital because information systems of the past have not necessarily met with the success that was envisaged. Numerous writers postulate that a high proportion of systems are failures in one sense or another. Given their high cost of development and their importance to the day-to-day running of organizations, this situation must surely be unacceptable. Research into IS failure has concluded that the primary cause of failure is the lack of consideration given to the social and behavioural dimensions of IS. Far too much emphasis has been placed on their technical side. There are good historical reasons why this has been the case, as discussed in Hirschheim's *Office Automation: A Social and Organizational Perspective*, the first book in the Wiley Series on Information Systems. The result has been something of a shift in emphasis from a strictly technical conception of IS to one where it is recognized that information systems have behavioural consequences. But even this misses the mark. A growing number of researchers suggest that information systems are more appropriately conceived as social systems which rely, to a greater and greater extent, on new technology for their operation. It is this social orientation which is lacking in much of what is written about IS. The first book in the Series, *Office Automation: A Social and Organizational Perspective*, goes some way in addressing this imbalance; the second, Jarke's *Managers, Micros and Mainframes: Integrating Systems for End-Users*, provides a complementary perspective. The third, *Critical Issues in Information Systems Research*, highlights key areas where research is needed.

The Series seeks to provide a forum for the serious discussion of IS. Although the primary perspective is a more social and behavioural one, alternative perspectives will also be included. This is based on the belief that no one perspective can be totally complete; added insight is possible through the adoption of multiple views. Relevant areas to be addressed in the Series include (but are not limited to): the theoretical development of information systems, their practical application, the foundations and evolution of information systems, and IS innovation. Subjects such as systems design, systems analysis methodologies, information systems planning and management, office automation, project management, decision support systems, end-user computing, and information systems and society are key concerns of the Series.

June 1986   Rudy Hirschheim
                                                                      Richard Boland

List of Contributors

John Banbury
Department of Computing Studies, Bristol Polytechnic, Bristol, UK

Richard J. Boland, Jr.
Department of Accountancy, University of Illinois at Urbana-Champaign, Urbana, Illinois, USA

Claudio U. Ciborra
Instituto di Informatica, Universita di Trento, Italy

Michael J. Earl
Oxford Institute of Information Management, Templeton College, Oxford University, Kennington, Oxford, UK

Charles R. Franz
Department of Management, University of Missouri, Columbia, Missouri, USA

Rudy Hirschheim
Oxford Institute of Information Management, Templeton College, Oxford University, Kennington, Oxford, UK

D. Ross Jeffery
Department of Information Systems, University of New South Wales, Kensington, New South Wales, Australia

Heinz K. Klein
School of Management, State University of New York, Binghamton, Binghamton, New York, USA

Rob Kling
Department of Information and Computer Science, University of California, Irvine, Irvine, California, USA

Tae H. Kwon
School of Business Administration, University of North Carolina, Chapel Hill, North Carolina, USA

Kalle Lyytinen

Department of Computer Science, University of Jyvaskyla, Jyvaskyla, Finland

Enid Mumford

Manchester Business School, University of Manchester, Manchester, UK

Daniel Robey

Department of Management, Florida International University, Miami, Florida, USA

Ronald Stamper

London School of Economics and Political Science, University of London, London, UK

E. Burton Swanson

Graduate School of Management, University of California, Los Angeles, Los Angeles, California, USA

Jon A. Turner

Graduate School of Business Administration Management, New York University, New York, New York, USA

Robert W. Zmud

School of Business Administration, University of North Carolina, Chapel Hill, North Carolina, USA

Contents

Introduction

Information systems research addresses a wide range of issues concerning the technology, development and management of information systems, as well as their organizational and social impacts. The work is diverse in both its topics and its outlets for publication. As a relatively young area of research, its findings are sketchy, scattered and sometimes dubious. This volume brings together and critically analyses a number of important issues currently facing the field.

This volume is not an attempt to unify the field, nor is it an attempt to clearly define its boundaries. It accepts the amorphous quality of the information systems area, and addresses a broad but not exhaustive set of topics within it. The term 'critical issue' was chosen with care. Being critical in a double sense is the organizing theme of this book. The intention is to move the field ahead by taking a number of issues deemed to be critically important to the field, and subjecting them to a critical analysis.

In creating the volume, seventeen scholars from a wide variety of national and academic backgrounds were asked to identify an issue of information systems research that they believed to be of major importance to the field. They were then commissioned to write a paper which summarized the work to date in that area, subjected that work to a critical review, and sketched a more hopeful and productive set of questions and/or methods for future work. They were instructed to be as openly critical of what had gone before relative to the issue they had chosen as they could, noting its shortcomings, conceptual confusions, and failed promises.

If the field of information systems is to have a cumulative development, we need to take a hard look at what it has really accomplished, or failed to accomplish, and be ready to learn from a productive criticism of our past. Journals primarily publish research that provides incremental findings within larger streams of work, and do not as frequently provide outlets for studies that are explicitly critical. But polite approbation serves neither the authors nor the field well. Critical reappraisals of the field offer the greatest hope for gaining new insights, reframing old questions, opening new issues, and challenging the beliefs and assumptions that have guided the field to this point.

The book is in two parts. In Part I, the chapters focus on issues associated with the practice of analysing and designing information systems. The chapters present a very broad view of practice, including its sociology of knowledge, the responsibility of its professionals, and the effectiveness of its tools and procedures. In Part II, the chapters focus on the social context of information systems. The chapters address the way we think about and research the organizational antecedents and consequences of information systems, their diffusion, and our ability to understand their repercussions in the wider network of changing social relations.

The placement of a chapter into one of these two parts is not always clear cut. For example, major criticisms of practice often rely on an analysis of the social theories that drive it. Similarly, an analysis of the organizational and social context is often concerned with the way it is, or is not, reflected in information systems practice. Nonetheless, this organizing scheme allows us to order the chapters, within each part, in something like a progressive development of their themes.

Kalle Lyytinen begins Part I with a challenging assessment of the underlying concepts that have justified our established methods of information system development. Ronald Stamper follows this stimulating survey with a critique of the theory of language implicit in our data models, and the implications for designing systems that can meet the pragmatic tests of meaning and action. Following these overviews of the implicit theories guiding our methods of practice, John Banbury critiques our understanding of the process of systems analysis, arguing that there are important responsibilities we fail to recognize in our fascination with method. Jon Turner then focuses on the actual creation of system designs, and exposes how little we know about the fundamental elements of design and the cognitive processes involved in designing. He then offers a research agenda to fill in some of the missing pieces.

The three concluding chapters of Part I explore practice at the level of applications development, and analyse problems with our understanding of software production in general, and of some major, emerging application areas. First, Ross Jeffery surveys the limitation of the models used to understand the software engineering process. Then, Enid Mumford focuses on some unasked questions in the burgeoning area of expert systems, and lays out a challenging set of research issues. Finally, Michael Earl critically surveys the models and methods being proposed to align an information system with its organization's strategy.

E. Burton Swanson opens Part II with a provocative survey of the way researchers in information systems and in organization theory have failed to satisfactorily explain why and how information systems are used and what effects their use has in organizations. Following this, Charles Franz and Daniel Robey analyse a number of published papers, showing the way information systems researchers have failed to match the organizationally relevant questions they asked with an appropriate research strategy. Tae Kwon and Robert Zmud then contrast the broader social science research programme on the diffusion of technology to our own fragmented efforts to understand the process of implementation.

The last four chapters in Part II deal with models and images available for understanding and evaluating the information system structures we find in the world today. First, Claudio Ciborra draws upon institutional theory from economics to identify a number of as yet unexplored issues in explaining the relation between information systems and organization structures. Heinz Klein and Rudy Hirschheim then draw upon recent social theory to expose our failure to understand the relation between shifts in societal norms, values, and beliefs and changes in our legitimated methods of information system development. Rob Kling then chastises our failure to understand and evaluate the complex social impact of information systems, proposing web models as a way to begin doing so. Finally, Richard Boland identifies some images, metaphors and fantasies that have misguided our ways of thinking about information, and reduced our ability to develop humanly satisfying systems.

The authors were challenged with a doubly critical theme, and we hope the reader will agree that they have succeeded in meeting that challenge. We expect that the volume will be of use to both practitioners and academics involved with the design and evaluation of information systems. We especially hope that young researchers will find in this volume some critical issues that they can make progress on, with their work then becoming an object for later criticism.

Part I

A focus on information systems practice

Critical Issues in Information Systems Research
Edited by R. J. Boland Jr. and R. A. Hirschheim
© 1987 John Wiley & Sons Ltd.

Chapter 1

A TAXONOMIC PERSPECTIVE OF INFORMATION SYSTEMS DEVELOPMENT: THEORETICAL CONSTRUCTS AND RECOMMENDATIONS

Kalle Lyytinen

ABSTRACT

Two important concerns for the information systems community are to understand the nature of information systems development (ISD) and the characteristics of methodologies to support ISD. To address these concerns a variety of theoretical constructs are needed that help the reader to understand the multifaceted nature of ISD and the requirements for methodology development. This chapter proposes the following six theoretical constructs for analysing ISD methodologies: (1) three *contexts* (relating to organization, language, and technology domains) which the development actions point to; (2) *object systems* identified by using one or more of the contexts; (3) *representation forms* and their intended use; (4) *super-contexts* which form a conceptual bridge between the basic contexts; (5) the *type of mappings* between contexts (descriptive and instrumental); and (6) *content of a mapping process* (deterministic or emergent). These constructs are applied to provide the basis for a comprehensive taxonomy to analyse several methodologies. By identifying essential characteristics the methodologies are grouped into five major classes. The result leads to several recommendations on how future research into ISD methodologies should proceed.

1. INTRODUCTION

Since the application of computers in administrative data processing began in 1954 it has become one of the key instruments for improving organizations' formal information processing activities. In three decades computer-based information systems (IS) have evolved from supporting peripheral, already formalized, systems, like payroll, to penetrating the whole organization. New applications and technologies have emerged such as MIS, transaction processing, decision-support systems, office information systems and so forth. It is therefore no surprise that many enthusiasts think of information technology as a major organizational problem-solver, increasing organizations' capacity to cope with external and internal complexity and improve their performance (Galbraith, 1977).

This widely held view in the IS community is not, however, in accord with the empirical evidence on how computer technology shapes organizational performance (Ouchi, 1978; Earl and Hopwood, 1980; Strassman, 1985). Numerous studies suggest that there is no causal relationship between the development of formal information systems and the improvement of organizational performance. Instead, empirical analyses reveal that information systems tend more often to be 'troublemakers' (Kling, 1980; Lucas, 1975, 1981; Turner, 1982). Accordingly, 'failure' rather than 'success' is common in systems development efforts.

The IS community faces a paradox: despite impressive advances in technology, problems are more abundant than solutions: organizations experience rising costs instead of cost reduction, IS misuse and rejection are more frequent than acceptance and use.

In this chapter we shall claim that one major reason for systems failure is the deficiency of systems development practice. It has long been a conventional wisdom that IS success depends on the attributes of the process producing it. For this reason the IS research community has produced a large body of literature trying to improve the state of the art in systems design. Numerous methods, tools and techniques have been put forward (Cotterman *et al.*, 1981; Olle *et al.*, 1982, 1983). One reason for the abundance of IS design approaches is that it is quite easy to develop a method, but difficult to get it accepted.

We argue, however, that the claim of a fundamental deficiency of systems development methodologies has not been taken sufficiently seriously to lead to a thorough and critical investigation of the basis on which current development methodologies build. There are few, if any, convincing studies that verify the efficacy of proposed approaches. In fact, we shall argue that proposed development approaches may even add to the crisis of IS failure. The reason for this is that they focus on a limited spectrum of development issues. Further, their assumptions about the nature of the systems development conflict with several empirical findings of its true nature (Boland, 1979; Boland and Day, 1982; Nygaard and Handlykken, 1981; Kling, 1985). Therefore, we shall argue that development methodologies have weaknesses, which can be summarized as follows:

—*they lack synergy with other IS research areas*. Most development methodologies neglect insights gained from implementation research, socio-technical design and so on.
—*they have a limited scope*. A majority of systems development methodologies concentrate on the design of the IS application and its life-cycle management (Kensing, 1984; Vitalari, 1984). Although this is an important concern, it ignores the need to understand social impacts and institutions surrounding systems design (Kling, 1984), to anticipate changes in the work-processes (Mumford, 1981; Kensing, 1984), to support problem-solving, goal-setting and analysis of assumptions (Vitalari, 1984) and so on. In particular, the legitimation of goals and other assumptions that determine the basic direction of information systems development (ISD) is held to be self-evident (see Klein and Hirschheim, Chapter 12 in this volume).
—*they have an inadequate conceptual base*. Most systems development methodologies have an ambiguous and narrow conception of the phenomena IS developers

confront. For example, few methodologies discussed in Olle *et al.*, (1982) provide a penetrating definition of the IS, its parts and purpose. In addition, lessons which could be easily drawn from systems thinking, such as stakeholder analysis (Mason and Mitroff, 1981), have not been widely addressed.

—*they lack or have limited theoretical foundations*. The field is quite naive with respect to theoretical foundations on which to base design approaches. At most, its theoretical basis is borrowed from systems theory, logic, artificial intelligence or semantics of programming languages. However, these notions have very little, if any, use when we try to deal with the hazards of social change introduced by the systems design (Kubicek, 1983).

—*they are unaware of the philosophical underpinnings of systems development*. Every systems development methodology is founded on assumptions about the nature of the knowledge we can obtain about the future IS. However, very rarely are these assumptions critically analyzed and their impact on the development practices evaluated and anticipated.

Our goal in this chapter is to examine the issues noted above. In particular, we shall:

—suggest theoretical constructs by which we can more carefully explicate the nature and content of IS design;
—identify theoretical foundations for various facets of systems design;
—use these constructs to classify some systems development methodologies;
—make recommendations on how to define a systems development methodology, how to compare methodologies, and how to select them, and finally pinpoint areas that are in need of more research.

The main message of this chapter is that systems development methodologies cannot simply deal with the problem of how one designs technically reliable and cost-effective information systems. Instead, we should regard systems development as a multidimensional social change. The choice of a development methodology should therefore take into account its sensitivity to the cultural, social, political and moral aspects of systems design (see Klein and Hirschheim, Chapter 12 in this volume).

The chapter is organized as follows: in section 2 we identify essential features of systems development and systems development methodologies; section 3 outlines taxonomic principles for classifying systems development; section 4 proposes a preliminary taxonomy of development methodologies using a number of development approaches as examples, and makes some recommendations that concern methodology definition, its assessment, methodology choice and its theoretical foundations. Section 5 summarizes the main findings of the chapter.

2. FEATURES OF SYSTEMS DEVELOPMENT

2.1 Information Systems Development — a Definition

We shall define information systems development as follows (Welke, 1981):

> *Information systems development* is a *change process* taken with respect to *object systems* in a set of *environments* by *a development group* to achieve or maintain some *objectives*.

The essential components in the definition are highlighted and illustrated in more detail in Figure 1. This definition is general enough to adopt a broad view of systems development. On the other hand, it is specific enough to shed light on its essential aspects.

Object systems consist of phenomena 'perceived' by members of the development group. They identify a target of change. In general, there are several object systems which a development group can identify. Further, object systems are often related, so that a change in one can induce a change in others. Members' perceptions of object systems need not coincide. Therefore identified object systems can be partially overlapping, disjoint and even conflicting. Object systems can be further characterized in terms of their context, underlying concept structure, representation form, ontology, and epistemology. These are discussed in more detail below.

Change process is an event in which phenomena, i.e. objects, properties and their relationships in object systems, come into being as a result of a development group's deliberate action. It can be further characterized in terms of its intentionality, intersubjectivity and uncertainty.

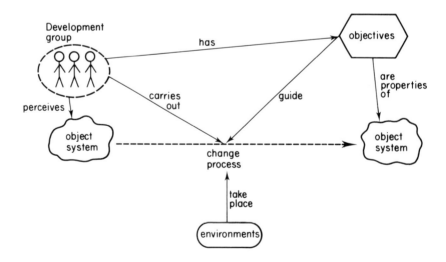

FIGURE 1 *Information systems development*

Systems development is intentional, to the extent it reflects a planned change. It is based on developers' intentions to change object systems towards desirable ends. Intersubjectivity means that the change process is founded on an intersubjective recognition of phenomena and on a mutual coordination of participant's actions. Systems development is not an artificial adventure, it is always embedded in a social and cultural milieu. Uncertainty entails that the change process is not a deterministic one. Developers are often uncertain whether the planned intervention can be carried out, and whether the resulting object systems will have the desired properties.

In general, we shall distinguish three types of uncertainty: *means uncertainty, effect uncertainty and problem uncertainty*. The first type deals with situations in which developers are unsure whether certain means can achieve a desirable end-state. The second type reflects situations in which developers are unsure of whether the end-state will have the desired properties. An intervention can coproduce changes that are not coincident and even conflicting with their wants. The third type expresses developers' uncertainty about which object systems they ought to approach and which would-be changes are needed to remedy a problematic situation. This type of uncertainty is associated with the 'error of the third kind', i.e. solving the wrong problem (Mitroff, 1980).

Environments should be viewed as 'webs of conditions and factors' which surround development processes (see Kling and Scacchi, 1982). They exert influence on development activities, organization, outcomes, and so on. Environments include labour, economy, technology, application, external and normative environments.

The notion of a *development group* entails that systems development takes place in a formally organized group. It is accomplished by a social body that has similarities with social institutions (Robey and Markus, 1984) in that it sets mutual expectations; it sanctions, punishes and gives rewards; it consists of positions and roles filled by people, and so on. A development group can organize itself in alternative ways that specify the set-up of its positions, roles, authority structures and decision-making rights (Scacchi, 1985).

Intentions in systems development are expressed by *objectives*. These are related to general value-orientations and represent what 'one ought to do' or 'what is good' (Klein, 1984). Objectives have several features that must be kept in mind when studying the IS change:

—they can be implicitly imposed, for example, by the methods used, or they can be explicitly agreed upon through an open negotiation, or superimposed by fiat;
—they can be clear or vague (ill-defined);
—they can be uni- or multifunctional;
—they can be conflictual or a-conflictual

The components of the definition of systems development form a complicated web of social, technological, and cultural phenomena. The components are not independent of each other, nor are they completely dependent. Rather, we can speak of a totality in which components' features are defined by their interactions with other components—they are thus emergent. A detailed specification of one component is a case of a constrained choice: a choice with regard to one component constrains our freedom to choose the others, for example, identified object systems are constrained largely by pursued objectives. Usually, a major part of these interactions are prefixed by a systems development methodology as will be shown below.

2.2 Features of Object Systems

Object systems have a variety of properties; these are illustrated in Figure 2. As is currently realized there are no objectively given object systems (Checkland, 1981). Rather people have viewpoints which enable them to perceive object systems. We call these viewpoints *object systems contexts* (Welke and Konsynski, 1982). Object system contexts form wholes with emergent properties: phenomena in each context are organized and structured as a whole (Israel, 1979) owing to their mutual intrinsic relationships. Object system contexts segment the domain of change into distinct action and perception realms. Phenomena in these segments are subject to different laws and they exhibit various regularities to the extent to which they are responsive to introduced changes (Etzioni, 1967).

The notion of the object system context indicates the open-ended, situation-dependent and cyclical nature of IS intervention. In the beginning, change is

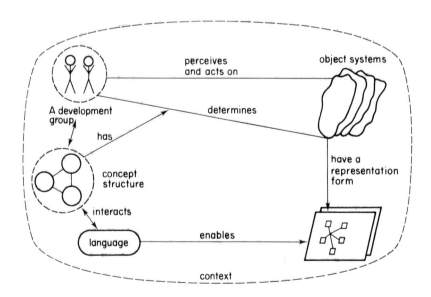

FIGURE 2 Object systems in systems development.

conditioned by the initial perception enabled by the language used. However, during the development process language and perceptions are in a constant flux.

As noted above, several overlapping and even conflicting object systems can be generated within one object system context. These are determined by *underlying concepts or theories* which classify, explicate and give order to its phenomena. For example, a computer can be viewed in terms of physical states, logical circuitry, or a high-level program execution process.

Object systems can be *represented* in multiple ways. Examples of representation forms are free form text, semiformal notation such as structured English, graphical descriptions, and formal mathematical notations. The chosen representation form depends primarily on the concept structure and its degree of accuracy and formality. Results of applying representation forms are called *object system representations*. Object system representations can serve different purposes: descriptive, predictive, prescriptive, interpretive, and reconstructive.

The *ontological dimension* reflects the fundamental existence of the object system: the basic stuff that is 'seen'. It can be composed of hard, tangible structures with a concrete material base, or it can be malleable, more vague phenomena with an ideal or cultural base. These ontological extremes are called realism and nominalism (idealism).

The *epistemological dimension* reflects how developers inquire into object systems and see phenomena in them. It affects what form the knowledge ('perception') adopts about the object system. There are two positions: positivism and antipositivism (humanism). If it is postulated that all knowledge can be expressed in statements of laws and facts that are positively corroborated by measurement, we speak of positivism. On the other hand, in the extreme case an antipositivist standpoint denies the possibility of positive, observer-independent knowledge, and instead emphasizes sympathetic reason in understanding phenomena (Hirschheim, 1985).

In systems development prior experiences, the analogies used and learned habits affect the choice of object systems (Vitalari, 1984, 1985). Systems development environments and the composition of development groups also have an impact. But the most influential factor is likely to be that of a systems development methodology.

2.3 Systems Development Methodology

We define an information systems development methodology as follows:

> An *information systems development methodology* (*ISDM*) is an organized collection of concepts, beliefs, values and normative principles supported by material resources. The purpose of the ISDM is to help a development group successfully change object systems, that is to perceive, generate, assess, control, and to carry out change actions in them.

Methodologies must meet several conditions to achieve their change mission. They must be written so that they can be taught, learned and transferred over a wide range of development situations. They must be understandable and socially acceptable. Often their use must be motivated by rewards and sanctions, because a methodology change requires people to change their working habits, thinking and language. Finally, ISDMs must be legitimized. Reasons to use them must be accepted and justified by those who decide on their use.

A single methodology does not usually cover all aspects of systems development. Methodologies are partial in their focus, but can be used:

(1) to identify problematic situations and object systems for change (information requirements analysis methodologies/change analysis methodologies (Davis, 1982)).
(2) to generate and analyse correctness of change actions (analysis and design methodologies, see Olle *et al.*, 1982).
(3) to assess and evaluate effectiveness and efficiency of change actions (cost–benefit and assessment methodologies (Kleijnen, 1980)).
(4) to carry out and implement changes (programming methodologies (Jackson, 1975), organizational implementation methodologies (Keen and Scott-Morton, 1978)).

The methodologies current use coincide quite well with our definition. All of them include concepts and beliefs that enable developers to identify and order phenomena. All of them suggest a pool of methods, languages and techniques (i.e. normative principles) for going about representing, selecting and/or implementing the change. Finally, all of them employ various resources: manpower, tools etc., for carrying out ISD.

On the other hand, methodologies differ in many ways. For example, they can sustain alternative beliefs about the type of uncertainty involved in systems design. For this reason they can prefer quite distinct development strategies. For example, approaches founded on the systems life cycle notion (Wasserman and Freeman, 1983; Yourdon, 1982; Cotterman *et al.*, 1981) presume means uncertainty, and propose a linear, stepwise development process. Other methodologies, such as Checkland's soft systems methodology (Checkland, 1981), concentrate on problem uncertainty. As a result they think of the development process as a learning cycle.

A methodology's organizing principles prescribing how the development group is to be arranged can specify a complete autocracy where systems development is done by outside experts or they can promote full-blown participation. A methodology's goals and values can be predetermined and fixed as in software engineering methodologies. However, other methodologies, like Checkland's, emphasize the fuzziness of human goals and values and the need to debate and reason about them.

We can see that object systems preselected in some methodologies have very little in common with those seen in others. Methodologies thus act like perceptual filters which identify certain phenomena at the cost of neglecting other. For example, Mumford's ETHICS (1983) and structured analysis and design approaches (DeMarco, 1979) have very dissimilar visions of the future IS.

In this chapter, we are particularly interested in the issue of how a systems development methodology guides the choice of object systems. We want to see what aspects of object systems are currently being disregarded by the currently used ISDMs. In order to focus attention on this, the following outline of taxonomic principles for classifying development methodologies is suggested which considers which object systems the ISDM proposes to the development group for change.

3. TAXONOMIC PRINCIPLES FOR SYSTEMS DEVELOPMENT

3.1 Three Object System Contexts

It is postulated that there are three object system contexts: *the technology context* (T), *the language context* (L), and *the organization context* (O). We believe that these three are exhaustive and segment the systems development domain into three distinct realms, which respond differently to introduced change.

The three contexts are hierarchically ordered. Technology, or in general, the physical world, is the basis for the language context, because language is always represented in some material carrier. On the other hand language is necessary for any organized social action that comes into focus in the organization context.

For all contexts the following general features will be discussed: definition of the context, nature of phenomena in the context, type of change in the context, nature and uses of object system representation, ontology and epistemology of object systems, and values embedded in the systems change.

3.2 Technology Context

3.2.1 General Features

By a *technology context* we mean a viewpoint which confines object systems to a view of how to efficiently process and store signs (data) in some material carrier. information systems in this context consist of work-processes, they are integrated user–machine systems (Davis and Olson, 1985).

During systems development there is a need to select a technology context, because in the final stage every information system is introduced as a technical system consisting of hardware, software, database, models, manual procedures and so on.

Developers confront phenomena in this context as mainly deterministic (Solvberg *et al.*, 1978), because they cannot reset the working principles of computers or other equipment. Accordingly, preferred reference disciplines are computer science, systems engineering and so forth.

In this context the *change* involves technological rationalization: either direct substitution or incremental aggregation (Kling and Scacchi, 1982). Change is about introducing faster computers, more efficient and reliable software, software packages with new functions and so on. An information systems change (technology change) can be achieved by designing from without by dividing the IS into smaller pieces and then tackling each sub-component separately. The development process can be represented in terms of a set of deterministic transformations (Lehmann, 1984). These transformations depict how the functional idea of the IS is gradually transformed into a real operational system.

In the technology context *object system representations* concentrate on the predictability of future events. Some representations, like programs also have 'prescriptive' purposes, i.e. to govern the operations of the computing equipment. Their preferred properties are formal rigor and associated capability to manipulate them. Both linear and graphical notations are widely employed.

The *ontological stance* is predominantly realism: technology consists of hard manipulable structures. The *epistemological stance* is positivism, i.e. knowledge about technology is objective and can be obtained by the empirical–analytic method.

The *goals* in the technological context emphasize the effectiveness of technological change: to minimize cost or maximize monetary benefits over the life-span of the IS. This can be expressed by several measures which represent systems quality attributes such as robustness, portability, efficiency of operation, fault-tolerance, and so on (Boehm *et al.*, 1977).

3.2.2 Object Systems in the Technology Context

Object systems in the technology context can be classified in two dimensions. The first concerns the nature of identified objects and their relationships. The second concerns the location of the chosen object system on a particular level of abstraction.

The first dimension focuses on designs 'through data' or designs 'through processes'. In the former, object system representations model relationships in stored and accessed data. In the latter, object system representations capture properties and relationships between processes. Structured analysis (DeMarco, 1979) is an example of a design approach which focuses on processes, because it studies mainly how data flows through a system. Database design methodologies (Yao *et al.*, 1982) are examples of approaches which focus on data, because they emphasize the role of the data structuring in the systems design. In general, a dividing line between these two approaches is often vague and more a question of emphasis. In some design approaches these two viewpoints are applied concurrently (Wedekind, 1981; Iivari and Koskela, 1983).

The second dimension places an object system closer to an abstract functional idea or to an operational system. There are numerous proposals for levels of abstraction in the literature (Senko, 1976; Wedekind, 1981; Iivari, 1983; Lehman, 1984). In this paper we shall rely on Lehman's (1984) classification and locate an object system on any of the following five levels: viewpoints and requirements, logical design, physical design, computational and structural design, and implementation-oriented design.

Table 1 combines these two dimensions, allowing the various classes of object systems in the technology context to be noted. In each class we can further distinguish single approaches by analysing which concept structures and representation forms are used. For example, ISACs (Lundeberg *et al.*, 1981), A-graphs and data flow diagrams in structured analysis (DeMarco, 1979) represent alternative object system representations that belong to the class of object systems restricted to the (logical) data flow design.

It is possible to find several underlying theories for the generation of object systems in this context, ranging from theories of program correctness and program structure (Jackson, 1975) to normalization theory (Date, 1982) and performance evaluation. All classes of object systems identified in Table 1 have been widely discussed in the literature. Many of the so-called 'structured methods' exhibit a series of object systems that abstract through processes (Yordon, 1982; DeMarco, 1979). Another example is ISAC (Lundeberg *et al.*, 1981). On the other hand database design methods and methodologies (see Yao *et al.*, 1982, and Olle *et al.*, 1982) employ mainly series of object systems that abstract through data.

TABLE 1 A taxonomy of object systems in the technology context

Abstraction level	Change in the focus		
	Development approach		
	Through data	Through processes	
Viewpoints Requirements	Local views of data	Processing functional needs	
Logical designs	Logical data design and canonization	Logical data flow design	
Physical design	Schema mapping and structuring (DBTG, relational, etc.)	Physical data flow design	Transformation
Computational structural design	Access paths, indexing, access method	Program design	
Implementation	Allocation to devices, buffering loading, conversion	Coding testing manual procedures	

3.3 Language Context

3.3.1 General Features

By a *language context* we mean a viewpoint which confines object systems to the use, nature, content, context and form of signs included into the IS. Seen in this light an IS provides a means and an environment for linguistic communication (Lyytinen, 1985).

The language context is necessary in systems development because an information system always has a symbolic function. Use of information systems is not just the physical transfer of material objects and their efficient manipulation. It is based on users' ability to see these transfers as having a common significance (language expressions) that goes beyond their peculiar physical properties.

Language expressions are subject to regularities that are based on human convention. These regularities define their significance in social contexts. Regularities are defined by such notions as syntactic correctness, meaning, coherency, veracity, impact and so on. However, owing to their conventional nature, linguistic regularities are much more malleable and vague than, and are therefore distinct from, laws of nature (Itkonen, 1978). Several reference disciplines such as linguistics, logic, philosophy of language, parts of psychology, sociology and anthropology, are relevant to this context. It is a common view among the students of language that theories related to language have a different scientific status (Pateman, 1983).

In this context, the IS change is about coming to an agreement on conventions that govern language use: its form, signification, use-intention and so on. Information systems development *qua* language change involves a language development and formalization process. During systems development languages evolve: new meanings and words are defined, new uses established and so on. Language formalization means that its use is made more systematic and institutionalized: syntax of language is restricted to preselected forms, and its use-patterns and contexts are fixed.

The IS research community has no generally shared view of the *nature of language change*. In some situations it can be understood in functional terms: language expressions are divided into smaller units and their relationships analysed to capture their meaning and to record acceptable configurations. Here, the language change is seen as a linear formalization and modeling process (van Griethuysen, 1982). In other situations it is understood as a learning process in which new word meanings are negotiated and their uses established by a collective inquiry. In this case the change resembles a hermeneutic circle (Gadamer, 1975; Boland, 1985) by which people can expand their 'horizon of expectations' to grasp alien new expressions.

In the language context *object system representations* vary from natural language expressions to more rigorous formal descriptions. Both linear and graphical notations can be employed. The degree of formality depends on the underlying concept structure. Object systems representations are used to describe, prescribe and reconstruct linguistic regularities.

The object systems' *ontology* ranges from realism to nominalism, and their *epistemological stance* from positivism to humanism.

In general there are no universal desirable properties for object systems generated about linguistic phenomena. They depend on the chosen concept structure and its preferred view of the linguistic phenomena.

3.3.2 Object Systems in the Language Context

Object systems in the language context are always based on some theory of linguistic regularities. We shall distinguish between five language (theories) views (Lyytinen, 1985). These are:

(1) Fregean core: a denotational study of language about the relationships between the world and language.
(2) The Chomskyan grammar: a generative study of language about the structural relationships between elements of language and how they are generated.
(3) Piaget's schema: a cognitive study of language about the relationships between the mind and linguistic behaviour.
(4) The Skinnerian response: a behaviouristic study of language about observable behaviour and language.
(5) Ordinary speaking: an interactionist study of language about relationships between language and human action.

TABLE 2 *Five language views*

Language view	Covered linguistic phenomena	Primary function of language	Basic elements of analysis	Nature of knowledge
Fregean core	semantics (syntax)	denotational	entity truth-value possible world	mathematical
Chomskyan grammar	syntax semantics	ideational	literal meaning sense relations syntactic structures	conceptual
Piaget's schema	semantics	cognitive	cognitive maps memory	psychological
Skinnerian response	pragmatics	behavioural	context variables, stimulus/response pairs	empirical
Ordinary speaking	pragmatics	interactionistic sense-making	context speech act illocution	rule-based

TABLE 3 Adoption of language views into the IS field

Language view	Information system definition	Main application stage	Main objects	Main references
Fregean core	A formalized IS is a mechanism able to store, communicate and process propositions about some application discourse	Stage: information requirements analysis (IRA) Task conceptual schema development	Categorization of the 'universe of discourse', Behaviour of the 'universe of discourse'	Bubenko (1983), Senko (1976)
Chomskyan grammar	An IS is a collection of time-varying sentence sets generated by a grammar	Stage: information requirements analysis (IRA) Task: design of natural language interfaces	Specification of correct sentences, Identification of significant sentences	Lehmann (1978), Colombetti et al. (1983), Pilote (1983), Laine et al. (1979)
Piaget's schema	An IS comprises linguistic structures that evoke cognitive processes within a decision-making context	Stage: information requirements analysis (IRA) Task: fit of data and cognitive style	Decision maker's cognitive schemata and styles, Cognitive development	Keen and Scott-Morton (1978), Mason and Mitroff (1973), Johnson (1984), Shneiderman (1981)
Skinnerian response	An IS is a system for collecting, sorting, retrieving and processing information used by one or more managers in the performance of their duties	Stage: information requirements analysis (IRA) Task: decision-making analysis	Reactions to linguistic stimuli, Prediction of decision maker's optimal behaviour patterns	Ackoff (1971), Bariff and Ginzberg (1982), Ein Dor and Segev (1978), Kendall and Kriebel (1982)
Ordinary speaking	An organizational IS is a system of communicative action that creates, sets up, controls, and maintains organization's contracts and reports on their status	Stage: information requirements analysis (IRA) Task: organizational change sense-making	Action patterns of organizational exchange, Control and coordination of commitments, Sense-making, Rules	Flores and Ludlow (1981), Ciborra (1985), Boland (1979), Goldkuhl and Lyytinen (1982, 1984), Lyytinen and Lehtinen (1984a)

The ontological stance in these approaches differs. Skinnerian response and Fregean core are based on some sort of realism. Chomskyan grammar and Piaget's schema have more affinity to idealism and 'ordinary speaking' advocates a type of nominalism. Epistemologically all except 'ordinary speaking', are variants of positivism. Table 2 lists some characteristics of each of these views (Lyytinen, 1985, p. 62).

Each language view suggests a distinct approach to studying an IS as a linguistic entity. Each language view has been used in the domain of IS. Table 3 characterizes how. Some object systems generated with these views are common in systems development methodologies. For example, the Fregean core and Skinnerian response views. As illustrated in Table 3, database design approaches use, in the early phases of systems development, some variant of the Fregean view. Management information requirements approaches study language mainly as a signal that leads to optimal decision-making behaviours. It is believed that the meaning is the behaviour triggered.

3.4 Organizational Context

3.4.1 General Features

By an *organization context* we mean a viewpoint, which confines object systems to the origin, nature, purpose and form of systematic relationships and interactions between people. Seen in this light an IS supports, enables or takes part in some organizational process involving human interactions: decision making, operative control, bargaining, sense-making and so on.

The organization context is necessary in systems development, because an information system must serve some manifest or latent organizational mission (Klein and Hirschheim, 1985). In terms of regularity of responsiveness, the realm of organizations has an intermediary status between two other contexts. The developers face organizations as if they were states of nature (Berger and Luckmann, 1967). But patterns of social relationships and interactions can be restructured — not as readily as symbols, but more readily as technology — by changing organizations' norms and requiring their compliance by power and sanctions. The organization context is thus more malleable than the technology context, but less so than objects in the language context (Etzioni, 1967). Examples of reference disciplines from which theories in the organizational context are drawn are social psychology, economics, political science, anthropology, organization theory, sociology and social philosophy.

In this context, *change* is about influencing social behaviours and arrangements by affecting an organizational situation. We can realize this in multiple ways depending on our preferred view of the organization. It can be understood in functional terms as done in classical systems analysis (Checkland, 1981); understood in terms of socio-psychological motives that resist or promote change as in Lewin–Schein's theory of organizational change (Keen and Scott-Morton,

1978); understood in political terms where change is an indication of power-play and an establishment of a sufficient political coalition to carry out the change (Kling and Iacono, 1984). We can represent it as a shift in how people 'read' organizations and how they attribute meanings to embedded situations (Boland, 1985; Checkland, 1981). There is no valid model of how an organizational change can take place. It can be comprehended as a linear, stepwise process, as a chaotic political battle, or as text to be studied by a hermeneutic cycle (Morgan, 1980).

Here *object systems representations* concentrate on describing and ordering social phenomena. They are mainly based on natural language or semi-formal descriptions. Graphical notations are widely employed side by side with narratives. An example of this is the ritual use of organizational charts to indicate control structures. They are mainly used to describe, but prescriptive and predictive uses are also possible.

The *ontological stance* of object systems in the organization context also varies. Most object systems adopt realism. Organizational phenomenology, on the other hand (Sanders, 1982; Boland, 1985), provides an example of a nominalist approach. The *epistemological stance* is mainly positivism. However, in recent years several anti-positivist approaches to organizational inquiry have been suggested (Burrell and Morgan, 1979; Morgan, 1983).

In general, *goals* of organizational change are presumed to be well-defined and agreed. This results in an a-conflictual view of the organizational change. However, conflict-based models of organizations emphasize an inevitable conflicting nature of organizations' goals and change. In general, the view taken depends on value-orientations. In most cases, these are claimed to be clear, uni-functional, a-conflictual and explicit.

3.4.2 Object System in the Organization Context

Well-defined and separate object systems in the organization context are hard to pin down, because their nature is determined by several layers of assumptions. The first layer is concerned with the epistemology and ontology of organizational analysis. The second layer distinguishes two classes of assumptions: the first is concerned with the individual/collective dichotomy, the second with the deterministic/voluntaristic dichotomy. Both of these dichotomies relate to the study of social phenomena and are not in themselves new to social theory. Their implications for social studies have been widely discussed (Burrell and Morgan, 1979; van de Ven and Astley, 1981). Here, we shall use them to identify principal concept structures that underlie object system generation. These two dimensions taken together lead to four regions where object systems can be located (see Figure 3).

The collective extreme is concerned with the macro-organizational characteristics. The individual extreme focuses on the individual or his position. The deterministic/voluntaristic dichotomy expresses the classical duality between social determinism and free will — the view that human behaviour is either determined by external forces and principles or is autonomously chosen and created by human beings.

Theories exhibited in Figure 3 are representative and have been selected among many available. The reason for our choice is that they illustrate some typical positions in the organizational literature and they also underlie most organizational views discussed in the IS literature.

Table 4 illustrates how each theory noted in Figure 3 has been applied in the IS context. Some of the theories noted in Table 4 have been widely adopted in the IS literature focusing on development methodologies. In fact, all widely applied methodologies can be located in the upper right region of Figure 3. This reflects the widely held belief in the IS community of the rational 'man' and 'organization'.

It is also evident from Table 4 that both the individual/collective and the determinism/voluntarism dimension affect our view of IS development. If one selects an individual alternative, one is inclined to emphasize the information systems' role in improving individual decision making or other individual task-performance such as problem solving. Individual decision making is the dominant view adopted in both classical MIS, and in the more recent DSS and office information systems approaches (Keen and Scott-Morton, 1978; Klein and Hirschheim, 1985). Organizational views in the left regions are oriented towards positions and individuals in management and professional groups. On the other hand, if one adopts a collective position, one focuses on the information systems' community role in management control, communication, bargaining, conflict

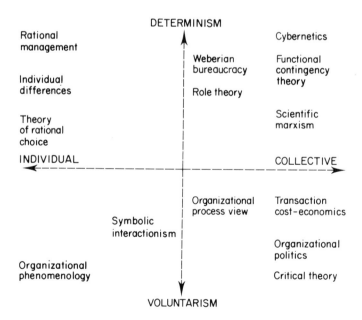

FIGURE 3 Representative theories for object system generation in the
organization context

TABLE 4 Organizational object system models

Theory	View of an organization	Role of an IS	References
Rational management	Organization is a decision-making unit that tries to optimize its function by a rational decision	To provide information that maximizes decision outcomes	Kleijnen (1980) Keen and Scott-Morton (1978) Huber (1981)
Individual differences	Organizational decision is affected by individuals' abilities and strategies especially their cognitive skills	To provide information that maximizes decision outcomes by adapting to individuals' information processing behaviour	Mason and Mitroff (1973) Keen and Scott-Morton (1978)
Theory of rational choice	Organization is a satisfying decision unit due to individuals' bounded rationality	To provide information for problem analysis, search, and choice phases in problem-solving	Cooper and Swanson (1979) Keen and Scott-Morton (1978)
Organizational phenomenology	Organization is an externalization of subjects' consciousness	A context for interaction to attribute meaning for individual experience	Boland (1979)
Symbolic interactionism	Organization is a set of meanings that arise from human interactions	A means for symbolic interactions	Goldkuhl and Lyytinen (1982) Boland (1979)
Weberian bureaucracy	Organization is an instrument for task accomplishment consisting of parts designed and meshed into a fine-tuned efficiency	A control and optimization mechanism	Ein-Dor and Segev (1978)
Organizational process view	Organization is collection of structures, conventional practices and programs	To support accomplishment of programs and practices	Keen and Scott-Morton (1978) Huber (1981)
Role theory	Organization is a set of stable roles that define mutual expectations	To adapt to existing role structure	Mumford (1983)

TABLE 4 (continued)

Theory	View of an organization	Role of an IS	References
Cybernetics	Organization is a goal-seeking, self-steering system maintaining homeostatic balance through feedback-based learning	Variety generating and filtering mechanism	Blumenthal (1969) Rochfëldt and Tardieu (1983) Espejo (1980)
Functional contingency theory	Organization is an adaptation mechanism to environmental and task-uncertainty based on contingencies	A means to cope with uncertainty	Olerup (1980)
Scientific Marxism	Organization is a set of practices and social relations embedded into a class-conflict	Serves class-domination and adaptation to capitalist value accumulation	Sandberg (1979, 1985)
Transaction-cost economic	Organization is any stable pattern of transactions between agents	Mediator in governing transactions	Ciborra (1984, 1985)
Organizational politics	Organization is an arena for political activity where actors engage in a conflict and negotiate for private interest	Instrument in a political game	Pettigrew (1980) Markus (1983) Kling and Iacono (1984) Franz and Robey (1984)
Critical theory	Organization is a means to advance personal autonomy, social cooperation, and democratic will-formation	An input and a means for a democratic debate	Lyytinen and Klein (1985) Lyytinen (1986)

resolution, maintenance and negotiation of meanings and world-views. This kind of view has often been adopted in approaches that criticize the individualistic, decision-oriented view of the IS (Ciborra, 1985; Goldkuhl and Lyytinen, 1984; Flores and Ludlow, 1981; Boland, 1979; Klein and Hirschheim, 1985). Instead these views concentrate on IS as a social and political phenomenon: how it affects communication patterns; authority and power structures; legitimation of organizational action; maintenance of belief systems and norms and so on.

If one selects determinism one sustains a view that the IS use is determined by causal factors which affect its organizational outcomes. If one prefers voluntarism one is inclined to believe that the IS use can be understood by more 'soft' notions such as enactment, interpretation of meanings, and socialization into local values, myths and rituals. Therefore determinism entails realism, whereas voluntarism typically embraces nominalism.

Deterministic stances tend to adopt closed models in understanding organizational behaviour, whereas voluntarism places more emphasis on open models (Boland and Pondy, 1981). The former emphasize object systems as efficient input–output transformations whereas latter focus on organizations' adaptation to task and environmental uncertainty.

3.5 Super-contexts

Information systems development must be able to represent, analyse, assess and carry out changes in all three object system contexts. Hence, systems development does not just produce changes in technology, communications or organizational behaviours, it also involves activities by which we find out how these changes are related to each other and how they are 'funnelled' through other contexts. Therefore good ISDMs recognize that they need to relate all three contexts in some way.

In real life all three contexts are intertwined and are only separable through a conceptual analysis. This can be easily ascertained by thinking of common systems description techniques and figuring out which contexts their different parts relate to.

To perform this kind of conceptual analysis we shall introduce a notion of *a super-context*. A super-context is a context by which a developer combines any two contexts to see how phenomena in these two contexts are interrelated. With a super-context a developer can bind together diversified phenomena when carrying out and analysing the IS change [1]. Figure 4 depicts the possible super-contexts that can be deployed during systems development.

In an ideal case all super-contexts exhibited in Figure 4 are covered in a systems development methodology. However, this is not always the case. For example, software engineering methodologies cover only the technology context, socio-technical methodologies cover only technology and organization contexts, and so on.

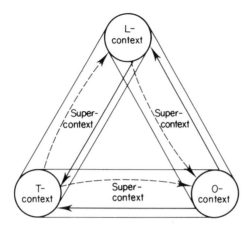

FIGURE 4 Super-contexts in systems development

In principle each object system context can serve as a starting point to build super-contexts. Those methodologies that cover only one object system context use this as a starting point (and end-point). In those methodologies that cover several object system contexts the choice of the starting point is more problematic. The traditional perspective has been to see information systems development as a technical innovation which has behavioural and social consequences. In this case systems development is targeted at the technological context, which is selected as the starting point, and possible courses of action in this context are evaluated using descriptive mappings to the organization context (which in most cases are assumed to be deterministic; see, for example, Bariff and Ginzberg (1982)). Others, like ETHICS, choose both the technology and the organization contexts as simultaneous starting points, where changes are developed in parallel and coordinated during the systems development.

In our opinion both these approaches are rather too narrow and do not fully take account of the complexity and the inner nature of systems development. We see information systems as organizational communication systems that are just technically implemented and which rely to an increasing extent on information technology (Land and Hirschheim, 1983). This perspective requires that the initial focus is put on the language context — in symbolic interactions and on language change to improve them. The technology context is always subordinated to language change and technology is just a component and a means to accomplish it (Goldkuhl and Lyytinen, 1982). In this case, the organization context is seen as a boundary environment which sets conditions and explains the need to intervene in both other contexts.

The role of super-contexts in systems development is to map desirable changes in one context onto others. This necessitates two kinds of mappings: *descriptive* and *instrumental*. Descriptive mappings permit developers to anticipate how changes in one context 'cascade' into other contexts. Descriptive mappings have been the main topic in social analyses of computing (Kling, 1980; Attewell and Rule, 1984). In general, this knowledge is needed to choose among available courses of action and for discussion of their possible outcomes. Descriptive mappings need not necessarily (and in most cases they are not) be causal. Descriptive mappings are depicted by broken arrows in Figure 4.

Instrumental mappings permit developers to translate planned changes in one context into changes in other contexts. Instrumental mappings are depicted by solid arrows in Figure 4. They express means–ends relationships between object system changes and can therefore be expressed as practical inferences (von Wright, 1971). Instrumental mappings are derivative, because they are based on knowledge about descriptive mappings. Instrumental mappings are mainly obtained by following rules included in systems development methodologies. Examples of systems development approaches dealing with various type of instrumental mappings are depicted in Figure 5.

The nature of the mapping process is to a large extent determined by the prior decisions concerning the object systems' ontology and epistemology that are included in the mapping process. In the mainstream of IS-literature, the mappings are assumed to be functional and deterministic (causal). For example, it is assumed that technical attributes of the new technology can be directly translated into social attributes, e.g. faster data flows entail faster and better decisions. Kling and Scacchi (1982) call these kinds of conceptions of organizational impacts of technological change 'discrete-entity' analysis. They criticize discrete-entity analysis for its

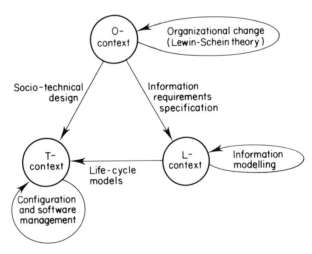

FIGURE 5 *Examples of development approaches dealing with instrumental mappings*

limitations and mechanistic bias and develop a richer family of models — 'web models' — which study technological change as a part of a larger social and technical mosaic in which the development and use of the focal technology is embedded. By so doing they relax some of the realist and positivist assumptions underlying the discrete-entity analysis.

In our opinion, Kling's and Scacchi's analysis can be expanded to cover all descriptive and instrumental mappings in all three super-contexts. We shall call conceptions similar to their discrete-entity models *deterministic* mappings, and conceptions similar to their web-models *emergent* and *contingent* mappings. In the extreme case the latter conceptions will assume that any mapping between two contexts (or within context) is contingent and has only emergent properties.

The above has important consequences for our understanding of the systems development process. If one applies only deterministic mappings, then one does not have any means uncertainty (in instrumental mappings) or effect uncertainty (in descriptive mappings). All knowledge about these mappings is completely context-independent and can be applied in every circumstance. On the other hand, if all mappings are claimed to be contingent and emergent then uncertainty in the systems development is extremely high. No generalizations can be made of its likely outcomes. Thus, if one assumes deterministic mappings then the systems development process can be thought of as a linear and well-defined sequence of transformations between and within object system contexts, which in the ideal case, can be fully automated. If one assumes that all mappings are contingent and emergent, every development process is dissimilar: no well-defined sequence of activities can fully capture its real emergent and situated nature.

4. TOWARD A TAXONOMY OF DEVELOPMENT METHODOLOGIES

4.1 General Principles

The following taxonomic criteria are used to develop a preliminary taxonomy of systems development methodologies:

(1) which object system contexts are covered by the ISDM and what is their role?
(2) which types of object systems are actually generated for each context when the ISDM is applied?
(3) what presentation forms are being used, and how are they employed?
(4) what is the ontology and epistemology of the object systems?
(5) which super-contexts are covered; what mapping types are analyzed within each of them?
(6) what is the nature of the analyzed mappings?

These criteria result in the taxonomic criteria of Table 5. The criteria are listed in the order of their relative importance. For us, the most important criterion

TABLE 5 Taxonomic principles for ISD methodology classification

Taxonomic criterion	Alternatives		
1. Contexts covered	Technology	Language	Organization
2. Object systems generated	Data Process Abstraction levels Type: disjoint, overlapping, conflicting	5 language views	4 main regions
3. Representation forms and their use	Natural language, semiformal, formal Descriptive, predictive, interpretative, reconstructive, prescriptive		
4. Ontology Epistemology	Realism and nominalism Positivism and antipositivism		
5. Super-context mapping type	6 + 3 super-contexts Descriptive and instrumental		
6. Nature of mapping	Deterministic and emergent		

is the number of contexts covered, because it separates methodologies that cover only technological change from those covering changes in more than one context.

The second criterion helps us to pick out those object systems that are generated for a given context in each methodology. We are also interested in whether overlapping and conflicting object systems are permitted.

The third criterion indicates the type of representation forms needed to depict object systems. We also reveal their major uses.

The fourth criterion classifies methodologies by the nature of their assumptions about the ontology and epistemology of identified object systems. These assumptions are important in determining which inquiring and interaction strategies are appropriate for a given stage or task of ISD.

The fifth criterion focuses on options which exist for methodologies to map changes in one object system context to another. It also helps to identify which linkages or types of mappings are 'seen' when one looks at the domain of change through the 'spectacles' of a particular methodology. These mappings are important for analyzing a methodology's development strategy and principles that guide selection and assessment of change alternatives.

The sixth criterion classifies the mappings in the methodology. If mappings are deterministic then a methodology appeals to the ideal of a well-defined, rational problem-solving process. If these mappings are emergent, then a methodology appeals more to the idea of a fuzzy social, symbolic and political change.

It should be noted that our taxonomic criteria do not focus on surface differences in the representation forms, concept structure, methods, or tools in methodologies, as is done in the majority of other methodology comparisons, such as in the CRIS effort (Olle *et al.*, 1983, Bemelmans, 1984) [2]. Although this area is an important research concern, we have a different goal. We aim at a classification which penetrates into the background theories and assumptions of ISDMs, by which developers draw insights and solutions to problems they confront in systems development situations.

4.2 Taxonomic Classification of Some Systems Development Methodologies

We have chosen several methodologies to be analysed [3]. These are ISAC (Lundeberg *et al.*, 1981), structured analysis and design (SA) (Yordon, 1982; DeMarco, 1979), NIAM (Verheijen and van Bekkum, 1982), CIAM (Gustafsson *et al.*, 1982), ETHICS (Mumford, 1982), development of decision-support systems as outlined in Keen and Scott-Morton (1978), the MIS-research framework by Mason and Mitroff (1973), information requirements specification approach discussed in Boland (1979), and information analysis and requirements specification approach suggested by Lyytinen and Lehtinen (1984a, 1984b).

The analysis is exploratory and tries to illuminate how we could use taxonomic principles to study development methodologies. The result of our analysis is depicted in Table 5.

Because of the large number of possible taxonomic classes (3×19 [4] $\times 15$ [5] $\times 4 \times 18 \times 2$) we have grouped our taxonomic space into larger (super) classes. Within each such class, methodologies share principal common features such as the context covered and the object systems generated. The classes used in our analysis are: technical design oriented methodologies, socio-technical methodologies, decision-oriented methodologies, sense-making-oriented methodologies, and communication-oriented methodologies.

Technical design oriented methodologies cover mainly contexts L and T, and their idea is to introduce change in the technology context to implement communications specified in L. Socio-technical methodologies cover T and O, and their principal concern is to adopt technological change into an organizational situation. The other three taxonomic classes cover contexts O and L, and their principal concern is relating communications and information supply with the phenomena in the organization context. They differ remarkably, however, in terms of object systems generated, especially in the organization context. In decision-oriented methodologies object systems in the organization context locate into the upper left region of Figure 3. In sense-making-oriented methodologies they can be found in the lower left region of Figure 3. In communication-oriented methodologies they are in the lower right region of Figure 3.

The first four of the included methodologies are either widely used in practice (SA and ISAC) or have been included in the CRIS-case (CIAM and NIAM)

TABLE 6 Taxonomic classification of some ISDMs

Methodology & taxonomic class	Object system contexts	Object systems generated	Representation forms & use	Ontology & epistemology	Super-contexts	Nature of mappings
ISAC technical design-oriented	P(O) P(L) W(T)	O: collective, mainly deterministic (functional) / L: Fregean core / Skinnerian resp. / T: process-oriented all levels covered disjoint object systems	graphs narratives descriptive	realist mainly positivist	P(I(T,T)) P(D(T,O)) W(I(L,T)) P(I(L,L)) P(I(O,L)) P(I(O,T)) P(I(O,O))	mainly deterministic
SA technical design-oriented	A(O) W(T)	O: collective, deterministic / L: none / T: process-oriented two highest levels covered disjoint object systems	graphs narrative descriptive predictive	realist positivist	A(I(T,T)) W(I(L,T)) A(I(O,L))	mainly deterministic
NIAM technical design-oriented	P(O) W(L) P(T)	O: collective, deterministic / L: Fregean core / T: data-oriented two highest levels covered disjoint object systems	graphs narratives descriptive	realist positivist	P(I(O,L)) W(I(L,L)) P(I(L,T))	deterministic

CIAM technical design oriented	W(L) P(T)	O: none (collective, deterministic) L: Fregean core T: date-oriented highest level covered disjoint object systems	predicate logic descriptive predictive	realist positivist	P(I(O,L)) W(I(L,L)) A(I(L,T))	deterministic
ETHICS socio-technical	W(T) W(O)	O: role theory (collective, mainly deterministic) T: through process all levels covered overlapping/conflicting object systems	narratives tables, graphs descriptive P(I(O,O))	mainly realist and positivist	A(I(T,T)) W(D(T,O)) A(I(L,T)) P(I(O,L)) W(I(O,T)) P(D(L,O))	mainly emergent
DSS decision-oriented	W(O) P(L) P(T)	O: individual, deterministic L: Skinnerian response/Piaget's schema T: not expl. covered overlapping/conflicting object systems	narratives tables descriptive predictive	mainly realist and positivist	W(I(O,L)) W(I(O,T)) W(D(T,O)) A(I(L,T)) A(I(T,T))	mainly deterministic

continued

TABLE 6 (continued)

Methodology & taxonomic class	Object system contexts	Object systems generated	Representation forms & use	Ontology & epistemology	Super-contexts	Nature of mappings
Mason's and Mitroff's MIS-programme decision-oriented	W(O) P(L)	O: individual/ deterministic L: Skinnerian response Piaget's schema disjoint object systems	narrative descriptive predictive descriptive	mainly realist and positivist	W(I(O,L)) P(I(L,L)) P(D(L,O)) P(D(O,O))	mainly deterministic
Boland's IRQ-determination approach sense-making oriented	W(O) W(L)	O: mainly individual/ voluntaristic L: ordinary speaking T: none overlapping/conflicting object systems	narrative descriptive interpretive	nominalist antipositivist	W(I(O,L)) P(I(L,L)) P(D(L,O)) P(D(O,O))	emergent
Lyytinen & Lehtinen's IRQ-determination approach communication-oriented	W(O) W(L)	O: mainly collective/ voluntaristic L: ordinary speaking overlapping/conflicting object systems	graphs narratives descriptive interpretive reconstructive	nominalist antipositivist	W(I(O,L)) W(I(L,L)) W(D(L,O)) P(D(O,O))	mainly emergent

Legend: P = poorly covered, W = well covered, A = assumed to be covered during ISD, D(O,L) = descriptive mapping from organization to language context

(Olle *et al.*, 1982). All these belong to the technical design-oriented methodologies because of their heavy interest in the technological change associated with systems development. Typical is the domination of design and engineering principles in the methodology design. Most mappings are instrumental, their nature is deterministic, and systems development is structured as a stepwise engineering process.

ETHICS is an example of the socio-technical methodology class. Typical for it is a keen emphasis on mappings between organization and technology contexts and the mutual adaptation of technology to organization context. Therefore both instrumental and descriptive mappings are covered in the T–O-super-context and they are mainly seen as emergent.

Examples of decision-oriented approaches to IS-design are Mason and Mitroff's MIS program and decision-support systems approach by Keen and Scott-Morton as documented in these works. Their focus is on the individualistic/deterministic corner of the organization object systems and the information needs of an individual to arrive at a decision. Thus the emphasis is placed on the instrumental and descriptive mappings between organization and language contexts. Language context is, however, greatly delimited. It is represented mainly as a parameter in the IS design model. Therefore the nature of mappings is mainly deterministic. The technology context in these methodologies is virtually non-existent.

Boland's approach is an example of a sense-making-oriented approach to IS design. The focus here is more on the individual/voluntaristic corner of the organization context and on the mutual interactions between language and the organization context. Mappings between the contexts are emergent and cyclical.

Lyytinen and Lehtinen provide an example of a communication-oriented methodology. The methodology focuses on the interactions between the language context and the organization context. The focus is on the collective use of language in coordinating and initiating interactions in the organization. Therefore, both these contexts are covered but the main emphasis is on the study of the communicative use of language.

Taking Table 6 as our base we can summarize the following features for taxonomic classes:

(1) *coverage of systems development methodologies*. It can be seen that the domain of change is conceived very differently in each taxonomic class. Technical design-oriented methodologies primarily address change in the technology contexts. In this sense, they see systems development mainly from a technical systems designer's point of view. The other taxonomic classes see other facets of the IS change such as: impact and adoption of technology to organization, individual learning and improvement of individual decision-effectiveness, collective sense-making, or the nature and type of contracting through the IS.

(2) *object systems generated*. Technical design-oriented methodologies view an organization narrowly, or it is not taken into a consideration. Generated

models are based on mechanistic and collective theories of organizational behaviour. Their models of linguistic phenomena are similarly founded on formal and mechanistic theories such as the Fregean core and Skinnerian response views. Other taxonomic classes such as sense-making-oriented and communication-oriented methodologies propose a wider spectrum of ways to view organizations and linguistic phenomena.

(3) *representation forms and their use*. Most taxonomic classes use representation forms in description. Some technical design-oriented methodologies use them also for prediction. The sense-making and communication-oriented classes on the other hand note also interpretive, reconstructive and prescriptive uses. Technical design-oriented methodologies prefer mainly formal or semi-formal representation forms. In the remaining taxonomic classes their importance is less emphasized.

(4) *ontology and epistemology*. Technical design-oriented methodologies regard symbols and organizations as behaving like computer systems and consisting of states of nature that can be designed from without by intervening and restructuring them in systems design. For example, their models of the communication situation is usually represented by a model of signal transmission through a channel; the organization as communication interaction structures (sociograms); the human as an information processor, and so on. In other methodology classes these requirements are relaxed as we approach sense-making- and communication-oriented methodologies.

(5) *super-context and mappings*. Technical design-oriented methodologies focus on principal instrumental mappings between language and technology contexts, i.e. how a specific communication pattern can be technically implemented in an efficient way. For this reason, descriptive mappings concerning job-satisfaction, power changes, etc. are disregarded. In the remaining taxonomic classes the coverage of mappings is wider. Unfortunately, each proposes a quite limited set of mappings covering just a particular aspect of interrelationships between two contexts. A good example is socio-technical methodologies, which offer a rich conceptual machinery to relate technological alternatives to the social system of work, i.e. roles, tasks, values and needs. They cannot, however, cope with other mapping types, such as interactions between organization and language, and thus if used alone, can result in a quite narrow view of the change.

(6) *nature of mappings*. In technical design-oriented methodologies, mappings are in the ideal case deterministic. This is especially true with instrumental mappings that go inside the technology context. However, the same schema is extended to cover changes from organization to language context, and from language to technology context. Other taxonomic classes offer a richer view of mappings. Some point out that changes in the language and organization contexts are cyclically related and therefore deterministic relationships between these phenomena cannot be found. Instead development outcomes depend

on the quality of interpretive and reconstructive processes by which developers try to understand and explicate emergent interactions between organizational and communication activities.

4.3 Recommendations

Our exploratory analysis reveals that approaches to IS development can be radically different. This raises several problems that need to be solved by the IS research community. For example, how can we compare different approaches, what kind of approaches should one choose in a given development situation, on which reference disciplines and frameworks should we base development methodologies and approaches on? We shall briefly address four issues and provide some general recommendations on how they might be tackled in future research. These issues are:

—the notion of a systems development methodology,
—methodology assessment,
—methodology selection, and
—theoretical foundations of systems development approaches.

It is clear that some of the suggestions to which the framework of this chapter leads are not completely new, but the proposed framework allows us to understand their interrelationships and significance better. Moreover, the framework provides a cohesive set of concepts from which many of the earlier findings can be logically derived. It therefore suggests an economical and concise starting point to develop a more encompassing theoretical foundation for ISD.

A systems development methodology has traditionally had the ring of a well-defined procedure which enables the developer to proceed in a step-by-step basis towards achieving a particular result. In the light of our discussion this notion appears to be too limited and rigid. First, the results of the systems development exercise depend on what object systems and contexts one wants to see. Therefore, results can vary, as will the process producing them. Second, the nature of the change process, especially the types of uncertainty involved in bringing about the result, may suggest that the goal of a well-sequenced process is just an idealistic illusion. Therefore, a methodology should be conceived in broader terms as a general way of thinking and going about developing an information system. This also suggests that IS research should develop a variety of *radically different ways* of defining what a systems development methodology is and what aspects of systems development it covers.

Most *methodology assessments* build on the assumption that it is possible to predict the outcomes of systems development. Therefore methodologies can be compared with respect to the means by which they help to achieve desired outcomes. The proposed framework suggests that only those methodologies which fall in the same taxonomic class should be compared, i.e. STS-methodologies cannot be compared with technical design-oriented methodologies because they differ in terms of their covered contexts. In addition, methodologies include quite different, if not conflicting, assumptions about the development environments (Lyytinen, 1986), embedded values and goals (Klein, 1981), and organizational forms the development group should adopt. This suggests that methodology assessment is fraught with many difficulties which have to be adequately recognized in future research. But this does not necessarily mean that methodology assessments are just a waste of time and energy. We should as a community be much more careful when trying to compare methodologies and when trying to validate the results of such comparisons. This necessitates that IS research should develop more refined taxonomic frameworks on which to base such assessments.

The issue of *methodology selection* deserves careful attention. In our opinion, in this choice the first issue to be addressed is the nature of change process a development group is facing. Assumptions must be elicited defining problems and possible solutions to those problems. In other words, the following questions must be dealt with:

(1) what is the nature of the development problem, in which context, and under what goals and assumptions it is valid (context analysis)?
(2) what are the stakeholders of the problem, and what are their goals and interests (stakeholder analysis (Mason and Mitroff, 1981))?
(3) what object system representations are needed to conceptualize and address the problem, to anticipate its repercussions, and how they are used (object system analysis)?
(4) what ontological and epistemological postulates are brought into the problem definition (postulate analysis)?

We believe, that only after dealing with these issues can the choice be made of the possible methodology relevant for carrying out the change process. An urgent research task is to study more carefully the processes and factors that may be useful in making this decision. Clearly it is not a decision that can be made by the DP-professionals alone, because their view of the change involved can be limited and biased. Top management, end-users, unions and so forth should have their say (Ciborra and Bracchi, 1983). In this connection, other issues also become critical, such as the learning problems related to the methodologies, problems of their use, organizational adaptation to the methodology change, organizational decision-making about methodologies and so on.

Theoretical foundations of systems development methodologies should be enlarged and their impact on the proposed methodologies should be more thoroughly analysed. Several research avenues are open to us here. First, the language context should be dealt with as an independent sphere of the IS change. This necessitates that the richness of insights gained from the study of language should be carefully adapted to the specification of methodologies. Second, the functional views of the organization context should be enlarged with more individualistic, pheno-menological and conflict views of the organizational behaviour (cf. Ciborra, 1985; Goldkuhl and Lyytinen, 1984; Boland, 1985; Klein and Hirschheim, 1983). In our opinion this will result in totally new insights about the nature and role of IS in organizational action. Third, more research should be directed to solving the issue of how to interlink object system representations in different contexts during concrete systems work. An example of a first attempt in this direction is the multiview methodology of Wood-Harper *et al.* (1985). However, more research is needed to clarify how this can be done with all object system representations. Fourth, the nature and type of mappings embedded in the methodologies should be more carefully analysed and based on results of empirical studies. An encouraging example of this kind of work is Kling and Scacchi's (1982) work on web-models.

5. SUMMARY AND CONCLUSIONS

If one looks at the recurrent reasons for IS failure, one can see numerous applied technical design-oriented methodologies which do not focus on the reasons for the failure. Most IS failures are caused by conceptual problems, data problems, and people problems (Lyytinen, 1986). These problems to a large extent relate to the changes in the language and organization contexts. However, in technical design-oriented methodologies these changes are either neglected or understood in too mechanistic and simple terms. In fact, their use can even strengthen a failure pattern, because they given an impression of well-defined, well-behaving phenomena.

All this suggests that the notion of a systems development methodology deserves a more thorough analysis in the IS research community than has so far been made. In this chapter we have made some progress in this direction. We have studied several methodological approaches by taking into account what they suggest one should see (and get) in systems development. Unfortunately, as our study indicates, most of the currently used methodologies limit their field of view too narrowly. This results in a paradoxical situation in their use. Instead of getting what one sees and seeing what one gets, one does not get what one sees, and one gets what one does not see. To remedy this situation we should more carefully reflect on what a methodology can lead one to see and (hopefully) get when one is engaged in systems development.

ACKNOWLEDGEMENTS

I am greatly indebted to Dick Welke who first introduced me to the idea of the object system, and Heinz Klein who carefully criticized earlier drafts of this chapter. Thanks also go to Rudy Hirschheim for the careful reading that improved the language of the chapter.

NOTES

[1] Super-contexts are not typical only of information systems development and research. For example, organization theorists and sociologists relate technology and organization (for example, Leawitt's diamond), or organization and linguistic phenomena (see, for example, Jelinek *et al.*, 1983). Their analyses can involve interactions between technology and organization (work-sociology, industrial relationships); organization and language (accounting) etc. Therefore, super-contexts have paradigmatic features when employed in systems development. These relate to their total coverage of all three super-contexts and their specific features discussed in section 3.5.

[2] Unfortunately, CRIS-effort (Olle *et al.*, 1982) has limited its focus to the design, i.e. to phases where it has been agreed that a system is needed (Olle *et al.*, 1982 p. 2). Although this simplifies methodology comparison and assessment, it does not necessarily improve the practice of developing successful information systems. The reason is that in this way CRIS just seeks better ways to diminish means uncertainty in systems design, and this radically limits the number of contexts and the type of object systems considered. However, the problems of systems development may not lie in those object systems considered when designing the system (and, in fact, in most cases they do not).

[3] It should be noted, that the approaches are quite different in their sophistication and usability. All included works are not proposals for methodologies in a literal sense. This is especially true for Mason and Mitroff (1973). Keen and Scott-Morton (1978) and Boland (1979). Rather, they are loose freameworks on which such methodologies could be developed in the long run. However, because we focus on underlying assumptions and viewpoints they can be compared to other more well-thought out approaches.

[4] There are ten object systems in the technology context, five object systems in the language context, and four main regions in the organizational context.

[5] There are three representation forms and five main uses.

REFERENCES

Ackoff, R. L. (1971) 'Towards a System of System Concepts', *Management Science*, **17**, 11, 661–671.

Attewell, P., and Rule, J. (1984) 'Computing and Organizations: what we know and what we don't know', *Communications of the ACM*, **27**, 12, 1184–1192.

Bariff, M., and Ginzberg, M. J. (1982) 'MIS and the Behavioral Sciences', *Data Base*, **13**, 1, 19–26.

Bemelmans, T. H. (Ed.) (1984) *Beyond Productivity: Information Systems for Organizational Effectiveness*, North-Holland, Amsterdam.

Berger, P. L., and Luckmann, T. (1967) *The Social Construction of Reality*, Penguin Books, Harmondsworth.

Blumenthal, S. C. (1969) *Management Information Systems: A Framework for Planning and Development*, Prentice-Hall, Englewood Cliffs, N. J.

Boehm, B. W., Brown, J. R., and Lipow, M. (1977) 'Quantitative Evaluation of Software Quality', Software Phenomenology — Working Papers of the Software Lifecycle Management Workshop, pp. 81–94.

Boland, R. J. Jr. (1979) 'Control, Causality and Information System Requirements', *Accounting, Organizations and Society*, **4**, 5, 259–272.

Boland, R. J. Jr. (1985) 'Phenomenology: A Preferred Approach to Research on Information Systems', in *Research Methods in Information Systems*, E. Mumford, R. Hirschheim, G. Fitzgerald and A. T. Wood-Harper (Eds.), North-Holland, Amsterdam, pp. 193–203.

Boland, R. J. Jr., and Day, W. (1982) 'The Process of System Design: A Phenomenological Approach', in *Proceedings of the 3rd International Conference on Information Systems, Ann Arbor, Michigan, Dec. 13–15, 1982*, M. Ginzberg and C. Ross (Eds.), pp. 31–45.

Boland, R. J. Jr., and Pondy, L. R. (1981) 'Accounting in Organizations: A Union of Natural and Rational Perspectives', BEPR Faculty Working Paper No. 811, College of Commerce and Business Administration, University of Illinois Bureau of Economic and Business Research, Urbana-Champaign.

Bubenko, J. Jr. (1983) 'Information and Data Modelling: State of the Art and Research Directions', in *Proceedings of Second Scandinavian Research Seminar on Information Modelling and Data Base Management, Acta Universitas Tamperensis, Ser. B*, Vol. 19, H. Kangassalo (Ed.), University of Tampere, Finland, pp. 9–28.

Burrell, G., and Morgan, G. (1979) *Sociological Paradigms and Organizational Analysis*, Heinemann, London.

Checkland, P. (1981) *Systems Thinking, Systems Practice*, John Wiley, Chichester.

Ciborra, C. U. (1984) 'Information Systems and Organizational Exchange: a New Design Approach', in *Beyond Productivity — Information Systems for Organizational Effectiveness*, T. Bemelmans (Ed.), North-Holland, Amsterdam, pp. 135–145.

Ciborra, C. U. (1985) 'Reframing the Role of Computers in Organizations: The Transaction Costs Approach', in *Proceedings of the Sixth International Conference on Information Systems*, L. Gallegos, R. Welke, and J. Wetherbe (Eds.), Indianapolis, Indiana.

Ciborra, C. U., and Bracchi, G. (1983) 'Systems Development and Auditing in Turbulent Contexts: towards a new participative approach', in *Information Systems Auditing*, E. M. Wysong, and I. de Lotto (Eds.), North-Holland, Amsterdam, pp. 41–52.

Colombetti, G., Guida, G. and Somalvico, M. (1983) 'Natural Language Reasoning and Analysis of Data Base Requirements', in *Methodology and Tools for Data Base Design*, S. Ceri (Ed.), North-Holland, Amsterdam, pp. 163–180.

Cooper, R. B., and Swanson, E. B. (1979) 'Management Information Requirements Assessment: The State of the Art', *Data Base*, **11**, 2, 5–16.

Cotterman, W. W., Couger, J. D., Enger, N. L., and Harold, F. (Eds.) (1981) *Systems Analysis and Design: A Foundation for the 1980s*, North-Holland, Amsterdam.

Date, C. (1982) *An Introduction to Data Base Systems* (3rd Edn.), Addison-Wesley, Reading, MA.

Davis, G. B. (1982) 'Strategies for Information Requirements Determination', *IBM Systems Journal*, **21**, 1, 4–30.

Davis, G. B., and Olson, M. (1985) *Management Information Systems — Conceptual Foundations Methods and Development* (2nd Edn.), McGraw-Hill, New York.

DeMarco, T. (1979) *Structured Analysis and System Specification*, Yourdon Inc., New York.

Earl, M. J., and Hopwood, A. G. (1980) 'From Management Information to Information Management', in *The Information Systems Environment*, H. Lucas, F. Land, T. Lincoln and K. Supper (Eds.), North-Holland, Amsterdam, pp. 3–12.

Ein-Dor, P., and Segev, E. (1978) 'Organizational Context and the Success of Management Information Systems', *Management Science*, **24**, 10, 1064–1077.

Espejo, R. (1980) 'Information and Management: The Cybernetics of a Small Company', in *The Information Systems Environment*, H. C. Lucas Jr., F. F. Land, T. J. Lincoln and K. Supper (Eds.), North-Holland, Amsterdam, pp. 291–310.

Etzioni, A. (1967) *The Active Society: Theory of Societal and Political Processes*, Free Press, New York.

Flores, F., and Ludlow, J. J. (1981) 'Doing and Speaking in the Office', in *Decision Support Systems — Issues and Challenges*, G. Fick and R. Sprague (Eds.), Pergamon Press, London, pp. 95–118.

Franz, C. R. and Robey, D. (1984) 'An Investigation of User-led System Design: Rational and Political Perspectives', *Communications of the ACM*, **27**, 12, 1202–1209.

Gadamer, H.-G. (1975) *Truth and Method* (translated by G. Barden and J. Cumming), Seabury Press, New York.

Galbraith, J. (1977) *Organization Design*, Addison-Wesley, Reading, MA.

Goldkuhl, G., and Lyytinen, K. (1982) 'A Language Action View of Information Systems', in *Proceedings of the 3rd International Conference on Information Systems*, Ann Arbor, Michigan, Dec. 13–15, 1982, M. Ginzberg and C. Ross (Eds.), pp. 13–30.

Goldkuhl, G., and Lyytinen, K. (1984) 'Information System Specification as Rule Reconstruction', in *Beyond Productivity — Information Systems for Organizational Effectiveness*, T. Bemelmans (Ed.), North-Holland, Amsterdam, pp. 30–55.

Griethuysen, J. J. van (Ed.) (1982) *Concepts and Terminology for the Conceptual Schema and the Information Base*, ISO/TC97 Computers and Information Processing, New York (ISO/TC97/SC5/WG3).

Gustafsson, M. R., Karlsson, T., and Bubenko, J. A. (1982) 'A Declarative Approach to Conceptual Information Modelling', SYSLAB Technical Report 8, Department of Information Processing and Computer Science, University of Stockholm.

Hirschheim, R. A. (1985) 'Information Systems Epistemology: An Historical Perspective', in *Research Methods in Information Systems*, E. Mumford, R. Hirschheim, G. Fitzgerald, and T. Wood-Harper (Eds.), North-Holland, Amsterdam, pp. 13–38.

Huber, G. P. (1981) 'Organizational Science Contributions to the Design of Decision Support Systems', in *Decision Support Systems: Issues and Challenges*, G. Fick and R. H. Sprague (Eds.), Pergamon Press, Oxford, pp. 45–56.

Iivari, J. (1983) 'Contributions to the Theoretical Foundations of Systemeering Research and the PIOCO-model', Ph.D. dissertation, *Acta Universitatis Ouluensis, Ser. A* 150, Institute of Data Processing, University of Oulu, Oulu.

Iivari, J., and Koskela, E. (1983) 'The Object System Model in the PIOCO metamodel of the Data System', *Acta Universitatis Tamperensis Ser. B*, Vol. 19, University of Tampere, Tampere, pp. 29–70.

Israel, J. (1979) *The Language of Dialectics — The Dialectics of Language*, Munksgaard, Copenhagen.

Itkonen, E. (1978) *Grammatical Theory and Metascience*, John Benjamins, Amsterdam.

Jackson, M. (1975) *Principles of Program Design*, Academic Press, London.

Jelinek, A., Smircich, L., and Hirsch, D. (1983) 'Introduction: A Code of Many Colours', *Administrative Science Quarterly*, **28**, 331–338 (Special issue on organizational cultures).

Johnson, P. E. (1984) 'The Expert Mind: a New Challenge for the Information Scientist', in *Beyond Productivity — Information Systems for Organizational Effectiveness*, T. Bemelmans (Ed.), North-Holland, Amsterdam, pp. 367–386.

Keen, P. G. W. (1981a) 'Decision Support Systems: A Research Perspective', in *Decision Support Systems: Issues and Challenges*, G. Fick, and R. L. Sprague Jr. (Eds.), Pergamon Press, Oxford, pp. 23–44.

Keen, P. G. W. (1981b) 'Information Systems and Organizational Change', *Communications of the ACM*, **24**, 1, 24–33.

Keen, P. G. W., and Scott-Morton, M. S. (1978) *Decision Support Systems: An Organizational Perspective*, Addison-Wesley, Reading, MA.

Kendall, K. E., and Kriebel, C. H. (1982) 'Contributions of the Management Sciences to the Evolution of Management Information Systems', *Data Base*, **13**, 1, 13–18.

Kensing, F. (1984) 'Towards Evaluation of Methods for Property Determination — A Framework and Critique of Yordon–DeMarco Approach', in *Beyond Productivity: Information Systems Development for Organization Effectiveness*, T. M. A. Bemelmans (Ed.), North-Holland, Amsterdam, pp. 325–338.

Kleijnen, J. P. C. (1980) *Computers and Profits — Quantifying Financial Benefits of Information System*, Prentice-Hall, Englewood Cliffs, N. J.

Klein, H. K. (1981) 'Design Ideals and their Critical Reconstruction', ISRAM DP-8105-2.2, ISRAM, Faculty of Business, McMaster University, Hamilton.

Klein, H. K. (1984) 'Which Epistemologies for Future Information Systems Research', in *Report of the 7th Scandinavian Research Seminar on Systemeering (part I)*, M. Saaksjarvi (Ed.), Helsinki Business School, Helsinki, pp. 60–90.

Klein, H. K., and Hirschheim, R. (1983) 'Issues and Approaches in Appraising Technological Change in the Office: A Consequentalist Perspective', *Office: Technology and People*, **2**, 1, 15–42.

Klein, H. K., and Hirschheim, R. (1985) 'Fundamental Issues of Decision Support Systems: a Consequentalist Perspective', *Decision Support Systems*, **1**, 1.

Kling, R. (1980) 'Social Analyses of Computing: Theoretical Perspectives in Recent Empirical Research', *ACM Computing Surveys*, **12**, 1, 61–110.

Kling, R. (1985) 'Computerization as an On-going Social and Political Process', in *Proceedings of the Working Conference on Development and Use of Computer-based Systems and Tools — in the context of democratization of work*, vol. II, Arhus Universitet, Arhus, pp. 309–328.

Kling, R., and Iacono, S. (1984) 'The Control of Information Systems Developments after Implementation', *Communications of the ACM*, **27**, 12, 1218–1226.

Kling, R., and Scacchi, W. (1982) 'The Social Web of Computing: Computer Technology as Social Organization', *Advances in Computers*, Vol. 21, Academic Press, New York, pp. 2–90.

Kubicek, H. (1983) 'User Participation in System Design: some questions about the structure and content arising from recent research from a trade union perspective', in *Systems Design for, with, and by the Users*, U. Briefs, C. Ciborra and L. Schneider (Eds.), North-Holland, Amsterdam, pp. 3–18.

Laine, H., Maanavilja, O. (Eds.) and Peltola, E. (1979) 'The Grammatical Data Base Model', *Information Systems*, **4**, 4, 257–267.

Land, F., and Hirschheim, R. (1983) 'Participative Systems Design: Rationale, Tools and Techniques', *Journal of Applied Systems Analysis*, **10**, 91–107.

Lehman, M. M. (1984) 'Program Evolution', *Information Processing & Management*, **20**, 1–2, 19–36.

Lehmann, G. (1978) 'An Interpretation of Natural Language in an Information System', *IBM Journal of Research and Development*, **22**, 5, 560–572.

Lehtinen, E., and Lyytinen, K. (1986) 'Action Based Model of Information System', *Information Systems*, **11**, 3 (in press).

Lucas, H. C. Jr. (1975) *Why Information Systems Fail*, The Columbia University Press, New York.

Lucas, H. C. Jr. (1981) *Implementation: The Key to Successfull Information Systems*, Columbia University Press, New York.

Lundeberg, M., Goldkuhl, G., and Nilsson, A. (1981) *Information Systems Development — A Systematic Approach*, Prentice-Hall, Englewood Cliffs, N.J.

Lyytinen, K. (1985) 'Implications of Theories of Language for Information Systems', *MIS Quarterly*, **9**, 1, 61–74.

Lyytinen, K. (1986) *Information Systems Development as Social Action — Framework and Critical Implications*, Department of Computer Science, University of Jyväskylä, Jyväskylä. (Ph.D. dissertation.)

Lyytinen, K., and Klein, H. (1985) 'Critical Social Theory of Jurgen Habermas (CST) as a Basis for the Theory of Information Systems', in *Research Methods in Information Systems*, E. Mumford, R. Hirschheim, G. Fitzgerald, and A. T. Wood-Harper (Eds.), North Holland, Amsterdam, pp. 219–236.

Lyytinen, K., and Lehtinen, E. (1984a) 'On Information Modeling through Illocutionary Logic', in *Report of the Third Scandinavian Research Seminar on Information Modeling and Data*

Base Management, H. Kangassalo (Ed.), University of Tampere, Tampere, Finland, pp. 35–118.

Lyytinen, K., and Lehtinen, E. (1984b) 'Discourse Analysis as an Information System Specification Method', Report of the 7th Scandinavian Research Seminar on Systemeering (Part I), Helsinki Business School, Helsinki, Finland, pp. 146–200.

Markus, M. L. (1983) 'Power, Politics and MIS Implementation', *Communications of the ACM*, **26**, 6, 430–444.

Mason, R. O., and Mitroff, I. I. (1973) 'A Program for Research on Management Information Systems', *Management Science*, **19**, 5, 475–487.

Mason, R. O., and Mitroff, I. I. (1981) *Challenging Strategic Planning Assumptions*, John Wiley, New York.

Mitroff, I. I. (1980) 'Toward a Logic and Methodology for "Real-World" Problems', in *The Human Side of Information Processing*, N. Bjorn-Anderson (Ed.), North-Holland, Amsterdam, pp. 187–195.

Morgan, C. (1980) 'Paradigms, Metaphors and Puzzle Solving in Organization Theory', *Administrative Science Quarterly*, **25**, 4, 605–622.

Morgan, G. (Ed.) (1983) *Beyond Method: Strategies for Social Research*, Sage Publications, Beverly Hills.

Mumford, E. (1981) 'Participative Systems Design: Structure and Method', *Systems, Objectives, Solutions*, **1**, 1, 5–19.

Mumford, E. (1983) *Designing Human Systems — The ETHICS method*, Manchester Business School, Cheshire.

Nygaard, K., and Handlykken, P. (1981) 'The Systems Development Process — Its Setting, Some Problems and Needs for Methods', in *Software Engineering Environment*, H. Hunke (Ed.), North-Holland, Amsterdam, pp. 157–172.

Olerup, A. (1980) 'On a Contingency Framework of Computerized Information Systems', in *The Information Systems Environment*, H. C. Lucas, F. Land, T. J. Lincoln, and K. Supper (Eds.), North-Holland, Amsterdam.

Olle, T. W., Sol, H. G., and Verrijn-Stuart, A. A. (Eds.) (1982) *Information Systems Design Methodologies: a Comparative Review*, North-Holland, Amsterdam.

Olle, T. W., Sol, H. G., and Tully, C. J. (Eds.) (1983) *Information Systems Design Methodologies: A Feature Analysis*, North-Holland, Amsterdam.

Ouchi, W. G. (1978) 'Coupled versus Uncoupled Control in Organizational Hierarchies', in *Environments and Organizations*, M. W. Meyer (Ed.), Jossey-Bass, San Francisco.

Pateman, T. (1983) 'What is a language?', *Language & Communication*, **3**, 2, 101–127.

Pettigrew, A. M. (1980) 'The Politics of Organizational Change', in *The Human Side of Information Processing*, N. Bjorn-Anderson (Ed.), North-Holland, Amsterdam, pp. 39–52.

Pilote, T. (1983) *A Framework for the Design of Linquistic User Interfaces*, Computer Systems Research Group, University of Toronto, Toronto. (Ph.D. dissertation.)

Robey, D., and Markus, M. L. (1984) 'Rituals in System Design', *MIS Quarterly*, **8**, 1, 5–15.

Rochfeld, A., and Tardieu, H. (1983) 'MERISE: An Information System Design and Development Methodology', *Information & Management*, **6**, 143–159.

Sandberg, A. (Ed.) (1979) *Computers Dividing Man and Work*, Arbetslivscentrum, Malmo.

Sandberg, A. (1985) 'Socio-technical Design, Trade-Union Strategies and Action Research', in *Research Methods in Information Systems*, E. Mumford, R. Hirschheim, G. Fitzgerald and A. T. Wood-Harper (Eds.), North-Holland, Amsterdam, pp. 79–92.

Sanders, P. (1982) 'Phenomenology: A New Way of Viewing Organizational Research', *Academy of Management Review*, **7**, 3, 353–360.

Scacchi, W. (1985) 'Applying Social Analysis of Computing to Systems Development', in *Proceedings of the Workshop on Development and Use of Computer-Based Systems and Tools*, Arhus University, Arhus, August 1985.

Senko, M. (1975) 'Information Systems, Records, Relations, Sets, Entities, and Things', *Information Systems*, **1**, 1, 3–13.

Senko, M. (1976) 'DIAM II: The Binary Infological Level and its Database Language — FORAL', *SIGPLAN Notices*, **2**, 2.

Shneiderman, B. (1981) *Software Psychology*, Winthrop, Cambridge, MA.

Solvberg, A., Aanstaad, P., Johansen, T., and Skylstad, G. (1978) 'An experiment in computer aided information systems development', in *Information Systems Methodology*, *Lecture Notes in Computer Science 65*, G. Bracchi and P. Lockeman (Eds.), Springer Verlag, Berlin.

Strassman, P. A. (1985) *The Information Payoff — The Transformation of Work in the Electronic Age*, Free Press, New York.

Turner, J. A. (1982) 'Observations on the Use of Behavioral Models in Information Systems Research and Practice', *Information & Management*, **5**, 3, 207–213.

Ven, A. H. van de, and Astley, W. G. (1981) 'Mapping the Field to Create a Dynamic Perspective on Organization Design and Behavior', in *Perspectives on Organization Design and Behavior*, A. H. van de Ven and W. F. Joyce (Eds.), John Wiley, New York, pp. 427–468.

Verheijen, G. M. A., and van Bekkum, J. (1982) 'NIAM: An Information Analysis Method', in *Information Systems Design Methodologies: A Comparative Review*, T. W. Olle, H. G. Sol and A. A. Verrijn-Stuart (Eds.), North-Holland, Amsterdam.

Vitalari, N. P. (1984) 'Critical Assessment of Structured Analysis Methods: A Psychological Perspective', in *Beyond Productivity: Information Systems Development for Organizational Effectiveness*, T. M. A. Bemelmans (Ed.), North-Holland, Amsterdam, pp. 421–434.

Vitalari, N. P. (1985) 'Knowledge as a Basis for Expertise in Systems Analysis: An Empirical Study', *MIS Quarterly*, **9**, 3, 221–241.

Wasserman, A. I., and Freeman, P. (1983) 'ADA Methodologies: Concepts and Requirements', *Software Engineering Notes*, **8**, 1, 33–50.

Wedekind, H. H. (1981) 'A Multipath Methodology for Developing Database Application Systems', in *ICS 81 Systems Architecture, Procs of 6th ACM European Reg. Conference*, Westbury House, UK, pp. 191–201.

Welke, R. J. (1981) 'IS/DSS: DBMS support for information systems development', ISRAM WP-8105-1.0, McMaster University, Hamilton.

Welke, R. J., and Konsynski, B. (1982) 'An Examination of the Interaction between Technology, Methodology and Information Systems: A Tripartite View', *Data Base*, **13**, 1, 41–52.

Wood-Harper, A. T., Antill, L., and Avison, D. (1985) *Information System Definition — A Multiview Methodology*, Basil Blackwell, London.

Wright, G. H. von (1971) *Explanation and Understanding*, Routledge & Kegan Paul, London.

Yao, S. B., Navathe, S. B., and Weldon, J.-L. (1982) 'An Integrated Approach to Database Design', in *Data Base Design Techniques: Requirements and Logical Structures*, S. B. Yao, S. B. Navathe, J. L. Weldon and T. L. Kunii (Eds.), Springer-Verlag, Berlin.

Yourdon, E. (1982) *Managing the System Life Cycle*, Yourdon Press, New York.

Critical Issues in Information Systems Research
Edited by R. J. Boland Jr. and R. A. Hirschheim
©1987 John Wiley & Sons Ltd.

Chapter 2

SEMANTICS

Ronald Stamper

ABSTRACT

This chapter advocates that research on information systems should employ the framework of semiotics, the theory of signs, in which one division, semantics, has been relatively neglected so far. A dangerous, commonsense notion of meaning serves most people working on the design of business information systems. Words, of themselves, are assumed to have meanings, making it easy and unproblematical to share information about an objective reality using corporate databases. This naïve position has been fortified by an army of semanticists who have developed a mathematical theory of great power and sophistication. Unfortunately, it proposes that we account for meanings by reference to a universe of discrete, identifiable individuals comprising all the past, present, future and possible worlds that are the subject matter of our information. The assumptions made by this mathematical theory beg all the important questions about meanings in a social system. Away from the laboratory bench, reality has to be created and maintained by a continuing social effort. Meanings are rooted in our culture and refined for specific business purposes by endless large- and small-scale negotiations. The semantic theories that rely upon the unwarranted metaphysical assumptions of mathematics can be superseded by a new approach better suited to the domain of information systems. This is possible if we make our starting point the study of actual social norms, as they are exhibited in legislation, for example. Formal methods for the analysis of meanings in business, legal and other social contexts can be devised. In particular, Legol, a legally orientated language, and Norma, a logic of norms and affordances, are touched upon. In the course of presenting this argument, the chapter introduces, or at least mentions, many different methods and problems for the potential researcher in the semantic issues of information systems.

1. INTRODUCTION

Information systems are those man–machine systems that enable us to get practical things done by using signs. (Signs are words and numbers, but also nods and winks, which represent past, present and future states of affairs that we wish to know about, judge or prescribe.) Information systems include business organizations which are usually studied from such points of view as logistics, finance and accounting, or human relations. However, in this chapter, I shall examine some aspects of organizations from a special point of view, the view of semiotics, the theory of signs, one branch of which is semantics.

An arrangement of computers linked by a telecommunications system does not constitute an information system. Such a technical system only processes information in the sense that it operates upon structures of symbols that are intrinsically meaningless [1]. Meanings are only conferred upon the symbols manipulated by computers when they are interpreted by the social system within which the technical system is embedded. When an organization uses a computer it must in some way or other establish the meanings of the signals being processed electronically, which, in a nutshell, is why semantics is one of the central research areas in our nascent discipline.

Notice that I have opened this chapter by raising an issue of semantics. Some people, I imagine, may object to my use of terms. I anticipated that by starting with brief definitions of two key expressions. In circumstances where such differences of opinion do not exist, there are no semantic problems. I shall argue that solving semantic problems is a major business activity closely related, at one end of the scale, to the resolution of industrial disputes by negotiation and legal disputes in the courts, or, on a much smaller scale, to the removal of differences of opinion by discussion many times a day in every office or workshop. These activities are among the most important ones that business people perform when they are working with information, but they are very difficult problems to research within the established information systems perspective. Semantics is potentially one of the most exciting and rewarding fields of enquiry for students of organizations.

Notice also that I started this chapter with the first person pronoun, contrary to usual editorial advice. My reason is to emphasize that meanings have no objective existence (contrary to age-old traditions from Plato to today's computer scientists). Meanings express personal views of reality. When there is a firmly established consensus, and only then, we can pretend that meanings are independent of people. Many semantic problems cannot be solved until one has established who is responsible for the meanings expressed. A misleading impression of objectivity is conveyed by the convention, usually adopted in scientific or academic works, of writing in the third person. From the pen of a politician we might see this device as verbal sleight-of-hand; it serves to present opinions, for which the author should accept responsibility, as though they were detached and objective knowledge. Even in scientific and academic work, it is dangerous, except in carefully chosen situations, to be lulled into dissociating any knowledge, meanings or information systems from the people responsible for them.

2. SEMIOTICS

To place semantics in context, let us examine that distressingly vague word 'information'. One meaning of special relevance here, because it is the most concrete, might be implied when, in response to the question, 'How much useful information have you got onto that disk?', I reply, 'About two megabytes, which is more than I expected!', where we are both talking about a quantity of signs. The word 'data' is often used in this sense but it is better to reserve this word for the *given* (Latin: *datum, -a*) items of information relative to some problem or other. The return to the original, pre-jargon usage helps to remove one common cause of confusion. But there is a more deeply rooted one that clouds our thinking: 'data' and 'information' are both employed as though we were talking of substances such as 'water', 'butter' and so on. This usage is unfortunate because it embodies the misleading metaphor of a mystical substance that persistently draws our thinking about this subject away from a simpler and more concrete approach to it.

(Incidentally, the extent to which language influences thought is one important aspect of semantics. The deeply ingrained metaphors out of which our language grows are discussed in Lakoff and Johnson (1980) and Ortony (1979) and the specific metaphor for information in Stamper (1973) and Stamper (1985a), whilst Reddy (1979) deals with the closely related, misleading metaphor that pervades most of our language about language.)

The simple primitive notion of a 'sign' is a far better one to use than the vague one of 'information'. You cannot show people information except in the simple sense of a collection of signs; so why not begin there, and demonstrate all kinds of signs and how they are used to get things done. Words, numbers, nods, winks, traffic lights, footprints, architects' models and even the position of a chair in a room may be among the examples you use in this process of ostensively defining 'a sign'. Indeed anything can function as a sign and be used to convey (notice the metaphor!) information. Having thus in the most basic manner introduced our primitive concept, we can build safely numerous different but precise meanings of the term 'information' to be used for different purposes [1].

The theory of signs is one of the least explored but most stimulating and fruitful ways of approaching the study of organizations. It helps to answer the question: how do we get things done through the use of words, numbers, nods and winks, diagrams, reports, speeches, rule-books and other signs? The treatment of information in computing and telecommunications is too narrow for the study of organizations as information systems. Semiotics incorporates the technical view but it constructs its main theses on the principle that our ability to use signs is rooted in our cultural and biological natures. Moreover, semiotics allows us to bridge the man–machine boundary with strong unifying ideas.

There are four different major branches of semiotics: pragmatics, semantics, syntactics and empirics. When we ask questions about the relationships between signs and the behaviour of people, we deal with *pragmatics*. *Semantics* deals with the issue of meaning, the relationships between signs and what they purport to represent. *Syntactic* questions concern themselves quite narrowly with the relationships among structures of signs, regardless of how people use them or what they mean; big signs such as sentences or computer programs are constructed from small signs such as words or expressions and these forms can be operated upon in essentially mechanical ways to produce new forms, as we do when making logical inferences or running a program. The fourth branch of the subject, *empirics*, focuses upon the very limited set of questions about the repeated use of signs and looks for answers in statistical terms; it is another expression to use for the large but misleadingly named 'information theory' of the telecommunications engineers. This classification helps us to partition a vast subject and it serves as a checklist drawing attention to the key aspects of any practical information systems problem.

3. SEMIOTICS AND PRACTICAL INFORMATICS

To illustrate this point, consider broadly what has to be attended to when we are building with computers and telecommunications a new information system. Ask ourselves who looks after each of the four aspects of the sign-system we are developing.

Syntactics gets the attention of the programmer who establishes the precise structure of all inputs and outputs and how the one is mechanically transformed into the other; these features are embodied in his programs.

Empirics receives attention when someone counts numbers of records and frequencies of transactions, and then designs codes that optimize the use of storage, routings that minimize message traffic and generally makes the hardware configuration efficient for performing the syntactic operations.

These two parts of the task fall principally to the software engineer. Notice that his work, strictly speaking, is totally independent of the meanings or social uses of the signals which their systems process. The other aspects are dealt with, if at all by the systems analyst, but perhaps we should extend his role or make him more conscious of it and give him the title 'information engineer'.

Pragmatics does receive some attention from the designer of the man–machine interface, but generally in the rather mechanical fashion which we associate with the applied psychologist or ergonomist who employs experimental methods to investigate how effectively people perform tasks of reading displays, typing commands, remembering procedures and so on. There is a very different kind of problem associated with the interpretation of signs in a social setting that we perform when we interview users about their information requirements; these cannot be investigated statistically but are dealt with using those simple hermeneutic procedures that are taught as systems analysis 'methodologies'.

Semantic issues are dealt with by the systems analyst but usually without his consciously doing so. Upon him devolves the task of designing and establishing the links between the character-strings in the formal system that the software engineer creates and the entities in the real world that those strings represent. For practical purposes, meanings are fixed by the chains of operations that bring inputs from their sources in real-world events and by the operations taking outputs to the events to be controlled. Data analysis brings us a little closer to a deliberate act of semantic investigation, but only marginally so, because it is insufficiently systematic and relies on the rather arbitrary intuitions of the analyst.

Thus the software engineer can give all his attention to the complex and demanding task of organizing the mechanical or formal aspects of a system whilst the information engineer attends to the informal, human aspects. However, the work of the information engineer comes first because he must brief the software engineer about the information required. Later, they are both involved in the maintenance of the system, one of them correcting mechanical defects or inefficiencies whilst the other helps the system to retain its useful place in the organization. 'Bugs' in the wider information system take the form of misunderstandings, failures of data to discriminate, unnoticed ambiguities, confusion of names, rigidity of the system faced with changes in business requirements, and so on. Thus we can classify system failures usefully into the syntactic and empiric ones handled by the software engineer, and the semantic and pragmatic ones which fall in the province of the information engineer.

If we wish to differentiate these two domains for academic purposes, we may call the knowledge required by the software engineer 'computer informatics' whilst attaching the expression 'social science informatics' to the disciplines upon which information engineering is built. All four branches of semiotics are needed in the study of social information systems. Semantics is singled out as the area perhaps most in need of research effort, but we need to see how each area connects up to the other branches of the subject.

The fourfold classification is not water-tight: the categories of problems invade each other. Consider how each of the other three relate to semantics.

Empirics sheds light upon the formation of meaningful relationships in the minds of people as events condition them to associate ideas; this behaviourist approach to semantics can be valuable, as Osgood and his followers have demonstrated (Osgood, 1957). Meanings in operational terms can sometimes be defined usefully in terms of the responses provoked by a stimulus regarded as a sign. These techniques apply when one can create, in the spirit of applied psychology, a standardized situation in which the behaviour of people may be observed and analysed statistically. The pattern recognition approach to semantics also belongs to empirics. The search for invariants can often be thought of as a search for meaning and meanings can be understood as structures. 'Meaning' has many meanings and empirics supplies several of them.

Syntactics supplies perhaps the most technically sophisticated analysis of semantic problems. The general approach it adopts is based on the encoding of expressions in one language (English, say) according to formal mechanical rules into other, canonical expressions, in a standard formalism (usually that of the mathematical theory of sets). This approach will be examined critically, in detail, below.

Pragmatics also has an important role to play in our thinking about semantics. Its position *vis-à-vis* syntactics needs to be strengthened because the latter has the benefit of a climate of academic opinion that accords superiority to whatever treatment of a problem is the most formal. I shall argue strongly in favour of a pragmatic approach strengthened with formalism as far as it is appropriate. Meanings depend upon what people do with signs, and I shall demonstrate that one can be formal without wearing the straitjacket of the classical syntactic approach.

4. A NEW DIRECTION FOR SEMANTICS

In the following sections, some of the established approaches to semantics will be examined. We shall find that they evade just those aspects of the problem that are most relevant to the running of a business.

The classical approaches either stay within the domain of language and make no attempt to connect signs to reality, or they naïvely assume that there is an objective reality that, given sufficient effort, we can know about in as much detail as we desire. We owe these approaches to linguistics and to logic. They fail in the business context, where people are more concerned with getting things done than with paraphrasing one another and because the reality of the world of business is not objective and ready-made. In fact, the logical approach, which dominates artificial intelligence, expert systems, database semantics and all the technologically orientated branches of informatics, indulges in fantasies of the kind that are legitimate in mathematical theorizing but not in running a business. We must swap platonic reality for the reality of action.

A new approach is required and I have already hinted at the direction to adopt, in the opening paragraphs. We have to keep the user of the signs at the centre of our vision and we have to relate the words he uses to the actions he performs or wishes to have performed for him. We also have to be less ambitious than the logician who aims to present us with 'meanings' fully expressed as formulae. Meanings belong to the human agents not to axiomatic systems. If only we can keep track of those agents and what they do, we shall devise a new semantics that can be applied successfully to business, legal and other social information system.

I shall attempt to offer the reader a number of research tools and methods, and, in doing so, I shall formulate a number of hypotheses which he might like to explore. My aim is to guide the researcher who is trying to escape the intellectual shackles of the mechanistic, positivistic view of information systems that looks daily less appropriate for our field of enquiry.

5. ESTABLISHED METHODS OF RESEARCH IN SEMANTICS

Research in the semantics of business information can draw upon linguistics, psychology, logic, mathematics, and, of course, philosophy. But we can start conveniently by looking at how questions of meaning tend to be treated by colleagues and practitioners in the information systems field.

Among the first to perceive the importance of these issues were those researching problems in database management. They soon recognized the value of describing the data independently of how they were to be stored or manipulated. It was likely to increase productivity if this complex task could be done once and for all for the benefit of all users. They saw the task as one of relating the contents of the database to the concepts used by managers to understand their business. The idea of a 'conceptual schema' to contain this information was developed by database researchers in the mid-1970s.

Attempts to create a definitive answer led to a programme of work by the standards organizations. First, in the USA, the three-part ANSI-SPARC (1975) architecture was devised incorporating an 'internal schema' representing (1) the data as they are organized in storage, (2) a series of 'external schemas' embodying the limited views of different sets of users, and (3) a grand 'conceptual schema' bringing these views together into a composite picture which could be controlled by a manager of information resources. They appeared to envisage the conceptual schema as embodying the solution to the semantic problem.

Their initial optimism gave way to more questioning. Kent of IBM wrote a book (1978) which pointed out how very much more complicated are these semantic issues than the current folklore admitted. Subsequent work by the ISO (Griethuysen, 1982) on the representation of the conceptual schema considered three approaches, the Entity–Relationship–Attribute model of Chen (1976), the Binary Network model of Nijssen (1979) and the Propositional Logic model as tools for semantics analysis. Most recently, in 1985, the relevant IFIP group initiated a series of conferences specifically focused on database semantics. If one looks closely at all of these one finds the syntactic outlook is dominant; I predict that the second wage of optimism will only yield more questions.

The errors in the ANSI-SPARC way of treating semantics are twofold. The basic one is their invocation of a naïve metaphysics by their use of the term 'conceptual'. This belongs to a stance of psychologism which treats semantics as an investigation of relationships of reference between linguistic expressions and concepts in the minds of people, these concepts being their meanings [2]. A more mysterious and unsatisfactory way of establishing meanings could not be chosen for a scientific treatment of the subject. In addition, despite the totally subjective nature of concepts when you come to investigate them, the same database community assumed that a single conceptual schema sufficed to unite the diverse external schemas of various user groups. Users could employ their own local language by adopting synonyms for items in the conceptual schema, and they could limit their domain of discourse to a subset of the conceptual schema, but they had to accept its overarching structure. Hence we see, despite all the subjectivist language of 'concepts', that they also adopt a naïve assumption of a single valid view of the world, a kind of sidelong view of the logical positivists' picture of reality. These two errors reflect the metaphysical assumptions widespread among a scientific community reared on a diet of natural science, engineering and mathematics, where a single objective reality is taken for granted as readily as a belief in the reality of mathematical concepts.

6. EARLY IDEAS FROM LINGUISTICS

Belief in a reality populated with concepts is to be found in the writing of the early language theorists such as the American, Sapir, and the Swiss, de Saussure. Even today it strongly influences the European school of semiologists, but that seems quite appropriate because their interests focus upon the fictional worlds of literature, cinema, theatre, and topics such as the language of politics. One might expect a more hard-headed set of criteria to govern the choice of theories for database management.

However, those earlier authors have something important to tell the DBMS scientists. There is an interesting idea called the Sapir–Whorf hypothesis which is relevant to database schema design. This hypothesis, that a person's understanding of the world is dictated by the language he speaks, cannot be proved or disproved in this loose form. One may easily generate evidence to favour the hypothesis by creating specific problem situations which have to be discussed in a vocabulary that tends to bias people towards certain solutions. This happens fortuitously quite often in practical business affairs as Whorf, himself, observed in his earlier profession as chemical engineer inspecting accidents. For example, he recalls (Whorf, 1956, p. 136) encountering a drying-shed for hides which had caught fire from sparks from the motor of a fan used to 'blow the air across them'; as he pointed out, had the design task in its formulation been to 'draw air across the hides', the engineer would probably have placed the fan on the exit side, and the overheating motor would have wasted its sparks upon the desert air. Evidence is easy to adduce against the hypothesis in its strongest form, which asserts that the speakers of any specific language may be debarred entirely from thinking the thoughts that another natural language makes possible. For example, one need only invoke the full richness of a natural language such as English to argue, that, whereas in Eskimo there are numerous different words for snow in its various manifestations, we are not debarred from describing the same phenomena in English, provided that we pay the cost of a less efficient encoding for those concepts, measured in numbers of words. But recoding a problem in an unbiased vocabulary takes time and effort (see Reddy (1979) for a discussion of this factor); business problems usually have to be solved in a hurry and as cheaply as possible; under such conditions a modified form of the Sapir–Whorf hypothesis will hold.

I propose a strong form of the hypothesis for database work. Consider, instead of natural language, the kind of formal language specified by a systems analyst to embody, within a database, a model of the reality in which the organization operates. The view of reality imposed by such a conceptual schema may indeed act as a straitjacket upon the thoughts of the computer-users in the application area covered by the database, in much the way that Sapir and Whorf hypothesized. Anyone who has used computer systems designed by other analysts will have experienced this kind of semantic obstacle. I propose that we should treat seriously the Sapir–Whorf hypothesis applied to formal or computer-based systems.

7. LOGICAL SYNTAX

The most promising of the formalisms examined by the ISO committee for specifying database schemata appears to be *predicate logic*. It has the advantage conferred by its rules of inference that add a power of reasoning to the more basic facilities of storage, manipulation and retrieval (Lee and Stamper, 1985). The process of deductive reasoning which predicate logic supports is not the only one we employ. It is relevant to the organization of a verbal and numerical account of a range of problems about which there is no deep-rooted dispute. The mechanization of deductive process does enable the machine to simulate some features of intelligent semiological behaviour but it certainly does not confer the overwhelming advantage upon the machine that some of its enthusiasts have claimed.

The value of first order predicate logic for consolidating the established ideas about conceptual schemas has been ably demonstrated by the ISO group and authors such as Bubenko (1983). Their approach is circumspect and makes no exaggerated claim for their chosen logical tool. However, some more passionate devotees of logic programming seem to assert that you might have your language bounded by the nutshell of first order predicate logic yet count yourself the king of infinite thoughts. Plenty of evidence suggests that the logical model of natural language fails in numerous particulars (for example, see McCawley (1981)). Predicate logic provides a neat, closed system but it does not facilitate the remaking of that neat structure, an activity essential to any business activity. To achieve that you would first have to step outside the formal shell, into the realm of natural language, in order to conceive new thoughts and reformulate the logical paraphrase of those thoughts, before returning to the comfort and security of the formalism. Logic helps us to specify a database schema more effectively but it cannot help us to escape from the closed-world assumption that it imposes upon its users; it has no open-endedness, no hooks shaped like question-marks, to lead the user to reconsider what it expresses.

The most radical treatment of semantics is offered by some logicians; their solution is to replace semantic questions with syntactic ones. Kowalski (1979, p. 9) puts this position clearly:

> It follows that it is unnecessary to talk about meaning at all. All talk about meaning can be re-expressed in terms of logical implication. To define the semantics of the clausal form of logic, therefore, it suffices to define the notion of logical implication.

This approach is quite acceptable for the highly constrained illustrative problems in logic textbooks, but dubious in real-life contexts. Hilbert introduced this formalist approach to the realm of mathematics because the naïve belief in a world of real but ideal mathematical objects had come under attack by Brouwer, who sccmcd prepared to outlaw a large part of the subject. Hilbert, in effect, said that we should forget about the supposed referents of mathematical expressions and concentrate on the forms of the symbols themselves. He proposed that a formal language, with formal rules of inference for mechanically deriving new combinations of symbols from old, would suffice, provided that one could demonstrate, in a theory of meta-mathematics, that the resulting system is consistent. The idea does not even work in the mathematical domain. Gödel showed that a system rich enough to account for elementary arithmetic cannot be shown to be consistent within the limits of that system's own rules of inference, and furthermore, he showed that, given any consistent set of arithmetic axioms, there are true arithmetical statements that cannot be derived from them. Despite these damning discoveries about formal systems, we may be on safe ground if we confine them to finite operations. That would mean relinquishing the use of recursion, and logic programming would be badly hampered by that constraint. If we were content to treat computer programs as self-contained 'board games' (formal systems) in which every 'position' (proposition) has to be derived using legal moves of the counters (rules of inference) from the prescribed 'starting position' (axioms), then we might agree with Kowalski.

Of course those who do not wish to tangle with semantic problems can treat logic as a purely syntactic system, one in which well-formed formulae can be constructed, divided into two categories, the valid and the others, and then operated upon by mechanical rules of inference which permit an initial set of valid formulae to be transformed into other valid formulae. That is an escapist luxury in which software engineers may justifiably indulge. The luxury of over-simplification for the sake of formal tidiness serves an important purpose in the design of software in the closed mechanical world of the computer, but it is denied to the information engineer, who is responsible for linking computer-manipulable language to the open-structured reality of business. Even the most vehement supporters of logic (and some can be extreme indeed [3]) have to step outside the confines of a purely formalist or syntactic treatment of logical semantics. The effectiveness of logic for the treatment of semantics depends upon the semantics of logic itself.

We now turn to examine the standard semantic treatment of logical languages. We shall discover that it employs the kinds of metaphysical assumptions that were criticized earlier: belief in the reality of concepts and the presumption that there is a single reality, a reality that owes as much to the mathematical imagination as to the world of practical affairs.

8. CLASSICAL FORMAL SEMANTICS – DANGEROUS METAPHYSICS

The usual treatment of the semantics of formal languages exploits a number of analytical tools which, in the domains of natural science, engineering and mathematics, seem entirely appropriate but rather dubious in the domains of practical business activities, legal matters, or the affairs of everyday life which are influenced by social forces. These analytical tools include truth-conditional semantics, set-theoretic models, and the dangerous appeal to possible worlds. We shall look at each of these critically.

This particular formal approach has been extended to the semantics of natural language. It has been followed very effectively in a research programme launched by Richard Montague between 1955 and 1970.

As Dowty, Wall and Peters say in their lucid *Introduction to Montague Semantics* (1981), 'A truth-conditional theory of semantics is one which adheres to the following dictum: To know the meaning of a (declarative) sentence is to know what the world would have to be like for the sentence to be true'. In the more mysterious formulation of its originator, Tarski, we need a rule schema to provide for every sentence, S, of the language, a formula saying:

S is true if and only if p

for example,

Snow is white is true if and only if snow is white

where the italicised sentence is the one we are investigating and the same words appearing as a clause at the end of the above sentence correspond to the conditions, p, which apply in any world where our sentence is true. This is a theory about the *correspondence* of the sentence, S, to an independently existing world. The idea is that we know the meaning of any sentence if we know precisely in which worlds it is true.

Notice the dangerously insinuated suggestion that there are other worlds than one which is here and now, other worlds where the truth of any sentence must be decided if we are to know its meaning. We shall return to this issue of possible worlds later.

Even without the problem of possible worlds, notice the two big assumptions being made. There is a definite, independently existing world (for without it we could not resolve semantic questions this way). There clearly is, or equally clearly there is not, a correspondence between a sentence and any world of which it might be stated. The first of these is again the naïve belief in one objective reality, the unsatisfactory belief embraced by the conceptual schema adherents. They also adopted the second assumption, that truth is a simple matter of correspondence of the database to reality, as evidenced by their discussions of database integrity. Personally, I cannot accept either assumption in the context of business affairs.

9. MODEL THEORY

The use of set-theoretic models is intended to clarify the process of establishing the correspondence of a sentence or other expression to reality. This is done by modelling the world using the very simple idea usually taken to be the root of mathematics, the idea of a set.

Model theory is well suited to supplying a semantics of predicate logic, the well-formed formulae of which tell us about the properties of and relationships among individuals, such as:

BOY(john) & LIKES(john,mary) & GIRL(mary)

This says, roughly, 'The boy, John, likes the girl, Mary'. We are expected to assume that the world consists of a collection of individuals, as many as we care to specify, including in this case the ones called *in our formalism* 'john' and 'mary' (note that only lower-case letters are used for individual names in the formalism) and *in our natural language* by the very similar symbols 'John' and 'Mary' (using upper-case (capital) letters for proper names). This set of individuals is the basis of our model and is called the 'universe of discourse'. The meaning of each individual constant (such as 'john' and 'mary') in the logical language is given by its correspondence to one of the members of this potentially vast set, the universe of discourse. The predicate names such as BOY, GIRL, LIKES and so on, have meanings in terms of structures based on the universe of discourse. One-place predicates, such as BOY or GIRL can be regarded as meaning (in the sense of referring to or corresponding to) subsets of the universe of individuals. Two-place predicates such as LIKES can be related to sets of ordered pairs of individuals such as ⟨John,Mary⟩ or ⟨Bill,Jane⟩ or ⟨Bill,Mary⟩ or ⟨Mary,Jane⟩ and so forth — if the first of each of these pairs actually likes the second, then that pair will belong to the set of ordered pairs that is the meaning or referent of LIKES.

A richer language includes quantification as an extra feature. The more complex expression

Ex.BOY(john) & LIKES(john,x) & GIRL(x)

contains an existential quantifier, as it is called, Ex., which may be paraphrased as 'there exists an individual, x, such that . . .'. It is needed to turn the rest of the formula into a genuine sentence otherwise

BOY(john) & LIKES(john,x) & GIRL(x)

would merely be a formula that is sometimes true, sometimes false, depending upon the interpretation given to the variable, x. There is not space in this brief chapter to show how to construct from the universe of discourse a set-theoretical structure to which Ex. refers. We can then use these correspondence-meanings assigned to the basic components of our formulae in order to calculate the meanings of larger expressions.

The semantic rules have to enable us to find the meanings of complex expressions from the meanings of their components. Thus, from the meaning of 'john' (the real individual we would call 'John' or sometimes 'Jack') and the meaning of BOY (the subset comprising among many others, my sons and yours, plus John (alias Jack) we mentioned above, as well as Ronald, the President of the USA but excluding Margaret, the Prime Minister of the UK, all our daughters, and so on), we can find the meaning of BOY(john). All we need do, according to the semantic rules, is to look into the gigantic set comprising all boys and check that it contains the one we call John or Jack who is always known unambiguously in the logic as 'john'. If it does then BOY(john) is true in the present world. Similarly we can fix the meanings of the other component expressions and then, by the composition rules, we finally compute the truth value or meaning of the whole expression as its correspondence to one of the special individuals, TRUE or FALSE.

The process seems simple and justifiable as a kind of thought experiment performed upon a universe of discourse as though upon objects spread out upon a table. The objection to it as a way of accounting for meanings is not only that it would be difficult to perform on any realistically sizeable universe. More importantly, the method will not work as an account of the meanings of many common sentences unless one recklessly extends the scope of the universe of discourse.

The method, as explained so far, has conveniently overlooked the problem of *time*. Remember that the boy, John, does not exist for ever and that people do not always like one another, so we confront the difficult problem of accounting for meanings in a changing world, a world of history and of plans. A Herculean labour has to be accomplished to make clear the meaning of brief sentences such as BOY(john) or LIKES(john,mary) when their correspondence to the fact has to be checked for every other world, past and future, that our universe of discourse contains. Times have to be introduced as additional individuals (numerous they are!) and propositions have to be indexed, e.g. BOY(john,t), where 't' is time variable. The process is even more elaborate for an existential sentence containing a variable, x. We must check each possible world for the meanings of the expressions LIKES(john,x,t) and GIRL(x,t) taking care to note the interpretation of x, each time we do it. This model-theoretic semantics will not get us far if we are capable only of modelling the world as it exists here and now. If we were limited to models of the here-and-now, our semantics would prevent us from finding the meanings of natural language expressions involving time.

Often enough in business meetings we discuss bridges that have not yet been built, employees who have not yet even read an advertisement, and hypotheses we strive to prevent from coming true. The problem is supposedly overcome, along with the problem of time, by incorporating into the universe of discourse, all manner of extra individuals including instants of time and possible worlds. Without their addition, we should be unable to build a rich enough theory of meaning. These vast additional assumptions about a plethora of totally inaccessible individuals destroys the delightful simplicity of the original set-theoretic model built upon a universe of discourse comprising objects we can point to. The unsatisfactory world of *concepts* has to return.

Frankly, no businessman should be content with a computer system giving him information, the meaning of which can only be established by its supposed correspondence to some imaginary world. In addition, he would find, if he took the trouble to follow the logico-mathematical argument, that the truth-conditional, model-theoretic semantics established the truth of a sentence in a way that bears little resemblance to the way in which actual people establish truth values in business situations. The standard approach to semantics, elegant though it may be in mathematical terms, fails to have any explanatory power when confronted with practical affairs.

10. INDIVIDUALITY AND IDENTITY — FURTHER PROBLEMS

To start with it is a gross and misleading assumption to suggest that the individuals in the universe of discourse already exist as individuals. Where does one thing end and another begin? Having assumed that this issue is already disposed of by common sense in defining a universe of discourse, the classical semantic theory is silent on this matter. But in everyday life it is not a matter of common sense. When a car is written off by an insurance firm after an accident, bought by a breaker, sold to a repair enthusiast, resurrected as a functioning vehicle, made to satisfy the Ministry of Transport test and insured again by the same firm, is the insurer dealing here with one car or two different ones? Again: a customer, having ordered 500 nuts and 1000 washers sends an alteration to order saying that they meant 500 bolts, later still they explain the 1000 washers should have been 1000 wipers; is the supplier now dealing with the same or a different order? Individuation is usually a matter of negotiation or the interpretation of established rules in these circumstances. Individuation has to be explained by any remotely satisfactory theory of business semantics.

Identity, also assumed to be established by common sense for all members of a universe of discourse, is difficult to account for in practical affairs. Take the kind of problem, common in manufacturing, which I encountered when I worked in the steel industry, the identification of work-pieces. A bloom weighing 20 tons enters a billet mill quite slowly as a single work-piece; but before it has entirely passed the first set of rolls, red hot steel of much smaller cross-section is being sheared into numerous billets travelling at 60 miles per hour. The identities of these new pieces need to be established and maintained because they differ in qualitatively significant ways depending upon the part of the bloom from which they originated (for example because of internal and surface deformities that may give rise to similar deformities in the billets). The identities of the red-hot billets of steel are difficult to establish and maintain in those circumstances until their serial numbers can be stamped on the much cooler metal. Without a labelling or tracking system, the concept of identity for billets of steel is of no practical use. The idea of a heavenly guardian-angel overlooking the welfare of each billet and vouching for its separate identity may seem ludicrous, but that is essentially what the exponents of model-theoretic semantics presume when they ascribe a definite, objective identity to each member of the universe of discourse. In fact, identity has to be constructed and maintained by people as they go about their practical affairs.

Numerous other examples of the identity problem in business and administration can be found. Among the most instructive, I think, are those giving rise to systems of registration needed to fix the individuality of such diverse populations as bank cheques, motor cars, contracts, satellite orbits, times and even places. In every case an essentially human system is required to establish and maintain identities, sometimes supported by large and expensive computer systems.

This problem is not new. Heraclitus (c. 500 BC) noted, 'You cannot step twice into the same river; for fresh waters are ever flowing in upon you', and 'The sun is new every day'. How do we establish the sameness of things, the stability of boundaries where everything is in a constant state of flux? Systemic individuality and identity also need to be accounted for, but classical logic has difficulty in this area too. Substances introduce yet another class of problems in identity and individuation. Difficulties for the predicate logic enthusiast abound.

11. MEANINGS DEPEND UPON CONSENSUS

I hope that I have indicated how naïve it is to base a theory of commonsense, practical, everyday semantics on the foundation of a ready-made, objectively given universe of discourse. Naturally, there are many ordinary situations where this approach is a useful approximation. In all those situations there exists a community of people who have reached a stable consensus about the issues they are dealing with. Routine engineering, routine natural science, routine accounting, routine administration can often be dealt with in this manner—were it not so, the computer would have had little use so far. But, as soon as there is a conflict of opinion about the interpretation of rules, or the drawing of boundaries, or the classification of things, the consensus is threatened. The naïve, mechanical solution has to be repaired by those involved in the problem arguing, negotiating or exercising superior power, one over the others, to resolve the dispute.

I am prepared to argue that doing business involves, even at the lower levels in an organization but especially in the higher levels of management, semantic problem-solving: for example, agreeing upon boundaries, identifying individuals, establishing and maintaining classifications, conjecturing ways of doing things that belong in no existing formal schema. Thus, if we are interested in studying business from the perspective of information systems, I believe that the paradigm usually accepted in the Management Information Systems community, of a system where facts about a definite world are stored, retrieved and manipulated, is inadequate. (For numerous concrete examples, see Stamper, 1985a.) We must also study the conflicts about meanings, ranging from the trivial to the epic, that are the daily bread of business existence.

Office work each day entails the resoltuion of thousands of small differences of opinion about the interpretation of rules and the drawing of boundaries. The work of Wynn (1979), in which she studies the conversations in a typical office dealing with the acceptance of orders and the investigation of customers' problems, illustrates this. She draws attention to the important cognitive tasks performed routinely by quite low-level employees, tasks that are overlooked by most systems analysts studying office procedures. Plans to automate office work need to take notice of the persistent demands to resolve minor semantic issues that fall to clerical staff. Although the uncovering of details of customer requirements and clarifying the understanding of the company's products are small tasks, such work cannot be performed by the machine. At best we can devise computer systems to facilitate such work. Office automation has to recognize the role played by the intrinsically human mode of reasoning that keeps the meanings of language in repair through endless cycles of small misunderstandings, minor conflicts and swift, polite renegotiation.

To find an example of a semantic problem of epic proportions, recall the history of the 1984/85 dispute in the British coal industry. A strike by the National Union of Mineworkers, lasting a whole year, can be looked upon as a dispute about the meanings of the terms 'pit' and 'uneconomic'. It was agreed that really uneconomic pits should close. However, one side, the Mineworkers and the Labour Party, held that a pit should be seen as including the community immediately dependent upon the mining activity for its existence, and that the economic assessment of viability should take account of all the social costs associated with a decision to close the pit or to keep it in production. The social accounting framework included obvious items such as the unemployment benefits which would have to be paid to those thrown out of work and the less obvious long-term costs of coal deposits made permanently unrecoverable. The other side, the National Coal Board and the Conservative government, insisted upon a narrower interpretation of the disputed terms. Taking the pit as the assets owned and run by the Board and the economic criteria as those in the balance sheet, they came to quite different conclusions about which pits should close. These semantic issues were resolved not by rational argument nor by negotiation, but by the exercise of superior power.

Practical semantic problems take one into politics on both the small and the grand scale. They also take us into legal disputes, where, I shall argue, we can find some of the best raw material for our research. In a non-hierarchical kind of organization, the most practical way to resolve semantic issues is by adopting the norms of rational argument conducted in open discussion. Our own community, the international scientific community, is a good example of a non-hierarchical institution. We can see the writing of this book and the critical and evaluative processes to which it will be subjected as concerned with some semantics issues.

12. SCIENCE AND SEMANTICS

The compilers of this book and all the authors contributing to it are engaged in a typical semantic exercise. Every one of us has been involved for many years in the information systems field, attempting to delineate an emerging academic discipline. In the light of our own individual experiences, we have written papers on the subject, capturing in the words available at the time our unique judgements on the relevant issues, methods of investigation, and so on. The uniqueness of everyone's experience guarantees disagreement among us. But through our disputations conducted at conferences, in common rooms, at seminars and through journals, we gradually generate a measure of consensus, which, like the still water on the lee side of an island, protects the regular undergraduate student and ordinary practitioner from the turbulent arguments that occupy much of the time of those working on the leading edge of knowledge. It will be interesting to see how far this book represents an emerging consensus or a further clash of views.

The analogy between the scientific community and an island in a storm tends to suggest that the scientific or academic community resolves its differences of opinion as though battling with the common natural enemy of ignorance — a view often purveyed by the media to the layman. A more accurate simile is that of warfare. Writers on the sociology of knowledge and science historians, with their accounts of internecine struggles between different 'paradigms', all support this view. The rules of engagement for this kind of warfare deserve notice if we are to examine the process. The struggle is conducted on two fronts: the intellectual and the institutional. The rules of engagement on the intellectual front are legislated by the philosophers of science, a self-appointed parliament where such names as Popper (1963), Lakatos (1976) and Feyerabend (1975) symbolize some of the main major 'political' parties represented. To some extent, scientific communities do apply the rules which these philosophers propounded in conducting their disputes, and even adopt them as guidelines in selecting their own methods of investigation. We have to remember that the rules of engagement relevant to one sphere of enquiry may not necessarily be appropriate to all others; the social sciences have probably suffered from the unwise imposition of principles found useful in physics. The rules of intellectual warfare, by which I mean the epistemological principles that govern the acceptance of scientific knowledge, are not themselves outside the combat but weapons used within it [4].

Often enough, scientific arguments are conducted as disputes about meanings of terms. Our own discipline illustrates this as it, even now, gropes its way towards a consensus on those key terms 'information' and 'system' and the expression 'information systems'. Take 'information': it is a dangerously vague term which can be given dozens of quite different but reasonably exact meanings, yet these crucial distinctions are dismissed regularly by writers in our field who employ naïve formulae such as 'information is what a computer distils from data to make it useful for managers' [5]. Language that fails to recognize well-founded distinctions loosens the intellectual grasp that we have on the affected subject, and conversely. Science can legitimately be viewed as a verbal activity directed at formulating and justifying semantic distinctions that improve our hold upon, or construction of reality.

I have deliberately drawn attention to one of the semantic issues in our own scientific domain in order to suggest that we can find relevant empirical material in the literature of science which openly records the process of semantic argumentation. Perhaps we can learn lessons about the resolution of semantic problems in business by reviewing the works of historians and sociologists of science from our different perspective. Obviously we might include in our research agenda the study of how semantic issues are resolved in our own discipline, where many live debates, even within the covers of this book, will cast light on the process.

13. IMPOSED CONSENSUS

Scientific disputes about the meanings of terms do not always get resolved by open debate. At least in the short-term the scientific community can be pushed into irrational directions by the exercise of institutional power. University politicians, despite the grand terms in which they proclaim their intellectual rectitude to the wider public, are quite prepared to exercise their organizational power for temporary local advantage. For example, by placing decisions about a department of Information Systems in the hands of committees containing no member with any knowledge of the subject, it is possible to turn it into an adjunct of the Computer Services department, simply because, to the ill-informed, 'information systems' seems to warrant such an interpretation. Should such a coup succeed, the wider consensus in the relevant international scholarly community would eventually reverse it. The history and current practice of science abound with examples of institutional power displacing rational argument. Once again, I suggest that a study of this and other disciplines' fortunes during their formative periods will afford numerous examples of the influence of institutional forces on the selection and bias of its key concepts.

The institutional forces are probably more important than the intellectual, no matter how fervently we try to persuade the world of the divine nature of the quest for truth. Power resides in our institutions, so their pre-eminence over any intellectual argument is not surprising. Intellectual criteria for resolving scientific issues hold sway only in so far as individuals supporting them are endowed with the necessary institutional power to enforce them. The rules of institutional engagement are those of the various societies, funding bodies, journals, teaching and research centres and relevant governmental institutions. These rules are localized and difficult to understand or even to be discovered outside their immediate context. The institutional weapons are widely known: agendas, appointments, confidential reviews, budgets, teaching loads, allocations of space and equipment, committee structures and, most importantly, decisions on the curriculum and the syllabus. Decisions on most of these matters are often taken covertly when, not infrequently, those involved have relatively little knowledge of the field and, even after the event, the process is seldom open to public scrutiny. The institutional struggle over contentious questions of semantics often takes place because the meanings of terms govern the ways in which money can be spent, and the unscrupulous institutional politicians will attempt to wrench words from their normal meanings in order to legitimate spending in ways that were never intended. Labels attached to budgets come under strong pressure to change their meanings for reasons of expediency.

The institutional mechanisms for establishing meanings in practical terms are complex and seldom understood fully by the protagonists. The degree and the manner in which different people are involved in the processes will influence the quality of decisions that are reached. The demand for efficiency tends towards limiting the diversity of those engaged in the process. To recognize that the sorting out of semantic problems is involved in decision-making is not encouraged by the usual mechanistic model which assumes that a consensus about meanings has been established. The design of information systems still tends, for the sake of imagined efficiency, to be performed by analysts with broad direction from management, and imposed on the majority of users. The participative methods of conducting analysis and design championed by Mumford (1981), and by Land (1982) and investigated by Hirschheim (1983, 1985), are capable of improving the quality of the semantics of the resulting system, especially when diverse groups will be sharing the data. This is an aspect of participation in systems work that has not received significant attention, so far. The institutional machinery specifically for developing information systems deserves the attention of the semanticist.

All practical business decisions tend to reinforce or to modify the meanings given to the language in which they are couched, but this aspect of decision making tends to be overlooked until the group involved detects a breakdown of consensus. The shifting of a semantic consensus in a business is probably of greatest importance at the most senior levels of an organization. Empirical work in such an environment is notoriously difficult because of the sensitivity of the process to the presence of an observer, even supposing that matters of confidentiality would permit that method. A participant observer is unlikely to see the situation outside the constraints of his personal semantic framework. Failure of consensus and the repair of the meaning-structure usually involves quite strong feelings which make those involved reluctant to be observed, so perhaps the best line of empirical study in this area is afforded by business archives and the historical method.

14. SEMANTICS AND BUREAUCRACY

The law is another field of practical problem solving where we see the processes of establishing boundaries and naming their contents enacted in slow motion, and therefore most instructively. We should begin by distinguishing two kinds of problems generated by laws. One is the bureaucratic problem of determining the consequences of rules which raise no questions of interpretation. The other, the genuinely legal problem, is the kind for which we employ the professional lawyer, and it occurs when each party in the dispute sees how to interpret the rules in a way that suits himself. The object of well-drafted administrative rules should be (among other things) to ensure that the bureaucrat will not be troubled by semantic issues of the kind that are meat and drink for the lawyer.

Bureaucratic rules, to function reasonably efficiently, must deal with domains where the ideas involved are well understood. Without this basis, to delegate the resolution of large classes of common but often complex problems to functionaries would be impossible. Where bureaucratic rationality wears thin is round the edges of its systems of rules, where complexity and infrequency of use leave the meanings of the words of the rules open to dispute. Such circumstances invite the functionary who is less than angelic to impose meanings that suit him more than the client. The functioning and malfunctioning of bureaucratic systems need to be examined from a number of semantic angles, especially now that computer systems have given us the ultimate in bureaucracy.

The research agenda for information processing in the office should include the study of the activities performed by staff as they interpret and round off the edges of formal rules. Applied blindly and mechanically, almost any system of rules can injure an organization, because no one can formulate them richly enough to deal with all the complexities of any everyday administrative situation. The unthinking introduction of computers and telecommunications into offices can dangerously attenuate the human ability to rehearse meanings, to maintain them, and to modify them as circumstances gradually shift. One approach to this set of problems may be through the empirical materials potentially available in the records held by both the bureaucracy and by the pressure groups that monitor the administrative actions relevant to their constituencies.

15. THE LESSONS OF THE LAW

We can use the methods of sociology as exemplified in such classic work as that by Crozier (1964). We can sharpen up our understanding of rules by reading Twining and Myers (1976). Another potentially good source of ideas is the legal activity of dispute resolution in the courts (for example, Murphy and Rawlings (1981) who examined the decisions made by the House of Lords during one full year, to reveal a disappointing lack of structure to the semantic argumentation by their lordships). But we lack, precise formal tools that will be necessary if we are to make our way towards computer support for the decision makers who encounter semantic problems, that is to say, decision makers at the higher levels in a business. This lacuna inspired a research programme that I hope will suggest a wide range of topics for investigation and also supply tools for the study of semantic problems.

The intention of the research programme was to explore the central theoretical issues of information systems and systems analysis by investigating the automation of bureaucratic rules. We soon realized that perhaps the most important and difficult of these theoretical issues concerns the relationship of the formal system to the real world of business. The pre-eminence of these semantic problems was emphasized by the response of the lawyers with whom we discussed the automatic application of complex rules to legally significant facts. They had little use for arguments based on logical inference compared with their need for support in resolving conflicts about meanings. We discovered a strong affinity between systems analysis and the process of legal drafting; both could be thought of as quests for meanings.

This work has led towards a set of formal tools for investigating semantics. Let me outline the main ideas.

The aim in studying a wide range of administrative law and business systems was to create a formalism in which legal, business and social norms, quite generally, could be expressed with maximum formality but without doing injustice to the informal human system. The work obtained its discipline and its concrete objective from the goal of formalizing norms in a manner that would permit them to be interpreted, in so far as that could be done mechanically, by computer. Where machine processing became inappropriate, then the formalism was intended to prompt and facilitate correct forms of human intervention, such as naming things, classifying them, making value judgements, exercising discretion in a multitude of ways. The resulting legally orientated language, called Legol, was developed with semantic problems in mind. We were attempting to base the language upon a theory of meaning suited to practical business affairs, quite different from the established semantic theories derived from mathematical modes of thought that were criticized above. Ideally, this Legol formalism would impose enough constraints upon the user to ensure that his specification of a system of data structures and rules would have well-defined meanings.

The basic theoretical idea is that meanings in business are relationships between signs (think of these as the character strings held in computers) and the actions that people perform to accomplish the purposes of the organization. One way of linking sign and action is familiar to anyone acquainted with the mathematical device of coordinates in geometry. First you must reach agreement on the location of an 'origin'. The relevant action is a shared ability to re-locate this origin every time one wishes to specify another point in space. Then, an expression such as (25,44) can be translated into actions by anyone who knows its meaning if he takes 25 paces from the origin to the West followed by 44 paces from that point to the North. He will then find himself located at the place called '(25,44)'. What we attempted to do was to provide a generalization of this concept of coordinates to embrace, in addition to the location of physical objects in physical space, the location of seemingly abstract social objects in socially created space. Ideally, an expression in these generalized coordinates should represent a set of instructions on how to locate the particular thing or state of affairs represented. Notice that the entities in the business or legal world are more likely to be such things as copyrights, contracts, levels of priority, which are located in our social space. The syntax of the expression representing each physical or social entity would capture the essential structural features of the actions needed to locate it.

For specifying business information systems, this clear means of translating sign-structures into actions would be an ideal solution. The task of the systems analyst would primarily be to establish meanings in a language of this kind by discovering and encoding the actions relevant to the conduct of the business. Firstly, he would declare the vocabulary of the system (the coordinate framework), and then he would establish the shape of the organization in the form of its norms of conduct (how you are allowed to move around the social space of the organization). The result would be as formally precise a specification of the business functions as one could achieve in describing a social system. Every organization, in so far as it is organized, acts as though its members were conforming to a set of rules only a few of which might be explicit. These are the essential features of the organization that the analyst must uncover. Put together, the norm system would define the structure in social space that would be analogous to a system of equations and inequalities marking out a geometrical pattern on a coordinate diagram. Our attempt to create better tools for specifying information systems has led us deep into the problems of semantics and towards novel methods of solving them.

The simple solution which we implemented in 1979 was called Legol-2.1. It employed the following inadequate but instructive semantic principles.

Every particular thing in the world had to be an instance of some 'entity'. The entities we subdivided into three types with a common (coordinate) structure:

SORT, CHARACTERISTIC, ANTECEDENTS, EXISTENCE.

Each of these corresponded to a pattern of behaviour which could be shared by the population of interpreters (such as the ability to find the origin, move to the North and West with uniformly long steps). The SORT is like the ability to sort things out. For example, put everything now surrounding you, as you read this book, onto a conveyor belt and let them be transported past another person — he would be able to recognize chairs, tables, filing cabinets, people, coffee cups and so on as they went by — the common nouns would designate the shared abilities to recognize these sorts of particulars.

We shall return to the CHARACTERISTIC later. It can take three different forms depending upon the type of entity we are dealing with.

The ANTECEDENTS would not arise in the sorting example above because all the objects listed were simple physical ones but you may possess, in addition to your furniture, family and crockery, some copyrights which are also assets. The problem about a copyright is that it is so abstract. To make sense of the kind of thing we call a 'copyright' we first have to make sense of the notion of a 'work' in which the copyright subsists. In this case 'work' is an ontological antecedent of 'copyright': it must have a prior existence. Even the notion of a work is abstract. The book you are holding in your hands is just one instantiation of the work which carries the copyright. One particular instance, the manuscript, is the ontological antecedent of the work you are (I hope) now enjoying. This is the same idea that we encountered in a geometrical coordinate system where the origin is the antecedent of the two selected directions which, in turn, are the antecedents of the distances moved in those directions.

Finally, we have to account for the EXISTENCE coordinate. Quite simply, this is the interval during which the translation of the whole coordinate structure into actions can be performed so that the instance represented can actually be found. It can be represented by a start time and a finish time recorded on some chronometer we care to nominate, but it may be a time period specified in another convenient way. For example, the start and finish of a member of your family would be the times of that person's birth and death; the start of a copyright, in the UK at least, is the day of publication and the finish is 50 years after the author's death. Thus the notion of existence is one that we explain in terms of the notion of successfully completing the pattern of actions represented in the semantic coordinate structure, the period during which all the ingredients contained in the coordinate recipe are available.

Now we can return to look at CHARACTERISTICS which vary according to the type of semantic recipe we have. Three types of entities are distinguished in this way: *things*, *conditions* and *states*. They are most easily understood using examples:

thing

SORT	IDENTITY	ANTECEDENTS	existence
person	John		2–11–43 to now
copyright	UK	work 'Love Song'	1917 to 1967

condition

SORT	CRITERION	ANTECENDENTS	EXISTENCE
fat	weight-watchers	person 'John'	11–10–85
married	UK	person 'John', person'Mary'	7–2–64 to 1–1–78
married	RC church	person 'John', person 'Mary'	7–2–64 to now

state

SORT	value	ANTECEDENTS	EXISTENCE
weight	250 lb	person'John'	11–10–85
distance	50 000 km	comet 'Halley', probe'x'	22–1–86

As you see the CHARACTERISTICS can be names, criteria or values. The entities we class as *things* appear to have a kind of independent existence. At least in the case of simple physical objects, things can be known by their SORT and IDENTITY alone, their EXISTENCE is a period of time defined by an ontologically prior knowledge of the individual. Thus we suggest by this semantic framework how times are basically established. The use of lower-case letters for the 'existence' attribute of things indicates this dependency.

In the case of *conditions*, all the attributes are needed to make up the full 'recipe' for meaningful action. As you see, John and Mary are married by virtue of two different CRITERIA, those of UK civil law and those of the Roman Catholic church, one of which permitted divorce on 1–1–78 although the other did not recognize it. The criteria are the relevant sets of norms or laws, or, in the case of the deplorable obesity of John, the criterion is the judgement of his weight-watchers group.

The *states* are like measurements. They relate entities to data-types in such a way that the algebraic structure of the data-type encodes a similar empirical or prescribed structure of relationships among the instances of that entity class. The VALUE will be a value of the entity type selected according to the norms of the measurement or state. You will notice 'value' is printed in lower-case to indicate this functional relationship.

This completes, except for one detail, the explanation of this over-simplified, Legol-2.1, semantic framework. There are also some constraints upon the existences of individuals and their ontological antecedents. In the case of a state, there *must* be a meaningful instance of the state during the existence of its antecedent(s), whilst in the case of a condition, it need not exist whenever its antecedents do (e.g. an arbitrarily selected Frederick and an arbitrary Mabel may never be married). The anomalous case is that of things which are permitted to exist outside the period of their antecedents' coexistence. If we did not allow this, we should only be able to construct with our Legol operators complex specific entities of ever more restricted duration and we should not be able to write laws that link events over time (e.g. earnings and tax liability). This anomaly in the temporal constraints enables us to avoid the semantic problem of signs or information. The overall effect of the semantic framework is to constrain the user of the system to write statements that are more than syntactically correct but semantically well-formed according to an action-orientated theory of meaning.

16. A FORMAL METHODOLOGY FOR SEMANTIC INVESTIGATIONS

The greatest problem of dealing with semantics in a formal way, without becoming enmeshed in the inappropriate metaphysics of mathematics, is one of obtaining any grip on the problem at all. The classical logical tools are all based upon the assumption that the fundamental semantic problems have already been solved before a logic can be used. This even applies to non-monotonic logic where it is assumed that new facts or axioms can be introduced, but without recognizing that meanings can change in any other sense. Within the classical framework, terms have meanings either because they are supposed to refer to objects in a universe of discourse or related structures (the modelling approach), or because they are implicitly defined by the axioms and the syntactic rules (the abstract axiomatic approach). The modelling approach evades the semantic issues and the axiomatic approach ignores them.

The Legol Project, which I have just touched upon, has proposed a radically new approach to the semantics of business, legal and other social information systems. It provides a formalism that is essentially open-ended, as the genuine problems of semantics require and not, as the classical methods provide, a closed, sterile formalism that presupposes that the semantic issues have all been resolved. The tabular framework, described above, into which each entity has to fit, can be seen as a means of generating questions about the meaning of the entity name: what criterion determines the existence of an instance of the entity? when does an individual start and finish its existence? what are its ontological antecedents? In the later version of the language touched upon below, these questions can only be answered by mentioning other individuals with their own sets of question-marks attached to them. The formal core written down can be interpreted by computer, but the question-marks define the links to the informal human system.

An open-ended formal semantic framework should be capable of being applied to the semantic problems introduced earlier in this chapter. It should be possible to characterize explicitly the differences of understanding that give rise to legal disputes, industrial relations problems, negotiating difficulties over contracts, and other common business disputes. In an experiment using the Legol formalism, a student was taught the method of semantic analysis to enable him systematically to unravel the meanings latent in the mind of an imaginary Member of Parliament (played by a Parliamentary Counsellor, one of the small group who draft all major legislation) who was trying to specify a new Bill. He did this by taking any expressions the MP introduced in his outline of the Bill and putting them into the semantic framework. (This is exactly the same method he would have applied had he been analysing the requirements of a 'user' of some proposed information system.) The constraints imposed by this framework then forced the analyst to ask questions about the details of how to interpret operationally each significant expression. This analytical process gradually drew forth the structure of the draft legislation which the MP had formulated in a vague intuitive way. (For a brief account of this, see Stamper 1984.) A system to support the analyst as he applies this technique to both sides in a conflict will create a new kind of decision support, a solution to the problem posed earlier of finding a rational way to proceed when the shared semantic framework breaks down.

Numerous other applications suggest themselves. Data analysis is greatly improved using a strict semantic framework. If one looks at the work on database semantics, one finds it is concerned with formal semantics, not with the semantics of relationships to a real world. Formal semantics deals with the translation from one formal representation to another with a preservation of 'meaning', in the narrow sense of being able to reverse the transformation. The computing fraternity acts as though formal semantics were the only kind available. The semantics we need in the study of information systems is one that deals with the intrinsically non-mathematical issue of how to relate the character-strings in computer stores or on mathematical blackboards to the world that we are pleased to call 'real'. So we are likely to find our apparently technical-looking questions leading us straight into the soft, suffocating embrace of philosophical enquiry.

17. THE NATURE OF REALITY FOR INFORMATION SYSTEMS RESEARCHERS

The thesis that semantics is a central issue in information systems research compels us to face deep questions about the nature of reality. Let me offer a solution, one that I believe will enable us to proceed with greater assurance on all fronts in our whole research field.

Earlier in this chapter I rejected the crude metaphysics entailed by model-theoretic semantics and its appeal to a universe of discourse populated by all kinds of imaginary individuals. I also hinted that we should reject the apparatus of formal semantics most often used in the computing milieu today, because it assumes a reality that is objective and independent from any person or group. Dispensing with these familiar ideas throws us back to the start, as far as formal methods are concerned. Our desire to study social systems makes us yearn to reject that notion, but can we afford the theoretical loss? I am convinced that there is a new route to follow. We find it and hold on to it by adopting two simple principles. They are ones that lurk within the Legol semantic framework set out above.

First: There is no world without an observer.
Second: The observer has no knowledge of the world
              without doing something in it.

These lead us to conjecture that a serviceable formalism for information systems might have well-formed formulae with the structure:

real state of affairs = agent + action successfully performed

or in the terminology of the language we are developing:

⟨realization⟩ : := ⟨agent⟩ ⟨affordance⟩

where the realization can itself be regarded as a complex agent, thus recursively generating worlds of any complexity centred on the one agent. The affordances (a term borrowed from James Gibson (1979)) are the patterns of behaviour which the environment afford the agent in question. The agent can be a person but it might well be a team, a company or even a whole nation-state.

A person enjoys knowledge of a social world and through it he can enjoy vicariously the worlds experienced by others, because the social world equips them all with the ability to use signs, the simple yet infinitely rich material out of which we construct our information systems. The agent also acquires the accumulated wisdom of the society by playing roles within social structures it has devised, often over long periods, to handle a range of problems beyond the capability of isolated individuals. These roles, laid down (mostly informally) in the cultural norms of the society, may be clarified by explicit rules in some subcultures, such as a bureaucracy. This picture accords with our understanding of business reality better than the mechanistic picture imposed upon anyone who embraces the assumptions of classical logical and computer science tools.

It would add excessively to the length of this chapter to provide more detail about the logic which we can build on the foundation of the two basic metaphysical principles enunciated above. The syntax and some illustrations can be found in Stamper (1986). It is called Norma as it is a logic of norms and affordances, norms being the social counterpart to the affordances that the physical environment provides an individual. In many important respects Norma is like Legol-2.1 mentioned above. For our purposes it is sufficient to highlight the fact that the formal structure is never complete. For every realization or well-formed formula, there are associated ones. In particular there are realizations marking its start and finish, each of which has its own start and finish, and so on until the action of time has been established with sufficient precision; there are realizations of the criteria, either norms or abilities, that make it possible to determine when the affordance has been realized; there is always an underlying agent that may have any number of constituent parts depending upon the detail of analysis a problem requires. Every one of these underlying realizations has its own underlying structure, and so on indefinitely as a series of questions that ask, 'What precisely do you mean when you say . . .?'

18. RESEARCH METHODS AND TOOLS

Reaching the end of this essay on semantic problems in information systems, it is time to summarize some key points. First, let us look again at the methods and tools available.

In order to study semantics in a business context it is necessary to have tools for characterizing meanings, especially with a view to exhibiting differential meanings. The tools of predicate logic and classical formal semantics are ill-suited to this task. The application-specific terms are either names of individuals or they are predicate names; the resulting structure is flat and uninformative and it is unstable if one attempts to deal with small shifts of meaning because the extension of a predicate is all one can give. Furthermore, these extensions can be very large and also fortuitous if defined by different agents who happen to have overlooked different individuals. The unreliability of the classical semantics rules it out for the study of meanings in the context of business.

Above the level of its vocabulary and the definitions of the referents of application-specific terms, predicate logic allows one to elaborate upon meanings by introducing 'axioms' (Sergot, *et al.*, 1986) or 'meaning postulates'

(Montague, 1974) in the form of implication clauses or asserted formulae. Unfortunately, there is nothing in the syntax or the semantics of predicate logic that would lead anyone to look for one kind of feature rather than another in building up this axiom system.

The Norma semantic theory appears to overcome these difficulties. It links comfortably with the informal system and allows levels of discrimination at any depth. Names of individuals are no different in principle from names of other affordances but the affordance structure as a whole is rich and informative. Also, as the schema is being specified, the syntax prompts one to answer, or at least declare of little concern, a series of questions that expose the subjects' meanings in gradually increasing detail. For example, starting and finishing events need to be clarified; beginning and ending phenomena can be asked about; ontological predecessors can be sought; part structures and roles prompt more questions; and so on. All these features give the investigator the opportunity to limit his attention easily to the relevant aspects of his problem, and to carry out his analysis just so far but no further than necessary.

Research is needed to develop these tools and the techniques for using them on business problems or legal issues. We are working at the London School of Economics on a computer system to support the analyst as he contends with semantics. It aims to facilitate both database schema design and dispute resolution. We hope that it will open up a new field of research into semantics, but there is scope for work on other systems of this general type. Observation of live problems, in which differences of meanings understood by groups or individuals can explain some aspects of organizational behaviour, provide an obvious method. It will be difficult to go beyond informal analyses until this kind of computer-based tool is available.

Meanwhile the informal methods of analysis should not be ignored. An earlier generation of semanticists are worth reading to sharpen one's wits for the task. Ogden and Richards, Dewey, Hayakawa, Korsybski, Whorf and so on are more help in trying to understand organizational semantics than are the more recent schools of writers engaged in building the formal tools based on classical logics. Law reports and analyses of political discourse are greater help than axiomatizations of legislation created by logic programmers. The formal tools I am proposing and developing will be aids to the use of these informal methods, not substitutes for them.

There are also other less precise empirical tools, such as content analysis which uses Osgood's semantic differential technique for comparing affective meanings, or statistical taxonomy which can be used to compare semantically significant clusterings of words used by different groups or individuals. These tools are steam hammers that cannot crack the smaller, more sophisticated nuts without destroying them. Nevertheless for some initial studies they should not be ignored.

Experimental situations may make the use of statistical techniques more acceptable. The kind of experiment I have used is the simulation game in which people solve problems cooperatively under pressure of limited time and limited communication channels. I first employed these methods when I worked in the steel industry. It was then (and I fear still is) fashionable to pretend that operational research workers can discover how the plant should run, so that they can build a simulation model from which a hundred years of experience can be obtained with the aid of a computer. The alternative procedure that my colleagues and I developed was to model the plant in such a way that the managers concerned with the day-to-day decisions could face the problems over which they were in regular disagreement. This gaming simulation exposed misunderstandings about the meanings of variables, the relevance of certain information and the nature of the sub-goals to be pursued. The result was an accelerated process of negotiation about their joint decision making. This kind of situation can be imitated in artificial games in which semantic problems are deliberately embedded. Experimental results based on replications of the game with different groups of subjects can be analysed statistically, and because they are not too far removed from practical situations, the results are likely to be instructive for business decision makers.

Yet another valuable method is that of semiotic analysis. Given a situation in which signs are being used to influence and draw together in common understanding the participants in a collective decision, the signs employed in the transaction may be classified and their modes of signifying questioned at many different levels. The whole sign situation can be taken first, then the isolated transaction, then its parts, verbal, gestural, proxemic, and so on. Relevant authors are Charles Morris, Pierre Guiraud, Umberto Eco and, with special reference to organizations, Stamper. The method is hermeneutic and it produces a sensitive perception of the forces at work without providing a basis for hard scientific conclusions, but that limitation does not matter if the object is to find ways of teaching people how to use information with greater insight.

For the study of business transactions at the normally inaccessible level of senior management where semantic issues are often dominant, we have a wonderful resource in business archives. These allow access to confidential communications and they enable us to look at processes that are enacted over a long period by a wide range of people who would be inaccessible to other research methods. Good archive material will span the organization from the top to the bottom of its hierarchy (Liebenau, 1986). Some similar research could be carried out using legal materials, which set out in historical perspective shifts of meanings as a result of disputes, exposed in fine detail by arguments in court proceedings and judgements. Historical methods such as these need to be brought into our field.

So we may conclude with the assurance that there are some relevant research tools for the study of business semantics. However, they are still undeveloped and a large part of our research efforts will have to be applied to improving these tools.

19. HYPOTHESES TO EXPLORE

This chapter has been almost exclusively about the important of semantics as a research field in the domain of Information Systems, and the need for new tools of enquiry. Some of the existing tools and research methods have been touched upon. It remains only to suggest some hypotheses that may be worthy of investigation. The following list includes many relating to the impact of information technology on the organizational performance. This is perhaps the aspect of the subject that has prompted our enquiry, but we cannot deal with it in isolation from the more general questions about organizational semantics.

Space permits only the listing of a series of hypotheses. A whole book would be needed to spell out the reasons for including each one and to explain what I consider their practical implications to be. It is not unfair to exploit the semantic ambiguity consequential upon this enforced brevity. Because the precise meaning of each hypothesis to me cannot be explained to you, the effect will be, I hope, to stimulate your own ideas. Meanings have to be made and ambiguity can sometimes be a stimulus to creativity.

The hypotheses can be classified in many different ways. The following classification has been adopted here.

(1) semantic norms within a community, group or team,
(2) processes of meaning formation within a group,
(3) the adaptation of individuals to the system of meanings within a group,
(4) institutional or multiple group semantics,
(5) resolution of conflict through semantic shifts,
(6) effects of market situations on semantics,
(7) impact of formal systems upon semantics,
(8) impact of information technology on semantics.

The order signifies that meanings essentially depend upon the consensus among a group, then individuals accommodate to prior semantic structures and alter them, as they grapple with problems that require multiple teams in a larger organizational framework, giving rise to conflicts that are resolved through semantic shifts. Finally, there are two important problem areas, the transactions induced by market situations and the impact of technology.

Individuals
*Semantic boundaries that are easy to operationalize concretely will not provoke passionate semantic disputes, but words and expressions that cannot be operationalized easily, even when used by groups that claim to have common objectives, will be given a diversity of meanings that will tend to be defended with passion.
*An individual joining a team to perform a task unfamiliar to him will not initially understand the meanings of task-relevant words.

*In any team, the more powerful members will have their use of language, including choice of meanings, imitated by the less powerful.
*Meanings depend on boundaries: start and finish, territory and agency, where actions can or cannot be performed. Some individual or group is responsible for directly judging these boundaries or for maintaining the criteria according to which they are determined.
*Every semantic boundary marks a shift between situations that the group concerned evaluates differently.
*Every semantic difference is underpinned by a difference of values.
*A person can tolerate several different semantic regimes and their associated value systems to an extent that decreases as the tangible effects of language used in one regime are significant within other regimes.

Groups
*Diversity of meanings used within a linguistic community will increase as power in that community is more widely distributed.
*The majority of semiological transactions in a community must serve to confirm the established semantic structure.
*The adaptability of a community to changing circumstances depends upon its ability to accept changes of meaning in its vocabulary.
*When a team develops a common vocabulary to support its performance of a shared task, a change of task requiring an overlapping, relevant vocabulary will result in new meanings for the original words and expressions.
*An individual or group, habituated to dealing with situations using one vocabulary, will evaluate negatively the problem characterizations or solutions produced by individuals or groups using another vocabulary that is not equivalent semantically.
*When people collaborate, they will disagree less about meanings when the relevant vocabulary is easier to operationalize.

Institutions
*Constituents of a team that are separated in order to do their work will display a gradual semantic drift that will increase with the lack of face-to-face contact among them.
*Two groups that operate independently, even when engaged on initially identical tasks, will generate task-relevant vocabularies with differences of meaning that will gradually increase over time.
*Contact between groups having semantically different languages for the same task will reduce the semantic differential to an extent dependent upon the amount of contact and the hierarchical level of the contact.

Conflict
*Failure of a semantic boundary is always associated with a conflict, whilst conflicts are frequently formulated as semantic differences.

*The successful protagonist in a conflict situation is likely to be the one having the richer vocabulary in which to characterize and understand the situation.

*Where a conflict has to be resolved by negotiation, each party will attempt to impose its own favoured meanings upon the words and expressions relevant to the solution.

*The vocabulary used in a negotiated solution to a conflict will have the meanings closer to those favoured by the more powerful party.

*Where meanings are firmly established by a wide consensus, conflicts will be more quickly resolved than they are without the background consensus.

*Meanings cannot be reformulated without the communication of evaluative information and information which convey inducements (threats or rewards) to comply with the new frameworks being advanced.

*Conflicts between parties of similar strength will tend to provoke a weakening of consensus about the meanings of relevant terms among those who are not partisan.

*Institutions that have no mechanism for generating conflicts about meanings or are unable to manage them creatively will be unable to adapt.

Markets

*When products or services that are difficult to differentiate operationally are marketed, the competitors will attempt to create spurious distinctions by creating synonyms for terms already established by the general consensus.

*When mutually substitutable and operationally readily distinguishable products or services are marketed, the competitors will attempt to reduce the precision of the meanings already established by consensus.

*In any competitive situation, the dominant party, if one clearly exists, will resist having to adopt the semantic norms of the culture at large and use every available strategy to take control of the meanings of the vocabulary relevant to its products or services.

Formal systems and technology

*Every data element in a formalized schema exhibits at least minor variations in usage among a population of users.

*Any formalized schema will fail to represent the view of reality favoured by some user.

*The diversity of meanings attached to the elements of a formalized schema will tend to vary in inverse proportion to the level of involvement of the users in its design.

*A decision maker dealing with real-life situations and working through the mediation of a formalized system will recognize the need for changes in the formalism only if there is feedback outside the formal system; the rate of perceived change will depend upon the amount of feedback, among other factors.

*An agent constrained to deal with a real-life (or even a complex, formalized situation) using the fixed vocabulary of some data- or knowledge-base, will recognize features of the situation or courses of action that cannot (concisely) be expressed in the formalism.

*Problem-solving methods that have only a closed-world semantic component will always produce solutions in a domain of practical affairs that degrade over time; the constant reformulation of meanings of the terms used in a formal system is essential for maintaining economy of expression and for adjusting to shifting values.

(You should recognize several hypotheses in this list that express aspects of the Sapir–Whorf hypothesis, especially in relation to formal systems.)

20. SUMMARY AND CONCLUSION

The message of this chapter can be stated briefly. A study of business information systems can derive much support from the theory of signs, or semiotics, which has four main divisions: syntactics, empirics, pragmatics and semantics. The computer-orientated community deals with the first of these, whilst Information Systems as a discipline concentrates upon the other two. In the rest of the chapter attention was focused upon semantics, which is a particularly difficult subject area. One of the reasons is that the emphasis of research in recent years has been upon the semantics of formal systems derived from the timeless, abstract world of mathematics. Logic and mathematics begin where the semantic problems that constitute the everyday concerns of business have already been solved, hence the present-day formal methods of semantics have nothing to contribute to solving practical, non-formal problems. A new direction is sought.

The new methods can employ formalisms provided that they do not assume a closed world. They have to represent the consensus, necessarily temporary, among the groups with conflicting views about the business problem. This new type of formalism has to remain open-ended, able to accept and indeed prompt refinements to the semantic model. An example of how to approach the design of an open formalism, Legol, was discussed briefly. More research is needed in this methodology domain.

The new tools in the making and many established ones statistical, hermeneutic, experimental and historical, can be invoked for investigating how people in business make and remake meanings in the processes of innovating and resolving conflicts. An extensive list of hypotheses was suggested.

NOTES

[1] The important meanings of 'information', besides the naïve one of 'a collection of signs', are the well-known entropy measure devised by Shannon (1948) for the engineering of telecommunications systems, the family of logical measures based on Carnap's logical theory of probability (Carnap, 1942) by Bar-Hillel (1964), and the subjective measures based on betting odds introduced in Stamper (1973). For a simple account of these see Stamper (1971) and for a detailed study of the meanings of the word 'information' in the business context, see the books Stamper (1973, 1987).

[2] This kind of psychologism is rampant in works on information systems. One finds many examples in the writing of some of the most respected authors on the subject, for example, Langefors and Sundgren (1975), especially Chapter 1, and Langefors and Samuelson (1976), especially Chapter 3. The idea is ancient and was given renewed impetus by Saussure in his *Course in General Linguistics* (1916).

[3] For example:

> There is only one language suitable for representing information — whether declarative or procedural — and that is first order predicate logic. There is only one intelligent way to process information — and that is by applying deductive inference methods. (Kowalski, 1980, p. 40)

[4] A most outrageous example of this was the argument advanced by the Secretary of State for Education and Science against the social sciences on the grounds that they did not conform to 'the Popperian paradigm', according to which, hypotheses are not genuinely scientific unless they are open to refutation by empirical observation. He did not find support for the abolition of the Social Science Research Council but petulantly he removed the word 'Science' from its name, changing it to the 'Economic and Social Research Council'!

[5] For examples of this naïve idea that information is a kind of mystical fluid see Stamper (1985c). Boland (1986) eloquently attacks the same misconception. The underlying reasons for the persistence of metaphors such as the mystical substance view of information is explained by Lakoff and Johnson (1980) and by Reddy (1979).

REFERENCES

ANSI-X3-SPARC (Standards Planning and Requirements Committee) (1975) 'Interim Report from the Study Group on Database Management Systems', *FDT* (Bulletin of ACM SIGMOD) 7, 2.

Austin, J. L. (1962) *How to Do Things with Words*, Oxford University Press, Oxford.

Bar-Hillel, Y. (1964) *Language and Information*, Addison-Wesley, Reading, MA.

Barnes, B. (1982) *T. S. Kuhn and Social Science*, Macmillan, London.

Barwise, J., and Perry, J. (1983) *Situations and Attitudes*, MIT Press, Cambridge, MA.

Berger, P. L., and Luckman, T. (1967) *The Social Construction of Reality*, Penguin, Harmondsworth.

Bloor, D. (1976) *Knowledge and Social Imagery*, Routledge & Kegan Paul, London.

Bloor, D. (1983) *Wittgenstein: A Social Theory of Knowledge*, Macmillan, London.

Boland, R. J. (1986) 'Fantasies of Information', *Advances in Public Interest Accounting*, 1, 49–65.

Bubenko, J. A. (1983) *Information Modeling*, Student Literatur, Lund.

Carnap, R. (1942) *Introduction to Semantics*, Harvard University Press, Cambridge, MA.

Carnap, R. (1950) *Logical Foundation of Probability*, University of Chicago Press, Chicago.

Chen, P. (1976) *The Entity-Relationship Model: Towards a Unified View of Data*, ACMTODS, 1, 1, pp. 9–36.

Crozier, Michel (1964) *The Bureaucratic Phenomenon*, University of Chicago Press, Chicago.

Date, C. J. (1977) *An Introduction to Database Systems*, Addison-Wesley, Reading, MA.

Davis, P. J., and Hersh, R. H. (1981) *The Mathematical Experience*, Harvester Press, Brighton.

Dowty, D. R., Wall, R. E., and Peters, S. (1981) *Introduction to Montague Semantics*, Reidel, Dordrecht.

Feyerabend, P. (1975) *Against Method*, Verso Books, London.

Gibson, J. J. (1979) *The Ecological Approach to Visual Perception*, Houghton-Mifflin, Boston.

Hardy, W. G. (1978) *Language, Thought and Experience*, University Park Press, Baltimore.

Hayakawa, S. I. (1963) *Language in Thought and Action*, Harcourt, Brace & World, New York.

Hirschheim, R. (1983) 'Assessing Participative Systems Design: Some Conclusions From an Exploratory Study', *Information & Management*, **6**, 6.

Hirschheim, R. (1985) 'User Experience with and Assessment of Participative Systems Design', *MIS Quarterly*, **9**, 4.

Jones, S., Mason, P., and Stamper, R. K. (1979) 'LEGOL-2.0: A Relational Specification Language for Complex Rules', *Information Systems*, **4**, 4.

Kent, W. (1978) *Data and Reality*, North-Holland, Amsterdam.

Korzybski, A. (1933) *Science and Sanity*, Science Press, Lancaster, PA.

Kowalski, R. (1979) *Logic for Problem Solving*, North-Holland, Amsterdam.

Kowalski, R. (1980) Quoted in a special issue on knowledge representation, *SIGART Newsletter*, No. 70.

Kuhn, T. S. (1962) *The Structure of Scientific Revolutions*, University of Chicago Press, Chicago.

Lakatos, I. (1976) *Proofs and Refutations*, Cambridge University Press, Cambridge.

Lakoff, G., and Johnson, M. (1980) *Metaphors We Live By*, University of Chicago Press, Chicago.

Land, F. F. (1982) 'Notes on Participation', *The Computer Journal*, **25**.

Langefors, B., and Sundgren, B. (1975) *Information Systems Architecture*, Petrochelli-Charter, New York.

Langefors, B., and Samuelson, K. (1976) *Information and Data Systems*, Petrochelli-Charter, New York.

Lee, R. M. (1984) 'Automating Red Tape: The Performative vs Informative Roles of Bureaucratic Documents', *Offices: Technology and People*, **2**, 187–194.

Lee, R. M., and Stamper, R. K. (1985) 'Ontological Aspects of Logical Databases', *Information Systems*, **10**, 3, 331–338.

Liebenau, J. (1986) Private communication, a research proposal, Business History Unit, London School of Economics.

McCawley, J. D. (1981) *Everything That Linguists Have Always Wanted to Know about Logic*, Blackwell, Oxford.

Methlie, L. B., and Sprague, R. H. (1985) *Knowledge Representation for Decision Support Systems*, North-Holland, Amsterdam.

Montague, R. (1974) in *Formal Philosophy*, R. H. Thomason (Ed.), Yale University Press, New Haven, Conn.

Morris, C. (1971) *Writings on the General Theory of Signs*, Mouton, The Hague. (A collection of his key works.)

Mulkay, M. (1979) *Science and the Sociology of Knowledge*, Allen & Unwin, London.

Mumford, E. (1981) 'Participative Systems Design: Structure and Method', *Systems, Objectives, Solutions*, **1**, 1.

Murphy, W. T., and Rawlings, R. W. (1981 & 1982) 'After the Ancien Regime', *The Modern Law Review*, **44**, November, 617–657, and January, 34–61.

Ogden, C. K., and Richards, I. A. (1923) *The Meaning of Meaning*, 10th Edn. (1949), Routledge & Kegan Paul, London.

Ortony, A. (Ed.) (1979) *Metaphor and Thought*, Cambridge University Press, Cambridge.

Osgood, C. E., Suci, G. J., and Tannenbaum, P. H. (1957) *The Measurement of Meaning*, University of Illinois Press, Urbana.

Popper, Sir Karl (1963) *Conjectures and Refutations*, Routledge & Kegan Paul, London.

Reddy, M. J. (1979) 'The Conduit Metaphor — A Case of Frame Conflict in Our Language about Language', in Ortony (1979).

Sapir, E. (1921) *Language: An Introduction to the Study of Speech*, Harcourt, Brace & World, New York.

Saussure, F de (1916/1983), *Course in General Linguistics*, translated by R. Harris, Duckworth, London.

Sergot, M. J., Sadri, F., Kowalski, R., Kriwaczek, F., Hammond, P., and Cory, H. T. (1986) 'The British Nationality Act as a Logic Program', *Comm. A.C.M.*, **29**, 4.

Shannon, C. E. (1948) 'A Mathematical Theory of Communication', *Bell System Technical Journal*, **27**, pp. 379–423 and 623–656.

Stamper, R. K. (1971) 'Some Ways of Measuring Information', *Computer Bulletin*, **15**, pp. 432–436.

Stamper, R. K. (1973) *Information in Business and Administrative Systems*, Wiley, New York, and Batsford, London.

Stamper, R. K. (1979) 'Towards a Semantic Normal Form', in *Database Architecture*, G. Bracche and G. M. Nijssen (Ed.), North-Holland, Amsterdam.

Stamper, R. K. (1980), 'LEGOL: Modelling Legal Rules by Computer', in *Computer Science and Law*, B. Niblett (Ed.), Cambridge University Press, Cambridge.

Stamper, R. K. (1984) 'Legal Drafting and Semantic Analysis', in *Gesetzgebung und Computer*, Th. Ohlinger (Ed.), J. Schweitzer Verlag, Munich.

Stamper, R. K. (1985a) 'Management Epistemology: Garbage In, Garbage Out', in Methlie and Sprague (1985).

Stamper, R. K. (1985b) 'A Logic of Social Norm for the Semantics of Business Information', in T. B. Steel and R. Meersmann (Eds.), *Database Semantics*, North-Holland, Amsterdam.

Stamper, R. K. (1985c) 'Information: Mystical Fluid or Subject for Scientific Enquiry?', *Computer Journal*, **28**, 3.

Stamper, R. K. (1985d) 'LEGOL Project Papers: An Annotated List of Papers Produced by the Project', Paper L0, The LEGOL/NORMA Project, London School of Economics.

Stamper, R. K. (1986) 'A Non-classical Logic for Law Based on the Structures of Behavior', in Martino, A. A. and Socci-Natli, F. (Eds.) *Automated Analysis of Legal Texts*, Elsevier, Amsterdam.

Stamper, R. K. (1987) *Information in Practical Affairs* Blackwell, Oxford (in press).

Twining, W., and Myers, D. M. (1976), *How To Do Things With Rules*, Weidenfeld & Nicolson, London.

Whorf, B. L. (1956) *Language, Thought and Reality*, MIT Press, Cambridge, MA.

Wynn, Eleanor (1979) *Office Conversation as an Information Medium*, Ph.D. thesis, University of California, Berkeley.

Critical Issues in Information Systems Research
Edited by R. J. Boland Jr. and R. A. Hirschheim
©1987 John Wiley & Sons Ltd.

Chapter 3

TOWARDS A FRAMEWORK FOR SYSTEMS ANALYSIS PRACTICE

John Banbury

ABSTRACT

Through dramatic decreases in cost and developments in technology computing has become far more readily available over the last ten to fifteen years. Furthermore, the technology is now more flexible, and so is more adaptable to specific applications, and capable of being applied in novel fields. Such developments are requiring the analyst to adopt a more complex (and realistic) view of the nature of user systems, and correspondingly, of the practice of design itself. The need for user involvement is receiving increasing emphasis for a number of reasons, while the practical and theoretical difficulties in doing so are becoming more widely realized.

Such developments are compelling the profession to reflect upon the nature of its subject matter and of its practice. This paper outlines a possible conceptual framework within which such matters may be considered. The framework is then used to explore the characteristics of a general approach for the development of information systems.

1. INTRODUCTION

It has been said many times that in the early days of computer application in organizations when computer technology was at a relatively rudimentary stage, the problems the analyst faced were predominantly technical. Since then the technology has advanced dramatically and has become more readily manageable in these respects within information systems analysis and design (ISAD); at the same time, increasing attention has come to be given to matters such as the modelling of the user system, societal issues such as data protection, and methodological issues such as user involvement in development.

In 1974, the Education Committee of the International Federation for Information Processing (IFIP) published its *Curriculum for Information Systems Designers* in the form of a set of guidelines for the advanced training of information systems analysts and designers. It was intended that courses based upon the curriculum should be multidisciplinary and vocational, and should prepare students for the equivalent of a higher degree.

In discussing whether this curriculum needed to be updated, Land [1] in 1980 critically examined a number of ways in which the situation facing the analyst (and the user) had changed since those early days. These were broadly:

(a) A changing climate of opinion regarding the *way* in which computer technology was introduced, and in particular its possible impact upon the rights of the individual, the quality of working life, and so on. The implication was that computing was perhaps no longer being seen as part of a 'technological imperative'; that it did not necessarily have to be regarded as 'having a momentum of its own'; that there was scope for choice in its *application*, as well as in the *methods* used to apply it.

(b) The changing view being taken of the ways in which Information Technology might impinge upon the organization in the light of dramatic developments in computing. Examples were: increasing emphasis on the user function; computing being used to stimulate decentralization rather than the hitherto seemingly inevitable centralization; office automation, with all that that implied — word processing, electronic mail, viewdata, etc.; an increasing emphasis on the support of, rather than the automation of decision processes, and the consequent opening up of possible new fields of application; the growth of personal computing, of dedicated systems, and of expert systems, all of which placed dramatic emphasis upon the role of the user in development.

(c) Decreasing emphasis being placed upon the 'life cycle' as the yardstick for discussing systems development, and an increasing recognition of the essentially evolutionary nature of the process. This reflected an increasing concern with the user's relationship with the system as exploratory and experimental, with a corresponding shift towards emphasizing prototyping approaches.

(d) The development of a variety of different *methods* of systems development ranging from the relatively 'hard', structured methods, to the softer approaches of the socio-technical school, and of 'soft-systems methodology' (Checkland).

(e) New ways of tackling the preparation of software via, for example: the development of automated tools; the development of new, general-purpose and special-purpose languages; new approaches to program design and to the organization of the programming task.

(f) A developing interest in the impact of Information Technology upon society at large, and in particular, a concern with its possible impact on, for example, employment, privacy, and the quality of working life.

Discussions concerning the continued suitability of the IFIP curriculum led to the conclusion that a revision was called for; the revised curriculum has since been developed [2].

A number of the matters referred to by Land touch on the nature of the user system. This concern arises either because of an increasing awareness of the perhaps over-simple, predominantly mechanistic view generally taken till then, or because the interest in extending the application of computing into novel fields (e.g. more personal computing, expert systems, decision-support systems) highlighted the need for a more complex view and, in particular, focused on the complementarity of user and computer systems [3]. Secondly, Land's paper raised questions concerning the adequacy of current understanding of the *process* by which systems analysis is carried out, and in particular of the part necessarily played by the user during the analysis of requirements.

Systems analysis as the means for designing computer-based systems is obviously not alone in its concern with such matters. Consideration of the nature of the process of design has received increasing attention from practitioners in a variety of fields in recent years [4]. Design as the realization of a desired outcome (a building, a sewing machine, a motorway) which meets a particular client's requirements, bears obvious similarities to design as the realization of a computer-based information system which meets a particular user's requirements. Much can be learnt from such developments, arising as they generally do in fields of practice with longer histories, and greater experience than our own. Certainly in the author's view, significant insights into the nature of systems analysis practice can be gained in this way, and the next section briefly reviews some of these developments.

2. DEVELOPMENTS IN THE THEORY OF DESIGN

Speculating and theorizing about the nature of design seems to have developed a new impetus in the 1950s, 1960s and 1970s, deriving at least partially from more general consideration of the subject of problem-solving then seen as a related process, for example as in operational research and management science [5].

Early attempts were made to formalize the process as a sequence of well-defined activities, to draw on the 'scientific method' as a possible paradigm, and to involve mathematical treatments and notions of optimality. The process of design was seen to involve analysis and synthesis components [6] — the analysis of a client's requirements, and their synthesis in terms of a specification of the 'form' required 'to fit the context'. It is interesting to note that emphasis at this time was also placed on the part that the designer's values, as well as the incidence of original ideas played in the process [7]. The engineer added three further phases to analysis and synthesis, namely, optimization, revision and implementation.

Subsequent consideration of such ideas led to two major conclusions, viz:

(a) design is not a strictly sequential process; and
(b) Rittel's contention that design problems are 'wicked' [8].

It is worth setting down his description of such problems in full '. . . [a] class of social system problems which are ill-formulated, where the information is confusing, where there are many clients and decision makers with conflicting values, and where the ramifications in the whole system are thoroughly confusing' [9]. The complexity of the problem situation implies the conclusion that all (in this case, architectural) problems are wicked. On the other hand many would no doubt claim that, on occasion it is still possible to abstract a well-structured problem from this confusion without doing undue violence to the rest [10].

Rittel also identified the related importance of 'argumentation' and negotiation within design, seeing the process as involving negotiation and compromise between parties with differing views and interests. This has led subsequently to the view of design as a learning process in which designer and client are steadily gaining new insights into both problem and solution.

Alexander [11] has focused more specifically upon the justification for user involvement in design, and upon ways of making it effective in practice.

This brief review of the development of other design practices, and particularly of architecture, and of the nature of the design process has highlighted the increasing emphasis that has come to be placed upon the generally 'wicked' (ill-structured) nature of the problems tackled, and the associated evolutionary nature of design. However ISAD generally takes place in the apparently more structured confines of the organization. It is pertinent to consider the significance of this, and its implications for the nature of the process of analysis.

3. ISAD IN THE ORGANIZATION

3.1 The Nature of the Organization

The term 'organization' implies order with a purpose in mind, and hence structure. Yet at the same time organizations are complex social institutions in which individuals with their own particular interests, values and concerns, necessarily interact with each other in the enactment of their work roles. In one sense, the structure of the organization is obvious. It is formally hierarchical in accordance with the distribution of authority within it, and it is broken down laterally into specialisms. At the same time, it is obvious that the freedom of action of those at the base of the hierarchy is more tightly constrained than it is at the apex, and the situations dealt with, again in formal terms, are correspondingly more structured. However, to leave it at that, and to focus solely upon this normative structure is largely to miss the point of the organization as *necessarily* a social institution with all the variety that that implies. Suffice it to say that to see the organization as having a simple unitary structure, with all individuals uniformly enacting their agreed work roles without even acknowledging the need to achieve a minimum of their cooperation, would be to adopt a view which would be generally quite unrealistic, and correspondingly unsatisfactory as a basis for design. Specialization and the division of labour further complicate the analyst's view of the organization, since they imply the need to delegate an appropriate degree of autonomy to the specialist in order to obtain the benefit of his use of his skills in the form of access to his 'tacit knowledge' [12]. Secondly, in general, decision situations in organizations are bound to contain uncertainty and ambiguity such that they can be handled only by relying upon the individual to use his judgement to a corresponding extent; this further calls for the delegation of significant autonomy to the subordinate. Such forms of delegation are not required, for example, merely to increase job satisfaction as an aid to motivation or on more humanitarian grounds; they are essential to the effective operation of the organization. Without appropriate access to these resources, the organization could not survive. Hence to cope with the social aspects of organization at least to this extent, and to introduce at least this degree of realism into his understanding of behaviour in organizations, and in particular of user information requirements, the analyst would need to adopt a more complex view, and see organizational situations in general as less than well-structured. The further need to achieve a degree of cooperation sufficient at least to make up for the ways in which the computer system will virtually inevitably fall short in practice adds to the complexity of this view. This implies the need for a shift away from reliance upon the simple functional model, grounded in what might be called 'production rationality' [13], as the basis for the analysis of user requirements, at least until the analyst has satisfied himself by reference to such a more complex view that his use of that model is justified in the particular circumstances he faces [14].

3.2 The Nature of the User System

ISAD is complicated by the fact that the user is not simply an individual acting as a private citizen and for example negotiating the design of some artefact for his personal and private use. In general he is more likely to be an employee, or a group of employees, negotiating with a fellow employee about matters which are going to affect the way in which particular work tasks will be performed in future. Furthermore, those who open negotiations may not even be those who will be the future end users of the proposed system, but perhaps their superior(s). In addition, representatives from other functional specialisms (e.g. Accounting, Sales, Production Scheduling) may also be involved, and put forward their various views about the proposed system. In general then, the user may be a complex of individuals forming some hierarchically arranged network, negotiating within the larger institutional framework of the organization.

Reference to the differences of view of the various members of the user system highlights the need for the analyst in general to see the organization for this purpose as pluralist rather than unitary, and as being made up of groupings of individuals, each group sharing a particular interest. In addition, each individual will also be serving his own ends to some extent [15]. Furthermore, aspects of more general organizational policies, e.g. concerning capital/labour substitution, or the centralization/decentralization of power, may also be involved, yet further complicating the nature of the user system. Such matters would need to be taken into account in representing the user system if the notion of *matching* the information providing system with the information requiring system is to have any meaning.

Finally, in regard to the relationship between the user system and its information requirements, the parent organization as some kind of whole, is bound to be seen as having a relationship with its environment which is to a greater or lesser extent shrouded in uncertainty and ambiguity [16]. In such circumstances, the further understanding of, and coming to terms with, its environment must rest upon the use of approaches which are to some extent exploratory and experimental. Arguably, in general such characteristics would also typify the relationship between a user system and its information requirements.

3.3 The Nature of the Process of ISAD

Reference was made in section 3.1 to the effectiveness of an organization being dependent in general upon individuals being delegated sufficient autonomy to enable them to draw upon their judgement and tacit knowledge in the performance of their work tasks. This would suggest that the analysis of information requirements aimed at supporting, and in particular complementing such activities would have to take place over an extended period. What information was required would not be immediately obvious to the individual concerned, and would be brought into consciousness, if at all, only via an extended dialogue [17]. Secondly, reference was made in section 3.2 to the members of the user system having differing views regarding the proposed computer system, views which would derive from the particular interests, etc., which they represented. Such differences would call for negotiation and bargaining between the parties concerned, as well perhaps as the straightforward wielding of power and authority if an adequate degree of consensus was to be arrived at. Further, such negotiations would need to continue in general throughout the process of analysis (and would need to involve the analyst as another interested party as well as prime mover in the project) as more of the relevant aspects of the requirements to be met by the computer system were revealed.

Both of these points lead to the view that the process by which the requirements are arrived at cannot be a deterministic one carried out by following a tightly prescribed set of steps. The outcome in general is bound to be emergent, and the underlying process essentially evolutionary and social [18].

This conclusion is similar to that arrived at by Rittel referred to in section 2 above in his treatment of wicked problems.

4. THE COMPONENTS OF DESIGN

Some insight into the structure of ISAD can be gained by looking at the components of design as it is widely viewed.

As was indicated earlier, design can be broken down into phases according to the method of identifying and ordering the significant elements, namely, analysis and synthesis. However, these terms are not sufficiently expressive of the underlying processes involved. Design must involve two parties—a client/user on the one hand and an expert on the other. (Obviously the two can exist in the same skull, but that is a special case!) The client/user has a specific 'problem' which he views in his own terms, and the expert has a general solution to a particular class of 'problem' — a building or a computer system. Their interchanges are aimed at reaching a sufficiently common understanding of the client's/user's 'problem' in terms which are interpretable and expressible as a particular application of the expert's general solution.

There are circumstances when the 'problem' is manifest as no more than a feeling of unease or dissatisfaction with some aspect of his situation, which he has lived with for some time. On other occasions, the 'problem' will be immediate, and such that he is quite clear about its nature — though still in his terms. Again, there are circumstances when the common understanding of the 'problem' that has been reached is interpretable in the form of a variety of technical 'solutions' and methods of implementation, such that the understanding has to be further elaborated in ways aimed at reducing the variety. There are other circumstances when a simple, well-defined 'solution' stands out a mile.

The term 'articulation' reasonably describes the process of movement towards an appropriate common understanding and specification of the client's/user's requirements, and 'realization' the interpretation of that understanding (specification) in the form of an appropriate artefact. Typically, each of these phases would contain analysis and synthesis elements. Furthermore, circumstances seem bound to arise when work on each of the phases would involve a retracing of steps already taken in the light of deepening insights into the client's/user's requirements. In general therefore, there cannot be a clear break between the two phases; they must overlap such that one merges into the other. In such circumstances, the stage which a design has reached is best distinguished in terms of whether the current major emphasis is upon the 'articulation' of the client's/user's requirements, or their 'realization' as a running system.

Churchman [19] identifies the need for a 'model of the user' as a prerequisite to the development of an appropriate information system. Such a model could be regarded as the outcome of the 'articulation' phase in this formulation, and would correspond broadly with the 'object model' referred to by Rittel [20]. The model would then need to be translated into a more appropriate, more technically oriented form to become the input to the 'realization' phase.

Such a representation of structure and process is helpful in that it is indicative of the kinds of activities that are undertaken during design. It is also broadly expressive of the changing orientation of the activity as design progresses — initially towards understanding user requirements, latterly towards more technical matters. Finally, its generality facilitates the relating of ISAD to other fields of practice.

5. A FRAMEWORK FOR INFORMATION SYSTEMS ANALYSIS AND DESIGN

A possible framework for ISAD will now be developed which draws upon the above discussion but also upon the more specifically systems analysis literature. In particular, the need is for a framework which will facilitate the development of a more principled basis for practice, for example via the development of ideas about relevant knowledge bases, the nature of the analyst's role, and so on. Churchman's contention that the analyst needs to model the user is a suitable starting point.

Modelling can reasonably be regarded as a means of simplifying the 'buzzing, roaring confusion' of reality by catching the essentials of a particular situation for the particular purpose. But to be able to identify what aspects *are* significant, the modeller must have some prior, general understanding of the situation. Waddington [21] refers to this prior understanding as a philosophy. A model thus embodies a set of assumptions about the particular reality with which the modeller is concerned. Checkland [22] goes further and describes a philosophy as a broad, non-specific guideline for action, and the illustrations he gives suggest that he sees such a philosophy embodying a particular value position. The analyst has an obvious need of a philosophy in Waddington's sense (Checkland, writing from a systems viewpoint, takes that for granted). However, since the analyst is associated with the introduction of change, arguably he also needs a Checkland-type view of a philosophy to legitimate what he does and the initiatives he takes, i.e. to justify his position to, say, his employers, his professional peers (as well as to himself) and perhaps to society itself.

5.1 The Analyst's Philosophy

Arguably then, the analyst's philosophy needs to contain two components:

(a) a set of soundly based and defensible beliefs about the nature of those aspects of reality which are significant in the conduct of systems analysis; and
(b) a set of soundly based and defensible beliefs about such matters as: the purpose of systems analysis; the nature of the analyst's role; and the way in which his role should be enacted.

These points are developed in sections 5.1.1 and 5.1.2 below.

5.1.1 Beliefs about the Nature of Reality

It can reasonably be assumed that the analyst is concerned with organizational performance and hence with goal-achieving and with the purposeful component of behaviour (via the provision of appropriate information). He is thus concerned with decision making. This would imply a focus upon decision processes, and decision situations, upon decision making in the organization, and upon the individual as decision maker.

The nature of a decision and of decision making is elusive other than from some rationalistic standpoint. Such a functionalist view may be helpful to the analyst, for example in giving a sense of direction at the start of an analysis. However, in general, the analyst's philosophy needs to be realistically rather than idealistically based to be a suitable source of 'prior understanding' for the model of the user system in its final form. This would suggest that the focus of this component should be the decision maker, and the structure of constraints within which he operates. The individual as decision maker implies a degree of autonomous action, rather than merely reaction, say, to a rule-based system. This would call for a set of beliefs about the nature of man as decison maker which owes more to the 'action frame of reference' [23], than to more behaviour-oriented models of man, based as it is upon the notion of human intentionality. Briefly, such a view would see the individual's actions being explained in terms of the meanings he assigns to the relevant aspects of the situation he sees himself facing, as well as to the action he chooses to take (and its outcome). This assignment of meanings is seen to take place against the background of the individual's current weighing of his own interests, values and concerns within the constraints of his social context. At the same time, it is regarded as being motivated on the basis of his background and environment.

This frame of reference can be elaborated as follows: the individual is viewed as irreducibly self-directing, but at the same time operating in circumstances that are to various degrees independent of his volition. Accordingly, human actions are envisaged as initiatives which are inexorably conditioned by the context. This elaboration is intended to draw attention to the significance of the organization's structure of constraints, and the part it plays in decision making. Such a view of man emphasizes the functions of both individuality and constraint, of process and structure in decision making.

Though this view may be appropriate in general for the analyst, nevertheless there are many circumstances in which a more mechanistic model might seem to be in order. Examples might be a situation where he is required to produce a system to support the performance of a relatively routinized task, when exceptions to the routine are to be dealt with outside the system; i.e. via some form of 'manual override'. A second example might be the provision of information about work schedules to work stations on an assembly line, where once again the operation of a manual override might be included in the system specification. The latter example emphasizes that though in such circumstances the worker might appear to all intents and purposes to be behaving mechanistically with regard to the system, the actual speed of the line and hence his work rate would almost certainly reflect the results of negotiation between management and labour, e.g. regarding rates. This example might be used to illustrate the possible shortcomings of a too-ready acceptance of the mechanistic model. Arguably, the work rate (as well as, for example quality performance) would reflect the underlying general degree of cooperation between management and labour (see section 3.1 above). This might well be affected by the general style of management, itself represented in the approach adopted by the analyst, for example in the form of the degree and manner of user involvement in systems design.

The implication of this discussion is that the general model of man as 'autonomous' is always appropriate, but that there are special circumstances in which the analyst may be justified in representing the user *as though* he is 'plastic' [24]. However, it is bound to be the case that the latter assumption should only be made after critical examination of the particular circumstances.

A related set of beliefs is required to provide the analyst with an appropriate view of the organization, or of the department within it. A view which is compatible with the above model of man [25] would see behaviour emerging as the outcome of members' actions at the intersection of the hierarchy (defined in terms of formally agreed work roles), and the individuals who occupy those roles (with their intentions deriving from their ends, definitions and involvements).

However, once again, as was suggested above, a more simple functionalist view may well be helpful on occasion to give a sense of direction at the start of an analysis. In addition, obviously, systems theories are a powerful source of insights in particular circumstances.

5.1.2 Legitimating the Work of the Analyst

Regarding the behaviour of practitioners in general, it seems reasonable to assume that the community of systems analysts (and their employers) would expect the analyst in general to behave more as a professional than as a technician, on the understanding that, for example:

(a)   the professional would be likely to put greater effort into taking independent initiatives in the forming and critical assessing of the organization's information function;

(b)   the professional would be more inclined to consider independently the interest of the organization as a whole — a systems perspective, rather than a more partial view, e.g. of local management, bearing in mind the significance of, for example, sectional interests;

(c)   the professional would be more concerned to maintain the authority, responsibility and standing of his position, and to hold appropriate ethical standards. He would expect to make a greater, independent contribution in line with professional ideals [26].

Such a view has obvious implications for the manner in which the analyst interprets and enacts his role. At its most obvious, for example, this would bear upon the extent to which he sees himself passively accepting the definitions and instructions of local management on the one hand, and being expected to contribute to the development of organizational policies regarding the future involvement of computing within the information function, in a manner compatible with other related policies (see section 3.2 above), on the other.

Similarly, such a view has implications for the philosophy he adopts, as well as for the way in which he approaches the conduct of an analysis (for example, for the extent to which he commences with strongly preconceived ideas regarding the form of a 'solution' and for the extent to which he sees analysis as in general necessarily being an interactive process as between analyst and user (see section 3.3)).

The above discussion leads on to a consideration of the relation between ISAD and management. The declared link with the purposeful component of organizational behaviour (see section 5.1.1), inevitably links ISAD with the managerial function of the organization. However, arguably the professional view of the nature of this link would be distinctive. In general, in a manner consistent with the adoption of a systems perspective the analyst would see himself as being primarily concerned with contributing to organizational effectiveness, rather than to local departmental efficiency [27]. This would imply an association primarily with organizational management *as a generality* (i.e. in a way which would imply similar treatment both in the commercial enterprise, the government office and the cooperative), rather than with individual local department managers, as the sponsors of individual projects.

Such views would in general be compatible with the adoption of the scientific attitude as it is usually propounded, for example that the individual is reflective and critical, and that his approach is grounded upon a reliance upon rigour, scepticism and imagination. Finally, arising out of the discussion in sections 2 and 3 above, as well as the nature of the articulation component of design in section 4 the analyst would in general see his role as being to facilitate and enlighten, negotiate and bargain, rather than primarily as the purveyor of a technical expertise, who is merely the instrument of a technological imperative.

No doubt many other matters could reasonably be raised under this heading. However, the above discussion is perhaps indicative of the nature of the general content of this component of the analyst's philosophy.

5.2 The Analyst's Approach

The previous section addressed the possible nature of an appropriate philosophy for the analyst as an essential component in the structure of ISAD practice. How does this relate to other aspects of ISAD practice? There is now a need to outline the ways in which such matters might be incorporated in a *general* approach to practice, for example in the form of more specific guidelines and recipes for action. In the course of a discussion of the development of his 'soft-systems methodology', Checkland puts forward a possible framework for considering practice. His particular focus at this point is upon the methodology, which he regards as being interposed between the philosophy and technique in relation to the part it plays in practice. Interpreting the term philosophy as '. . . a broad non-specific guideline for action . . .', and a technique as '. . . a precise specific programme of action which will produce a standard result . . .', he sees a methodology as being

'. . . intermediate in status . . .' between these two. In particular, he sees it as '. . . lacking the precision of a technique but . . . a firmer guide to action than a philosophy' [28].

Such a structure for practice has the appeal of generality. At the same time it can be used in conjunction with an understanding of the nature of the underlying process of design, as a basis for deepening that understanding via the identification of the bodies of knowledge which would be called upon in applying it. Furthermore, it ties in broadly with design as consisting of articulation and realization in that it embodies a similar progression. From an initial focus upon the development of an appropriate understanding of the user system, attention moves to the identification of possible models of that system and thence to the more technical aspects of change in the form of possible solutions and their implementation.

The term, methodology, has become widely used in ISAD in particular, and is sometimes used as a synonym for both method, and technique. Checkland therefore sees the need to define the term more precisely for the purpose he has in mind. He sees a methodology not as another word for method, but as '. . . a set of *principles of method which in any particular situation has to be reduced to a method* uniquely suitable to that . . . situation'. Interpreted in this way, a methodology would have general applicability in that it would enable the analyst to come to grips with the richness of the reality, e.g. of the full range of possible types of user systems (see sections 3 and 4), through its adaptability, and by allowing the use of insights, which the greater precision of a technique would rule out.

Checkland then outlines his methodology in a way which is compatible with this interpretation. His discussion is helpful in highlighting both the nature of the progression from philosophy to technique, as well as critical attributes of the underlying process (e.g. its emergent character) [29]. The analyst's general approach can usefully incorporate the spirit of Checkland's methodology.

The approach can usefully be examined from three standpoints:

(a) as embodying the articulation component of design as it is discussed in section 4, from the development of the necessary understanding of the user system and the analysis of its requirements, to their expression in the form of a suitable model of that system; and thence to the interpretation of the model, and its translation into the specification of a hardware/software system (see section 4);

(b) as a social process (see section 3.3), i.e. consisting of social interaction between individuals with their particular interests, values and concerns, their viewpoints and expertise, and producing an outcome which is essentially evolutionary (or emergent); and

(c) as a process designed to perform a specific function, and so having a set of sub-functions which can be inferred, such as: negotiation of the brief; delineation of the 'focal task' the proposed system is to support; identification of data sources; and the like.

It should be noted that consideration of the process by which the specification of requirements of the user system is eventually realized in the form of an implemented hardware and software system has been excluded from this discussion. This process with its strong emphasis upon the more technical aspects of the design, has its own particular characteristics which do not accord readily with those associated with the understanding and modelling of the user system, and its requirements.

The implications of the three standpoints set out above will now be considered.

(a) The performance of the articulation component of ISAD as it has been discussed in this paper would call for access to two main categories of knowledge:

(i) *Situational* — dealing with the nature of the situations the analyst meets in a way compatible with the 'beliefs about the nature of reality' component of his philosophy (see section 5.1.1). This would cover appropriate theories of organization, and of bringing about change in organizations [30], of information and of information systems and their functions, of decision making in organizations; and so on.

(ii) *Technical* — dealing with the technology of computing and its use in information systems; with the ways in which computing affects the organization and its members. This would facilitiate the design of computer systems which more nearly suited their user system needs in their organizational contexts, having regard to the ever-widening range of choice within the developing technology.

A further category of knowledge can also be identified which emerges out of the interrelation between (i) and (ii) namely:

(iii) *Process* — dealing with the nature of the (evolving) relationship at the man/computer interface, and at the higher-level, user system/ information system interface, having regard to its exploratory nature.

(b) To fall in line with the general need for the analyst to take initiatives during the analysis, the design of the steps in the approach would need to take him from the idealism of the normative model (which as has already been suggested, he might use to give a sense of direction to negotiations within the user set) to the realism of more social models compatible with the model of man. The need for the process of analysis to be treated as a social process would imply that each step in the approach would have to be designed with this in mind, for example progression through the analysis would be evolutionary via social interaction [31]. As an ordered series of steps, it would 'guide' the analyst through an analysis, and highlight the relevant features of the situation and the bodies of knowledge relevant to those features. It would thus produce a general orientation to the specific practice of the analyst, whilst at the same time providing him with a framework within which he might assess what to do, how to do it, and to what extent, and which allowed him to consider the potential of the situation. Finally, the steps in the approach would need to be adaptable to particular situations via the omission of particular steps, e.g. when dealing with the support of well-structured work tasks.

(c) The elaboration of the process of ISAD on purely functional lines into a set of sub-processes would facilitate the development of a rationale necessary for the delineation of the steps in the approach. Such a view, for example, may also facilitate the elaboration of necessarily complementary relationships between user and system, and between the more formal and the less formal information systems which support the performance of the work task; as well as, say, the feedback loops that are required (and hence the necessary organizational links established) between the Information Providing System and the User System to ensure the former's continuing appropriateness in context.

Space does not permit any further elaboration of this framework here.

6. CONCLUDING REMARKS

This chapter has identified the need for a shift in the focus of concern in systems analysis away from the more technical aspects towards more generally social matters. One possible outcome of this shift is the need for a deeper understanding of the nature of ISAD practice itself, and the processes which practising involves. On the assumption that the purpose of ISAD is the production of a design, parallels have been drawn with other forms of practice which are similarly associated with design, as one useful source of insights. Seeking such an understanding draws upon the belief that the developments that have taken place in the last 10–15 years no longer justify the view that ISAD practice is necessarily dominated by the nature of the current technology of computing. The analyst is no longer an 'instrument of the technology'. Furthermore, he makes significant choices throughout an analysis which deeply affect the form in which user requirements are seen, analysed and met [32]. Subsequent discussion has therefore been concentrated upon the development of a framework within which ISAD practice might usefully be examined for furthering both teaching and research.

This discussion has drawn heavily upon the belief that a critical component in such a framework is the view that is taken of man (and so also of organization) as the focal element in the user system, namely that he is autonomous, etc. Such a view is in sharp contrast to the more typical simple, functional view. Obviously, there are many circumstances when the latter view is defensible. On the other hand there are many circumstances when a more complex (and, arguably more realistic view) is called for. It is suggested that in practice this latter view is the general case, of which the former is a special case [33].

A second critical component is the view that is taken of the process of analysis, namely, that it is in general a social process, with all that that implies for the way in which an analysis is appropriately conducted.

Whilst both of these points can be straightforwardly related to similar views in the more general, design literature, nevertheless there is an obvious need to examine them and their implications in greater depth. Such matters as the nature and content of the implied 'system specification of requirements', as well as the means for the effective management in practice of the interface between 'articulation' and 'realization', are obvious candidates for further research. In section 4 it was suggested that the model of the user could be regarded as the interface between the articulation and realization components of design, and that this model would need to be translated into a more technically oriented form to become the system specification. Furthermore, in sections 1 and 3.1 it was implied that the analyst needed to take a more realistic view of the nature of the user system and hence to embody more of its complexity in his modelling. For representing situations for which simple mechanistic modelling was adequate, arguably the straightforward functional specification was sufficient. But when 'more of the complexity' of the user system is to be included, what further matters would need to be covered, and in what terms might they be handled?

Underlying the discussion in the early part of the chapter is the implication that it is the ways in which contemporary computer technology interacts with the more social aspects of the organization, that is generally being left out of account. This would imply the need for research aimed at examining these matters, for example with a view to typifying the technology from this *user point of view*, so that they can be dealt with appropriately in the system specification, as well as the more technical functional aspects.

Under these circumstances, the choice of software/hardware configuration for a particular application cannot be regarded as a purely technical matter to be decided on predominantly economic criteria; account would also need to be taken of these other matters [34]. This complication seems likely to call for some toing and froing between articulation and realization phases as the implications for the user system of particular configurations, which are suitable on purely functional grounds, are explored from this broader viewpoint; this would make the interface fuzzy.

Some progress has already been made in delineating the general approach discussed in section 5.2. However, much more effort needs to be put into the further consideration and development of such an approach, as well as, ultimately its testing in practice. Finally, this discussion has approached the development of a framework for systems analysis practice primarily from consideration of the nature of the user system and of the process of information requirements analysis. There is an obvious need to complement this with the development of a similar, and related, framework for the process by which the 'system specification' is eventually interpreted in the form of the running hardware/software system.

NOTES

[1] Land, F. F. (1980) 'Is a Revision of the IFIP Curriculum Needed?', London School of Economics Working Paper.
[2] Buckingham, R. A., Hirschheim, R., Land, F. F., and Tully, C. (1986) *Information Systems Education: Recommendations and Implementations*, Cambridge University Press, Cambridge.
[3] See, for example, Rosenbrock, H. H. (1977) 'The Future of Control', *Automatica*, **13**, 389–392; Cooley, M. J. E. (1973) 'Dialectics of the Man/Machine Interaction', Proc. Design Activity Int. Conf. Design Research Society UK, 1973; Archer, L. B. 'Computer Design Theory and the Handling of the Qualitative' (1973), Royal College of Art, London.
[4] See Bazjanac, V. 'Architecture Design Theory: Models of the Design Process' for a review.
[5] There are cross-references to the work, for example, of C. West Churchman, one of the pioneers of OR and management science in the USA and of John Luckman, then at the Institute of Operational Research in the UK.
[6] It should be noted that the term 'design' is widely regarded at least by architects as referring only to that component of the process which leads to the production of a specification. This specification is then 'realized' in the form of a building.

It is likely that a second group (e.g. of civil, or structural, or construction engineers) similarly sees itself as designing when it takes this specification and translates it into three-dimensional form, since analysis and synthesis would appear to be similarly involved.
[7] Archer, L. Bruce (1966) 'Systematic Method for Designers', Council of Industrial Design, HMSO, London.
[8] Rittel, C. G. (1972) 'On the Planning Crisis: Systems Analysis of the First and Second Generations', *Bedriftsokonomen*, No. 8, 390–396. Note also the earlier reference [5] Churchman, C. W. (1967) 'Wicked Problems', *Management Science*, **4**, 14, B-141 and 142. R. A. Ackoff refers to such problems as 'messes'.
[9] There are similarities to the ways in which a social scientist describes an organization, and parts within it. Rittel emphasizes that there is always more than one possible interpretation of a 'wicked' problem, the one chosen depending upon the analyst's *Weltanschauung*. The particular interpretation chosen determines the solution. Furthermore, he suggests that every wicked problem is a symptom of another, 'higher-level' problem.
[10] Checkland, P. (1981) in *Systems Thinking, Systems Practice*, (John Wiley, Chichester, pp. 154–155), distinguishes between 'structured' and 'unstructured' problems. He suggests that in the latter case, the analyst is concerned not so much with problems, as with problem situations, in which problems are differentially perceived by the various parties concerned — including the analyst. His 'soft-systems methodology', which is essentially an evolutionary approach is aimed at dealing with such situations. (See Banbury, J. (1984) 'A Note on the Incorporation of the Social Dimension in Practice', Bristol Polytechnic Working Paper, for a discussion of Checkland's methodology from this point of view.)

[11] In discussing the development of the built environment, Alexander (Alexander, C. (1979) *The Timeless Way of Building*, and Alexander, C. *et al.* (1975) *The Oregon Experiment*, Oxford University Press, Oxford) has argued that there is a need for design as a process to match the 'organic order' of the community in which it takes place. To this end, he sees the need for in-depth user involvement in the design process at the local level. He envisages overall coordination of such local projects as being appropriately carried out via the identification (again through participation) of the ways in which the 'whole' needs to be developed (its policies?). To be acceptable for consideration, local projects are required to contribute in identifiable ways to the furtherance of these policies; thus coherent development of the whole is achieved.

To the extent that the organic analogy has also played a significant part in deepening understanding of organizations as social systems, similar arguments may apply to the development of information systems therein.

[12] Polanyi, M. (1962) 'Tacit Knowing: its Bearing on Some Problems in Philosophy', *Reviews of Modern Physics*, **34**, 4, 601–616.

[13] The functional model assumes that the organization, or part thereof, has a simple and well-defined function which is readily identifiable, which uniformly determines behaviour. 'Production rationality', a related term, relies upon simple mechanistic modelling of production, and quantitative measures of performance (e.g. yield, output, fuel consumed), as the sole basis for representing the organization — i.e. normative models. This would be reasonable enough if it was used only as a means of giving a sense of direction to the parts of an organization, but not if it became the only basis for representing behaviour.

[14] This would imply a perhaps more sensitive application of, say the more structured methods of analysis, based as they are upon simple, mechanistic modelling along purely functional lines.

[15] See, for example, Burns, T. (1966) 'On the Plurality of Social Systems', in *Operational Research and the Social Sciences*, J. R. Lawrence (Ed.) Tavistock, London, for a discussion of this view. Burns refers to three analytically separable systems of behaviour, viz. formal authority, political and career systems which jointly influence the individual's actions. This view is elaborated in the paper by Tom Manuel in Buckingham *et al.* (1986) [2].

[16] See, for example, Burns, T. and Stalker, G. M. (1966) *The Management of Innovation*, Tavistock, London.

[17] The process involved might be broadly analogous to the 'knowledge elicitation' process referred to by the designers of expert systems — e.g. Addis, T. R. (1985) *Designing Knowledge-based Systems*, Kogan Page, London, Chapter 3. Also H. M. Collins, R. H. Green and R. C. Draper (1985) Where's the Expertise?: Expert Systems as a Medium of Knowledge Transfer in *Expert Systems 85*, Martin Merry (Ed.), Cambridge University Press, Cambridge.

[18] See Manuel, T. in Buckingham *et al.*. (1986)[2].

[19] Churchman, C. W. (1968) *The Systems Approach*, Dell, Chapter 7.

[20] Rittel (1972) [8].

[21] Waddington, C. H. (1977) in *Tools for Thought*, Paladin, London, Chapter 1, suggests that 'the only way to make a robot anything more than an adding machine is to provide him with a philosophy. He cannot even see to any purpose . . . unless there is built into his system some sort of model of the kinds of things or processes that he may expect to encounter'. He refers to this model as a philosophy which he describes as '. . . a mental machinery for dealing with a large variety of things . . . and interpreting them into something which has "meaning"'.

[22] Checkland, P. (1981) [10], Chapter 6, p. 162, illustrates his version of a philosophy with '. . . political action should aim at a redistribution of wealth in society' and '. . . industrial expansion should be balanced against environmental degradation'. (He has no

need to emphasise the Waddington-type component of philosophy because the context in which he is writing presumes the systems viewpoint.)

[23] See, for example, Silverman, D. (1970) *The Theory of Organisation*, Heinemann, London, Chapter 6.

[24] The terms 'autonomous' and 'plastic' are used by M. Hollis in *Models of Man*, Cambridge University Press, Cambridge, 1977.

[25] See, for example, Burns, and Stalker (1966) [16], Preface to the second edition, pp. xi to xv for a description of such a compatible view.

[26] These characterizations of a dimension, the poles of which are Professional/ Technician, were a by-product of some empirical work undertaken by T. Manuel, D. Singh and the author.

[27] See, for example, Churchman (1968) [19], Chapters 3 and 7, and Ackoff, R. A. (1980) 'From Information to Control', in *The Human Side of Information Processing* N. Bjorn-Anderson (Ed.), North-Holland, Amsterdam.

[28] Checkland, P. (1981) [10], p. 16.

[29] Checkland, P. (1981) [10], Chapter 6. Though it is intended for wider application the methodology developed has much of the character implied by the discussion in section 3.3.

[30] Bearing in mind the association between computerization and bureaucratization for example, there would be a need in particular to cover theories of bureaucracy—its manifestation and origins, its 'dysfunctions', the bureaucratic personality and so on.

[31] It is difficult to convey what such a requirement means in practice by description alone; it is more straightforward by discussion of an example. Though Checkland does not formally present his methodology in such terms, certainly he has strong interaction between users and analysts in mind. Five of the seven specified stages, as he puts it, '. . . necessarily (involve the) people in the problem situation'. As he says of Stage 2, the Problem Situation Expressed, '. . . the best studies have been characterised by . . . a readiness to collect as many perceptions as possible from a wide range of people with roles in the problem situation, and by a determination not to press the analysis in systems terms at all'; of Stage 5 which is designed to generate 'debate' between the systems-based, conceptual model (arguably, an idealized view) on the one hand, and the reality on the other as this is represented by '. . . concerned participants in the problem situation', as a way of stimulating the identification of '. . . possible changes (in the problem situation) which might be introduced in order to alleviate the problem condition'. This could be interpreted as using a normative model to give initial (and defensible) direction to the analysis, then moderating the model to a more realistic one as the analysis proceeds (see previous paragraph of main text). Finally, a further stage of discussion and negotiation occurs at Stage 6 about what kinds of changes might be 'desirable' and 'feasible' in the reality of the problem situation in the light of the debate of Stage 5 and prior to taking action to improve the problem situation at Stage 7 (all the quotations are from Checkland, P. (1981) [10] Chapter 6). Such a process is obviously strongly interactive between users and analysts throughout; the process is thus evolutionary during these stages, and ends with an outcome which is emergent—i.e. it is a social process, and the steps have been designed as such.

[32] The empirical work referred to in note [24] above was a pilot study aimed at exploring the nature of the analyst's freedom for manoeuvre, and the influences that bore upon the choices he made.

[33] Checkland, P. (1981) [10], p. 191, makes a similar claim for his 'soft-systems methodology' *vis-à-vis* 'hard-systems methodology'.

[34] Checkland, P. (1981) [10], for example, examines the 'feasibility' and 'desirability' in the context of the possible changes to be considered as a basis for selection. In ISAD, however, it seems likely that eventually it will be possible to be more specific than this whilst retaining his 'user-oriented' approach to evaluation.

Critical Issues in Information Systems Research
Edited by R. J. Boland Jr. and R. A. Hirschheim
© 1987 John Wiley & Sons Ltd.

Chapter 4

UNDERSTANDING THE ELEMENTS OF SYSTEM DESIGN

Jon A. Turner

ABSTRACT

The act of designing is central to the field of information systems, yet little is really known about what design is or how people go about doing it. If we are to develop an understanding of design that will allow us to effectively teach it and improve upon it, we must understand what the elements of design are, and what cognitive processes are invoked in doing design work. This chapter first reviews research on the cognitive process of design, and shows how poorly we understand design activity. It then reviews some ways design is portrayed in engineering and architecture, and proposes a set of basic elements that constitute design in the information systems field. These elements serve as an initial vocabulary for describing what must be accomplished in creating an information system design. Finally, some directions for a research program to help us better understand the process of design are proposed.

1. INTRODUCTION

Quite simply, the fact is that we do not understand very much about designing complex, computer-based information systems. I mean that we don't know what system design consists of, we don't know how it is done, and we don't know how to teach it. Furthermore, our lack of knowledge about the process of system design is the greatest single barrier to improving our ability to apply information technology (IT) and to increasing system development productivity, a major goal of most information system departments, executive management, and the industry as a whole.

This is not to imply we can't design information systems, for that is obviously not the situation. There are many examples of successful systems. But we do not understand well the *process* of design. And without that understanding we can never systematically apply it, or improve it.

In this chapter I will review research findings on the cognitive process of design, describe how design is characterized in engineering and architecture, propose a way to conceptualize design that is useful for IT, and suggest further avenues of research. My goal is to draw together what is known about information system design so the process may be better understood.

The problem of understanding design is not unique to information systems. There is little agreement as to what the process of design involves in other fields, for example, architecture or engineering (Alexander, 1964). The situation is just more pronounced in information systems. Engineering and architecture are fields that consistently produce objects through a process of design. And the computer itself is one of the best examples of an artifact that was the result of conscious conceptual and practical design activity.

But information systems are different than most other artifacts in three ways. First, they are abstract and not materialized in a form that is easy for people to comprehend as a whole. After a building is constructed it is quite straightforward to understand it and to respond. It is not easy to visualize an information system. Relatively few people have the skill or perspective needed to comprehend it, even after it is constructed. People come in contact with only a portion of the system allowing them to form, at best, a partial view.

Second, an information system needs to correspond to a complex, non-specific set of human behaviors as well as a set of explicit data transformations. It must reflect accurately the tasks that people perform and the interactions among them. Rather than being an arbitrary form, such as a building, an information system has a structure that is dictated by a group of poorly understood, inconsistent human activities. Third, because an information system is eventually represented by a computer program, its correctness is subject to verification. A building, by comparison, cannot be judged correct, only appropriate.

These distinctions in the form of the artifact suggest differences in the process of design. Design of an information system must not only accommodate the normal design activities involved in engineering and architecture, it must also provide means for comprehending human behaviors and representing them in a consistent fashion. It must reconcile the imprecision of human activity with that of precisely specified operations required by a computer. These transformations must be explicitly stated rather than left to accepted convention. Consequently, the design of an information system is more demanding and more mysterious than that of many other artifacts.

There are two basic strategies used for the design of information systems: the life-cycle approach; and evolutionary design, best typified by prototyping. The life cycle approach consists of three overlapped and interlocking activities: analysis, design, and implementation. While these activities are all highly related and frequently inseparable, it is usual practice for a description of the system to be produced in each phase as a means of conveying the information gained and decisions made to following stages. This is particularly true when more than one person is working on a project and they must communicate. Thus, the analysis phase produces a requirements statement or needs analysis, while the design stage produces program specifications or data flow diagrams (with a data dictionary, pseudo-code, and structure diagrams). The implementation stage, of course, produces running code. These stages could also be considered different levels of abstraction, or detail of the system. Most of the methodology that comprises software engineering applies to the implementation stage, or the later portion of the design stage that concerns program design; or are conventions for describing a system at one phase or another [1].

In contrast, prototyping combines all of these activities in one step. A preliminary understanding of the requirements are gained and a working system is built immediately. Adjustments are accomplished by feedback obtained from actual use by the client. Complexity is introduced through refinement over time. In a prototype, the requirements statement, or data flow description *may never* exist separately from the materialization of the system.

In both of these approaches the quality of the resulting system is determined largely by the degree to which the designer understands the requirements or needs of a system. Both approaches suggest that requirements analysis is performed top down, from general to detail. Requirements analysis is assumed to be accomplished as part of a closely spaced sequence of activities at the beginning of a project in the life-cycle approach. In prototyping, requirements analysis is performed continuously over the duration of the project. Both rely on a dialogue between designer and users to elicit an expression of needs. [2]

In both approaches, there is relatively little methodology to guide the designer, or the user for that matter, in obtaining an expression of needs. The presumption is made that (1) users know what information they need, and (2) they will freely disclose it if asked. As Ackoff (1967) points out, this is unlikely to be the case since most users do not know what information they need (and, incidentally, wouldn't know what to do with it if they received what they requested). As Davis (1982) notes, 'simply asking prospective users of the information systems to specify the requirements will not suffice in a large percentage of cases', because of constraints on individuals as information processors, the variety and complexity of the information requirements, and the patterns of interaction among users and designers in defining requirements. If this were not enough, free disclosure assumes an absence of organizational politics, which in most settings is unrealistic (Keen, 1981).

If simply asking users to state these requirements won't suffice, then different and expanded approaches are needed. Yet, the prescriptive literature is silent on what these approaches might be, or how the process really works [3]. If a true understanding of this process is to emerge, it must be based on the cognitive activities individuals invoke when designing.

2. RESEARCH

One way to characterize design problems is that they consist of a set of initial conditions and a *goal* but no immediate procedure that will guarantee attainment of the goal. Beginning at the initial state, operators or transformations are used to move from one state to another until a final state is attained (hopefully the goal). In real world design problems, however:

the goals are typically fuzzy and poorly articulated and cannot be mapped directly into properties of the design. Thus, the exact configuration of the final state is not prescribed. A part of the design process consists of formalizing and refining design goals into functional requirements that can be matched by properties of the design. Even so, it is usually difficult to tell how well a design meets a particular functional requirement. In addition, the functional requirements often cover different dimensions and the trade-offs between them are rarely well specified. (Malhotra, 1980, p. 120).

This characterization of real world design problems contrasts sharply with the idealized formulation presented above. It suggests that the goal is evolved along with adjustments in initial conditions rather being known *a priori*. It focuses on *properties* of the design *solution* and how well they match the functional requirements derived from the design *goal*. Properties of a design solution arise from a combination of design *elements*, indivisible units with certain characteristics, and the design *organization*, the way the design elements interact and fit together [4]. More importantly, it shows the central role of dialogue in clarifying some of the ambiguities. In practice, however, only some of them will be resolved and the issue becomes identifying what guides the discrimination between significant and insignificant.

Malhotra (1980) in studying dialogue between people attempting to solve real world problems found that it consisted of the translation of design goals into functional requirements that candidate designs must meet and the generation of designs to meet the requirements. He concluded that the dialogues were more complex than they appeared on the surface; they often consisted of implied requirements, the examination of partially proposed design elements to test the violation of some unstated goal, the substitution of possible design solutions for the original one, and the combination of design components into a solution. Much of this process was *implicit* and *unstated* [5].

From this study it appears that generation of solutions seems to consist of attempting to find design elements that meet functional requirements of the problem and then tying them together into a *coherent* design. This corresponds roughly to bottom-up design. Although this was not the only design strategy exhibited in Malhotra's study of dialogues, it was the predominant one and it seemed to be encouraged by the fragmentary presentation and elaboration of requirements.

The results of this study suggest that problem definition and solution generation are not independent activities; they are interrelated. Consideration of potential solutions raises questions about potential requirements which then give rise to new requirements. Requirements and solutions migrate together toward convergence. The fragmentary nature of the dialogues suggest that they play an important role in stimulating cognitive processes, rather than solely conveying predetermined information.

The prototype development strategy seems to match this problem definition/solution generation process more naturally than does the sequential and compartmentalized life-cycle approach, which may partially account for the popularity and success of prototyping and evolutionary design as implementation strategies in end-user computing (EUC). This is not an either/or situation, but rather an observation that in the life-cycle approach it may be unrealistic to expect that requirements will ever be completely articulated at the beginning of the project, and unless provisions are made to capture design solutions that are generated as part of the requirements definition activity, important information may be lost.

A related question is whether, for any design situation there exists a solution that is clearly superior. If no superior solution exists, and there are several acceptable ones with little to choose among them, then the solution generation and evaluation problem is quite different. Instead of searching for *the* correct solution, an acceptable solution only need be recognized.

One way to investigate this issue is to see whether people working separately on the same problem arrive at similar solutions. Turner (1985) studied the similarities and differences in solutions generated by experienced students who were all given the same design problem [6]. The analysis revealed many more differences than similarities. There was wide variance in what was included in solutions; arcs, names and contents of data flows were different, as were processes. Subjects made a number of different assumptions, many in direct conflict with the written description of the problem.

Further analysis showed that there appeared to be four different strategies used by subjects to decompose the problem. The first and most common was a functional decomposition strategy, the grouping of activities around major business functions being performed. There was, however, considerable variation in the functions selected as the basis of decomposition and the ways they were interconnected. The second strategy followed was process-orientated. Subjects recognized certain common information processing functions, such as updating a file, and grouped these together. The third strategy, similar to the first, was functional decomposition with the function selected because they occurred at the same time. The fourth was a combination of the first three.

When questioned, subjects could explain the logic of their approach to decomposition quite clearly, but they were unable to convince their colleagues (the other subjects) of the superiority of their approach. Turner concluded that how subjects thought about the problem influenced their decomposition strategy, and how they thought about a problem was largely a function of their *background* and *experience*.

One possibility is that these results are due largely to the use of students as subjects rather than experienced professional information system designers. Malhotra (1980) in another study asked experienced subjects to design a query system. An analysis of the resulting designs showed wide variation in approaches taken and in solutions. The researchers concluded that the sub-goals and solution strategies generated from higher-level goals seemed to vary widely and there did not seem to be an orderly procedure for generating sub-goals. The selection of sub-goals appeared idiosyncratic and to depend strongly on past experience. In a follow-up study, where subjects were to design the query system in more detail,

Malhotra found the solutions were all different—in module content, data structures, and algorithms. In addition, the solutions contained errors, inconsistencies, and unwarranted assumptions. He concluded that unlike engineering, it was difficult to tell whether information system design was complete or consistent, or even met functional requirements.

In summary, the common wisdom about the design of information systems is that it is an ordered process, performed at the beginning of a project (in the life-cycle strategy), a methodology which when applied will produce the same result; that it is top-down, moving from general to specific; and that definition of requirements precedes design solution. Research findings suggest the opposite. Design is ad hoc and associative, the process is individual and experientially biased, the solutions produced by different designers are usually different, much of design proceeds bottom-up, and solution and problem definition are intertwined.

Furthermore, there does not seem to be a common procedure for producing a design solution; different methods of problem decomposition are used, there seems to be no common mechanism for producing sub-goals, different operators are invoked, unwarranted assumptions are made, solutions are rife with errors, and there are no ways short of actually building a system to uncover errors and inconsistencies. In short, there does not appear to be convergence on one solution for any particular situation, nor do there seem to be strong problem-solving models that underlie design in information systems.

3. DESIGN AS PORTRAYED IN ENGINEERING AND ARCHITECTURE

The art of industrial design has been defined as 'selecting the right material and shaping it to meet the needs of *function* and *aesthetics*' (Archer, 1964) [7]. These two factors, functions and aesthetics, fundamentally different in nature and likely to be in conflict, must be reconciled by the designer, and this, then, is the design problem.

Design is considered an art because the rules for moving from one configuration, or state, to another, the *operators* as they would be called in computer science, in either of the two domains (functions or aesthetics) are not well-defined. Neither are the states.

Functions spring from a fundamental understanding of the purpose of an object, or the activity being performed. While it is quite possible to work out (by scientific methods) who likes what, in what circumstances, there are no immutable truths in aesthetics. Its essence is *choice* with the aim of *appropriateness*, and the criteria are the center of gravity of *all* prior choices. A special problem is that the designer must not only be aware of his own standards and values, he must also understand those of others, and foresee their probable future choices. In a majority of cases, aesthetics is handled more quickly and appropriately by intuition, provided there is an adequate body of prior experience to base it upon, than by a formal method. What tends to be missing in descriptions of information systems design is acknowledgement of the role of aesthetics, or any activities based on intuition.

Arriving at a solution by strict calculation is not regarded as designing because the solution is seen as arising automatically and inevitably from the interaction of the method of solution and the data. In this regard the process of calculating is considered to be non-creative. The selection of a solution method, or the representation of a problem in a form that permits it to be solved by calculation may be considered design if this does not follow directly from a statement of the problem. It is characteristic of creative solutions that they are seen to be apt *after* the fact and *not* before. Consequently design may be said to involve creativity and originality.

Design suggests purposeful seeking after solutions rather than idle exploration. It also implies that certain *limitations* exist, often in the form of obstacles or gaps, which constrain acceptable solutions. In information systems design, understanding the problem involves not only understanding needs, but also these constraints, and in many cases, these constraints are unstated, or implied. Thus, the need for a *fundamental* understanding of the object being designed (or the design situation).

The art of design is that of *reconciliation*. In general, design of industrial objects involve three categories of factors: human factors (motivation, ergonomics, and aesthetics); technical factors (function, mechanism, and structure); and business factors (production, economics, presentation, and support). Some of these factors, such as economics, relate to matters of fact that are susceptible to measurement and optimization. Others, such as aesthetics, relate to matters of value which can only be assessed subjectively. This variation in the quality of factors is characteristic of design problems.

It is the nature of design problems that they often begin with an analytical phase involving objective observation and inductive reasoning. In contrast, the creative phase at the heart of the process requires subjective judgement and deductive reasoning. Once these crucial decisions have been made, the process proceeds with detailing of the design, for example, producing working drawings in architecture, or a working prototype in information systems [8]. The design process is, thus, a *creative sandwich*. The bread of objective analysis may be thick or thin, but the creative act is always in the middle.

There still remains the crux of the design problem, the *creative leap* from specifying the problem to finding a solution. Industrial designers appear to establish a first approximation based on *prior experience* (Archer, 1964). This means finding connections between the goals, in terms of the attributes of a good solution, and the facts of the situation as mediated by the designer's knowledge and experience. Constraints serve to bound the problem, rule out certain solutions and provide useful clues to hidden needs or where possible solutions may be found.

Designers appear to search their minds for solutions by examining all kinds of *analogies* (Archer, 1964). They look at other people's design solutions to determine whether something along those lines would answer their problem. They look at phenomena and artifacts in the most unlikely fields. If this process still yields no result the designer tries to *reformulate* the problem in a manner that permits one of the solutions previously uncovered to be used. Only as a last resort does the designer attempt deductive reasoning, proceeding from analysis of data to necessary conclusion.

In computer science terms, the industrial designer attempts a backwards, depth-first search from potential solutions (based on prior experience) to parameters of the problem, with missing data and constraints serving as cues to potential solutions, evolving the problem [9], or bounding the search. If no solution is found the designer constructs a new network composed of solutions to similar (and dissimilar) problems used by others [10]. The designer then attempts to reformulate the problem in a manner that permits use of an uncovered solution. If one is still not found, the designer attempts a forwards, breadth-first expansion of the problem to see if it leads to a solution.

Experience acts both to define the set of initial acceptable solutions and to influence how facts and sensory data are interpreted. Observers contribute to their perception of the phenomenon before them from their own experience by either addition or subtraction. This requires a delicate balance. One needs a group of wide and rich range of experiences to stimulate flexibility and fantasy in thought in order to recognize those aspects of the design problem that are *important*. Yet, this must be done without biasing what is observed. I believe experience serves an important role in focusing the designer's attention on key (pivotal) aspects of the problem, while permitting him to disregard the great majority of (irrelevant) data.

A frequent mistake in information systems design is to presume that the objective portion of design involving, for example, documenting an existing system, constitutes *all* of the design activity. This view is incorrect because it does not recognize the creative decisions involved in defining the form the system will take and in recognizing the aspects of the problem on which to concentrate. But how shall the form of a system be described and what are the factors involved in information system design? A new vocabulary of design would be useful.

4. AN INITIAL SET OF INFORMATION
SYSTEM DESIGN ELEMENTS

It is my belief that experienced information systems designers consider implicitly (that is, have developed refined procedures, or schemas, for) the following elements of design. These represent a set of elements that form an initial vocabulary of design. No time sequencing of activities is implied; many take place in parallel. Nor, are these activities likely to be the way people *think* about design. The cognitive processes involved in design seem to be associative and individual, and are at a much more detailed level. The elements presented are an *external* view of the design process— a *checklist* of issues that must be resolved when designing an information system. They form a useful way of discussing the process.

Identification of these elements is based on my experience as a designer of information systems, my intuition, and my observations of industrial designers. They are presented here to make them explicit and in the hope that, as such, they will serve as a new, somewhat more useful, description of information system design.

4.1 System Concept

Industrial designers make a distinction between a design *idea* and any one *embodiment* of it. The design idea is an invention, an abstraction, while the finished design is one of many possible embodiments of it. For example, in a patent application, the invention and a material embodiment of it are described separately. The description of the invention is interpreted literally and is deemed to cover all of the variations that the inventor wishes. The description of the material embodiment is interpreted freely and is regarded merely as an exemplar.

In order to serve as a guide in making consistent decisions and to resolve conflicts in information systems design, a system *concept* is needed. The concept is the rationale, or underlying theme of the system, for example, *minimal,* or *simple.* An elaboration of what the system should do is not the concept. The concept is a distillation of the system, its essence — analogous to the design idea used by industrial designers.

In OS/360 (IBM) the design concept was *complete*; one common operating system would support the company's complete line of computers and that system would have a complete set of features. While JCL permits almost infinite adjustment and configuration of the operating system, it is complicated, time consuming to learn, and difficult to use. Another design concept (user-friendly) would have produced a different solution, for example, TOPS-20 (DEC).

4.2 Boundary

The boundary defines what is inside the system, what is external to it, and what crosses between the two. The boundary establishes the scope of the system and, consequently, its size and complexity. If the boundary is set too wide, the system becomes so complex as not to be buildable; if it is set too narrow, the system is trivial. Boundary decisions are particularly important in explaining (predicting) resistance to the implementation of a system based on an analysis of the redistribution of power.

4.3 Division of Labor

Decisions concerning the allocation of tasks between a computer and the human operator are another key design issue. A large number of combinations are possible, ranging from fully automatic, with the operator playing a role only when a malfunction occurs, to completely manual with the operator performing all tasks. In most practical systems, tasks are allocated to either computer, or human. The question then is the basis upon which this allocation decision is made, for example, by selecting the processor that is best suited to perform the task, or the one that is least loaded at the time [11].

Too often the operator's job follows implicitly from the design of the computer (applications) portion of the system. It becomes the by-product of prior design decisions, rather than the impetus for them. Consequently, it is important to identify the tasks an operator will perform and insure that they make sense from the standpoint of what is known about worker behavior, performance, and working life quality.

Most of the effort expended in design is directed at identifying the functions an application system is expected to perform. The trade-off is usually between functionality and complexity (cost). I maintain that these functions follow largely from prior decisions (such as system concept and boundaries) and the activities being performed [12]. This makes it all the more important that these design decisions be explicit.

4.4 System Structure

The structure of a system consists of two parts: the processing organization, representing the work organization, or flow of the system; and the data structure, the way data elements are related. If the system is considered as transforming inputs to outputs, work organization refers to the manner in which these transformations take place. At one extreme, a unit of input can be completely transformed into output, invoking, in sequence, all of the necessary steps. Such an approach is responsive, because it permits predicting when the output will occur, but it incurs a high overhead and presents difficulties in control. At the other extreme, the input can be held until all of the input of a particular category is assembled. This method is efficient (in terms of resources), but it is difficult to predict when output will arrive. Efficiency and functionality of actual programs depend on data structures actually selected.

4.5 Decomposition

In order to cope with the complexity of most application systems some method of decomposition (i.e. problem expansion) is needed. The approach most frequently prescribed by design methodologies is top-down, breadth-first expansion. This, however, is just the opposite of the way industrial designers approach their problems. I suspect that information system development methodologies that support bottom-up, depth-first expansion and permit associative (ad hoc) thinking will be more successful than methodologies currently used.

Two basic strategies are followed in decomposition: functional, where the system is successively divided into parts on the basis of the business activity taking place; and data processing, based on the generic processing activity involved. The method of decomposition is highly leveraged because it influences how designers perceive the problem (its representation), what aspects of the problem receive attention (solutions and their parameters), allowable operators, and the value of the design produced.

4.6 Operating Sequence

Identification of the set of time-ordered actions that must be performed in order to accomplish the purpose of the system. It is a useful check to insure that all needed functions have been defined and that those that have are used.

4.7 Performance Measures

Every system requires a control structure to monitor proper operation. Sometimes, as in file maintenance, this becomes a major portion of the system. Identifying performance measures that will be used to monitor performance is a cue in designing the control structure.

4.8 Extent of Change

Most systems represent an incremental change from some prior condition. Recognizing the extent of change imbedded in a system is another aspect of identifying the amount of resistance a system is likely to produce, and consequently, the risk involved in implementation.

4.9 Summary

These eight elements are dimensions within which an information system exists. Design is a search for conflicts among objectives and the means of resolving them, and constraints that bound the problem. These dimensions become the *space* in which design is played out.

The system concept is necessary to maintain consistency among design decisions. Boundaries establish the complexity of the system [13]. Division of labor and system structure are basic design dimensions that establish the configuration of the application. Decomposition reflects the way the designer and others perceive the system. Operating sequence, performance measures, and extent of change are cues to prompt for often-overlooked factors.

Design at this top-level should not be confused with detailed design at the system or program level. Detailed design is concerned with expanding the design in a particular instance. Although execution of detailed design may influence top-level design, it addresses different issues and is much more constrained and directed.

There are two categories of design factors: subjective and objective ones. Subjective factors concern the items discussed above. Objective factors follow from them. The difficulty in the past has been that we have not acknowledged, explicitly, the presence of subjective factors, with the result, that, in many cases, objective factors appear to be arbitrary.

5. IMPLICATIONS FOR RESEARCH

The discussion above has been based on experience and conjecture. One obvious starting point is to search, empirically, for evidence of the presence (or absence) and importance of these notions. For example, good and poor information systems designs (based on some objective criteria) could be compared in an attempt to establish the role a strong systems concept played (embodied in the good systems, while lacking in the poor ones). The good systems could be analyzed to see if they had selected operating points on the above dimensions that are consistent, while the poor systems may not have resolved these issues explicitly. Expert designers could be interviewed (observed) to determine the extent to which they consider these issues, and this could be compared with the behavior of poor (novice) designers. Although this research line is difficult from a methodological standpoint and subjective, I believe we need more detailed studies of the process of design to reveal what really goes on and to generate new conjectures for investigation.

A second line of research would investigate the design process, in more detail, at the cognitive level. While there have been no studies of information systems designers to determine the way that problems are represented and operated on, work has been done in understanding how people represent problems in other domains. Chi (1981), in studying the representation [14] of physics problems in relation to the organization of knowledge in experts and novices, has shown that the quality of problem representation influences the ease with which a problem can be solved and the quality of the resulting solution. Her results show that the categories into which experts and novices sort problems are different, although both are able to construct an enriched internal representation of it. Experts appear to categorize problems by underlying physics principles, a kind of deep structure, while novices categorize problems by their surface structure. With learning, advanced novices began to categorize problems by principles with gradual release from dependence on the physical characteristics of problems.

Chi's notion is that a problem can be at least tentatively categorized after some gross preliminary analysis of its features. After a potential category is activated, the remainder of the representation is constructed with the aid of knowledge associated with the category as an internal schema [15]. For experts, the schema includes potential solution methods. She concluded that experts perceive more in a problem statement than do novices. They have a great deal of tacit knowledge that can be used to make inferences and deviations from the surface features of the problem. Their selection of an approach (principle) to apply to solving a problem appears to be guided by this *derived* knowledge. The actual cues used by experts are not the labels themselves but what they signify.

The findings of Chi's study are consistent with the notions of the information systems design process set forth here. Problems and solution methods are bound together in a schema: bottom-up (data-driven) recognition of problem categories followed by top-down application of processing rules. This would be a reasonable explanation of the patterns found in Malhotra's dialogues. Chi's work suggests that we should be more interested in the ways designers represent problems and the operators they appear to apply in executing designs. Finally, to the extent the parallel holds between solving physics problems and designing information systems, if general principles of design exist they have not been recognized. We must continue the search.

6. CONCLUSION

I have argued that we do not understand very well the process of designing information systems. Design appears to be much more ad hoc and intuitive than the literature would lead one to believe. Solutions and problems are interrelated, and solutions are an integral part of problem definition. It is naïve to think that a problem has only one proper solution; there may be many. Consequently, notions of closure and completeness must be re-thought. A good portion of information systems design involves aesthetics, yet there is no discussion of the aesthetic in the field. Rather than pretending that it does not exist, it would be far better to acknowledge the importance of aesthetics and make it a central subject of attention and research. Subjective does not mean arbitrary. We should refrain from attempting to quantify subjectivity, although we certainly must understand its components.

We need more awareness of the top level factors that drive detailed design. These design dimensions should be made explicit and they should receive the same amount of attention that we lavish on such detailed design issues as data structures. In research, we need to understand how designers represent and manipulate problems. If we focus the energy and attention on these issues that they deserve, I'm confident that a major contribution will be made.

ACKNOWLEDGEMENT

The helpful comments of Professor William Sasso are gratefully acknowledged.

NOTES

[1] While these conventions are important for the purpose of consistency and in communicating detail design they do not *directly* contribute to an understanding of requirements. The detailed design is seen to follow from a statement of requirements.

Some authors contend that this documentation is never read and is impossible to keep consistent (McCracken, 1981).

[2] It is symptomatic of our lack of understanding of the process of design that the most useful skill in accomplishing this activity, interviewing, is not included in most courses or textbooks.

[3] Davis does identify the broad strategies for determining information requirements as: asking; deriving from an existing system; synthesis from characteristics of the current system being used; and, discovering from experimentation with an evolving system. The difficulty is that, in practice, all of these strategies are used.

[4] For example, part of the solution for an interactive system may be a set of data elements arranged in screen formats which are then invoked in different sequences under particular conditions.

[5] Malhotra noted that the dialogues were composed of cycles, each one broken into a number of mutually exclusive states he defined as (1) goal statement, (2) goal elaboration, (3) solution outline, (4) solution elaboration, (5) solution explication, and (6) agreement on solution. A diversity of content underlay this apparent regularity of structure. For example, although discussions and solution suggestions always follow discussion of requirements, the solution that is outlined need *not* apply to the requirements that precede it. New requirements are often uncovered in the process of examining solutions and these may start their own design cycles. This behavior suggests that design involves a strong associative component and that deeper structure, to the extent one exists, has yet to be revealed.

[6] Data flow diagrams, used to represent solutions, were compared on the basis of (1) boundaries, (2) data flows, including arcs, names, and element contents, and (3) process functions as represented by lower-level diagrams.

[7] *Function* is the purpose or function the finished product is to perform and this must be understood by the designer and represented in the product. *Aesthetics* are subjective considerations based on judgements that are shaped by values of the designer. They fall into two broad categories: descriptive aesthetics, which deals with empirical facts about perceivable qualities of an object and the statistics of preference; and ethical aesthetics, which is concerned with good or bad taste, or appropriateness.

[8] It is well known in architecture that in executing the detailed design conflicts arise and inconsistencies are revealed that require a rethinking of the creative phase. Often the original creative solution is abandoned and a new one conceived for the new situation.

[9] Review of Malhotra's dialogues suggests that a good portion concerns verification; obtaining feedback from the client that the designer has understood some specific aspect of the problem.

[10] I suspect that this step has a lot to do with injecting creativity into the solution as the process of attempting to understand someone else's way of thinking (why the solution works) stimulates your own thought.

[11] Turner and Karasek (1984) provides a more complete discussion of this topic.

[12] Or, as Davis observes, deriving the functions from an existing information system.

[13] Brooks (1975) has observed that management's usual response when a system has slipped schedule and over-run cost is to add more manpower, which will only make the system later and cost more. The proper reaction is to trim the size of the project, which in our terms would be to make the boundary smaller and to reduce the number of functions.

[14] An internal cognitive structure constructed by a person to stand for, or model, a problem.

[15] A schema is the category and its associated knowledge. That is, interpretation and processing rules consisting of both declarative and procedural knowledge, relating to the category. In Chi's study, the category was equated to the label a person used to access

a related unit of knowledge and the knowledge was expressed as a network and production rules.

REFERENCES

Ackoff, R. (1967) 'Management misinformation Systems', *Management Science*, **14**, 4, b-147–156.
Alexander, C. (1964) *Notes on the Synthesis of Form*, Harvard University Press, Cambridge, MA.
Archer, L. B. (1964) 'Systematic Methods for Designers', *Design*, **181**.
Brooks, F. P. (1975) *The Mythical Man-Month*. Addison-Wesley, Reading, MA.
Chi, M. T., Feltovich, P. J., and Glaser, R. (1981) 'Categorization and Representation of Physics Problems by Experts and Novices', *Cognitive Science*, **5**, 121–152.
Davis, G. B. (1982) 'Strategies for Information Requirements Determination', *IBM Systems Journal*, **21**, 1, 4–30.
Keen, P. G. W. (1981) 'Information Systems and Organizational Change', *Comm. of the ACM*, **24**, 1, 24–32.
Malhotra, A., Thomas, J. C., Carroll, J. M., and Miller, L. (1980) 'Cognitive Processes in Design', *Journal of Man–Machine Studies*, **12**, 119–140.
McCracken, D. D. (1981) 'A Maverick Approach to Systems Analysis and Design', *Systems Analysis and Design: A Foundation for the 1980's*, North Holland, New York.
Turner, J. A., and Karasek, R. A., Jr. (1984) 'Software Ergonomics: Effects of Computer Application Design Parameters on Operator Task Performance and Health', *Ergonomics*, **27**, 6, 663–690.
Turner, J. A. (1985) 'The Process of System Design: Some Problems, Principles and Perspectives', Technical Report GBA 86–101, New York University, Center for Research in Information Systems.

Critical Issues in Information Systems Research
Edited by R. J. Boland Jr. and R. A. Hirschheim
© *1987 John Wiley & Sons Ltd.*

Chapter 5

SOFTWARE ENGINEERING PRODUCTIVITY MODELS FOR MANAGEMENT INFORMATION SYSTEM DEVELOPMENT

D. Ross Jeffery

ABSTRACT

Because of the great backlog that exists in the development of new information system applications, there is need for improved methods for software development. There appear to be two key issues of concern to the IS community and they are the subject of exploration of this chapter: (1) What are the management strategies and policies which will provide improved system development productivity in the IS environment? (2) What order of productivity improvement is obtainable if these strategies are developed for the 4GL environment, and what other factors will impact the productivity in this environment? Specifically, the chapter provides a review of the literature on the factors which influence software development productivity, and outlines areas of research which now need to be addressed.

1. INTRODUCTION

There is a high level of concern about system development productivity within the information systems community. This is evidenced by:

(1) conferences such as 'People, Performance, Productivity' (SMIS 1981),
(2) significant books by authors such as DeMarco (1982), Boehm (1981), and Keane *et al.* (1984),
(3) publications in the computing press such as 'Call for New View of Software Production' (Hutchins, *PCW* August 1985),
(4) government-sponsored programs such as the STARS program (Druffel *et al.*, 1983) in the USA and the ESPRIT program in Europe.

This interest reflects the enormous project backlog which currently exists. Alloway and Quillard (1983) have found this backlog to be of the order of 374 per cent of the current capacity to supply. Furthermore, they state that it is currently 'impossible' for information systems departments, end-user programming, or packaged software to satisfy that demand. For this reason, improved productivity through faster development methods and better system development management is now a critical objective for the IS community.

This chapter presents a review of the research which has been carried out to determine the factors which are important in influencing software development productivity. It also outlines areas of research which now need to be addressed.

Following a discussion of the general ways in which productivity improvement might be achieved, the chapter summarizes the productivity research carried out to date to determine the likely areas which can lead to improvement. This research is subdivided into prescriptive and descriptive model types to provide a structure for discussion. The major areas discussed are:

(1) the work environment and group interaction,
(2) hardware characteristics,
(3) source language characteristics,
(4) programmer experience,
(5) the problem type,
(6) the development environment.

The chapter concludes with a critical summary of the research to date and suggestions for the direction of future research.

2. PRODUCTIVITY IMPROVEMENT

Productivity improvement can be achieved through two basic means: technological change and management. Kendall and Lamb (1977) felt that 'management can have more influence on productivity of the programing staff than any technology now in use', and this theory has limited support in the research of Jeffery and Lawrence (1979, 1981).

There is no doubt that technological change has the potential to provide significant productivity improvements, such as was achieved with the move from machine language to assembly-level languages, and again with the move to high-level languages. However, without the correct form of management it is also quite possible that potential productivity improvements will never be realized.

Some evidence of this is shown in later work of Lawrence and Jeffery (1983). A key finding of their work in traditional COBOL development environments was that newer technological changes, such as on-line program development and on-line testing, did not provide any productivity improvement. Yet productivity improvement was often stated to be one of the major reasons for adopting this type of change. These results were confirmed in later studies (Jeffery and Lawrence, 1985). At the same time it was found that the management and technical ability of a programmer's supervisor was highly correlated with programming productivity. It is suggested, therefore, that the management of a new technology will be just as important as the development of that technology if we are to achieve the desired productivity improvements.

Strassmann (1982) reinforces this in his work, stating:

> What we need right now is not more technology but much improved management and analytic tools that would aid us in chanelling a specific information technology investment with a much better understanding of its economic objectives.

Despite the weight of opinion as to the importance of management in productivity improvement, a vital consideration which always needs to be highlighted is the distinction between:

(i) those aspects of technology which have the potential for order of magnitude improvement, and

(ii) those which may result in small percentage increases.

Order of magnitude improvement can be achieved when the technology changes the process of software development, thereby allowing a substantial reduction in the number of job steps necessary to complete the task. An example of this happened with the move from assembly-level languages to third generation or high-level languages. In this case the reduction in job steps occurred because it was no longer necessary to determine the processing logic at such a low level of detail.

A significant technical change in the MIS environment recently has been the adoption of fourth generation languages (4GLs) as the implementation language. These languages have been selected because of their promised productivity advantages (see Duffy, 1984). Order of magnitude productivity improvements have been claimed (see, for example, Martin (1982)), but little research has been presented to provide evidence in support of this claim.

The second category is when the change allows only smoothing or tuning of the existing development process. This may have been the case with the introduction of on-line testing, mentioned above, but the productivity improvement possible was never consistently realized in the environment studied. It is likely that management of these types of change is critical in achieving the desired objective.

Two issues which are therefore of vital concern at this point in time are:

(1) *What are the management strategies and policies which will provide improved system development productivity in the MIS environment?*

(2) *What order of productivity improvement is obtainable if these strategies are developed for the 4GL environment, and what other factors will impact the productivity in this environment?*

The task of system development management encompasses both planning and control responsibility. Effective planning requires that the planner has an awareness of the appropriate relationships between the critical variables. For example, the manager needs to be aware that there is a relationship between project size and effort, and between elapsed time and the number of staff working on the project. Thus one of the prerequisites of effective system development management is an understanding of the appropriate models of the process.

The commercial MIS manager traditionally has very few models which can be used with confidence, for the following reasons.

(1) Very little research has been carried out in the MIS environment. Yet MIS is the predominant computing application today.

(2) Practically all models currently available have been developed in the 'technical' environment. For example, the COCOMO model (COnstructive COst MOdel) developed by Boehm (1981) was established using a database of 63 projects of which only seven were business applications. Furthermore, four of these seven applications were significantly larger than the norm for the MIS environment. Until verified in this environment, these models must be viewed with some uncertainty.

(3) System development in the MIS environment has recently undergone significant change with respect to the implementation languages and the system development methodologies in use. Until recently practically all systems were implemented using third generation languages very similar to or the same as those used in the 'technical' environment, but in the last three to five years more and more systems are being implemented using fourth generation languages for which no models are available. In addition, evolutionary design methods, prototyping, and various data modelling based system design methods have become more popular.

Given these compelling limitations of the current models and the changes which have occurred in the MIS environment, we need to:

(1) determine the applicability of the models developed in other environments to the MIS environment, and

(2) establish appropriate models for the design and implementation environments now in use.

3. A REVIEW STRUCTURE FOR MIS PRODUCTIVITY RESEARCH

Empirical research into productivity in the system development process had its beginnings in the 1960s with publications such as those of Nelson (1967) and Sackman *et al.* (1968). These two studies provided a contrast still evident today in that Nelson was reporting on a large field study into many variables that might effect the system development process, whereas Sackman carried out a laboratory experiment into the effect of on-line and off-line computer access on programming performance. The use of field studies continues, as evidenced recently by Vessey (1985), as does the experimental approach evidenced by Harel and McLean (1985).

There are many classification systems that could be used to order the research into system development productivity. The most appropriate here is to investigate the literature according to the model classification used. This was done by Jeffery and Vessey (1980) when such prescriptive models as those developed by Putnam (1978) were compared with such descriptive models such as those developed by Walston and Felix (1977). This is similar to the categorization used by Shooman (1979) in which he divided the literature into 'resource deployment models', again using the Putnam model as an example, and 'cost estimation models' such as those in Walston and Felix (1977) and Wolverton (1974).

Basili (1980) also classifies the research into different model types. His structure uses the categories:

(1) static or dynamic models,
(2) single-variable or multi-variable models,
(3) theoretical or empirical models,
(4) micro or macro models.

This approach does not draw a distinction between descriptive and predictive models, but is instead more concerned with the form of the equation which expresses the model, the basis for the derivation of the model, and the level of detail in the model. For example, the Putnam model is a dynamic staffing model in which manloading follows a pattern of gradual build-up and then decline. It can also be described as a multi-variable, macro model. Detailed discussion of particular models, however, is left until section 4.

Significant contributors to the research into system development productivity models have been Putnam (1978, 1979, 1980, 1981, 1983), Boehm (1976, 1981, 1983, 1984), and Basili (1980, 1981, 1983, 1984). Of these, Boehm and Putnam have developed comprehensive software development cost models which can be used for software cost prediction. Their models are similar in that they are based (in part) on the same theoretical foundation, proposed by Brooks (1975) in *The Mythical Man-Month*. Brooks argued that the addition of staff to a project which was behind schedule would delay that project even further. In other words, when the staff size is increased productivity will decline. In line with this theory, the Putnam and Boehm models both contain a trade-off between elapsed time and development effort, such that if elapsed time for a project is reduced, the total development effort to produce the system will be increased.

Bailey and Basili (1981) argue that each software development environment is significantly different and therefore requires its own model to describe that environment. To this end they then describe a modelling approach that can be used for an organization to establish its own software development models. This is in contradistinction to Boehm who supplies a set of models which, he argues, can be selected from for any particular environment.

4. THE PUTNAM MODEL

This model is partly based on Norden's work (Norden 1958, 1963) into manloading patterns for project management. Norden's study of research and development projects indicated that there were 'regular patterns of manpower buildup and phase-out'. He proposed that each phase of a project has a manpower increase and decline pattern that follows a Rayleigh curve shape. Kitchenham and Taylor (1984) point out that in models such as this:

> The development is considered to be a set of unsolved problems (The problem space) and work progresses until the set is exhausted. Problem solving is assumed to be a sequential process in time such that the occurrence of solution may be modelled by use of the Poisson model, with associated exponential interevent intervals.

Putnam's equation for this manloading relationship is:

$$y = 2Kat(\exp(-at^2)) \tag{1}$$

where y = manpower utilized at time t,
  K = total effort, that is area under the curve,
  a = a shape parameter governing time to peak,
  t = time.
The shape of this curve defines the rate at which effort is applied to the project over the project life cycle. Examples of this curve shape are given in Figure 1. In addition:

$$a = 1/2t_d^2 \tag{2}$$

where t_d = time at which peak effort occurs. In Figure 1 these are t_1, t_2 and t_3. If these equations are applied to the design and coding stage only of a computer system, then:

$$y_1 = 2K_1at(\exp(-at^2)) \tag{3}$$

where y_1 = design and coding effort at time t, and K_1 = total design and coding effort.

This makes the assumption that the general shape of the Norden/Rayleigh curve applies to both the total system life cycle and also the design and coding stage of that life cycle. Other authors have researched this curve shape (Mapp, 1978; Parr, 1980; Basili and Beane, 1981) and have found some support for the curve shape. Glass (1984) found that this curve shape provided a good fit for Australian MIS projects provided a horizontal shift factor was added so that the curve did not have to pass through the origin. In this research, the manloading patterns of nine MIS projects were analyzed and it was found that the shifted Norden curve shape provided a better fit to the actual manloading patterns than either a parabola shape or a trapezoid shape.

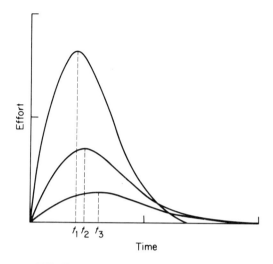

FIGURE 1 Life-cycle effort curves.

In the derivation of his model Putnam takes equations (2) and (3) to derive:

$$y_1 = K_1/t_0^2 t(\exp(-t^2/2t_0^2)) \tag{4}$$

where t_0 = time of peak design and coding effort.

The next step in the derivation is a relationship:

$$t_0 = t_d/6^{1/2} \tag{5}$$

This relationship carries the assumption (empirically based) that the design and coding stage of the system life cycle peaks at approximately 0.4 of the total life cycle peak effort. Thus:

$$\begin{aligned} y_1 &= K_1/t_d^2/6\,t(\exp(-t^2/2t_d^2/6)) \\ &= 6K_1/t_d^2 t(\exp(-3t^{2/t^2}_d)) \end{aligned}$$

but

$$K_1 = K/6 \tag{6}$$

then:

$$\begin{aligned} y_1 &= K/t_d^2 t(\exp(-3t^{2/t^2}_d)) \\ &= D\,t\exp(-3t^2/t_d^2) \end{aligned} \tag{7}$$

where $\quad D$ = difficulty = K/t_d^2 $\tag{8}$

This equation shows the manpower for design and coding at time t. For the entire life cycle the productivity (PR) is equal to total lines of code divided by total effort, but total effort on a project includes overheads. Thus effort for the design and code stage only can be expressed as:

$$xK/6$$

where $O < x < 1$

Now

$$PR = Ss/K$$

where PR = average productivity and

Ss = number of statements in the end product.

Therefore

$$SS = PRK \tag{9}$$

From empirical data Putnam finds that there is a relationship between productivity and the difficulty factor K/t_d^2. This is expressed as:

$$PR = C_n D^{-2/3} \tag{10}$$

Thus the slope of the log productivity versus log difficulty curve is $-2/3$. Substituting in equation (9) we get:

$$
\begin{aligned}
Ss &= C_n D^{-2/3} K \\
&= C_n (K/t_d^2)^{-2/3} K \\
&= C_n K^{1/3} t_d^{4/3}
\end{aligned}
\tag{11}
$$

The variable C_n is called the 'technology factor' and is a project constant which subsumes:

(i) the state of technology being applied to the project,
(ii) the environment in which the development is undertaken,
(iii) the development process used.

The equation shows a relationship between the size of the system (Ss) and two variables: development effort (K) and elapsed time (t_d). The relationship is such that if t_d is decreased K must increase since Ss is assumed constant for a project. This relationship therefore shows productivity (Ss/K) declining if elapsed time is decreased and increasing if elapsed time is increased.

5. THE BOEHM MODEL

Proposed by Boehm (1981, 1983, 1984), this model has also been discussed by Kitchenham and Taylor (1984). It is a hierarchical set of three models described by Boehm as Basic COCOMO, Intermediate COCOMO, and Detailed COCOMO. The complexity of the model increases in these levels along with the stated accuracy obtained in estimates using the model. As in the Putnam model there are underlying equations describing relationships between effort, size, and elapsed time. Similarly to Putnam's, these relationships are non-linear and take the functional form:

$$\text{Effort} \quad = a.\text{Size}^b$$

and

$$\text{Elapsed time} = c.\text{Effort}^d$$

The values of the model parameters a, b, c, and d depend on the 'mode of development' and the level of COCOMO model in use. For example, for a development using small teams in a familiar in-house environment Basic COCOMO provides the effort estimation equation:

$$\text{Man-months} = 2.4 \ (\text{KDSI})^{1.05} \tag{12}$$

where KDSI = thousands of delivered source instructions. Elapsed time is given by the equation:

$$\text{Elapsed time} = 2.5 \ (\text{MM})^{0.38} \tag{13}$$

where MM = man-months derived from equation (12).

Boehm allows for three modes of development:

(1) organic — small teams, familiar in-house environment;
(2) Embedded — complex hardware, software, operational interrelationships;
(3) Semidetached — somewhere between (1) and (2).

In addition intermediate and detailed COCOMO incorporate additional independent variables (called cost drivers) which influence the value of the equation parameters. These cost drivers are introduced because of their effect on productivity and thus the size/effort relationship. These cost drivers are (Boehm, 1981):

- Product attributes
  - required reliability
  - database size
  - software product complexity
- Computer attributes
  - execution time constraint
  - main storage constraint
  - virtual machine volatility
  - computer turnaround time
- Personnel attributes
  - analyst capability
  - applications experience
  - programmer capability
  - virtual machine experience
  - programming language experience
- Project attributes
  - modern programming practices
  - use of software tools
  - schedule constraint

From this it can be seen that the Putnam and Boehm models have similarities in terms of:

(1) the functional form of the equations;
(2) the variables in the basic equations (size, effort, and elapsed time).

The Boehm model, however, explicitly incorporates additional independent variables, whereas in the Putnam model they are subsumed within the C_n constant. Further both models assume the functional form of the equations used without apparent theoretical or empirical support.

From these models four aspects arise as worthy of research:

(1) verification of the effect of elapsed time variation on effort in the MIS environment,
(2) the most appropriate functional form to use for size, effort, elapsed time equations,
(3) the importance and stability of Boehm's 'cost drivers' and variables like them in the MIS environment, and
(4) whether the MIS environment is sufficiently stable to allow different organizations to use the same set of estimating equations or whether each organization needs to develop their own as suggested by Bailey and Basili.

6. PRODUCTIVITY FACTORS

The three authors discussed in section 5 all agree on one point: factors other than project size and elapsed time will impact the effort required to complete a project. In Boehm's model they are called cost drivers, in Putnam's model they influence the value of the constant C_n, and in Bailey and Basili's modelling approach they are input to the determination of organization's unique model.

These productivity factors have been discussed in the literature and the most complete framework to investigate them is given by Benbasat and Vessey (1980) after Chrysler (1978), who characterize the variables affecting programmer performance as being:

1. Organizational Operations Characteristics
    - Programming methods standards
    - System documentation standards
    - Work environment
    - Group interaction
2. Computer Hardware Characteristics
    - Memory size
    - Storage devices
3. Source Language Characteristics
    - Instruction set
    - Self-documentation
4. Programmer Characteristics
    - Innate ability
    - programming experience
    - Source language experience

5. Programming Problem Characteristics
   - Functions of program
   - Degree of integration
6. Software Engineering Characteristics
   - Structured design
   - Structured programming
   - Testing aids
   - Database management systems
7. Programming Mode Characteristics
   - Batch entry
   - On-line entry

This list is the most recent and complete in the research literature, and is therefore used here to provide a categorization to outline the research findings to date pertaining to system development productivity. It needs to be emphasized that this chapter reviews only the productivity research, and therefore does not address the literature which has as its concern aspects such as system quality or user satisfaction. It is recognized that these are also worthwhile objectives of the system developer but beyond the scope of this work.

6.1 Organizational Operations Characteristics

Programming and Documentation Standards

There has been little published research in the area of the impact of standards. In particular, any *productivity* impact of programming or documentation standards has not been investigated. See section 6.6 below for discussion of the closely related research on the use of structured programming.

Work Environment and Group Interactions

Bartol and Martin (1982) report that:

> the amount of empirical research which has focused on personnel issues related to the management of information systems is relatively small [and] much of this research has addressed individual dimensions.

They summarize the literature in group dimensions and the work environment, discussing the Myers (1978), Basili and Reiter (1981), and Hill (1975) papers.

Myers (1978) carried out an experiment to compare debugging performance when groups were given different facilities. The groups were:

(1) testing using terminals after access to the program specification only;
(2) testing using terminals after access to the specification and source listing;
(3) manual testing using code inspection and walkthroughs.

In this experiment, care was taken to control for certain factors, such as programming experience, but very little control was exercised over the manner in which the debugging was carried out. Thus even though one group was using code inspection/walkthrough it is not known whether the groups used the same method for the walkthroughs or inspections. This lack of control over the debugging methods used may account for the high individual variability that was found in the study.

The work of Basili and Reiter (1981) reports on an experiment comparing the use of teams versus individuals, and also on methodological versus ad hoc approaches to system development. The task was to design and implement a compiler for a 'simple high-level language and simple stack machine'. The systems averaged 1200 lines of high-level source code. It was found that chief programmer teams performed better on a number of programming metrics than individuals or ad hoc teams. These metrics did not include productivity, however, but some of the metrics collected such as number of computer job steps, number of compilations, and number of program changes may have productivity implications. It is not possible, however, to draw any productivity related conclusions from this research.

Hill (1975) reports on a study into the relationship between project productivity and personal compatibility within the analyst team. It was found that lower interpersonal compatibility was associated with higher productivity. It was argued that this may result (1) from a low need for interpersonal communication in the task, or (2) from the possibility that the task was non-routine and heterogeneous groups perform better in this environment.

In addition to these writers, Jeffery and Lawrence (1985) report increased productivity associated with increased perceived ability of programming supervisors. In this study each programmer was asked to rank their immediate supervisor, using Likert scales, on a number of factors such as helpfulness and ability. It was found that the higher the perceived competence of the supervisor, the higher was the programmer's productivity. This result was in agreement with research into supervisor relationships in other work environments. In the same study it was found that the work environment, the programmers peer relationships, and perception of the task were not associated with any productivity change.

Cheney (1984) found significant productivity relationships with the programmers perception of:

(1) supervisor feedback,
(2) participation in relevant decisions, and
(3) suitability of the organization structure to the task.

This adds additional insight into the findings of Jeffery and Lawrence (1985), but since Cheney measured programmer productivity as the supervisor's assessment of the programmer and many of the independent variables under study involved the programmer's assessment of the supervisor, correlations might measure factors other than pure productivity relationships. For example, if a supervisor and programmer establish good informal relationships they would tend to rate each other highly and a perceived productivity advantage may accrue regardless of actual job performance.

Bartol and Martin (1982) rightly conclude that considerable research still needs to be done in the areas of motivation, work-group organization, and leadership style if our understanding of these aspects of system development are to be improved. The research to date has indicated that productivity improvement is possible. The extent of that improvement, and the methods best used to achieve it have not been studied.

Another area concerning the work environment that has received considerable research attention is that of user involvement in systems development. Ives and Olson (1984) review the literature but identify only two studies (out of approximately thirty) which have investigated productivity related aspects. Powers and Dickson (1973) looked at the effect of user involvement upon the time to develop the system and Thurston (1959) looked at time to complete and elapsed time. Neither studies supported a productivity benefit through user involvement. Walston and Felix (1977) found a productivity disadvantage in user participation in the definition of requirements, lines of code per period of time dropping by 58 per cent when participation moved from 'none' to 'much'. Once again the question of 'quality' may be seen to be important in interpreting these results.

One of the problems facing the reader is the quality of the research. Ives and Olson (1984) find good reason to conclude that:

> much of the existing research is poorly grounded in theory and methodologically flawed; as a result, the benefits of user involvement have not been convincingly demonstrated.

Given this, and the few studies carried out, it is not possible to draw any conclusions on the productivity implications of user involvement in systems development.

Another approach to the information systems work environment has been the use of Information Centres. Murray (1984) reports on the basis of one case study that productivity improvement of the order of 24:1 had been experienced, but from his discussion it is not possible to determine the validity of this claim. Here is an example of findings which are in need of rigorous testing. Our problem is not so much one of insufficient models, but insufficient testing and validation of the existing models.

In summary, the research in this area has been able to provide some valuable insights into the productivity impact of group behavior and the work environment.

The research, however, is poorly grounded in theory and is not able to provide us with a set of models which could be used to understand the productivity effect of a wide range of possible changes that may be contemplated in the information systems work environment.

6.2 Computer Hardware Characteristics

The research in this area is relatively slim, most likely because hardware characteristics have not been seen as having large potential to impact system development productivity.

One study which did investigate the productivity impact of hardware, although not hardware characteristics, was Walston and Felix (1977). They found that there was a productivity disadvantage associated with concurrent development of hardware and software. They also found productivity effects with computer access, but unfortunately the method of analysis used in the study left many doubts as to the conclusions which could be drawn. In their study they investigated 68 independent variables likely to impact system development productivity and identified 29 of those as having significant productivity correlations. However, the database consisted of 60 projects written in 28 high level languages on 66 different computers. Furthermore, each independent variable was investigated separately, and so the degree of multicollinearity is unknown.

Boehm (1981) includes hardware characteristics (computer attributes) in his model, as noted above in section 5.

6.3 Source Language Characteristics

The impact of language on productivity has been investigated most recently by Harel and McLean (1985) in their study comparing Focus with COBOL for report programs. They found that in the Focus language programmers took less time to code a task than in COBOL. The major limitation of this study was the choice of a reporting task, since presumably a report generator (as is contained in Focus) should require less effort than COBOL for this type of task.

Duffy (1984) reports that in a survey of fourth generation language users in South Africa it was *believed* that fourth generation languages had led to increased system development productivity.

Another inter-language comparison was the non-controlled experiment of Holtz (1979) who compared ADF with COBOL for screen design and processing function specification. He reported 'significant improvement in programmer productivity' when using ADF. Munnecke (1980) also reports large productivity gains when using MUMPS rather than COBOL in a case study environment. Similarly Prywes *et al.* (1979) state that the Model II language is 'much shorter (approximately one-fifth) than the equivalent high level procedural language program', but no study is reported to support this statement.

Again, there has been little controlled productivity research, but it appears from the research reported that significant productivity benefits might be expected from the application of different languages to tasks suitable to the language. The scientific determination of the magnitude of any productivity improvement and the methods needed to achieve that improvement are yet to be determined.

6.4 Programmer Characteristics

Experience

Many investigators have studied the impacts of personnel experience. Cheney (1984) investigated three programmer characteristics:

(1) self-esteem,
(2) experience,
(3) mathematical aptitude,

and found significant productivity correlations with self-esteem and experience. The qualification on the Cheney findings outlined above in section 6.1, however, still applies. Boehm (1981) also includes experience and capability variables in COCOMO.

The research findings with respect to experience are not clear-cut, however. Chrysler (1978) found programming experience to have a significant positive effect on productivity, as did Lucas and Kaplan (1976) and Thadhani (1984), but Nelson (1967), Sheppard *et al.* (1979), Behrens (1983), and Jeffery and Lawrence (1979, 1985) could not find such a relationship. Gayle (1971) also could not support an improvement in programming productivity with increased experience.

Three possibilities arise.

(1) With respect to Cheney's (1984) findings, supervisor assessment of productivity measures a different and probably more complex characteristic than lines of code per period of time, and thus different findings might reasonably be expected. For example, a programmer might be perceived by the supervisor to be very productive and in consequence given additional organizational or supervisory responsibilities which reduces the lines of code per period of time from that programmer. This programmer would be highly productive in Cheney's metric, but say average if using loc/period of time.

(2) Even when using lines of code per period of time as the measure, conflicting results will arise because of the productivity effect of task difficulty and task type on the performance achieved. Thus programmers, experienced or inexperienced, might average say eight lines of COBOL code per hour because more experienced programmers are given the more difficult tasks.

(3) More experienced programmers may implement a given task in fewer lines of code than less experienced programmers, thus implementing a given task

in fewer lines of code and taking less time, resulting in the same coding rate as the inexperienced programmer.

These issues are as yet unresolved in the research. More often than not, the researcher is really interested in personnel skill and uses experience as a surrogate. The suitability of experience as a surrogate is open to doubt.

6.5 Programming Problem Characteristics

The relationship between program characteristics and time taken to complete the programming task was investigated by Chrysler (1978). He studied 14 program characteristics and found that 74 per cent of the variance in programming time could be explained by the variables:

Stepwise regression	r^2
1. Output fields	.279
2. Input files	.447
3. Control breaks & totals	.525
4. Input edits	.581
5. Output records	not provided
6. Input fields	.725
7. Input records	.740

These results were not, however, supported by Jeffery and Lawrence (1979) who found that the relationship between time and program characteristics was unstable. Chrysler (1978) analyzed 36 programs from one organization whereas Jeffery and Lawrence (1979) analyzed 93 programs from three organizations. The instability found is evidenced in Table 1.

Further investigation was carried out by Jeffery and Lawrence (1985) when 196 COBOL programs from 17 organizations were divided according to program type. Significant productivity difference (10 per cent) level was found only for processing type programs, where lower productivity was ascribed to the complexity of the algorithmic type programming represented in this category. It appears therefore, that differences in coding rates in COBOL cannot be ascribed to the type of program. Once again this need for thorough testing of a model is evidenced.

TABLE 1. Correlation coefficients for three organizations

		Correlation with time
No. of files	Org. 1	.34
	Org. 2	.61
	Org. 3	.16
No. of data types	Org. 1	.81
	Org. 2	.46
	Org. 3	.52

TABLE 2. Structured programming research and productivity

Authors	Study type	Dependent variable	Finding for structured programming
Sime *et al.* (1973)	Laboratory	Time	positive
Weissman (1974)	Laboratory	Time	no effect
Lucas & Kaplan (1976)	Laboratory	Time	no effect
Sime *et al.* (1977)	Laboratory	Time	no effect
Green (1977)	Laboratory	Time	positive
Sheppard *et al.* (1979)	Laboratory	Time	no effect
Walston & Felix (1977)	Field	Productivity	positive
Lawrence (1981)	Field	Productivity	no effect
Vessey (1985)	Field	Productivity	no effect
Hugo (1977)	Survey	Time	positive

6.6 Software Engineering Characteristics

An excellent and thorough review of the literature on structured programming was provided by Vessey and Weber (1984). They discuss the work of Green (1977), Hugo (1977), Lucas and Kaplan (1976), Sheppard *et al.* (1979), Sime *et al.* (1973, 1977), Weissman (1974), and Lawrence (1981).

Few of these studies are directed specifically at productivity, but they all include some consideration of effort and therefore have productivity implications. The results of these studies are summarized in Table 2 which shows the impact of the use of structured programming on the dependent variable. The findings again reveal a confusing picture, with almost equal numbers showing either no effect or a positive effect for structured programming.

Vessey and Weber (1984) find the results 'inconclusive' and the experimental methods used generally poor. They conclude:

1. the theory enunciating the effects of structured programming on software practice is rudimentary and inadequate
2. this lack of theory has inhibited the formulation of hypotheses
3. until the theory has been developed, it is not possible to identify the strategic hypotheses
4. existing empirical work reflects the shoddy state of the theory

Practitioners are generally convinced as to the benefits of structured programming but these benefits are seen to be wider than productivity and may be reflected in lower maintenance costs, for example, rather than lower development time. There is no doubt though that research efforts need to be better focused than has been the case in this particular area.

6.7 Programming Mode Characteristics

The most reported study in this area is that of Sackman *et al.* (1968) whose laboratory study comparing debugging performance in on-line environments with that in off-line environments found faster debugging under on-line conditions. These results contrast with those of Jeffery and Lawrence (1979) who, in a field study, found no productivity advantage for the programming task in on-line environments. It appears, therefore, that in the work environment other performance effects wash out this factor.

7. CONCLUSIONS

The productivity research to date has had mixed success. If criteria for the evaluation of research include:

(1) Is the research well grounded in theory?
(2) Has the research methodology been appropriately selected?
(3) Has the research been well executed to achieve the research aim?
(4) Has the analysis been appropriate to the study?
(5) Is the research well documented?
(6) Are the conclusions drawn appropriate?

then it can be said that on many counts the research has failed; but in any discipline, particularly young disciplines, there are many instances of less than ideal research efforts. This point is brought out by Ives and Olson (1984) as discussed above, and also by Weber (1985).

The literature surveyed in this chapter reveals a relatively coherent, if incomplete, picture with respect to productivity models for information systems development.

The time-sensitive cost models have been developed out of theories concerning the process of system development. In the simplest form they rest on a relationship between project size, effort, and elapsed time, such that if attempts are made to compress elapsed time on a project below optimum, then effort will rise.

This basic relationship is then enriched by the additon of factors concerning the organization, hardware, source language, programmer, task, and construction technique used. Much of the research in these aspects has been exploratory; the studies have often not been well grounded in theory; many of the studies have not been well designed; and some of the results are of dubious validity. An example has been given concerning programmer experience and the use of structured programming. It is considered axiomatic that more skilled programmers will be more productive, but the research has not come to grips with the measurement of programmer skill, using years of experience quite often as an unsatisfactory surrogate.

Looking at the research from the six perspectives given above it can be concluded that much of the research to date is not well grounded in theory, but this is a problem which should be expected in a relatively new discipline. As the discipline matures, the insights are gained, and the theories developed. The empirical testing of these theories through the enunciation of testable hypotheses is then a reality. Perhaps we have been guilty of too often carrying out empirical tests when there is too little theory to suggest the real reason for the tests, or the expected results from those tests. The result of this can be seen in the contradictory findings of the literature, as evidenced above, when quite often a measure is taken but the meaning of that measure in the context of a research hypothesis is not understood, or in some cases not considered.

In terms of the research methodology used, its execution, and the analysis, it has been noted by other writers that in new technology areas the interest is always on the latest innovation. In information systems we also see too many new models, too many new effects, and too little validation of those models or findings. For these reasons, the conclusions drawn are not always appropriate.

8. RESEARCH DIRECTIONS

From this survey of the literature it is apparent that there is considerable research that needs to be carried out in the IS field. This research must include theory formulation as well as empirical testing so that the research findings can be well grounded and the hypotheses developed in light of the relevant theory.

From the literature survey contained in this chapter, the following research topics are suggested:

(1) *Verification of the Putnam–Boehm type cost models in the commercial MIS environment.* These models were developed in large technical systems environments. Their applicability in the commercial MIS environment has not yet been established by empirical research. Further testing is necessary to establish their applicability, and to resolve the conflicts that exist between them.

(2) *Exploratory investigation of the impact of fourth generation languages on the system development process.* Industry has adopted 4GLs with enthusiasm, yet almost no research has been conducted on appropriate models for the 4GL development environment. The lack of theory supporting this type of research is a drawback in this research, but exploratory work can form the basis for the development of theory.

(3) *Further controlled empirical research into cost drivers.* It is known that individual differences in productivity are large, yet we are still not able to ascribe these differences to stable causal variables. Controlled experimental research is needed to improve the management models so that appropriate motivational and control techniques can be consistently applied in the system development process.

REFERENCES

Alloway, R. M., and Quillard, J. A. (1983) 'User Managers' Systems Needs', *MIS Quarterly*, 7, 2, 27–41.

Bailey, J. W., and Basili, V. R. (1981) 'A Meta-model for Software Development Resource Expenditures', *Proceedings, Fifth International Conference on Software Engineering*, pp. 107–116.

Bartol, K. M., and Martin, D. C. (1982) 'Managing Information Systems Personnel: A Review of the Literature and Managerial Implications', *MIS Quarterly/Special Issue*, 49–70.

Basili, V. R. (1980) 'Resource Models', in *Tutorial on Models and Metrics for Software Management and Engineering*, V. Basili (ed.), IEEE, London, pp. 4–9.

Basili, V. R., and Beane, J. (1981) 'Can the Parr Curve Help with Manpower Distribution and Resource Estimation Problems?', *Journal of System and Software*, 2, 1, 59–69.

Basili, V. R., and Freburger, K. (1981) 'Programming Measurement and Estimation in the Software Engineering Laboratory', *The Journal of Systems and Software*, 2, 47–57.

Basili, V. R., and Perricone, B. T. (1984) 'Software Errors and Complexity: An Empirical Investigation', *Communications of the ACM*, **27**, 42–52.

Basili, V. R., Selby, R. W., and Phillips, T. Y. (1983) 'Metric Analysis and Data Validation Across Fortran Projects', *IEEE Transactions on Software Engineering*, **SE–9**, 6, 652–663.

Basili, V. R., and Reiter, R. W., Jr. (1981) 'A Controlled Experiment Quantitatively Comparing Software Development Approaches', *IEEE Transactions on Software Engineering*, **SE–7**, 3, 299–320.

Behrens, C. A. (1983) 'Measuring the Productivity of Computer Systems Development Activities with Function Points', *IEEE Transactions on Software Engineering*, **SE–9**, 6, 648–652.

Benbasat, I., and Vessey, I. (1980) 'Programming and Analyst Time/Cost Estimation', *MIS Quarterly*, **4**, 2, 31–43.

Boehm, B. W. (1981) *Software Engineering Economics*, Prentice-Hall, Englewood Cliffs, NJ.

Boehm, B. W. (1983) 'Seven Basic Principles of Software Engineering', *The Journal of Systems and Software*, 3, 3–24.

Boehm, B. W. (1984) 'Software Engineering Economics', *IEEE Transactions on Software Engineering*, **SE–10**, 1, 4–21.

Boehm, B. W., Brown, J. R. and Lipow, M. (1976) 'Quantitative Evaluation of Software Quality', *Proceedings of Second International Conference on Software Engineering*, pp. 218–231.

Brooks, F. P. Jr. (1975) *The Mythical Man-Month*, Addison-Wesley, Reading, MA.

Cheney, P. H. (1984) 'Effects of Individual Characteristics, Organisation Factors and Task Characteristics on Computer Programmer Productivity and Job Satisfaction', *Information and Management*, 7, 209–214.

Chrysler, E. (1978) 'Some Basic Determinants of Computer Programming Productivity', *Communications of the ACM*, **21**, 6, 472–483.

DeMarco, T. (1982) *Controlling Software Projects*, Yourdon Press, New York.

Druffel, L. E., Redwine, S. T., Jr., and Riddle, W. E. (1983) 'The STARS Program: Overview and Rationale', *Computer*, **November**, 21–29.

Duffy, N. M. (1984) 'Fourth Generation Languages: Some Planning and Implementation Issues', *Proceedings of Joint International Symposium Information Systems*, Sydney, April 9–11, pp. 166–188.

Gayle, J. B. (1971) 'Multiple Regression Techniques for Estimating Computer Programming Costs', *Journal of Systems Management*, **February**, 13–16.

Glass, A. (1984) 'The Applicability of Resource Utilization Models to Medium-scale Software Development', Honours thesis, University of New South Wales.

Green, T. R. G. (1977) 'Conditional Program Statements and their Comprehensibility to Professional Programmer', *J. Occup. Psychol.*, **50**, 93–109.

Harel, E., and McLean, E. R. (1985) 'The Effects of Using a Nonprocedural Computer Language on Programmer Productivity', *MIS Quarterly*, **9**, 2, 109-120.

Hill, R. E. (1975) 'Interpersonal Compatibility and Work Group Performance' *Journal of Applied Behavioral Science*, **11**, 2, April-May-June, pp. 210-219.

Holtz, D. H. (1979) 'A Nonprocedural Language for On-Line Applications', *Datamation*, **April**, 167-172.

Hugo, I. St. J. (1977) 'A Survey of Structured Programming Practice', *AFIPS Conference Proceedings*, pp. 741-752.

Ives, B., and Olson, M. H. (1984) 'User Involvement and MIS Success: A Review of Research', *Management Science*, **30**, 5, 586-603.

Jeffery, D. R., and Lawrence, M. J. (1979) 'An Inter-organisational Comparison of Programming Productivity', *Proceedings of 4th International Conference on Software Engineering*, pp. 369-377.

Jeffery, D. R., and Lawrence, M. J. (1981) 'Some Issues in the Measurement and Control of Programming Productivity', *Information and Management*, **4**, 169-176.

Jeffery, D. R., and Lawrence, M. J. (1985) 'Managing Programming Productivity', *The Journal of Systems and Software*, **6**, 1.

Jeffery, D. R., and Vessey, I. (1980) 'Models, Metrics, and Management of IS Development', *Information and Management*, **3**, 89-93.

Keane, J. F., Keane, M. and Teagan, M. (1984) *Productivity Management in the Development of Computer Application*, Prentice-Hall, Englewood Cliffs, NJ.

Kendall, R. C., and Lamb, E. C. (1977) 'Management Perspectives on Programs, Programming and Productivity', presented at GUIDE 45, Atlanta, Georgia, November, pp. 201-211.

Kitchenham, B. A., and Taylor, N. R. (1984) 'Software Cost Models', *ICL Technical Journal*, **May**, 73-102.

Lawrence, M. J. (1981) 'Programming Methodology, Organizational Environment, and Programming Productivity', *The Journal of Systems and Software*, **2**, 257-269.

Lawrence, M. J., and Jeffery, D. R. (1983) 'Commercial Programming Productivity — An Empirical Look at Intuition', *The Australian Computer Journal*, **15**, 1, 28-32.

Lucas, H. C., and Kaplan, R. B. (1976) 'A Structured Programming Experiment', *Computer Journal*, **19**, 136-138.

Mapp, T. E. (1978) 'Applicability of the Rayleigh Curve to the SEL Environment', Unpublished paper, University of Maryland, pp. 1-19.

Martin, J. (1982) *Application Development without Programmers*, Prentice-Hall, Englewood Cliffs, NJ.

Munnecke, T. (1980) 'A Linguistic Comparison of MUMPS and COBOL', *Proceedings of National Computer Conference*, pp. 723-729.

Murray, J. P. (1984) 'How an Information Center Improved Productivity', *Management Accounting*, **March**, 38-44.

Myers, G. J. (1978) 'A Controlled Experiment in Program Testing and Code Walkthroughs/Inspections', *Comms. of the ACM*, **21**, 9, 760-768.

Nelson, E. A. (1967) 'Management Handbook for the Estimation of Computer Programming Costs', System Development Corp., Santa Monica, California, March.

Norden, P. V. (1958) 'Curve Fitting for a Model of Applied Research and Development Scheduling', *IBM J. Rsch, Dev.*, **2**, 3.

Norden, P. V. (1963) 'Useful Tools for Project Management', *Operations Research in Research and Development*, John Wiley, New York.

Parr, F. N. (1980) 'An Alternative to the Rayleigh Curve Model for Software Development Effort', *IEEE Transactions on Software Engineering*, **May**, 291-296.

Powers, R. F., and Dickson, G. W. (1973) 'MIS Project Management: Myths, Opinions, and Reality', *California Management Rev.*, **15**, 3, 147-156.

Prywes, N. S., Pnueli, A., and Shastry, S. (1979) 'Use of a Nonprocedural Specification Language and Associated Program Generator in Software Development', *ACM Transactions on Programming Languages and Systems*, **1**, 2, 196-217.

Putnam, L. H. (1978) 'A General Empirical Solution to the Macro Software Sizing and Estimating Problem', *IEEE Transactions on Software Engineering*, **SE-4**, 4, 345-360.

Putnam, L. H. (1983) 'Slim Perspectives', Vol. 1, Edition 1 & 2, *Quantitative Software Management*, Virginia.

Putnam, L. H. (1981) 'SLIM A Quantitative Tool for Software Cost and Schedule Estimation', *Proceedings of the NBS/IEEE/ACM Software Tool Fair*, San Diego, CA, March, pp. 49-57.

Putnam, L. H. (1980) 'The Real Economics of Software Development', Presented at Symposium on The Economics of Information Processing, December.

Putnam, L. H., Putnam, D. T., and Thayer, L. P. (1983) 'A Method to Measure the "Effective Productivity" in Building Software Systems', *Proceedings of The International Society of Parametric Analysts*, **2**, 1, 95-143.

Putnam, L. H., and Fitzsimmons, A. (1979) 'Estimating Software Costs', *Datamation*, **September**, 189-198.

Sackman, H., Erikson, W. J., and Grant, E. E. (1968) 'Exploratory Experimental Studies Comparing Online and Offline Programming Performance', *Communications of the ACM*, **11**, 1, 3-11.

Sheppard, S., Curtis, B., Milliman, P. and Love, T. (1979) 'Modern Coding Practices and Programming Performance', *IEEE Computer*, **12**, 41-49.

Shooman, M. L. (1979) 'Tutorial on Software Cost Models', *Workshop on Quantitative Software Models*, IEEE THOO67-9, pp. 1-19.

Sime, M. E., Green, T. R. G., and Guest, D. J. (1973) 'Psychological Evaluation of Two Conditional Constructions Used in Computer Languages', *Int. J. Man-Mach. Studies*, **5**, 123-143.

Sime, M. E., Green, T. R. G., and Guest, D. J. (1977) 'Scope Marking in Computer Conditionals — A Psychological Evaluation', *Int. J. Man-Mach. Studies*, **9**, 107-118.

Strassmann, P. A. (1982) 'Information Technology and Organizations', Presentation at IT '82 Conference, London.

Thadhani, A. J. (1984) 'Factors Affecting Programmer Productivity during Application Development', *IBM Systems Journal*, **23**, 1, 19-35.

Thurston, P. H. (1959) *Systems and Procedures Responsibility*, Harvard University Press, Cambridge, MA.

Vessey, I. (1985) 'An Empirical Study of Some Factors Affecting Program Development', Unpublished paper, University of Queensland, May.

Vessey, I., and Weber, R. (1984) 'Research on Structured Programming: An Empiricist's Evaluation', *IEEE Transactions on Software Engineering*, **SE-10**, 4, 397-407.

Walston, C. E., and Felix, C. P. (1977) 'A Method of Programming Measurement and Estimation', *IBM Systems Journal*, **16**, 1, 54-73.

Weber, R. (1985) 'Toward a Theory of Artifacts: A Paradigmatic Base for Information Systems Research', Unpublished paper, University of Queensland, April.

Weissman, L. M. (1974) 'A Methodology for Studying the Psychological Complexity of Computer Programs', Ph.D. dissertation, University of Toronto, unpublished.

Wolverton, R. (1974) 'The Cost of Developing Large Scale Software', *IEEE Transactions on Computers*, **23**, 6.

Chapter 6

MANAGERIAL EXPERT SYSTEMS AND ORGANIZATIONAL
CHANGE: SOME CRITICAL RESEARCH ISSUES

Enid Mumford

ABSTRACT

Managerial expert systems present many critical non-technical issues for information systems research. This chapter first discusses the general importance of undertaking research in this area. Then, it considers the expert system design task, and describes how research can help to better understand the design problems involved. The chapter then explores some of the organizational consequences of designing and using managerial expert systems. Finally, the chapter asks: how can we influence the course of future developments in managerial expert systems, and what are the ethical problems associated with expert system design?

1. THE RESEARCH AREA

There are many definitions of expert systems. An expert system has been described as

> a computing system which embodies organized knowledge concerning some specific area of human expertise (medical diagnosis, chemical identification, economic geology, structural analysis, number theory, chess, etc.) sufficient to be able to do duty as a skilful and cost-effective consultant. (Michie, 1980)

and as

> a general purpose, problem-solving program that mimics human intelligence. (Shallis, 1984)

and

> a high level intellectual support for the human expert. (Fiegenbaum, 1983)

Expert systems produce answers to problems that require reasoning, pattern matching, the acquisition of new concepts and judgement. In short they provide answers to questions that require intelligence (Michie, 1980).

Feigenbaum (1983) believes that the key factor in the performance of an expert system is knowledge. This knowledge is of two types: first, what he calls the facts of the domain — the widely shared knowledge that is written in textbooks and journals and generally accepted; second, heuristic knowledge — the rules of thumb that experts develop on the basis of experience and which, combined with book knowledge, give them their expertise.

Feigenbaum sees the principal problems in developing expert systems as: first, knowledge representation — how do you represent the knowledge of a domain of work as data structures in the computer in such a way that they can be easily accessed for problem solving? — second, knowledge utilization — how should the inference machine be designed to enable this knowledge to be used for problem solving? — third, knowledge acquisition — how do we get the knowledge out of the head of an expert in order to put it into the computer? This is often seen as the critical bottleneck in artificial intelligence.

Technologists therefore define their major areas of research interest as managing data inside the computer and as transferring knowledge from the human being to the machine.

Researchers interested in organizational issues will range more widely. An understanding of why expert systems are taking their present form and how they are impacting on organizations requires a study of the philosophy and values of the designers and their sponsors. It also requires an examination of: how the design task has been defined; the nature of the design decisions that have been taken, including technological decisions; the skills, knowledge and interests of the project group responsible for design and the processes which they use to move from problem identification to system implementation.

Organizational researchers are also extremely interested in how users interact with expert systems, how they make use of them and how they, and their work, are affected by them.

Expert systems differ according to who is going to use them. Some, for example medical diagnostic systems, will be systems which incorporate the knowledge of a group of experts for use by other experts in the same group — doctors will create systems for doctors. Others, will be handing over the knowledge of an expert group to a group of non-experts — accountancy systems to be used by people who are not accountants, for example. It is this last kind which is likely to be most controversial.

Expert systems can also, in theory, be used in three different ways: one, with the user as a client who is seeking answers to problems; two, with the user as instructor, adding to the system's knowledge; three, with the user as a pupil, learning from the system and increasing his or her knowledge (Michie, 1980). In reality a user may be doing all three of these activities at one and the same time.

The extent to which human expertise can be replaced by computers is not yet known. It can be argued that an important aspect of any client–expert interaction is that concerned with relationships. The client wants to talk to the expert, communicate fears and anxieties and establish trust and confidence. Information alone is not enough. But, research in England has shown that the opposite can also be true. Patients may prefer to give symptoms to a computer, particularly if their medical condition is due to behaviour which is not socially approved. They are also more likely to tell the truth to a computer. This may, of course, be less due to the superior capabilities of computers than to the poor social skills of some doctors [1].

If the undesirable consequences of new technology are to be avoided, we need to be able to predict these and research can help us to do this. Accurate prediction is never easy. Most predictions of the future are derived from experiences in the past, yet today technological developments progress so quickly that past experience may be a poor guide to future strategy for change.

One way of approaching this problem is to keep careful records of what is happening today, examine future developments and hypothesize their impact, and then monitor whether these predictions prove to be accurate. Sackman (1967) has made a plea for 'real time' research in which continuous measurements of new systems effects are used to estimate and influence future system performance.

Knowledge engineering is likely to have dramatic human effects, many of which will have a powerful influence on the acceptability of this new science. We need to monitor the nature of these effects and communicate them to designers, experts and users so that informed decisions can be made.

Here is another important area for research. Effective communication between researchers and non-academic groups is not easy. Attempts to communicate research knowledge to managers, trade unions and workers in industry have largely proved a failure.

Yet there is an important need for all interested groups to be aware that the results of knowledge engineering may be both threatening and benign to individuals, groups and organizations. They need also to be aware that many of the claims for these systems are over-stated and untested. The words 'artificial intelligence', 'knowledge engineering', 'expert systems' can arouse fear and anxiety in non-technologists. They can also make technologists believe that these new systems are further advanced and more sophisticated than is, in fact, the case.

Efforts must be made to bridge the communication gap between academics concerned about the social effects of new technology and their potential audiences. Politicians and users need to be able to make realistic assessments of likely benefits and drawbacks, while technologists need to be constantly aware of the social consequences of the decisions which they are taking. Michie (1980) has stressed the need to avoid the mistakes of the physicists in the 1930s who, in his view, were *laissez faire* about what they were doing.

The difficulty of making accurate forecasts about the future has already been referred to. One reason for this inaccuracy is the tradition of carrying out single variable research. In the past, it has been regarded as scientific to try and isolate single variables and then study their effects. But in the real world, in contrast to the laboratory, the reality is more complex. In industry, an expert system will be introduced into a work situation which already contains people with predetermined attitudes to technology, an industrial relations climate which may be positive or negative, and a set of long established management–worker relationships. All of these factors will affect the way in which the new system is received and used. Research therefore needs to be directed at identifying the significant variables that affect attitudes to change, and at gaining an understanding of the relationships between these variables.

Research also needs to be carried out on how expert systems are actually used, in contrast to how their designers intended them to be used. For example, an expert system introduced by an American court to assist judges to match sentences to the offender and his crime, was used by the lawyers for the defence and prosecution to assist their plea-bargaining activities.

Research into the human consequences of expert systems is essential. Research must tell us what an expert system can take away from a human being, but it must also inform us on what can be added to a situation. Can there be more, rather than less, opportunity for human contact because more time is available? Can more people have the opportunity to become experts, rather than fewer?

There are many other fascinating questions to which research can provide answers but such knowledge is only of value if it is fed into the design of new systems so that adverse consequences are avoided and posible gains are achieved. There must also be a willingness to change course if we find that we are on a technological route where the human losses outweigh the economic gains. In 1927 Mary Parker Follett gave a lecture in which she said

> I cannot wholly agree with those historians who say that the study of history should help us predict situations — it should help us create situations.

Technological history should be as much a guide to what not to do in the future, as it is to what we should be doing.

Knowledge engineering is now developing very rapidly and many companies are identifying business areas in which they could use expert systems. It is likely that in the next two to five years the computer industry will produce a wave of artificial intelligence products that will turn into a tidal wave by 1990. A forecast by International Resource Development Inc. of Norfolk, Connecticut, estimates that the United States market for expert system products and services will grow from $66 million in 1983 to $8.5 billion in 1993. The future market is expected to be located primarily in the home, factories and offices. To date, around one hundred expert systems have been built. Some are experimental, others are in use in the companies which built them, and a few others are for sale. (*Microelectronics Monitor*, 1984).

Along with these developments has come the setting up of new research institutes. In Europe, the British Government's Alvey project is sponsoring research into knowledge engineering, and the European Commission has its Esprit project. The Turing Institute is being set up by industry and the University of Strathclyde to develop AI and three of the largest European computer companies, ICL, Bull and Siemens, have formed a joint research institute for knowledge processing. But all this research effort is technology-focused. Its long-term goal is to develop computer systems that surpass human capabilities in reasoning, problem-solving, sensory analysis and environmental manipulation. This goal may be a long way off, however, and some AI experts do not see it being achieved within the next fifty years.

In parallel with this research or, better still, as part of it, there is a pressing need for studies of the behavioural, economic and political factors which influence the choice, design, implementation, use and acceptability of expert systems. Research into other forms of technology application, for example production control systems, has shown that managers do not want to buy expensive industrial relations trouble. If a system is likely to cause this they will not introduce it.

Sophisticated expert systems are still very expensive to produce although the declining costs of computer hardware are increasingly moving them towards cost-effectiveness. In Europe, the focus of scientific research has been on expert systems which address engineering problems and in which human variables play little part. When they are used to solving serious managerial problems, which some of the most successful American ones do, the financial savings are likely to be considerable. But the use of expert systems by managers and others will affect the structure and operation of many businesses, and the nature of this kind of impact needs to be identified through research.

Another area of research interest is the time required for an innovation to be accepted and used, and this is very often underestimated. First, the knowledge that the expert system exists has to diffuse to potential users and this can be a slow process. It has been suggested that a period of eight to ten years is required to move from a 10 per cent to a 90 per cent take-up. Second, it has to be seen by potential users as cheap, reliable, useful and non-controversial (Council for Science and Society, 1981). Third, whereas previous computer developments have had their greatest impact on the lower levels of the labour force — clerks and draughtsmen are examples — expert systems are likely to affect many of the professions. Professional groups are normally excellent at protecting their own interests. Dentists, for example, have always successfully fought off attempts to dilute the profession through the use of dental auxiliaries trained to do simple fillings.

It can be hypothesized that expert systems which are cost-effective, reliable, and adaptable and do not cause industrial relations problems at lower levels in the company, or professional resistance at higher levels, will come in relatively quickly. Other kinds may take much longer or never be accepted at all. Research can help us to develop the former and avoid the latter.

2. THE DESIGN OF EXPERT SYSTEMS

What is involved in the design of an expert system? To answer this question let us take as an example an expert system designed to solve a particular business problem. This is likely to be a system in which the knowledge originally held by experts is transferred to another, non-expert, user group, rather than a system to help experts to be more expert.

We need to consider what influences design practice today, what are the current defects and limitations of the present approach and how these can be overcome. The author will also provide an example of what she considers to be good design.

Broadly, the design of an expert system needs to cover the following stages (Wilkerson, 1985).

(1) The identification of a suitable business problem.
(2) The initial prototyping of the solution to check its feasibility.
(3) The creation of a project team. This should consist of a mix of experts, knowledge engineers — who act as the link between the human expert and the system — and future users.
(4) The creation of a steering committee. This is important if the expert system is to be used internally. The steering committee should include representatives from top management, particularly top management from the future user area. In some circumstances it may be advisable to include a senior trade union official.
(5) The development of a project plan.
(6) The training of project team members in the technology, problem area and methods of systems design.
(7) The creation of an initial design.
(8) The development of a basic shell.
(9) The testing of this in the user environment.
(10) Installing the system in the user environment and training the users.
(11) Enhancing the system.
(12) Adapting it to changing business needs.

The successful management of each one of these steps is crucial to the success of the eventual system.

All management needs, and usually has, a business philosophy and a set of values that guide its internal management practices and its relationships with the outside world. This philosophy should influence the way it approaches the design of an expert system and should be known to all the participants in the design process. A management with a humanistic value system, or even one that for reasons of expediency wishes to make expert systems acceptable to its staff, will have two objectives. The first will be to create a system that enables it to operate more effectively in its business environment; the second will be to create a high-quality work environment for its staff, particularly those who will be interacting directly with the new system. The aim should be to arrive at what the Americans call a 'win–win' situation in which every group gains something and there are no victims. This second objective may be difficult to achieve, but it can be striven for even though the end result is not perfect.

If at stages (1) and (2) a problem is selected that is not critical to the success of the business then the expert system is unlikely to arouse much interest. Similarly, if a group is threatened with loss of job or skill there is likely to be a period of upheaval and conflict before the system is accepted, if it ever is.

The research requirement here is the development of methods to assist the choice of business problems which can be solved more effectively with the assistance of expert systems. This requires the ability to identify and assess appropriate criteria for choice; for example, these might include such factors as problem complexity, problem volatility, high cost in terms of efficiency and effectiveness, high cost in terms of quality of working life.

Management and human considerations have to be taken account of at every stage of the expert system design process. If a project team that is predominantly technical in background and interests is selected at stage (3), it is likely to focus on technical variables only and to be unaware of, or ignore, the critical business and human interests. The team members are likely to concentrate on what happens inside the computer and to pay little attention to the equally important external factors. This problem can be avoided by the kind of training that is provided at stage (6) and training is another important area requiring research.

Given that training should be broad-based and cover project management, team building, user participation, organizational design and a sound knowledge of the business problem to be addressed, there is still a need for knowledge of the correct mix for different design groups and problems. There is also a need to learn how best to impart this kind of information and skill.

Stages (7) and (8) — making an initial design and building a basic shell — cover the tasks of creating a knowledge base and an inference structure. They are where most of the government and industry research funding is located, and of course they are very important. They are the nub of an expert system, without them the system would not exist. It is here that the very difficult problem of how knowledge can be obtained from an expert has to be addressed. At present this is usually done by a knowledge engineer asking an expert to describe what he or she does.

This approach seems to have originated in the tradition of systems analysts interviewing users individually to obtain an understanding of their jobs. It was never satisfactory in this early use and research has demonstrated that a participative approach, in which users are helped as a group to think systematically about their needs and problems, produces better and more acceptable systems (Mumford, 1981). Here is another important research area. What are the best means for assisting experts to think clearly and logically about how they use their knowledge, and is this best done individually or in small groups? Can it even be done at all, or does the nature of expertise mean that the more expert the person, the less his or her knowledge can be brought into the open and minutely examined.

The computer uses a series of causal links and logical deductions as the basis of its problem solving. Its reasoning is based on a series of 'if . . . then' statements. At one time it was thought that human beings reasoned in a similar manner. Research is now suggesting that this is not the case and that experts solve problems and make decisions by recognizing situations as instances of things with which they are familiar. Johnson (1984) describes how a physician attempts to connect a patient's symptoms with a known category of disease, so that procedures associated with the management of that disease can be used to cure the patient. Only when the disease is unfamiliar does the physician revert to general principles.

In addition to the difficulty of understanding how human beings reason, there is the additional problem that experts are poor at communicating the nature of their expertise. They may no longer consciously understand why they do certain things, or they may misinterpret what they do and report inaccurately (Nisbett, 1977). Unfortunately for knowledge engineers the expert usually knows more than he is aware of knowing or is able to communicate (Fiegenbaum, 1979).

It has been argued that eliciting knowledge from a single expert is not a good way of addressing a complex problem. Experts differ in their views and few experts will have a broad enough knowledge to span a total problem. But if experts need to be brought together in groups to discuss their approaches to problem solving and to agree on a common approach, then more research is required into methods for helping groups to think and talk cooperatively and analytically about their knowledge and skills.

It is the knowledge engineer who must handle and successfully resolve these communication problems. He or she must be able to express and systematize the knowledge of experts so that a team of programmers can convert it into working computer codes (Fiegenbaum, 1983). This is not an easy task and we are still a long way from understanding how best to accomplish it.

Stages (9) and (10) — testing in the user environment and installing — are crucial to the success of the system. When expert systems are designed in a laboratory environment and then handed over to the real users it has been found that they often prove to be far less effective than has been anticipated. Real world problems may be very different from those tackled in the laboratory. (Fiegenbaum, 1983).

Implementation strategy is therefore another important area for research. Much research has already been carried out into the implementation of computer-based systems for clerical workers (Mumford, 1979). But it seems probable that the introduction of expert systems will create even more serious difficulties. Because most experts are influential and in positions of high status, these systems are likely to affect powerful groups in the organizations in which they are used. These groups will support or oppose them according to their interpretation of how their personal and group interests are likely to be affected. Strong opposition may be difficult to overcome.

Opposition to change is usually very expensive. If systems have to be modified because they do not fit user needs or contain errors, then the costs of adjustment and error rectification will occur. Research has already shown that error rectification is the most costly element in systems design. [2] If systems are designed but not implemented, then there will be heavy financial costs without any compensating financial returns. These can lead a small firm into bankruptcy.

Strategies for implementation that resolve conflict, generate interest and enthusiasm and give users some control over the use and modification of expert systems are therefore essential. Research into how these things can be achieved for more, as well as less, powerful groups in an organization, is important.

Another problem with expert systems is that users may not trust them. How can they know that the answers which they are getting from the systems are correct? Good expert systems will provide clear, logical explanations of how they arrive at decisions, but these may not always convince the user. A different problem, experienced by the author, is that people may trust them too much. She has successfully used an expert system to configure a complex computer application although she has no knowledge of configuring.

This is where the notion of participation needs to be discussed in more detail. It has already been argued that eliciting knowledge from a single expert can lead to systems which other experts do not like and will not use. It can also be argued that omitting users from the design processes can be equally risky. An expert system designed with user participation from stage (1) is unlikely to founder at stage (10). If users are equal, or dominant, partners in the design team, with experts and knowledge engineers seeing their role as helping them to develop the best possible system for their needs, then there is likely to be a high degree of user acceptance. Users will welcome an expert system that enhances their efficiency and effectiveness and improves their quality of working life, and which they have designed themselves.

Similarly, users need to be constantly involved in stages (11) and (12)— enhancing the system and adapting it to changing business needs. A static expert system will rapidly become obsolete; a dynamic one, participatively designed, will bring increasing benefits.

Most textbooks on systems design now pay lip-service to the notion of user involvement. But there is very little concrete advice on how to manage the processes of participation. Yet successful participation depends on good management and on someone occupying the difficult role of 'group process facilitator'. Increasingly users will wish, and need, to be involved in systems design and implementation. Here again there is a need for a knowledge of 'best practice', and knowledge requires research.

User participation in the design of a system to be used in their own organization is not difficult to initiate, user involvement in systems designed for general business use is less simple and there are a number of research questions that require an answer. For example, is it possible to build 'frameworks' or 'shells', which users can then rebuild to meet their specific needs? Can a system designed by one user group to meet its own needs be redesigned by another which has somewhat different needs?

Despite the evidence of its success in creating good, acceptable, systems, many organizations are still reluctant to involve users in the design of their own systems. Companies which make participation a part of their standard practice are therefore very useful models for the rest of the world. The Digital Equipment Corporation in Boston, Massachusetts, is one of these. Here is a description of its approach.

The Digital Equipment Corporation is one of the most experienced designers of expert systems and is particularly famous for two related systems, XCON and XSEL. Digital manufactures computer systems which are not standardized but built to individual customer requirements. The manufacturing process is therefore complex and has to cater for many hardware and software variations. XCON is an expert system that handles what is called the configuring task. This ensures that the modules associated with a particular system are fitted together accurately and with all the necessary components. Before the development of XCON configuring was carried out manually by manufacturing specialists. This manual process was time-consuming and error-prone. The complexity and variety of the computer systems manufactured meant that it was impossible for any human to remember the detail of all of them.

Digital's rapid growth required either an increase in the number of these specialists, or the provision of some sort of productivity tool to assist them in this work. XCON has greatly reduced the number of mistakes at the manufacturing stage and this has enabled Digital to make major financial savings. Furthermore, it has enabled the company to process increasingly large numbers of orders without taking on considerable numbers of additional staff.

XSEL is also directed at reducing configuring errors, this time when systems are being sold and cost estimates given to customers. This configuring has traditionally been carried out by the salesmen and they too made errors which cost Digital money. If they forgot a component in their estimates, the customer would be undercharged. A system to help the salesman configure would therefore add to the financial savings already accruing from XCON.

The Intelligent Systems Technologies Group decided to design XSEL using a design methodology developed by the author, called ETHICS (Mumford, 1983). ETHICS (Effective Technical and Human Implementation of Computer-based Systems) is an ethical design approach that caters for human needs such as job satisfaction, and for job and organizational design. It aims to create systems which are administratively efficient and managerially effective and which increase the quality of working life for the users. It is highly participative.

The Digital approach was to proceed as follows.

(1) To create a project group consisting of engineering experts, knowledge engineers and salesmen users.

(2) To provide this group with comprehensive training, including technical, human and organizational skills and knowledge, project management and participative design.
(3) To involve experts and users jointly in the design process from stage (1). Initially the engineering and manufacturing experts were dominant as they described the knowledge required in configuring. Later, the users — the salesmen — played the major role, describing their configuring problems and the kind of system they needed to assist them. A large number of salesmen were involved in these discussions. If any could not be physically present at meetings, ideas were sent to them over the electronic mail and their reactions sought.
(4) Great attention was paid to the salesmen's job satisfaction and to ensuring that XSEL increased this.

The result, today, is a non-threatening system which everyone likes. Digital saves money as there are fewer configuring errors and therefore fewer customer complaints; the customers have systems that are technically satisfactory; the salesmen have a system that prevents them from making mistakes and, as a result, losing face with customers. It is a 'win–win' situation and has been consciously designed to be this.

Digital is now using this participative approach for the development of a number of its expert systems. Two features of it are of interest. One, Digital recognizes that designing expert systems is a multidisciplinary activity and incorporates in its design groups people from different academic backgrounds. It also provides each group with training in the business, behavioural and technical aspects of expert systems design. Two, it associates a behavioural science research programme with the design processes, providing grants to academics to study many of the problem areas discussed in this paper.

Approaches that are narrow, technology-dominated and not backed by research run the risk of creating expert systems which are not attractive to human users. One can envisage the following, all developed at great expense.

1. The 'idiosyncratic' expert system.
   This is the system which no-one uses because they do not like its singular approach to problem solving. This kind of system appears when knowledge is derived from a single expert.
2. The 'threatening' expert system.
   This kind of system replaces experts with non-experts. It causes great resistance from experts and there is now a danger that firms will lose their human knowledge base. A chemical plant that uses an expert system to decide when an accident requires that a plant be shut down, runs a serious risk when there is no human on the staff with the knowledge to check the decision.

3. The 'catch 22' expert system.

This is an extreme example of 2. For example, the doctor who is sued by relatives because he ignores an expert system's diagnostic decision and the patient dies — or who is sued because he does what the system tells him and the patient dies.

In addition there will be the 'inaccurate' expert system, the 'irrelevant' expert system, the 'inappropriate' expert system, and many others equally disturbing.

In the future it is likely that there will be many similar expert systems competing with each other. The ones that best meet business needs, are non-threatening and acceptable to users, are easy and interesting to use and enhance the quality of working life are the ones that will sell. The function of research is to provide the knowledge which enables these kinds of systems to be built.

3. RESEARCH INTO THE EFFECTS OF EXPERT SYSTEMS

The organizational consequences of an expert system are not a set of random events or the products of a malign technology, they are the direct result of a set of inputs. Some of the most powerful of these inputs are those associated with the system design process and the decisions that are taken, or not taken, then. Therefore if we want to understand why expert systems have certain consequences we have to examine how systems are designed.

Such an examination needs to cover the philosophy and values of the designers and their sponsors, the way in which the design task has been defined, the nature of the decisions taken, including technological decisions, the skills, knowledge and interests of the project group who have responsibility for design and the processes which they use to move from problem identification to system implementation. The objective or subjective choices which a project group makes at each stage of the design process are what causes the organization to change. A different set of choices or different weightings for individual variables will result in different organizational consequences.

The problem is no longer one of technological determinism, if this has ever been the problem. If technology produces unexpected and undesirable consequences this is due to either an inability or an unwillingness to think through the relationships between inputs and outputs and to recognize the complex and varied nature of the inputs that influence the design task. If undesirable consequences are intended and expected, then this can be something more sinister — a value position which says we are trying to achieve certain technological or economic goals and all other interests will be subordinated to these.

This is the position of writers such as Braverman (1983) who argue that technology is used by capitalist management to increase productivity by reducing the intervention of the human being in the production process and exerting tighter controls over any initiative that still remains. Such a strategy leads to the deskilling of the human being and the transfer of decision taking to the machine. Other writers argue that the totalitarian nature of many of the institutions which control technology make it difficult, if not impossible, to open any real dialogue between experts and users, technocrats and parliamentarians, planners and people (Pacey, 1983).

These views seem unduly pessimistic. Braverman's derive from a marxist philosophy in which the interests of the capitalists inevitably lead them to exploit the workers. Yet the history of technology suggests that many innovations pass through a cycle in which early applications, because of their lack of sophistication, are deterministic and can deskill, while later applications become increasingly able to cope with complexity and variety, thus permitting those who work with them to tackle different tasks and use different levels of skills. The history of office automation would appear to fit this model.

The second view, which is put forward by Pacey and others, suggests that democracy is losing influence in our modern age. This view is counterbalanced by that of Salomon (1981) who sees the introduction of technology as a social process, just as open to democratic control as any other social process.

The researcher can help throw light on these ethical dilemmas through a careful documentation of what is actually happening in society.

One way in which the researcher can obtain a more accurate understanding of the effects of technology is through avoiding the study of single variables and focusing instead on the total situation — the mix of variables, including new technology, that comes together and interacts to produce certain consequences. Russell Ackoff (1979) has written,

> Managers are not confronted with problems that are independent of each other, but with dynamic situations that consist of changing problems that interact with each other. I call such situations messes . . . managers do not solve problems: they manage messes.

This emphasis on the total situation is not new. In 1927 Mary Parker Follett was saying:

> All industrial psychologists feel that Dr. Mayo has added a very valuable contribution to their work by his insistence on 'the total situation'. And we must remember that we should always mean by that not only trying to see every factor that influences the situation, but even more than that the relations of these factors to one another.

Despite this good advice many researchers are unwise enough to make forecasts of social change as a result of predicting from one variable alone, usually technology.

It is suggested that research in the future needs to be concurrent with events rather than historical, multidisciplinary rather than from the perspective of a single discipline, focused on the total situation — the technology and its social and organizational context — rather than examining the impact of one or two variables, and qualitative as well as quantitative so that it can take account of values as well as behaviour (Mumford, 1985).

Predictions about the future are always dangerous and usually incorrect but it is still useful to make them, if only to enable us to learn from our mistakes. It can be hypothesized that with expert systems the greatest impact will be on those who hold knowledge, such as doctors, lawyers, and accountants. Their roles and skills may be considerably altered. If the doctor is using an expert system to assist his diagnosis then he needs to get accurate information about the patient's symptoms and feed these into his computer but he does not need to do much more. If he is wise he will use this newly available time to counsel the patient and to offer advice and sympathy (Shallis, 1984). Donald Schon (1983) believes that these social skills are new and important competences that reflective practitioners will want to acquire.

It has also been suggested that specialist skills will be associated with those aspects of knowledge where the human expert disagrees with the computer. This is the area of new knowledge, or knowledge revision, and the computer depends on the human expert to keep it up to date (Council for Science and Society, 1981).

Research must be objective, but it can never be value-free. In the future researchers, and others, must work to ensure that expert systems act as helpful assistants, easing and speeding up the work of the human expert, providing teaching and training aids, and giving factual information. They can be of particular assistance to the poor, sick and old. In these roles they will be providing social benefits while remaining acceptable to managers, doctors, teachers, trainers and social workers.

But, like all technology, they can be used in a more threatening way. A report on new technology by the Council for Science and Society describes how the hand-mule, developed by Crompton to ease his own labour, was used, fifty years later, to eliminate the skill of the spinner. Today, CAD seems to be removing the skill of the design draughtsman and there appears to be no reason why expert systems could not be used in a similar way to remove the skills of professionals, if society and the professional groups allow this to happen (Council for Science and Society, 1981). In 1927 Mary Parker Follett told a conference 'no executive should abdicate thinking on any subject because of the expert'. The same comment is equally true today if we substitute 'expert system' for expert.

It can also be hypothesized that, in the long term, if specialist knowledge is constantly transferred into computers, the spread of this knowledge could be greatly reduced so that advances have to come from a small group whose job is enhancing expert systems. This group is unlikely to be practitioners with the result that the development of new knowledge from practical experience may become less common than it is today (Council for Science and Society, 1981).

One important feature of expert systems is that they are not being introduced on their own. They are part of a complex set of microelectronic developments which, together, can affect many aspects of work and life. Some groups will resist these developments successfully, others will not have the power to do so, others again may actively welcome them. The result could be a society more divided than it is at present (Council for Science and Society, 1981). One way of reducing undesirable consequences is to give people choice — the option to use the new technology or not, with alternatives readily available. Students who prefer human teachers to machines should have them, managers who want to take their own decisions should be able to. It is not technology that forces itself upon us but the economic philosophies of those who press its case.

The human situation ten years from now is very difficult to perceive and almost certainly the major influences will be political rather than technical. Yet technology will be a major contributor to change as it always has been. Some AI experts forecast revolutionary change. Donald Michie in a recent BBC discussion programme suggested that from 1995 to 2010 machine intelligence would outstrip human intelligence. Other AI experts are more cautious and see technical change arriving more slowly and less dramatically.

The Working Party report of the Council for Science and Society (1981) asks the question 'will the concept of work, as we know it today, still be present in twenty years?' On balance they think that it will.

The way technology develops and is used will depend on political, economic and social factors — in particular how those groups with power wish it to be used. If economic goals predominate then it will be used to increase profits and social costs may be regarded as unimportant. If social goals are strong and society is egalitarian, liberating and humanistic then it will be used for the general good, and losers and victims will be few. It is the responsibility of the researcher to assist the monitoring of consequences and to identify the nature of the stimuli that cause them. It is also the responsibility of the researcher to draw the attention of managers and politicians to consequences which are having adverse effects for particular groups in society. The researcher can provide powerful evidence even if others take the decisions.

Knowledge engineering and expert systems are still in their infancy and much technology provides a history of wrong assumptions and disappointed expectations. Computers still have their limitations. They have to be 'spoon-fed' with knowledge, and not all knowledge can be turned into a form acceptable to a computer. Communication is not just information, it includes emotion, relationships, intention and anticipation (Weizenbaum, 1976).

Two statements can be made with some confidence about the future. One is Weinberg's Law of Twins — that people do not have these very often (Weinberg and Weinberg, 1979). Most of the time things stay more or less the same. The second is that a great deal of new technology is used in ways, and for purposes, of which its inventors never dreamt. When presented with something new, society avoids the revolutionary and uses innovation to do better, or more easily, something that is old and familiar.

One challenge for the researcher interested in the development of technology is to keep our knowledge of available and possible technical options alive. Very often new technical routes are closed down by vested interests before there is an opportunity to explore their advantages for society.

4. HOW CAN WE INFLUENCE FUTURE DEVELOPMENTS?

Influence comes from power, persuasion and understanding. If we are to control the future, we need to understand what is happening now — the nature of the 'total' situation and how technology fits into this. We also need to know how to move forward and pass from one total situation to another. Advice comes from many quarters. Weizenbaum (1976) says we must ask if there are objectives that are not appropriately assignable to machines. The Working Party of the Council for Science and Society states that if we want to influence the course of economic development then we need to change the incentives which act upon individuals and organizations. Shallis (1984) suggests that,

> people should first decide what goals they seek and then choose how best to achieve those goals.

Meanwhile, the technologists continue with their research largely untroubled by the possible social consequences of what they are doing. Weizenbaum (1976) suggests that

> the artificial intelligentsia argue that there is no domain of thought over which machines cannot range . . . The proposition that judges and psychiatrists know nothing that we cannot tell computers follows from the much more general proposition subscribed to by the artificial intelligentsia, namely that there is nothing at all which humans know that cannot, at least in principle, be somehow made accessible to computers.

Shallis (1984) predicts

> the technologists will present the possibilities; society, they will argue, must choose, reject or modify these possibilities.

He believes that our concern now should be with the processes of choice.

This brings us back to the notion of participation which was discussed in the section on the design of expert systems. Mary Parker Follett, although remote in time from expert systems, gave a lecture in 1927 in which she referred to, not knowledge engineering, but organization engineering. She said,

> there are three chief problems of organization engineering: how to educate and train the members of the organization so that each can give the most he is capable of;

secondly, how to give to each the fullest opportunity for contribution; thirdly, how to unify the various contributions, that is, the problem of coordination, confessedly the crux of the business organization.

Our problems are not very different. How can we help people to develop and increase their human potential? How can we provide them with opportunities for influence and choice, recognizing that there are many interest groups in society and each wants something different from the others? How do we get people working enthusiastically together to achieve a set of commonly agreed objectives? And how can more and better research help us to achieve all of these things?

The involvement of groups of experts and users in the design of expert systems should help avoid some of the potential problems, such as deskilling or a reduction in personal control over work. People do not willingly design adverse futures for themselves. But other democratic processes are required to ensure that there is an opportunity for choice on how and where expert systems are used.

An interesting research question here is how the role of the technical systems designer will alter in the future. In the field of expert systems this is the knowledge engineer. This democratic association of experts and users in the design process is unlikely to come about without his or her agreement, interest and cooperation.

It can be suggested that one reason why serious user involvement in systems design has never become common is because the professional designer has been reluctant to change his or her role to one who teaches others how to design. Is this less likely to happen in the future? Technical specialists have also liked to think that they are 'working at the frontiers of knowledge'. Expert systems represent yet another new frontier to attack. Why should users share in the pleasure and excitement of doing this?

The answer may be that powerful groups will insist on being involved. Few medical systems have been designed without the active cooperation of doctors and this situation is unlikely to change with medical expert systems. The research problem then becomes how to assist user participation. How can experts who will be future users of a system examine their own cognitive processes, and those of their colleagues, and build these into a system that will assist them? There are many difficult questions to be answered here.

The ideas of Mary Parker Follett have been quoted several times in this paper. It must be remembered that she was also the creator of what she called 'integrated solutions'. Decisions which aim at providing benefits for all interested parties. She contrasted these with domination in which only one party gains, and compromise in which neither side gets what it wants.

The challenge for the future is to design expert systems which contribute to 'integrated solutions'. All those involved—designers, experts, users, and society—should gain from this technological breakthrough; the objective must be to have no losers. If this is our goal surely we are clever enough to make it happen.

Progress can never be separated from values, for it is our values that influence us to take one innovative route rather than another. H. G. Wells (1932) saw the future of humanity residing in what he called 'disintegrated integrity' — the ability to stand back, look at things objectively and criticize our own behaviour. These should be the particular talents of the researcher.

Here then are two powerful principles for the development of expert systems. Let us seek to achieve both integrity and integration. And let us use the objectivity and insight of good research to help us do this.

5. ETHICAL ISSUES

The question of values leads us logically to a discussion of some of the ethical issues associated with the design and introduction of expert systems. There are many of these and most are not unique to knowledge engineering but stem from our traditional approach to science and technology.

First there is the question of how we define progress, particularly technological progress. There is always a paradox about technology. It brings with it a mix of advantages and disadvantages. Vallee (1984) notes that the same technology that precipitates human crises may also be the technology that ultimately solves them.

Progress can only be defined in terms of values — as a vision of the world that we are both trying to achieve and succeeding in reaching. The problem here is that each group has its own vision. Pacey (1983) argues that there is

> a consistent tendency for experts to see only those parts which are of direct technical interest. They reduce the globe to an 'expert sphere' which they know in detail, leaving a completely different view — a 'user sphere' — which they ignore.

This may be true of academic experts locked into the specialisms of their universities. It is increasingly less true of those experts who manufacture technology. They are increasingly forced to consider user needs by the pressures of having to sell their products in a highly competitive market.

But there is often excessive optimism about the contribution that a particular technical innovation will make to progress, however this is defined, and this may be true of artificial intelligence and its offshoot, expert systems. Rozak (1976) has said,

> To claim that the computer will ever master our messy human realities — or indeed improve upon the mind's way of dealing with them is . . . a sign of the madness of our time.

Another human tendency that influences the development of technology and our view of progress is the search for simple solutions. A great deal of the rationale behind the design of expert systems is based on a desire to take the complex skill of an expert, reduce this to a set of simple formulae, and place these formulae inside a computer. Pacey (1983) suggests that political and industrial pressures, personal values and professional culture may all foster the temptation to look for a simple solution to any worrying problem, often in the form of a technical fix.

Because technology often has a certain glamour and its development is exciting we tend to view it as a commodity that is useful in its own right, and forget about the importance of its ability to meet clearly defined and expressed community needs. This can result in a number of technical solutions, developed at great expense, lying around on shelves unable to connect with real world problems. The British Viewdata communications system was an example of this in its early days.

Many of these difficulties stem from a lack of breadth of vision. An inability to see the world as a complex, untidy network of social needs and processes and a desire to define it in neat and simple terms. We all have our own visions of the world and our own notions of progress which stem from our personal experiences, objectives and ideas of what is improvement. The technologist is particularly prone to criticism in this respect because he is translating his vision of the world and its needs into a set of physical objects, many of which affect the lives of others.

Pacey (1983) suggests that the 'tunnel vision' of the technologist is not due to a lack of integrity, or even to conscious laziness, it is a result of professional commitment to his own branch of expertise. It is also influenced by a human desire for success which encourages him to focus on the most successful developments in his field. And there may also be a desire for power. 'Politicians want power over people, technologists want power over projects.'

Jacques Ellul (1980) is another 'technology watcher' who argues that the important question associated with knowledge engineering is not technical, it is ethical. He believes that what he calls 'technique' is having an increasingly strong influence on our society and is now generating its own ethics. He says:

> The reality is the insidious ethics of adaptation, which rests on the notion that since technique is a fact we should adapt ourselves to it. Consequently, anything that hinders technique ought to be eliminated, and thus adaptation itself becomes a moral criterion.
> The development of technique has thus resulted in a new morality, which has two characteristics.
>
> 1. It is behavioural (in other words, only correct practice, not intentions or motivations, counts) and
> 2. It rules out the problematics of traditional morality (the morality of ambiguity is unacceptable in the technological world).

By this Ellul means that things are now either black or white, wrong or right, there are no issues which are unclear and neither good nor bad.

Ellul believes that we must now seek an ethics which can play the traditional role of ethics, that of giving man personal control and the possibility of developing personal relationships and human society. His ethics would be those of non-power, freedom, conflict and transgression. By non-power he means that man has to choose that he will not do all that he is capable of doing. The logic of technique, in his view, demands that what can be done must be done.

By freedom he means that we must try and free ourselves from technique. He compares the danger of technique to the danger of nature for prehistoric man, something that has to be mastered and made to work in man's interest. Non-power and freedom generate conflict and conflict is itself an ethical value. Conflict implies difference and negotiation, while technique is unifying and totalizing. It leads to what Ellul (1980) calls 'the seamless society'.

By transgression he believes that we must be able to transgress the constraints imposed by technique.

> We must destroy the illusion of progress, the illusion that technique leads us from one achievement to another . . . technique, while it liberates us from one thing deprives us of something else at the same time, and that something else is usually of the spiritual order.

This is excellent philosophy but it still leaves us with the question of 'what do we do to follow it?'. We clearly need a much broader, more diverse and flexible approach to technology. One that views technology as part of a 'total' human system and is as much concerned with ends — improving the human condition — as it is with means — designing the machines.

Must we ask computer societies to develop 'ethical guides' to shape their practice? These have been around since the days of Francis Bacon but they do not seem to have exerted much influence on behaviour. Must we have more, and better, independent groups to monitor technology — such as technology consumer societies? Do we need more public awareness and discussion of technology, more pressure groups and more control over it by the public? We need all of these things.

If we follow Ellul's advice, technology, whether space science, robotics or knowledge engineering, should be kept firmly in its place. It should be useful and it should work, but it should not demand tremendous sacrifices from those who come into contact with it. The final question is, 'Are we being asked to pay too high a price?'. We are moving into a new environment which we do not understand, we need to have a clear vision and a firm set of human values if we are to survive.

ACKNOWLEDGEMENTS

The author would like to express her thanks to Gerhard Friedrich, Bruce MacDonald and Wendy Wilkerson of the Digital Equipment Corporation's Intelligent Systems Technologies Group. They have contributed many of the ideas in this chapter.

NOTES

[1] Personal communication from Professor John Anderson, Professor of Medicine, London University.
[2] Contribution by T. Capers Jones at the DSSD Users Conference, Topeka, Kansas, 1983.

REFERENCES

Ackoff, R. (1979) 'The Future of Operations Research is Past', *Journal of The Operational Research Society*, **30**, 93.
Braverman, H. (1983) *Labor and Monopoly Capital*, Monthly Review Press.
Council for Science and Society. (1981) *New Technology: Society, Employment and Skill*, CSS.
Ellul, J. (1980) 'Technique and Non-power', in *The Myths of Information: Technology and Post-industrial Culture*, K. Woodward (ed.), Routledge & Kegan Paul, London.
Feigenbaum, E. A. (1979) 'Themes and Case Studies of Knowledge Engineering', in *Expert Systems in the Microelectronic Age*, D. Michie (ed.), Edinburgh University Press, Edinburgh.
Feigenbaum, E. A. (1983) *The Fifth Generation*, Addison-Wesley, Reading, MA.
Follett, Mary (1927) 'The Psychology of Control', in *Psychological Foundations of Business Administration*, H. C. Metcalf (ed.), A. W. Shaw (now McGraw-Hill), New York.
Johnson, P. E. (1984) 'The Expert Mind: A New Challenge for the Information Scientist', in *Beyond Productivity: Information Systems Development for Organizational Effectiveness*, Th. Bemelmans (ed.), North-Holland, Amsterdam.
Michie, D. (1980) 'The Social Aspects of Artificial Intelligence', in *Microelectronics and Society*, T. Jones (ed.), Open University Press, Milton Keynes.
Microelectronics Monitor, April–September, 1984, compiled by the Technology Programme of UNIDO, PO Box 300, A-1400 Vienna, Austria.
Mumford, Enid (1979) *A Participative Approach to Computer Systems Design*, Associated Business Press.
Mumford, Enid (1981) *Values, Technology and Work*, Martinus Nijhoff.
Mumford, E. (1983) *Designing Human Systems*, Manchester Business School, Manchester.
Mumford, Enid (1985) 'From Bank Teller to Office Worker: the Pursuit of Systems Designed for People in Practice and Research, in *Proceedings of the Sixth International Conference on Information Systems*, Gallegos, Welke, Wetherbe (Eds.), December 16–18, 1985.
Nisbett, R. E. (1977) 'Telling More than We Know: Verbal Reports on Mental Processes', *Psychological Review*, **84**, 231–259.
Pacey, A. (1983) *The Culture of Technology*. Blackwell, Oxford.
Rozak, T. (1976) 'The Computer—a Little Lower than the Angels', Review of Weizenbaum's Computer Power and Human Reason in *The Nation*, 1 May.
Sackman, H. (1967) *Computers, Systems Science and Evolving Society*, Wiley, New York.
Salomon, J.-J. (1981) *Prométhée Empetré*, Pergamon, Oxford.
Schon, D. (1983) *The Reflective Practitioner*. Basic Books, New York.
Shallis, M. (1984) *The Silicon Idol*, Oxford University Press, Oxford.
Vallee, J. (1984) *The Network Revolution*, Penguin, Harmondsworth.
Weinberg, G., and Weinberg, D. (1979) *On the Design of Stable Systems*, Wiley, New York.
Weizenbaum, J. (1976) *Computer Power and Human Reason*, W. H. Freeman & Co.
Wells, H. G. (1932) *The Work, Wealth and Happiness of Mankind*, Heinemann, London.
Wilkerson, Wendy (1985) *Guide to Expert Systems Program Management*, Digital Press.

Critical Issues in Information Systems Research
Edited by R. J. Boland Jr. and R. A. Hirschheim
© *1987 John Wiley & Sons Ltd.*

Chapter 7

INFORMATION SYSTEMS STRATEGY FORMULATION

Michael J. Earl

ABSTRACT

As most large organizations seek to align IS investment with business strategy and exploit IT for strategic advantage, they are formulating IS strategies. Academics, consultants and practitioners are increasingly active in experimenting with and evaluating new strategic frameworks, strategy formulation methodologies and concepts of strategic management. This chapter surveys the current state of the art and suggests which are the more promising approaches in practice, which are the areas in need of both research and development, and what are realistic expectations in the near term.

1. INTRODUCTION

It is widely agreed that information technology (IT) is becoming a strategic resource. The convergence of data processing, communications and automation technologies, the reducing cost trends in computing and the advances in software, provide business with new strategic options in a political and economic context which both needs technological innovation and is encouraging it — a context of global competition, economic uncertainty and industry deregulation. As evidence, we see IT being exploited by firms to make spectacular strategic thrusts, becoming a driving force which is eroding and fusing boundaries within and between sectors, facilitating survival in smokestack industries and fostering new firms making a business of information. A stream of persuasive articles has emerged to make these points (Parsons, 1983; McFarlan, 1984; Benjamin *et al.*, 1984; Porter and Millar, 1985). Indeed we can generalize that IT can be applied strategically in at least four different ways:

— to gain competitive advantage;
— to improve productivity and performance;
— to enable new ways of managing and organizing;
— to develop new businesses.

One consequence of this, it is asserted (King, 1986), is that IT and information systems (IS) should no longer be considered just a support activity serving management's planning and control needs and automating business operations. They also should be harnessed to support the firm's strategy and structure

(Scott Morton and Rockart, 1984; Parsons, 1983), be managed and exploited as a potential strategic weapon (McFarlan, 1984; Porter and Millar, 1985) and even be considered as inseparable from strategy in general (Kantrow, 1980).

These perspectives therefore have led to renewed demands to plan the use of IT and information systems strategically (Earl, 1983; Lucas and Turner, 1982). Strategic planning for information systems of course is not a new idea. It has been advocated and developed for some years, as works by King (1978), McLean and Soden (1977) and others demonstrate. However, to the former rationales of ensuring top management direction, defining a hardware path and systems framework, forecasting resource requirements, allocating scarce resources effectively and controlling information processing are now added the needs to exploit the strategic opportunities afforded by IT and to align IT with business strategies. Certainly information systems strategy formulation and IT planning are priority concerns of both information systems executives and their top managements (Earl, 1983; Dickson *et al.*, 1984).

A new research area thus has arrived, potentially combining at least the bodies of knowledge about information systems, business strategy, organizational behaviour, technology management and industrial economics. Indeed, practitioners have been experimenting in information systems strategy formulation, consultants have been developing new methodologies and academics have begun to evaluate both the techniques and the outcomes. The results of these endeavours, although often preliminary and suggestive rather than robust and prescriptive, are helping to define the area, guide management policy and practice and show where further research is needed. At the same time judicious observers retain a healthy scepticism about some of the strategic outcomes of IT applications and experienced executives are concerned that some of the strategic frameworks entering information systems discourse are superficial, some of the strategy formulation techniques are jejune, some of the prescriptions too generalized and many expectations over-optimistic. Consequently there is a huge scope and need for research in this area.

This chapter therefore seeks to evaluate significant work to date and suggest ways forward. In such a fast-moving area it is important to assess ideas and developments with a view to helping practitioners make management policy choices. Equally all of us researching and experimenting in the field need to take stock, critically appraising our collective efforts in terms of practical utility, theoretical validity and knowledge development. More bluntly, it is perhaps time to differentiate reality from rhetoric and distinguish the probable from the improbable.

Analysing the current literature and drawing on my own ongoing research in the area, four sets of issues can be identified to form a topical research programme:

(1) frameworks for analysis,
(2) strategy formulation methodologies,
(3) information technology policies,
(4) strategic management.

A fifth area might be research into the effects of strategic application of IT — the *ex post* success of strategic IS developments, the impact on organizations and the wider economic, social and political consequences. Important as this work is, however, it is not directly relevant to the *formulation* of IS strategies and thus is excluded from consideration in this chapter.

2. FRAMEWORKS FOR ANALYSIS

Three sorts of frameworks are emerging, which can be labelled *awareness*, *opportunities* and *positioning*. Most of these are either descriptive and interpretative drawing on case or field studies and action research or derivative and analytical based on the more prescriptive models of business strategy. Most are 'conceptual' in that they provide maps and rubrics rather than 'practical' offering tools and techniques for detailed analysis and prescription. Consequently they are often powerful pedagogic devices and provide useful meta-models for organizational assessment.

Awareness frameworks are typified by those of Benjamin *et al.* (1984) and Parsons (1983). The former derived a 'strategic opportunities framework' to help executives determine where strategic opportunities for use of IT exist. Conflating the two parameters underpinning the axes of their matrix in Figure 1 they formulated two questions that senior executives should ask: (a) can IT be used to make a significant change in the way we are doing business in order to gain competitive advantage and (b) should we exploit IT to improve our approach to the marketplace or to improve internal operations? This framework was derived by interpreting the impact (and perhaps the initial intention) of several recent clever uses of IT

	Competitive market place	Internal operations
Significant structural change	Merrill Lynch Cash management account	Digital Equipment Corporation Expert system configuration design
Traditional products and processes	American Hospital Supply Customer order entry	United Airlines Teleconferencing in operations control

FIGURE 1 Strategic opportunities framework (Benjamin et al.)

Level of impact	Effect of IT
Industry level	Changes fundamental nature of the industry
Firm level	Influences competitive forces facing the firm
Strategy level	Supports the generic strategy of the firm

FIGURE 2 Parson's impact framework

in diverse industries, four of which are referenced in Figure 1. In my experience this model is very valuable in raising senior executive awareness of the strategic potential of IT; and when coupled with exemplar cases demonstrates how the new information technologies create new business opportunities and offer new business methods. The model is evangelical; it persuades, it whets the appetite, and may indicate by analogy *areas* where opportunities lie.

Another awareness framework developed from studying the competitive use of IT in more than a dozen companies is that of Parsons (1983). His three-level framework is intended to help senior managers assess the current and potential impact of IT on their businesses. Parsons's impact framework, which I have reduced to its bare essentials in Figure 2, in its detail is derivative of Porter's (1980) influential models of competitive strategy. It is thus potentially useful in demonstrating that exploitation of IT can and should be aligned with competitive strategy. However, the framework has practical limitations in helping companies do this. An obvious point (discussed later) is whether a competitive strategy has been formulated beforehand, especially in Porter-like terms. Then in practice the framework has to be applied not at the firm level but at the level where particular product-market strategies are formulated or where Porter's five competing industry forces are played out. Further, Porter's generic strategies of cost leadership, product differentiation or niche concentration often turn out to be too simple a statement, the reality often being a complex and changing mix of strategic positioning especially in both young and recovery businesses. So again the framework is valuable in the classroom and does provide a general rubric for examining whether 'IT is a competitive weapon in my business'. Indeed it provides a framework for checking that application of IT is being aligned with strategic need.

The pedagogic value of both these awareness frameworks arises in part from their generalization. Conversely the disadvantage is that they are not sector-specific and it is becoming commonplace for executives to pronounce that their company or sector is different and 'nobody can quote me examples relevant to us'. A further criticism is that these frameworks do not help in the detailed search and analysis that is required to discover, study and evaluate specific opportunities to apply IT for strategic advantage. This, however, is the aim of the opportunity frameworks discussed next.

Opportunities frameworks perhaps are more prescriptive than awareness frameworks. They tend to provide more detailed techniques or models for analysis and identification of strategic uses of IT. As implied above, they need to be focused on a firm's specific context and activities, generic strategy models being too abstract.

Building on Porter's (1985) more recent work on competitive advantage, Porter and Millar's (1985) frameworks typify this second generation. They offer one particularly useful tool: the analysis of a firm's value chain (Figure 3) to see where either the physical or the information processing component of IT can transform the value chain to the firm's advantage — perhaps in any of the four strategic ways indicated in my introduction. As suggested in Figure 3 a firm performs a set of distinct technological and economic activities which create value and which fall into nine generic primary and support categories. A company's value chain is a system of interdependent activities where in principle IS and IT can be exploited

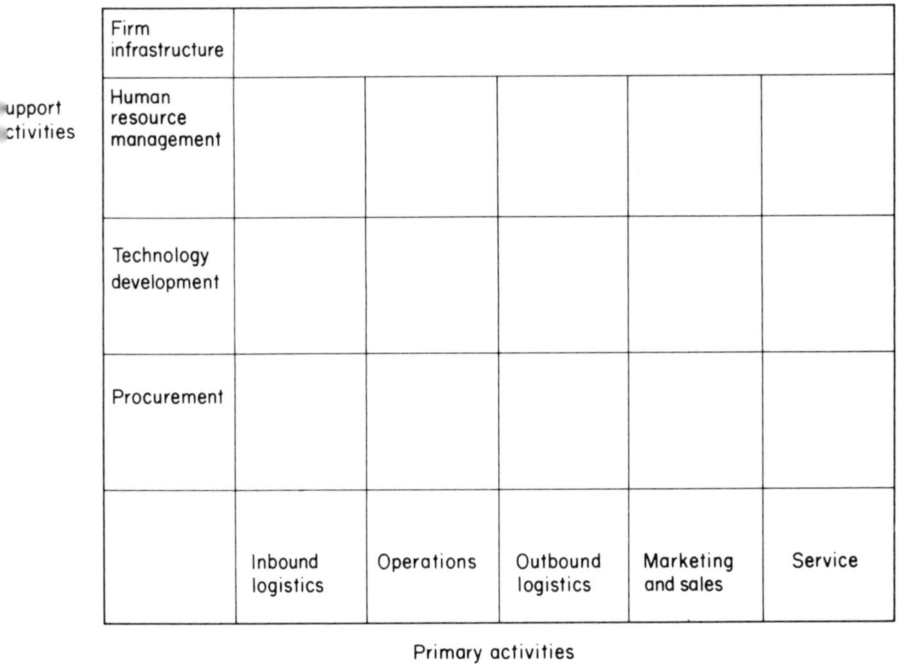

	Firm infrastructure					
Support activities	Human resource management					
	Technology development					
	Procurement					
		Inbound logistics	Operations	Outbound logistics	Marketing and sales	Service

Primary activities

FIGURE 3 IT and value chains (Porter and Millar)

to improve their execution, optimize their linkage and aid their coordination, both within the firm and between the firm and its customers and suppliers. This framework is useful for at least four reasons. First the value chain provides a structure in which, with a little 'customization', any firm's activities and functions can be analysed. Second, the linkages between value activities can be portrayed and examined to establish where application of IT can provide missing links or enhance relationships. Third, the framework encourages analysis of the wider industry value system of which the firms's value chain is a part, searching for potential exploitation of IT to reach into the firm's competitive environment. Finally, the value chain both is simple to understand and looks for strategic opportunity in operational terms.

A similar concept to the value chain is the customer resource life cycle of Ives and Learmonth (1984) who posit thirteen activities involved in nurturing, winning, maintaining and supporting a customer. When matched with an inventory of any information technology's capabilities, it provides another tool for seeking opportunities to use IT for competitive advantage. Runge (1985) has proposed such a framework for the application of telecommunications-based information systems to link up and perhaps tie in a firm's customers. Indeed more micro frameworks like this, which seek to match a particular technology with specific application areas are more likely to help line, commercial and IS managers in their search for strategic opportunities. Further examples might be models which match service and user characteristics of marketing and distribution activities with value-added network capabilities, or manufacturing operations and control characteristics with integrated computing, communication and automation possibilities or finance and accounting problem attributes with expert system capabilities. Formulation of such detailed models requires field studies at the level of applications in order to understand what makes a good fit between the technology and the application, to learn from the creativity that is being demonstrated in different sectors and to derive robust rubrics which translate across industries and yet help individual firms and their managers.

The importance of practical opportunity frameworks has been recently emphasized by Wiseman (1985). He points out that conventional information systems thinking has been heavily influenced by Anthony's (1964) planning and control systems frameworks (and, it should be added, by the decision-making models of Simon (1977) and others). Strategic uses of IT, Wiseman suggests, must be viewed from a radically different perspective and their identification be facilitated by new opportunity frameworks.

Positioning frameworks have been developed to help executives assess the strategic importance of IT for their business with a view to understanding how the information systems function should be *managed*. A well-known example is McFarlan et al.'s (1983) strategic grid (Figure 4) which, by assessing the past and future strategic impact of IT on the business, indicates one of four metaphors which suggest how information systems should be staffed, organized and planned.

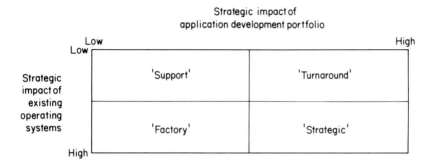

FIGURE 4 Strategic grid (McFarlan et al.)

For example, in support situations, IT budgets may be smaller, IS planning shorter-term, IS management lower-profile and IS managers lower-status than in strategic contexts. Turn-around situations may require a revolution and factory situations require consistent steady attention. Typically the assessment has to be done at divisional business unit level since strategic contexts and IS histories differ across organizations. However, there generally will be implications for both the division and the parent organization. In a sense, the grid is a tautology — 'if IT is important then so is management of IT and vice versa' — but for organizations seeking to understand what they should do in the new information age, it is no less useful for that. What the grid does not do is help uncover potential strategic applications, as opportunity frameworks seek to do, and so it must be used to guide information systems administration issues not to assess IT potential. Indeed a 'support' business could have some actual or potential strategic IT systems — and as technology advances, a firm's position in the grid could change, so that in practice the analysis should be repeated periodically.

The research issues raised are twofold. First firms do need such positioning frameworks to help them determine how to manage IT appropriately. However, the next generation of positioning frameworks should perhaps be less bland by becoming contingency-oriented, seeking to assess not only the strategic importance of IT but also factors such as organization structure, management style, dominant technology and business environment in order to give more situational management guidance. Some of these questions are addressed later (as IT policy issues), but Camillus and Lederer (1985) have offered an analogous contingent framework for the design of computer-based information systems. For example, they map alternative approaches to the management and design of information systems, as reflected in hardware configurations, IS design posture and IT policies, against the dimensions of a firm's preferred organizational structure and its adopted generic business strategy.

The second research need is for positioning frameworks that guide any firm on how to *strategically* manage IT given that firms increasingly perceive the strategic

Strategic context	Characteristic	IT strategic planning
IT is the means of delivering goods and services in the sector	Computer-based transaction systems underpin business operations	Infrastructure-led
Business strategies increasingly depend on IT for their implementation	Business and functional strategies require a major automation, information, communications capability and are made possible by these technologies	Business-driven
IT potentially provides new strategic opportunities	Specific applications or technologies are exploited for developing business and changing way of managing	Mixed

FIGURE 5 Modes of IT strategic planning

importance of IT and that the forces of an information society bring new threats and opportunities to most firms. For example, based on field studies and action research, I have developed a framework which seeks to indicate a preferred mode of IT strategic planning according to the IT strategic context in which the firm or business unit is placed (Figure 5). Organizations in sectors where goods and services are delivered or underpinned by IT need to emphasize their technology requirements in IT strategic planning. Organizations that find their business strategies increasingly depend on IT for their implementations have to identify business needs first in their IT strategic planning. In organizations where IT may provide new strategic opportunities, a mix is required of business direction, user vision and enabling technological support.

The hypothesis underpinning Figure 5 was suggested by four (probably related) findings which are relevant to the later section of this paper on strategy formulation methodologies. First, whilst many firms are experimenting with IT strategic planning, it was clear that there was no universal mechanism either emerging or in place; different contexts prompted different emphases. Second, despite claims in some articles that seemingly successful businesses had explicitly analysed their business strategy and then worked out an IT strategy to fit, certain leading firms in key sectors actually had been technologically led or had tacked along a route driven sometimes by technological opportunity and sometimes by obvious business need. Thirdly, in some cases, delivery of business needs would have been impossible without a major technological push, which, however, was made with only a general vision of the future of the business. Finally, and more recently, it became apparent that in some sectors the emphasis changes over time. In banking for example, investment in efficient and integrated technological infrastructure has been essential in order to deliver banking services and build a foundation upon which to develop new products. But today, leading banks having been content to leave much of IT strategy to the technologists are increasingly beginning to consider market opportunities and business needs as their IT strategic planning evolves.

Thus my strategy modes hypothesis is an early example of the positioning frameworks needed to identify appropriate strategic management of IT. Whilst information management lessons from the past together with strategic management paradigms can provide a base from which to derive these frameworks, the new era of IT poses new issues and added complexity. IT *is* 'different' — organizations are still learning, the technology changes rapidly, and much of the effort and resource required is complex and not readily visible. At the same time many of the available business strategy models seem to relate to a world which real organizations do not inhabit and to be conceived at a level which offers little guidance for information management.

With a workable set of awareness, opportunity and positioning models, we would be creating for managers a three-level complementary set of frameworks for analysis to show what is possible, help identify applications and guide how to get there. As suggested in Figure 6, each type of framework has a different purpose, scope and use. Awareness frameworks now need to be realistic for executives in sectors where exemplars so far have not been developed and reported. Opportunity frameworks need to be more application- and technology-specific. Positioning frameworks need to be more contingency-based.

3. STRATEGY FORMULATION METHODOLOGIES

It is commonly asserted that the opportunities created by IT exceed its effective utilization or management's ability to assimilate it. Indeed Parsons (1983) sees this 'strategic gap' as critical in the 1980s. The awareness, opportunity and positioning frameworks discussed above have of course been developed to help

Frameworks / Quality	Awareness	Opportunities	Positioning
Purpose	Vision	Ends	Means
Scope	Possibility	Probability	Capability
Use	Education	Analysis	Implementation

FIGURE 6 Frameworks for analysis

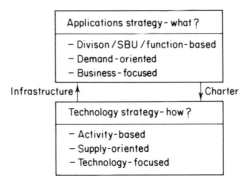

FIGURE 7   Information systems strategies delineated

remedy this gap. However, within organizations both senior management and information systems executives are searching for IT strategy formulation methodologies which provide a more substantive and ongoing procedure both for directing the application of IT and for gaining strategic advantage from it.

However, the concepts, discourse and practice of IT strategy formulation tend to be confused. There are several reasons for this. The terminology of strategy and planning in general is often loose. Top managers tend to be concerned as much about the spending and activity of the IS function as about the potential impact and use of IT. And, of course, we are still learning how to plan IT strategically. I find that the delineation of IT management issues depicted in Figure 7 helps executives resolve the confusion and provides a distinction which is useful in research. It distinguishes between information systems (applications) strategy and information technology (delivery) strategy.

Once this delineation is understood it is surprising how often it is admitted that general managers with inadequate experience and qualifications have been addressing the technology strategy and IT executives who cannot know all about business needs have been driving the applications strategy. Even more commonly, steering committees seem quite confused about which of these levels of strategy is their concern. In research, the distinction, although not always explicit, is usually clearer with much recent work concerned about applications while earlier work often focused on technology.

As implied by the connecting lines, however, the two levels are not entirely separable — applications needs suggest the charter for IT and the technology posture provides the infrastructure which underpins applications. Indeed Lucas and Turner (1982) contend that 'effective control of information processing (much of which can be achieved through technology strategy)' is a necessary prerequisite to the integration of technology with strategy (applications strategy). However, we do seem to have two areas of research often requiring different paradigms and methods. In this section the demand side, or applications level, is addressed; the next section on IT policies is concerned with the supply side.

The type of strategy formulation methodology sought by organizations in their desire to introduce a strategic orientation to IS planning is one which explicitly aligns IT investment with business needs and goals. A typical methodology is the 'critical success factors' approach as proposed by Bullen and Rockart (1984) and practised by many consultants. In short, it is a structured, sequential procedure aimed at identifying business goals, agreeing on those few tasks activities and processes (critical success factors) needed to achieve the goal-set and deriving the IS applications required to achieve or support the critical success factors. Rockart (1979) earlier proposed the technique as a means of identifying chief executive officer information needs and clearly the concept is potentially transferable into other areas. The three obvious research questions arising from this—and similar methods—are: does it work, when does it work, how do you make it work?

Answers to all three sets of questions are beginning to appear, mainly from case study and action research projects at this stage (Boynton and Zmud, 1984; Shank, Boynton and Zmud, 1985; Rockart and Crescenzi, 1984), and these largely equate with my own unstructured observations. For instance, it seems that in view of the conceptual level of the critical success factors approach, it is better suited to top-level IS planning than detailed information requirements analysis. Indeed my own field evidence suggests that the method is effective in identifying business goals and critical tasks and processes and in suggesting where IS and IT may have most potential, but is less helpful in pinpointing or prescribing either actual IS applications or their detailed requirements. However, most observers report that the method facilitates dialogue between IS managers and senior executives, helps in direction-setting and defining priorities, provides a structure which is top-down, is intuitively understood by user and line managers and is business-driven. To these claims I would add that the method is not too complex and time-consuming to apply, allows business goals and strategy to be explored without seeming to be challenging or openly setting strategy, and can be repeated as conditions change.

When does it work is less clear. Sullivan (1985) advocates it in diffused organizations (those which are decentralized and/or served by distributed technology) where infusion of IT (the impact, importance and strategic significance of IT) is not too high. My own experience is that it works best where there is an available business strategy or where strategic analyses have been done beforehand but that it also provides a start-up methodology for organizations where strategic thinking needs to be done for the first time or anew.

Making the method work reportedly is dependent on factors such as precision of the formal method, senior management understanding of the business, senior management champions, education of the staff analysts, focusing on concrete needs and applications, breadth and depth of analysis and interviews and back-up by events to examine alternative requirements and IS development tools to produce

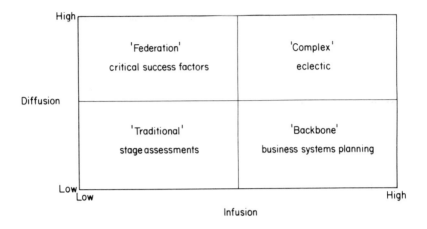

FIGURE 8

early solutions. McLean (1983) concluded in a study comparing the 'critical success factors' methodology with methods such as IBM's Business Systems Planning that either approach could work in different situations with appropriate supporting factors. But practitioners do need to know how to choose; hence the importance of 'when' and 'how' research. McLean did suggest that each approach was effective in appropriately skilled hands. Certainly understanding what skills and attributes are needed for IT strategy formulation is an important practical research need.

Another angle on how to choose appropriate strategy formulation methodologies would be the contingency paradigm. Sullivan (1985) postulates four schools of planning according to his measures of diffusion and infusion (Figure 8) defined above. Here the detailed business, data and structural analysis of IBM's Business Systems Planning is seen to fit 'backbone' environments which are a contingent opposite to 'federation' environments where the Critical Success Factors method is held to be appropriate. A third school suggested is the derivatives and variants of Gibson and Nolan's (1974) 'Stages Theory'. These stage assessments of applications, technology, management and users are thought to fit contexts low on both diffusion and infusion. Certainly Sullivan's 'eclectic' category — where the firm develops its own approach to fit its unique needs — is plausible for those advanced organizations that have a complex structure and depend on IT. However, my own investigations, while sympathetic with Sullivan's view that different approaches may be required in different situations over time, suggest a more complex picture shown in the 'three-legged model' of Figure 9.

My model implies that three approaches to information systems strategy formulation are required in parallel for all organizations, although one particular approach may be dominant in some situations and at some times. I will present this model because it raises another set of research questions.

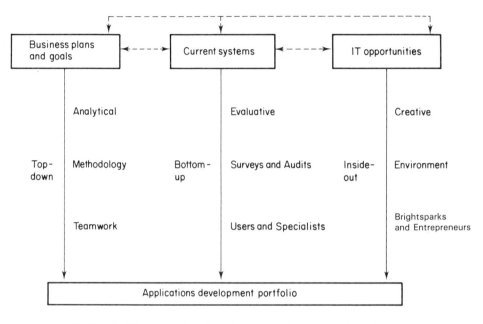

FIGURE 9 IT strategic planning: a multiple methodology

For most organizations then, it is not suggested that no one methodology is likely to fit all their current needs or always be the preferred approach. However, there is usually the desire and need for a formal attempt to match IS investment with business need. Leg one of my model suggests this: identification of business plans and goals followed by deduction of IS/IT needs using an analytical approach with a formal methodology such as Critical Success Factors and involving general, line and IS management. The methodology must cope with business strategies that are ill-defined or not easily interpreted in IS terms, or indeed cope with situations where no formal strategy is to be found. It has to be easily understood and used by line and general managers and give clear directions (but not specifications) of IS needs. Apart from the research questions posed in discussing the example of methodology of Critical Success Factors, development of other methodologies to fit this leg might be aided by action research.

The second leg recognizes the need to understand applications in place. This is for at least four reasons: top management often do not know the state of the art, some current systems will be either outdated or under-exploited, strategic advantage often can be built out of, or suggested by, existing systems and anyway we have to develop from where we are, not from where we would like to be or from 'a greenfield site'. Thus evaluative methods are appropriate here where both users and technologists judge the business and technical quality and potential of current systems.

Simple audit techniques or more elaborate Stages Surveys fit this leg. However, they could be improved by research on appraisal techniques, on measuring systems performance and quality and on the organizational politics that surround such audits. We know enough from management accounting and control research to suggest that such 'audit' activity is more complex than it seems. For example, methodological problems abound, such as how to relate cause and effect or the selection of criteria for evaluation or from which or whose stance to audit. Sociopolitical issues arise, not least the tendency for most actors to justify or defend decisions, actions and outcomes after the event. Psychological problems exist, such as the stresses created around audits and the role behaviours of the actors involved.

The third leg specifically addresses opportunities afforded by IT. This is much more creative and seems to need investigative studies (judging from some firms who have made spectacular IT-based strategic strikes) or awareness and creativity events (judging from educational and interventionist experience) plus an environment which stimulates innovation. Recent work by Runge (1985) emphasized just how important informal IS planning processes, product champions and entrepreneurial attitude and involvement are in enabling innovative use of IT. The research questions thus become obvious — what conditions are required to foster innovation through IT — organizational, technological, managerial and environmental — and how can these be created and managed alongside the equally necessary but more conventional IS planning, organization and control procedures. This set of issues is further examined below. Such is the processual nature of the questions, however, that longitudinal studies will be important in this work and 'change process' as well as 'factors approach' research strategies (using Benbasat's (1984) taxonomy of research methods) will be required.

This model, so far, like many others has concentrated on factors internal to the organization. Increasingly as IT becomes a competitive weapon, creates networks and changes sectors and their competitive forces, an external orientation is also required. I have begun to attempt this within my three-legged model by incorporating opportunities and threats analyses into leg one, strengths and weakness analyses of external stakeholders into leg two and exemplars and future studies into leg three. Two research needs immediately arise. There is remarkably little practical guidance available on competitor and environment analysis from an IS perspective. Second, there is a need to develop our ability in futures and scenario construction.

To return to the general argument, however, my three-legged model suggests that a multiple methodology is necessary for IT strategy formulation. It seeks to combine top-down, bottom-up and 'inside-out' approaches because strategy formulation is much more complex than any one technique can handle, requires inputs from organizational processes as well as structured techniques, and has to cope with ever-changing external demands, internal capabilities, management histories and technological possibilities. Figure 10 further postulates how different legs of the model may be emphasized in different strategic contexts — building

IT strategy mode	Emphasis in strategy formulation
Infrastructure-led	Bottom-up / Leg 2
Business-led	Top-down / Leg 1
Mixed	Inside-out / Leg 3

FIGURE 10 Strategy modes and methods

on Figure 9. In sectors where IT has become the principal means of delivering goods and services, it becomes essential to evaluate the firm's (and its competitors') current and potential systems investment and infrastructure as a guide to action. In firms where business strategies increasingly depend on IT for their implementation, it becomes imperative to identify business strategies first and derive IS needs second in order to guide IT investment. In firms seeking new strategic opportunities, but not obviously driven by, or dependent on, IT the inside out approach needs to be emphasized in order to create a facilitative environment for exploitation of, and innovation through, IT. This further development of my multiple methodology model thus suggests that the general contingency argument of Sullivan (1985) is worth developing and that detailed situational analyses of IT strategy formulation mechanisms, such as Pyburn's (1983) association of IS planning style to environmental, organizational and technological factors, should be fruitful. It also suggests that concepts of strategic management should be pursued — as argued later.

4. INFORMATION TECHNOLOGY POLICIES

Technology strategy as depicted in Figure 7 is concerned with the 'supply side' and thus comprises both technological issues such as infrastructure plans and policies and administrative issues such as the organization's preferred methods of staffing, controlling and organizing IS resources. The first set of issues in this new age of IT remains relatively unexplored at the policy level, probably because we are still working out the options, understanding the technologies and unsure when an inherently technological question becomes a policy issue. On the other hand there are puzzles facing IT executives and nostrums clung to by anxious chief executives which deserve some attention. Three examples may illustrate the need for, and nature of, the research questions which arise.

A recurring issue is hardware and vendor policy. I have heard IT directors variously and persuasively argue that dealing with one major supplier leads to better long-term relations and mutual understanding, that a two-supplier policy protects service levels and keeps pressure on prices and that a multi-vendor policy is inevitable in a multiple technology world. What is the empirical evidence on this question and are normative statements possible? Likewise, it is often stated that technology strategy involves making judgements about the technological future, taking technological risks and making trade-offs between, on the one hand, early adoption, technological leaps or leading edge postures and, on the other hand, waiting for cost reductions, advancing incrementally or following risk-averse paths. Do we have other than anecdotal evidence on these policy questions and are we developing practical approaches to technological forecasting in the IT industry? Then there is the question of infrastructure or architecture, comprising conflicts such as architecting a vision versus building to an applications-led plan, choosing between proprietary and open architectures and whether to rein in new technologies or encourage variety and experimentation.

These three sets of technology policy issues may be too big and multivariate for conventional research. Their shape may be changing too rapidly owing to technological change and they may need deeper technological knowledge than many of us possess. Nevertheless, they contain questions which practitioners frequently face and often ask.

Administrative issues are concerned with what often is referred to as 'managing IS as a business within a business'. Much of our body of knowledge has been influenced by the work at the Harvard Business School on the management of DP from the late 1960s onwards. However, as IT becomes strategic and the technologies multiply, the management policy questions become yet more complicated — and more crucial. As Lucas and Turner (1982) pronounce, senior management who lack confidence in their organization's ability to manage information processing will not want to risk the future of the firm on a strategy that depends on IS. Therefore continued research on the management control, organization and staffing of IS is important in general but can contribute to resolving contemporary policy questions such as funding the IS function, approving IS projects, charging out the new technologies (such as telecommunications or information centres), running steering committees, managing major IT projects and coordinating responsibilities for multiple technologies. In firms where IT is seen as a strategic resource resolving these questions could make a difference between innovative and radical exploitation and ordinary and incremental application.

For example, claims have been made that leading firms in many sectors invest more in IT than their competitors (Kearney, 1984) while others such as Strassman (1985) would challenge the assertion. This is clearly an empirical question in its own right, but in more managerial terms do firms perceive and decide IT expenditure as investment or managed cost or discretionary cost or what? And do they, or should they, treat IS proposals as any other capital project and accept all seemingly profitable projects, as finance theory might suggest, or should they vary their appraisal methods (and funding provisions) according to the strategic nature of the project as some firms are beginning to attempt?

If we wish to stimulate innovative projects and create an enabling environment in the spirit of leg three of Figure 9 should we introduce free or discounted tariffs for telecommunications usage. Alternatively, as one major bank which is adopting a low-cost information processing strategy has done, do we apply flat tariffs on a full charge-out basis to limit total costs? If we want to encourage exploitation of IT for competitive advantage, is it important that the management control system protects line managers' 'bottom-lines' from the initial investment costs, as might be suggested by innovation research; or are organizational solutions more effective in supporting innovation, such as placing product champions in key areas, as might be deduced from research into decision support systems by Curley and Gremillion (1983).

Then there are organizational matters. For example, while steering committees seem to yield applications strategy benefits of top management direction and support, better IS planning and user/DP understanding, they seem to contribute little to questions of technology strategy such as computing capacity, vendor policy or DP performance measurement (Drury, 1984). So are other mechanisms required to steer IT where it is perceived to be strategic? And as businesses work out new mission statements for IS and specify charters to delineate responsibility for various technologies are we sure that such formal organizational approaches are effective in promoting strategic change through IT? The chances are that we have to design organizations in the information age with processes as well as structures in mind and encourage and accept more informality than has been implied in latter-day administrative recipes for the DP era. Furthermore the concept of the IS function as a business within a business has its limits, for strategic information processing cannot be managed entirely as a functional specialism and in isolation of the business and its environment at large. We need to develop richer concepts of strategic management of IT.

5. STRATEGIC MANAGEMENT

The notion, and need for, 'strategic management' can perhaps be best developed through seven propositions. First, *if* a firm does perceive IT as a strategic issue, strategy becomes much more than a set of strategy formulation techniques. As argued by McCosh *et al.* (1978), four complementary strategic management tasks are essential — giving strategic direction, creating a strategic culture, designing a strategic organization and developing strategic managers. The remaining six propositions indicate what kind of research programme may be needed to advance our thinking along these lines.

If IT is perceived by a firm to be strategic, it can no longer be managed as a support or service activity and thought of as a specialist activity. Its profile and management will be elevated in the organization (Earl, 1983) but also IT will have to become an integral part of the firm's planning, control and operations. Inevitably responsibility for identification, analysis, development and implementation of strategic information systems will have to be distributed to all commercial and operational areas of the organization. In turn information management may well become more concerned with coordinating activities, ensuring cross-functional linkages, planning infrastructure and developing and assisting executives in exploiting IT, much as suggested by Porter and Millar (1985).

If IT is to be a mechanism for creating competitive advantage, then the external focus, product/service development characteristics and marketing orientation of the resultant information systems will be more reminiscent of industrial innovations than of traditional computer applications (Runge, 1985). Accordingly, tidy-minded internal structures and mechanistic environmental scanning techniques will rarely promote innovative uses of IT. It is more likely that firms will need to learn how to breed and husband 'fanatics' and 'entrepreneurs' (Quinn, 1985). They will have to avoid the rigours of structures and systems (Peters and Waterman, 1982). They may need to think of customers and other competitive actors as potential aides in innovation (von Hippel, 1982). Overall, they may have to design their organizations more as 'organized anarchies' (Cohen *et al.*, 1972).

If a firm operates in a sector whose infrastructure is founded on IT, finds its business strategies dependent on IT or again sees IT providing new tools and weapons, information management will be concerned with managing strategic change. Quinn (1980) see three major patterns in those firms who are successful at this. Awareness and commitment must be created, a task which is concerned not only with education, motivation and control, but also is likely to require political astuteness and management of the sort proposed by Pfeffer (1981) and others. Progress is liable to be made incrementally—continuously, constantly and gradually building understanding, working out viable routes and pulling people together. Indeed integration of processes and interests is thirdly required because substantive strategies form through fermentation, rather than analysis, and their implementation has to be worked at and over time becomes inseparable from formulation.

If a firm's business is technology-based or it is making a business of information by providing information and information-processing services, it probably requires some of the management practices found in successful 'hi-tech companies'. Maidique and Hayes (1984) conclude that this requires business focus, adaptability, organizational cohesion, entrepreneurial culture, sense of integrity and 'hands-on' top management. This picture is similar to that suggested by the previous propositions and hallmarked by periodic shifts between chaos and continuity.

If IT is agreed to be strategic, affecting the firm's future and requiring consideration of environmental matters as well as internal functioning, both IT executives and line and general managers need to interact with and manage their environments. For instance, in today's IT world, IT executives must understand, influence and work with policy makers in government, PTTs, supplier industries and the like. Commercial managers must understand, influence and work with actors in their competitive environments to maximize IT opportunities and minimize IT threats. External IT forces no longer can be considered uncontrollable.

If the above six propositions are generally true then managements have much to learn. Indeed organizational learning seems to be a prerequisite for technological change (Argyris and Schon, 1978) and the stages theory of computer management was founded on premises about how organizations learn (Gibson and Nolan, 1974); yet Argyris (1977) has shown that *organizations* do not learn easily. In the particular field of IT planning, I have found that it takes four to five years to produce acceptable strategic plans (Earl, 1986) and that the early benefits are mainly educational and motivational. Meanwhile, at the individual level, the innovative, creative, entrepreneurial and political attributes of strategic management may be as much born as made.

The implications of these strategic management propositions are similar for both research and practice in information systems strategy formulation. It should be clear that the centralized, functional and structural leanings of traditional information systems management frameworks and paradigms are inappropriate. More flexible, business-oriented, organizationally focused and eclectic approaches and perspectives are required. Like many of the studies cited here, much of the research will need to be multidisciplinary, if not interdisciplinary, and research strategies must include interpretative casework, longitudinal investigations and change process studies. Like the organizational learning required for strategic management, this may take some time.

6. CONCLUSION

The twin desires to exploit IT for strategic advantage and to give strategic direction to IS are pushing most large organizations into formulation of information systems strategies. The four areas discussed present a rich menu of information management issues and a varied programme for research.

First, promising frameworks for analysis are being developed and three overriding research needs stand out:

(1) More awareness frameworks are needed at the level of specific sectors. These may be inductively derived from case examples and/or deductively or 'inspirationally' derived where economic analysis or strategic vision may have to come first.

(2) Opportunities frameworks need to be both application/activity specific and technology specific. Deductive models can be derived from business analysis techniques, inductive models suggested from field studies and all such

frameworks further validated by monitoring and evaluating outcomes (see below).
(3) Positioning frameworks to identify appropriate management of IS resources could benefit from a contingency orientation. This requires more cross-sectional fieldwork as well as continuing development of normative theories of information management.

Then both IT strategy formulation methodologies and IT policies are under constant development and review. Again three issues have been identified:

(1) A contingency theory is required in order to prescribe which methodologies are effective in what situations and over time.
(2) Techniques embodied in the various methodologies need both further development and more rigorous appraisal. Examples include 'top-down' analytical planning tools, 'bottom-up' evaluative techniques, 'inside-out' processes and 'external' surveys and studies.
(3) Technology and administrative policies need continuous examination as IT advances and organizational learning proceeds. How to formulate policies is one set of questions; the effectiveness of alternative policies is another.

All these research questions need both longitudinal work to unravel the organizational and management complexities and plot the effects of time and cross-sectional work to compare experiences, identify contingent factors and generalize.

The concepts of strategic management of IT present a more complex set of propositions and challenges. Different in theme and assumptions from much conventional work on information management, strategic management research is needed to identify new questions as much as to seek immediate answers. Two forms of work should help:

(1) Organizational studies, often multidisciplinary or interdisciplinary in nature, at the organizational level to plot or enquire how strategies actually evolve and strategic initiatives are identified and pursued.
(2) Scholarship on, and replication of, previous research done in similar areas such as the management of technology and innovation.

This chapter deliberately focused on strategy formulation and not strategic impact. However, research on the organizational, sectoral and societal impacts of 'strategic' applications of IT should provide feedback on the appropriateness of frameworks for analysis, the effectiveness of strategy formulation methodologies and IT policies and the requisites of strategic management.

Finally, most of this research programme is managerial in both flavour and intent. Accordingly we need to encourage research and development not only by academics, but also by consultants and practitioners. Indeed they have built much of the foundation of this new research area. There still remains much to be done.

REFERENCES

Anthony, R. N. (1964) 'Planning and Control Systems: A Framework for Analysis', Harvard Business School, Division of Research.

Argyris, C. (1977) 'Organisational Learning and Management Information Systems', *Accounting, Organisations and Society*, **2**, 2.

Argyris, C., and Schon, D. A. (1978) *Organisational Learning: A Theory of Action Perspective*, Addison-Wesley, Reading, MA.

Benbasat, I. (1984) 'An Analysis of Research Methodologies', in *The Information Systems Research Challenge*, F. W. McFarlan (Ed.), Harvard Business School Press, Boston, MA.

Benjamin, R. I., Rockart, J. F., Scott Morton, M. S., and Wyman, J. (1984) 'Information Technology: A Strategic Opportunity', *Sloan Management Review*, Spring.

Boynton, A. C., and Zmud, R. W. (1984) 'An Assessment of Critical Success Factors', *Sloan Management Review*, Summer.

Bullen, C. V., and Rockart, J. F. (1984) 'A Primer on Critical Success Factors', CISR Working Paper No. 69, Sloan School of Management, MIT, June.

Camillus, J. C., and Lederer, A. L. (1985) 'Corporate Strategy and the Design of Computerised Information Systems', *Sloan Management Review*, Spring.

Cohen, M. D., March, J. G., and Olsen, J. B. (1972) 'A Garbage Can Model of Organisational Choice', *Administrative Science Quarterly*, March.

Curley, K., and Gremillion, L. (1983) 'The Role of the Champion in DSS Implementation', *Information and Management* (6).

Dickson, G. W., Leitheiser, R. L., and Wetherbe, J. C. (1984) 'Key Information Systems Issues for the 1980s', *MIS Quarterly*, September.

Drury, D. H. (1984) 'An Evaluation of Data Processing Steering Committees', *MIS Quarterly*, December.

Earl, M. J. (1983) 'Emerging Trends in the Management of New Information Technologies', in *The Management Implications of New Information Technologies*, N. Piercy (Ed.), Croom Helm.

Earl, M. J. (1986) 'Formulating Information Technology Strategies', in *Managing New Information Technology*, N. Piercy (Ed.), Croom Helm.

Gibson, C. F., and Nolan, R. L. (1974) 'Managing the Four Stages of EDP Growth', *Harvard Business Review*, January–February.

Ives, B., and Learmonth, G. (1984) 'The Information System as a Competitive Weapon', *Communications of the ACM*, December.

Kantrow, A. M. (1980) 'The Strategy–Technology Connection', *Harvard Business Review*, July–August.

Kearney, M. C. (1984) 'The Barriers and the Opportunities of Information Technology — A Management Perspective', Institute for Administrative Management and Department of Trade and Industry, London.

King, W. R. (1978) 'Strategic Planning for MIS', *MIS Quarterly*, March.

King, W. R. (1986) 'Developing Strategic Business Advantage from Information Technology', in *Management Information Systems: The Technology Challenge*, N. Piercy (Ed.), Croom Helm.

Lucas, H. C., and Turner, J. A. (1982), 'A Corporate Strategy for the Control of Information Processing', *Sloan Management Review*, Spring.

McCosh, A. M., Rahman, M., and Earl, M. J. (1978) *Developing Managerial Information Systems*, Macmillan.

McFarlan, F. W. (1984) 'Information Technology Changes the Way You Compete', *Harvard Business Review*, May–June.

McFarlan, F. W., McKenney, J. L., and Pyburn, P. (1983) 'The Information Archipelago — Plotting a Course', *Harvard Business Review*, January–February.
McLean, E. R. (1983) 'Strategic Planning for MIS: An Update', Information Systems Working Paper 4–83, Graduate School of Management, UCLA.
McLean, E. R., and Soden, J. V. (1977) *Strategic Planning for MIS*, John Wiley.
Maidique, M. A., and Hayes, R. H. (1984) 'The Art of High Technology Management', *Sloan Management Review*.
Parsons, G. L. (1983) 'Information Technology: A New Competitive Weapon', *Sloan Management Review*, Fall.
Peters, T. J., and Waterman, R. H. Jr. (1982) *In Search of Excellence*, Harper & Row.
Pfeffer, J. (1981) *Power in Organisations*, Pitman, London.
Porter, M. E. (1980) *Competitive Strategy*, The Free Press, New York.
Porter, M. E. (1985) *Competitive Advantage*, The Free Press, New York.
Porter, M. E., and Millar, V. E. (1985) 'How Information Gives You Competitive Advantage', *Harvard Business Review*, July–August.
Pyburn, P. J. (1983) 'Linking the MIS Plan with Corporate Strategy: An Exploratory Study', *MIS Quarterly*, June.
Quinn, J. B. (1980) *Strategies for Change: Logical Incrementalism*, Dow Jones-Irwin.
Quinn, J. B. (1985) 'Managing Innovation: Controlled Chaos', *Sloan Management Review*, May–June.
Rockart, J. F. (1979) 'Chief Executives Define Their Own Data Needs', *Harvard Business Review*, March–April.
Rockart, J. F., and Crescenzi, A. D. (1984) 'Engaging Top Management in Information Technology', *Sloan Management Review*, Summer.
Runge, D. (1985) 'Using Telecommunications for Competitive Advantage', Unpublished D.Phil. thesis, University of Oxford.
Scott Morton, M. S., and Rockart, J. F. (1984) 'Implications of Changes in Information Technology for Corporate Strategy', *Interfaces*, **14**, i, January–February.
Shank, M. E., Boynton, A. C., and Zmud, R. W. (1985) 'Critical Success Factor Analysis as a Methodology for MIS Planning', *MIS Quarterly*, June.
Simon, H. A. (1977) *The New Science of Management Decision*, Prentice-Hall, Englewood Cliffs, NJ.
Strassman, P. A. (1985) *Information Payoff: The Transformation of Work in the Electronic Age*, The Free Press, New York.
Sullivan, C. H. Jr. (1985) 'Systems Planning in the Information Age', *Sloan Management Review*, Winter.
Von Hippel, E. (1982) 'Get New Products from Customers', *Harvard Business Review*, March–April.
Wiseman, C. (1985) *Strategy and Computers*, Dow Jones-Irwin.

Part II

A focus on the organizational and social context of information systems

Critical Issues in Information Systems Research
Edited by R. J. Boland Jr. and R. A. Hirschheim
©1987 John Wiley & Sons Ltd.

Chapter 8

INFORMATION SYSTEMS IN ORGANIZATION THEORY: A REVIEW

E. Burton Swanson

ABSTRACT

Although modern organizations have over the last two decades undergone a revolution in the adoption and application of computer-based information technology, information systems are not as yet a principal subject of study by organization theorists. In support of the search for an understanding of information systems within organization theory, existing literature is reviewed here in terms of a typology of basic research questions associated with information system use. Specific deficiencies in our present knowledge of information systems in organization theory are thereby identified, enabling a number of suggestions to be made for adjusting the current research agenda.

1. INTRODUCTION

In the view of one observer of information systems research:

> While most other areas of management knowledge have been very critically re-examined, the question of computer impact has led a charmed existence. Despite the billions of dollars we spend annually on new computer systems, we have little systematic information about how computers actually 'work' in organizations. (Robey, 1981, p. 679)

Robey's remark provides the point of departure for the present chapter, the broad purpose of which is to review and organize what is known about how computer-based information systems 'work' in organizations, and to suggest likely new directions for adding to this body of knowledge.

A principal motivation for the chapter is the informal observation that relatively few researchers are presently attending to this basic question. As seen here, two classes of researchers have a stake in the answer: management information systems (MIS) researchers, and organization theorists. Neither group has made the answering of this question a central focus of its concerns, although a small number of individual researchers of varying disciplinary persuasion have done so. One is inclined to ask why.

In the case of MIS research, the difficulty may be illustrated by focusing briefly upon two problems which have, in contrast, attracted substantial interest: the problem of information requirements determination, and the problem of measuring information system success.

Both problems are taken very seriously, by MIS practitioners and researchers alike. From the practical point of view, it is easy to see why. Builders of information systems confront the issues necessarily, both in professional principle, and in practice. On the one hand, the determination of information requirements is the acknowledged first step in embarking on a building program. On the other, establishing information system success provides the justification for a building program just concluded. The two problems thus bracket all system development work, from beginning to end.

Ah, if only we (MIS researchers) possessed the solution keys to these two puzzles, all else might be easy. But we don't, of course, and it's not.

The difficulty is this: the keys are not ours to possess as such, from the vantage point at which we most frequently work. They presume the existence of answers to the more fundamental questions of how computers actually do and should work in organizations. Thus seen, any determination of information requirements must be based upon the organizational use to which the information is to be put. Similarly, the success of any information system must be measured in terms of what it accomplishes in the organization.

The keys thus lie in the organizational realm, beyond the conventional confines of system development methodology. And the implication, therefore, is that most MIS research is too narrowly focused at present to answer its own basic questions.

It is natural to turn to organization theory for assistance. (Here the term 'organization theory' will be used in the broad sense to cover such diverse areas as organizational behavior, organizational design and development, and management strategy and policy.) Alas, when one does so, the initial impression is likely to be one of disappointment. Although information systems are organizational phenomena, they are not as yet a principal subject of research by organization theorists. Further, with few exceptions, information systems are ignored as a major variable in organization design.

In the meantime (over the last two decades) modern organizations have undergone a revolution in the adoption and application of information technology. From the viewpoint of organization theory, how should this revolution be understood? Is there not a research agenda here somewhere? With the gnawing feeling that the answer to the second question is 'yes', the present chapter faces up to the first question.

The chapter proceeds in the section which follows by reframing the issue of how information systems work in organizations in terms of a typology of basic research questions. This typology is then employed in a selective review of the literature, divided among three succeeding sections. A conclusions section completes the chapter.

2. BASIC RESEARCH QUESTIONS

The typology of basic research questions shown in Table 1 was developed, so that the research on information systems in organization theory could be classified and related. The typology features two dimensions: unit of analysis and explanatory focus. It was felt that much of the research literature in organization theory could be 'carved naturally' along these two characteristic features. However, it should be noted that both features, and thus the domain carved, are associated with conventional research methodology, rather than with the subject matter itself. Specifically, unit of analysis is fundamental to research methods based in sampling and inferences to populations. Explanatory focus is fundamental in turn to all forms of causal modeling and analysis.

TABLE 1 A typology of research questions

Unit of analysis	Explanatory focus	
	Determinants	Effects
The individual	What are the determinants of an individual's information (system) use?	What are the effects of an individual's information (system) use?
The organization	What are the determinants of an organization's information (system) use?	What are the effects of an organization's information (system) use?
The market	What are the determinants of a market's information (system) use?	What are the effects of a market's information (system) use?

In the case of unit of analysis, it was recognized that much of the literature may be divided between that which employs the organization as the basic analytic unit, on the one hand, and that which employs the individual participant as the basic unit, on the other (Pfeffer, 1982). In addition, recent interest in the market as an alternative to the hierarchical organization (Williamson, 1975), suggests the inclusion of market as a third unit of analysis along the first dimension.

In the case of explanatory focus, it was decided to distinguish between research which identifies determinants of information (system) use, and research which identifies the effects of information (system) use. That is, it was decided to classify the research according to whether information (system) use was the dependent or the independent (or mediating) variable of interest.

The typology thus presents a three by two matrix of six basic research questions, all of which address information (system) use. In this context, the parenthetical inclusion of 'system' is in acknowledgement of the fact that the literature includes substantial research which addresses information use which is not system-based, as well as that which is system-based. In organization theory, there exists, in fact, more of the former than the latter. Thus, while it is the latter which is of principal interest, the former should in theory be closely related, and is incorporated in the review for this reason.

In summary, it will be assumed that the basic research questions are mutually exclusive and exhaustive of those needed for our examination of information system use in the context of organization theory. The worthiness of this simplifying assumption will rest entirely on the insights generated by the review. Several cautionary notes are in order before proceeding, however.

First, it is noted briefly that the inclusion of the market as a unit of analysis is in lieu of other alternatives, e.g. the organization population (Hannan and Freeman, 1977), which also involve more than the single organization, and might provide different perspectives. The selection of the market as the analytic unit in the present circumstance may thus mask these other perspectives.

Second, because the typology of questions is based in conventional research methodology, as indicated above, it should be understood that the review framework lends itself in particular to research typically employing such methods, i.e. research in which organizational action is viewed as purposive and rational, or externally constrained and controlled, rather than dependent largely on process and social construction (Pfeffer, 1982). Thus, the review may be shaped more by literature associated with systems rationalist perspectives than by that associated with segmented institutionalist perspectives (Kling, 1980).

Further, the appropriateness of conventional research methodology itself necessarily remains open to question. This issue will be taken up again briefly in the concluding section. (See too, Mumford *et al.*, (1985) and Markus and Robey (1985).)

Finally, the review framework offers only a means for the juxtaposition of research around the basic questions posed. As such, it poses a challenge and provides direction for theory builders; it builds no theory itself, however.

The discussion which thus follows will be in three parts, along the unit of analysis dimension of the typology. The nature of the discussion will vary sharply between these parts, however, given the particular focus of the present review, as well as the nature and extent of the available literature.

Of primary interest will be the organizational unit of analysis, the second of the three to be discussed. This unit corresponds precisely to the principal focus of present interest, viz. organization theory. For this reason, specific determinants and effects of organizational use of information (systems) are enumerated and considered in some detail.

In contrast, the discussion of the individual unit of analysis, which immediately follows this section below, will be abbreviated, and will serve largely to position the subsequent discussion. For more extended consideration of determinants and effects within this section, the reader will be referred instead to a number of substantial reviews of this extensive literature.

The discussion of the market unit of analysis will also be comparatively short, largely because of the relative paucity of reviewable work in this area.

Given the scope of the issues addressed, references will be heavily employed throughout, to point the reader to sources of more in-depth discussion.

3. INDIVIDUAL DETERMINANTS AND EFFECTS

What are the determinants of the individual's information system use? This question has motivated substantial MIS research to date, much of which is characterized as 'implementation theory'. Illustrative work includes Swanson (1974), Lucas (1978), and Schultz *et al.* (1984). (For a comprehensive review of the implementation literature, see Kwon and Zmud, Chapter 10 in this volume.)

From this MIS research, constructs such as user involvement in system development (Swanson, 1974; Ives and Olson, 1984) and user psychological type and cognitive style (Mason and Mitroff, 1973; Huber, 1983) have been introduced into the MIS literature. Among the other suggested determinants of an individual's system use are: management support, user knowledge, system characteristics, job characteristics, and goal congruence. (Schultz *et al.* (1984) present an integrated model.)

What are the effects of an individual's information system use? In principle, the individual's job performance should here be a focus of MIS research attention. Unfortunately, perhaps because of the difficulties of addressing this effect directly in the field, researchers have tended to focus instead on surrogates, and, in particular, on individual 'user satisfaction' with the system (Bailey and Pearson, 1983; Ives *et al.*, 1983).

Comparatively few MIS researchers have studied other effects of individual information system use. Exceptions include Mumford (1971), whose work has long been concerned with system impacts upon job satisfaction, Kling (1978), who has surveyed the impacts of computer use on several job characteristics, and Argyris (1971), who has described the 'challenge to rationality and emotionality' posed by systems to the individual management user.

In contrast to MIS research, organization theory has focused for the most part on individual information use which is not system-based. Of central concern have been two issues: the generation and exchange of information among organizational participants, and the use of information in individual decision making.

The generation and exchange of information among organizational participants constitutes the subject of the field of organizational communication within organization theory. Historically, the concept of 'organizational communication' has not been well articulated by researchers in this field (Porter and Roberts, 1976). However, it is generally understood to be 'the exchange of information between a sender and a receiver and the inference of meaning between organizational participants' (O'Reilly and Pondy, 1980, p. 121). Thus, from this viewpoint, the individual is seen as participating in an organizational network, made up of interpersonal information exchanges among members.

While the context of this research is therefore fundamentally organizational, much of its work has been based nonetheless on the individual as a unit of analysis. (An exception is a number of studies comparing the communication efficiencies of alternative configurations of small group.) For substantial reviews, the reader is referred to Guetzkow (1965), Porter and Roberts (1976), O'Reilly and Pondy (1980), and Huber (1982).

Perhaps the most important contribution of the literature in organizational communication has been its articulation of the individual communication role. Here a number of useful theoretical constructs have been introduced. Examples include: gatekeeper (Allen and Cohen, 1969; Pettigrew, 1972); boundary-spanner (Tushman, 1977; Tushman and Scanlan, 1981); liaison (see, for example, Galbraith, 1973); and participant and isolate (Roberts and O'Reilly, 1979). Such roles are generally regarded as relatively stable within a communication network, thereby conditioning the information access use of each individual member.

Social-psychological constructs such as status, credibility, trust, influence, and mobility aspirations (Roberts and O'Reilly, 1974) are further typically related as other determinants of performance in the communication role.

Organization theorists have also focused extensively on the 'bounded rationality' of the individual decision maker (March and Simon, 1958), and on the nature of the individual's information-processing limits. As constraints of human nature, these too constitute significant determinants of individual information use. Significantly, however, in this research literature, the decision-making context receives emphasis, rather than the communication role. Information is seen as used by the individual primarily for his or her own decision-making purposes.

Given this context, the effect of information upon decision making has also formed a natural focus of study. In particular, the phenomenon of information overload has received considerable attention (O'Reilly, 1980). Here it should be noted too that MIS researchers have also examined the information overload issue (see Chervany and Dickson, 1974).

For a more detailed discussion of the use of information in individual decision making, the reader is referred to Ungson *et al.* (1981) who present a review of the research in terms of three descriptive approaches (1) model-fitting, whereby correlational, regression, or functional models are used to explain the various ways in which information is integrated, weighted, or traded-off by a decision-maker; (2) process-tracing, in which the protocols, or procedural aspects of the individual's information processing are characterized and (3) theories of decision-making style, which propose certain characteristic patterns, or typologies of information processing, to explain general variation among individuals. For a useful review which integrates this literature within an organizational context, the reader is referred further to O'Reilly (1983).

A thorough review of the literature on individual determinants and effects of information (system) use is beyond the scope of this chapter. From our cursory overview we may nevertheless draw several conclusions.

First, there exists little linkage between studies of individual information system use and studies of individual information use which is not system-based. This is apparently due to strong differences in conceptual focus among the research schools. On the one hand, the MIS is the center of interest; on the other, it is communication among individuals, or individual decision making. In each case, the researcher tends to circumscribe his or her own study such that individual information use is understood in an exclusive context. The individual is seen as using a MIS, or as communicating with others, or as making decisions. The individual is not seen as engaged in all these activities, and in allocating his or her attention among them. (Mintzberg's well-known research provides a model of the type of study too infrequently conducted. See Mintzberg, 1973.)

Given this problem of conceptual focus, it is noted that the emergence of new office system technology, which aims specifically for the integration of traditional interpersonal communication and computer-based information processing, offers particularly suitable contexts within which to establish needed linkages (see, for example, Bikson, *et al.* (1985)).

Second, there has been relatively more attention paid to determinants than to effects of individual information use, by both MIS and organization theory researchers. This may be in part because the importance of individual information use tends to be taken somewhat for granted by both groups of researchers. But whatever the reason, an unfortunate result is that we can say comparatively little about the variety of circumstances and ways in which individual information use is itself consequential for the individual and the organization.

Finally, among the effects of individual information use, there has perhaps been undue attention given to individual decision making, as opposed to individual action and behavior in the organizational role. Indeed, decision making seems often to be taken as an end in itself, with the result that little insight is obtained into impacts of both decisions and information upon the organization.

Renewed interest in the phenomenon of uncertainty absorption (March and Simon, 1958), whereby inferences drawn by a decision maker from a body of evidence are communicated without this same evidence to others within the organization, .with the consequence that judgements as to the validity of these inferences are made problematic, might therefore be a useful means of correcting the current imbalance of research emphasis. (See also Swanson (1978) and Wildavsky (1983).)

4. ORGANIZATIONAL DETERMINANTS AND EFFECTS

The determinants and effects of an organization's information (system) use are seen here as the most important of the basic research questions presented by the typology in Table 1, given the present focus on organization theory. These organization-level questions can be seen as bracketed by a micro-theory of individual information (system) use, as discussed in the previous section, and a macro-theory of market information (system) use, to be discussed in section 5. In principle, any organization-level theory should be formed within both of these micro- and macro-contexts.

In reviewing the literature for the present section, an attempt was made to expand upon the basic questions of the determinants and effects of an organization's information (system) use, by developing itemized lists of specific determinants and effects suggested by various authors. Results are presented in Tables 2 (determinants) and 3 (effects). Both tables feature the rationales presented by these authors for the selected determinants and effects. Where possible, opposing views are included, to highlight substantive issues both old and new.

Tables 2 and 3 thus display accumulations of assertions about an organization's information (system) use, from multiple and overlapping theoretical perspectives. Consistencies and inconsistencies among these assertions suggest those points at which these perspectives coincide or collide.

The determinants of an organization's information (system) use, as summarized in Table 2, include: environmental uncertainty, environmental instability, environmental assumptions, task uncertainty, task variety, task complexity, equivocality, core technology, organizational size, rational objectives, organizational intrusiveness, distribution of information benefits and costs, strategic representation, and symbolic commitment. The concepts associated with these determinants are not mutually exclusive; however, each receives distinctive treatment within the literature.

Among the suggested determinants of an organization's information use, the nature of the organization's environment and task receives particular emphasis within organization theory. Briefly, environmental heterogeneity and instability (Items D.1 and D.2) engender the fundamental organizational need for knowledge. How an organization meets this need, however, depends upon the assumptions made as to the analyzability of this same environment (Item D.3), and on the intrusiveness of the organization in its information searches (Item D.10). Lack of knowledge about the environment will in any event be reflected in the organization's uncertainty about its task (Item D.4). Task variety and complexity (Items D.5 and D.6) contribute further to the burden of reducing this uncertainty.

Thus, the exigencies of information processing in coping with task uncertainty may be viewed as the central problem of organization design, as proposed in particular by Galbraith (1973, 1977). Here, the role of the formal vertical information system receives explicit interpretation, viz. the provision of additional processing capacity within the hierarchy.

TABLE 2 The determinants of an organization's information (system) use

D.1 Environmental heterogeneity.

'Under conditions of relatively undifferentiated environments that are quite stable, organizations should be able to cope with the information-processing requirements without elaborate information technology. It is when the organization faces a complex and rapidly changing environment that information technology is both necessary and justified' — p. 246, Pfeffer and Leblebici, 1977.

'Diversity is a relatively enduring characteristic of an economic or political community and organizations operating within this diversity would create permanent information systems that sort environmental elements into appropriate segments' — p. 583, Leblebici and Salancik, 1981.

D.2 Environmental instability.

'The increased turbulence of post-industrial society will cause organizational information acquisition to be more continuous, and the increased complexity will cause it to be more wide-ranging' — p. 933, Huber, 1984. See also Pfeffer and Leblebici, 1977.

'High volatility will result in less formal, more variant use of information, which allows more subjective interpretations and more judgmental decision making' — p. 583, Leblebici and Salancik, 1981.

D.3 Environmental assumptions.

'Organizations characterized as conditioned viewing assume an analyzable environment and are not intrusive. . . . The viewing is conditioned in the sense that it is limited to the routine documents, reports, publications, and information systems that have grown up through the years' — p. 289, Daft and Weick, 1984. See also Daft and Macintosh, 1978, 1981.

D.4 Task uncertainty.

'The greater the uncertainty, the greater the frequency of replanning. The greater the frequency of replanning, the greater the resources, such as clerks, computer time, input–output devices required to process information about relevant factors' — p. 52, Galbraith, 1977. See also Pfeffer and Leblebeci, 1977; Tushman and Nadler, 1978.

D.5 Task variety.

'When variety is high . . . individuals are frequently confronted with unfamiliar, novel, and unexpected events. Internal representations may not cover these contingencies. Preplanning is not possible, so a greater need exists for information acquisition on an ongoing basis' — p. 211, Daft and Macintosh, 1981. See also Daft and Macintosh, 1978.

D.6 Task complexity.

See DeBrabander *et al.*, 1972; Stabell, 1976; Christensen, 1982; Culnan, 1983.

continued

TABLE 2 (continued)

D.7 Equivocality.

'Equivocality presumes a messy, unclear field. An information cue may have multiple interpretations. . . . findings suggest that when equivocality is high, organizations allow for rapid information cycles among managers, typically face-to-face, and prescribe fewer rules for interpretation' — p. 2, Daft and Lengel, 1985.

D.8 Core technology.

(In seeking to seal off core technologies from environmental influences) 'It appears that not only "adaptation" but also "absorption" and "manipulation" require increasing amounts of information processing. . . . (As) labor-intensive solutions tend to be very expensive, information technology appears to be a viable alternative' — p. 14, Christensen, 1982.

'The organization's core technology should also influence scanning activities. Boundary spanning theory suggests that staff individuals in long-linked organizations should acquire external information directly and transmit it to line employees, thereby performing a gatekeeping function' — p. 195, Culnan, 1983.

D.9 Organization size.

'At higher levels (in a hierarchy), experience suggests that large organizations make more use of formal information and control systems' — p. 166, Banbury and Nahapiet, 1979. See also DeBrabander et al., 1972; Stabell, 1976; Christensen, 1982.

D.10 Rational objectives.

'In virtually every case information systems were designed to achieve some rational organizational objectives. Normally this involved more efficient use of resources . . . or better response to environmental contingencies . . .' — p. 686, Robey, 1981.

Situational equivocality (Item D.7), closely related to uncertainty, is also proposed to play an explanatory role, in particular, in the choice among alternative information media.

The size of the organization (Item D.9) and the core technology which it employs (Item D.8), two basic demographic variables, have also received attention as likely determinants of organizational information use. The rational objectives of the organization (Item D.10) are also seen as a natural determinant of its need to know.

But an organization needs not only to inform itself; it must represent itself to others with whom it interacts. Much organizational information is thus 'two-faced' in its origins, i.e. it is intended for consumption by others, apart from the organization itself (Swanson, 1978). Among the determinants of information use in this political context, organization theorists have cited the organizational need for strategic representation and symbolic commitment (Items D.13 and D.14). The overall distribution of information benefits and costs within the organization (Item D.12) may also be understood as a determinant of information use in this same context.

TABLE 3 *The effects of an organization's information (system) use*

E.1 Departmentalization.

'. . . information technology will have substantial effects upon the pattern of departmentation in the company. The main effect should be the aggregation of previously separate information-processing activities into the computer center' — p. 48, Whisler, 1970.

(In a study of manufacturing concerns) 'Neither is there any evidence that automation of plant functions by on-site computers leads to the consolidation of departments . . . and a reduction in their number' — p. 32, Blau *et al.*, 1976.

E.2 Hierarchy.

'When a technology that displaces people is adopted, if that displacement takes place fast enough and in sufficient degree to offset organizational growth, a decrease in the number of levels in the organization should result' — p. 47, Whisler, 1970. See also Leavitt and Whisler, 1958.

'Contrary to Whisler's assumption, . . . computer use tends to increase rather than decrease the number of administrative levels in the plant hierarchy. The reason probably is that a computer system serves as an impersonal mechanism of control, which makes it less disadvantageous for top management to be separated by the workflow by many hierarchical levels' — p. 32, Blau *et al.*, 1976.

E.3 Span of control.

'It has been found . . . that the average span of control in organizations is related to the degree of centralization of control. . . . Control is increasingly centralized as a consequence of computer use. Therefore, a reduction in the average span of control . . . should take place' — p. 46, Whisler, 1970.

'Automation permits structural elaboration because impersonal control can be substituted for direct supervision, and the span of control can be widened' — pp. 684–685, Robey, 1981.

E.4 Functional differentiation.

'. . . through enhancing the managers's own information processing and handling capabilities, it permits the manager to control and coordinate more complex, differentiated organizations' — p. 247, Pfeffer and Leblebici, 1977. See also Whisler, 1970; Robey, 1981.

'We would hypothesize . . . that information technology would be positively associated with both vertical and horizontal differentiation in organizations' — pp. 247–248, Pfeffer and Leblebici, 1977.

'. . . by generally increasing the information processing capacity of positions in the organization, the implementation of information technology may make less division of labor and task specialization necessary in the organization' — p. 75, Pfeffer, 1978. See also Stabell, 1976.

continued

TABLE 3 (continued)

E.5 Centralized control.

'By permitting more information to be organized more simply and processed more rapidly it will, in effect, extend the thinking range of individuals' — p. 269, Leavitt and Whisler, 1958. See also Whisler, 1970.

'Information technology, particularly computer technology, enhances the information-processing capability of persons, leading to possible alterations in the systems of control and governance' — p. 70, Pfeffer, 1978.

'We hypothesize that information technology, through its provision of more rapid and accurate performance feedback, would be associated both with more decentralization and less formalization' — p. 248, Pfeffer and Leblebici, 1977.

E.6 Delegation of decision-making authority.

'Specifically, what will tend to occur is a relocation of human choice-making and goal-setting in the newly established decision systems to higher organizational levels than was true in precomputer systems' — p. 69, Whisler, 1970.

'Using outcome measures, less emphasis would be given to process (rules of procedure), and more decision-making authority could be delegated to subordinates' — p. 248, Pfeffer and Leblebici, 1977.

'. . . what appears to be greater decentralization may simply entail the delegation of more routine decisions whose outcomes are more closely controlled' — p. 681, Robey, 1981. See also Robey, 1977.

E.7 Evaluation.

'Those things that are measured tend to be used, particularly if they are easy to process, and those that are not measured are not used in the evaluation process' — p. 81, Pfeffer, 1978.

'It is difficult to develop forms or computer systems that assess the process by which a job is done. Conversely, outcome measures can be implemented using information technology, and indeed, information technology facilitates the collection of a multitude of outcome measures, and their comparison and summarization' — p. 76, Pfeffer, 1978.

'It is hypothesized that information technology is associated positively with the use of formal written reports and detailed statistics, and is inversely related to the use of oral evaluations of performance' — p. 248, Pfeffer and Leblebici, 1977.

E.8 Formalization.

'Information technology enhances the possibility of monitoring compliance with procedures and rules . . . At the same time, however, because of the ability to obtain rapid feedback on organizational performance, the implementation of rules and procedures is less necessary' — p. 77, Pfeffer, 1978. See also Pfeffer and Leblebici, 1977.

continued

TABLE 3 (continued)

E.8 Formalization (*continued*)

'By allowing easy and timely linking to a broad set of individuals with common referrent bases, terminal-oriented communication seems to facilitate an organic style of organization; and if the task/environment so demands it facilitates a good fit' — p. 17, McKenney, 1985.

'. . . post-industrial technologies will cause decision processes to be more formalized. . . . advanced communication devices will increase the accessibility of any source of information, formal or informal. Since the attractiveness of informal sources is largely a function of their ready accessibility, the proportion of information that is formally acquired and processed will increase' — p. 936, Huber, 1984.

E.9 Power.

'While there are reasons to expect a CIS to centralize organizational control, instances of no change outweigh the incidence of change in this research. . . . Where CIS does not produce changes in structure, it reinforces existing structure' — p. 684, Robey, 1981. See also Kling, 1980; Kling and Scacchi, 1980; Danziger *et al.*, 1982.

'The computer, because of its importance in assessing and controlling organizational performance, is likely to increase the centrality of any subunit where it is housed' — pp. 82–83, Pfeffer, 1978. See also Bariff and Galbraith, 1978.

'. . . control is not a simple zero-sum relationship and . . . various groups may experience enhanced power and decision-making opportunities after computerization' — p. 1189, Attewell and Rule, 1984. See also Bjorn-Andersen and Pedersen, 1977; Markus, 1983, 1984.

'. . . in terms of effective organizational control, or in terms of the distribution of influence within the organization, the most likely outcome is an increased concentration of power' — p. 73, Pfeffer, 1978.

E.10 Lateral relations.

'Common computer-based techniques . . . are frequently used to coordinate lateral activities in organizations' — p. 684, Robey, 1981. See also Malone and Smith, 1984.

E.11 Stability and Rigidity.

It is more difficult to change computerized decision systems, because it is more expensive. Also, change is less likely to occur, because fewer people have a real grasp of the logic involved in these systems' — p. 89, Whisler, 1970.

continued

TABLE 3 (continued)

E.11 Stability and Rigidity (continued)

(From MIS) . . . 'organizations seem to have the capacity to learn primarily those lessons that are self-sealing because they maintain the status quo' — p. 117, Argyris, 1977.

'They filter away conflicts, ambiguities, overlaps, uncertainty, etc. and suppress many relevant change signals and kill initiatives to act on early warnings' — p. 47, Hedberg and Jonsson, 1978. See also Starbuck, 1975; Hedberg et al., 1976; Dery, 1981.

'(A) possibility is that the coordination mechanisms actually used inside large firms will come to resemble the structure of a decentralized market more than that of a rigid hierarchy. For example, the widespread use of electronic mail, computer conferencing, and electronic bulletin boards can facilitate what some observers have called ''adhocracies'' that is, rapidly changing organizations with many shifting project teams composed of people with different skills and knowledge' — p. 26, Malone and Smith, 1984.

E.12 Job Routinization.

'One major effect of information technology is likely to be intensive programming of many jobs now held by middle managers and the concomitant ''deprogramming'' of others' — p. 270, Leavitt and Whisler, 1958.

'On balance, clerical jobs have become more routinized' — p. 141; 'As the wave of change moves on, the pattern of change in supervisory jobs should eventually approximate that at the clerical level' — p. 132, Whisler, 1970.

'With the advent of computers, middle managers spent more time on such functions as communication, interpretation, and counsel. . . . Repetitious, routine aspects of their jobs disappeared' — p. 281, Hunt and Newell, 1971.

'Surveys of workers' perceptions of the new technology generally contradict the deskilling/job degradation thesis' — p. 1187, Attewell and Rule, 1984.

E.13 Institutionalization.

'. . . technologies are institutionalized and become myths binding on organizations. Technical procedures of production, accounting, personnel selection, or data processing become taken-for-granted means to accomplish organizational ends. Quite apart from their possible efficiency, such institutionalized techniques establish an organization as appropriate, rational, and modern. Their use displays responsibility and avoids claims of negligence' — p. 344, Meyer and Rowan, 1977, quoted in Pfeffer, 1982, p. 247.

E.14 Competitive Advantage.

'In any company, information technology has a powerful effect on competitive advantage in either cost of differentiation' — p. 156, Porter and Millar, 1985.

In summary, the proposed determinants of organizational information (system) use may be roughly classified into three general groups. The first group focuses on the organizational need to know about its environment and its task; the second group is based on the organization's need to influence; the third group includes demographic variables which interact with variables in the first two groups.

We consider next the effects of an organization's information (system) use. These are summarized in Table 3, and include effects associated with: departmentalization, hierarchy, span of control, functional differentiation, centralized control, delegation of decision-making authority, evaluation, formalization, power, lateral relations, stability and rigidity, job routinization, institutionalization, and competitive advantage. As with the determinants discussed above, the concepts associated with these effects are not mutually exclusive; however, each receives distinctive treatment within the literature.

From Table 3, it is seen that, in contrast to the literature associated with the determinants of information system use, the literature associated with hypothesized effects presents a rather confused picture. Much of this confusion surrounds the early work of Leavitt and Whisler (1958), as amplified by Whisler (1970). Here, the long-term effects of modern information technology are foreseen: the aggregation of departments engaged in information processing activities, a flattening of the management hierarchy, a reduction in the average span of control, increased functional differentiation, a tendency toward centralization, and less delegation of decision-making authority (Items E.1 through E.6). In each case, other organization theorists have drawn opposite conclusions, however, as illustrated, and the disentangling of competing rationales is seen to be problematic.

Information technology is further seen as leading to an increased use of outcome-oriented measures in the organizational evaluation process (Item E.7). Its implications for overall formalization (Item E.8) are mixed, however. While monitoring is facilitated within the hierarchy, the need for formal rules and procedures may be lessened. And, lateral relations (Item E.10) may be strengthened by information technology, both formally and informally.

Leavitt and Whisler also saw information technology as leading to the routinization of jobs (Item E.12) at the lower and middle levels of the organizational hierarchy. Here again, other researchers have not come to the same conclusion. There has been mixed support, too, for the argument that computerization may be associated with increased organization stability, and, dysfunctionally, rigidity (Item E.11).

Implications of information systems for the power structure of the organization (Item E.9) have also been drawn. It has been variously suggested that these systems enhance the power of the subunits that possess them, that power tends to be more concentrated, and that existing structure of whatever form tends to reinforced. Clearly, however, such consequences do not follow in general in tandem.

Institutionalization (Item E.13) is also an effect to be expected from information systems penetration of the organization. Here, information systems practices become a taken-for-granted aspect of organizational life. Unfortunately, there have as yet been few information systems studies of this type. (However, Zucker (1984) proposes such a study of micro-computing adoption.)

Lastly, information technology has most recently been asserted to have important implications for an organization's competitive advantage (Item E.14). These implications will be discussed further in the section to follow.

In summary, the effects of information systems upon the organization are as yet poorly understood. Early attempts to explicate these effects appear in retrospect to constitute more of a technological forecast, than a theoretical statement within which the role of information systems is consistently articulated. Subsequent work has identified problems with the rationale behind this forecast. However, constructive theoretical progress has been minimal.

5. MARKET DETERMINANTS AND EFFECTS

In general, the sharing of information among individuals and organizations engaged in a market transaction will be understood to constitute use of information in a market context, i.e. market use of information. A general discussion of this phenomenon in terms of economic theory is beyond the scope of this review. However, the market use of information systems in particular is deserving of discussion.

For present purposes, shared use of an information system by two or more organizations or individuals engaged in a market transaction will be understood to constitute market use of the system. As will be discussed below, the information system used may belong to one or more of the parties to the transaction. Or, it may belong to a different party altogether.

While use of information systems in a market context has received little systematic study to date, it is a current subject of substantial interest, and a promising area for significant future research.

Much of this current interest comes from MIS practitioners and researchers who are focusing on the use of an information system as a 'competitive weapon'. (See, for example, McFarlan, et al., 1983; Parsons, 1983; McFarlan, 1984; Ives and Learmonth, 1984; Cash and Konsynski, 1985; Beath and Ives, 1986.) This work has been inspired in large part by the more general theory of Porter (1980, 1985), who has himself spoken directly to the role of information technology in competitive strategy (Porter and Millar, 1985).

Porter argues that advances in information technology produce opportunities for competitive advantage across all industries, with substantial implications for changes in industry structure and the rules of competition, in addition to the spawning of new businesses. The argument is constructed upon the concept that all business activities and products have information as well as physical components, and that current opportunities to exploit the information components in support of product differentiation and cost minimization strategies are of particular significance. Among these opportunities are those in which the organization encourages usage of one of its information systems by certain of its customers or suppliers, sometimes thereby increasing the 'switching costs' for those with whom it does business.

Information systems shared by two or more enterprises in this fashion constitute one type of 'inter-organizational information system', of which there exist increasingly numerous examples (Barrett and Konsynski, 1982; Cash and Konsynski, 1985). Adopting Porter's point of view, these systems have arisen in substantial part in pursuit of competitive advantage, which may accordingly be seen from the perspective of this paper as one determinant of information system use in a market context.

What are the corresponding effects of such use of inter-organizational information systems? Here, we ask a question which is largely unexplored, beyond the implications suggested by Porter.

Transaction cost theory (Williamson, 1975; Ouchi, 1980; Williamson and Ouchi, 1981) might suggest that many inter-organizational systems built by organizations as 'competitive weapons' constitute transaction-specific human-capital investments in support of the development of idiosyncratic exchanges which, while constituting market exchanges in form, develop into bureaucratic, or even clan-assisted exchanges in significant substance. The effect, in other words, is the development of 'intermediate governance mechanisms', apart from the pure market, bureaucracy, and clan forms. (Barney and Ouchi, 1983, suggest a number of these intermediate mechanisms.)

Thus, use of an information system in a market context, as defined above, is not to be equated with use of an information system in a free market's interest. Where built as competitive weapons, the design and use of inter-organizational systems may, in fact, involve the creation of significant market entry and exit barriers (Cash and Konsynski, 1985).

Transaction cost theory is thus promising for the study of the use of information systems in a market context. To date, however, with the exception of Ciborra (1984, 1985), who proposes that the functions of computer-based information systems in general be reframed in terms of 'exchange support systems', and Beath (1983), who has applied the transaction cost model to MIS project management, there has been little application of the theory to an understanding of information systems in organizations. Treacy (1985) has, however, recently proposed that transaction cost theory be applied to the study of the effects of information technology on industry boundaries.

Apart from inter-organizational systems owned by one or more of the parties to a market transaction, independent organizational systems also exist for the expressed purpose of facilitating specific types of marketplace transactions. These systems are owned and employed by a third party who provides information services to one or the other of the first two parties, or to both. Inter-organizational systems of this type constitute information enterprises, in basic support of market, rather than hierarchical transactions. Their distinctive feature is the creation of a secondary market in the transaction-related information itself. The potential value of this information apparently lies in the increased efficiencies to be obtained in the primary transaction market. Examples have been offered by Lee (1986), who further describes alternative technologies for these enterprises, including videotex, database retrieval, and knowledge engineering.

Thus, marketplace inefficiencies based in imperfect information among participants may in general be viewed as giving rise to opportunities for information enterprises. And, for this reason, such inefficiencies may also be considered among the determinants of a market's information system use (by means of an information enterprise). Similarly, efficiencies in these same markets are in principle the consequential effect of the successful information enterprise.

With these informal remarks, we have of course merely scratched the surface of the subject of inter-organizational systems and the market use of information systems. For this reason, caution in drawing conclusions is clearly warranted. We venture several such conclusions, nonetheless.

We conclude first of all that the use of information systems in organizations may not be understandable in general in the absence of studies which examine usage in a market context. In other words, among the significant determinants and effects of information system use in organizations are those which are best understood at the market level of analysis.

In our view, inter-organizational information systems may differ fundamentally from those that are local to a single organization. Because they incorporate market transactions, these systems should probably be studied in part by analyses which transcend the conventional organizational unit. Research which focuses in a more limited way on the 'competitive weapons' of single organizations may, in fact, tend to produce 'half-truths', given that other market participants are ignored.

It is admittedly not wholly clear how inter-organizational systems should most profitably be studied. The unit of analysis itself no doubt requires refinement beyond the present informal definition. However, transaction cost theory is seen here as providing a useful point of reference and departure.

6. CONCLUSION

We return to the question which motivated the present chapter. Given that modern organizations have undergone (and continue to undergo) a revolution in the adoption and application of computer-based information technology, how should this revolution be understood, from the viewpoint of organization theory?

In seeking an answer to this question, we have reviewed the existing literature associated with information systems in organization theory, in the context of identifying the determinants and effects of information system use at the individual, organizational, and market levels of analysis. Though our review has necessarily been more selective than it has been exhaustive, given the scope of our inquiry, we may conclude nonetheless that existing theory is in general both underdeveloped and badly fragmented, and poorly suited to answering the question raised.

In reviewing the literature associated with the determinants and effects of individual information use, we have found little linkage between studies of individual use of interpersonal sources. We have also found more attention paid to determinants than to effects, and, where attention is given to effects, an undue concentration on individual decision making for its own sake as opposed to individual action and behavior in an organizational context.

With respect to the literature associated with the determinants and effects of organizational information system use, we have found a reasonably well articulated contingency theory in which a number of likely determinants are identified based on the organizational need to know. This theory fails to incorporate other determinants based on the organizational need to influence, however. Further, with regard to effects, theory has as yet provided little predictive or explanatory power, and the general picture is one of substantial confusion and contradiction.

A nascent literature associated with market use of information systems was seen to hold substantial promise for future development. However, the current focus on inter-organizational systems as 'competitive weapons' is viewed to be too narrow for the theory needed.

In conclusion, we must ask too whether conventional research approaches are adequate to the theoretical synthesis needed. Individual studies theoretically and methodologically contained within single cells of our typology may in particular be too impoverished for the task at hand. What may be needed instead are studies imbedded in more general theoretical contexts, which absorb the research artifacts, viz. causal precedence attributions and levels of analysis, with which we routinely work. In present terms, this suggests that determinants of information system use must be integrated with effects, and that individual, organizational, and market contexts be jointly incorporated within individual research studies.

How might these more general contexts be devised? In the case of determinants and effects, we might heed Weick's observation that 'Most managers get into trouble because they forget to think in circles. . . . Managerial problems persist because managers continue to believe that there are such things as unilateral causation, independent and dependent variables, origins, and terminations' (Weick, 1979, p. 86). So too do our research problems persist, it might be added. Weick recommends instead the construction of causal maps containing feedback loops in which stability among relationships may be understood. In this way, the separate, arbitrary identities of determinants and effects may be dissolved, and a more comprehensive understanding reached.

Sensitivity to historical context in the development, persistence, and dissolution of such stable relationships among information systems and organizational variables is similarly needed. In the absence of such sensitivity, which may be cultivated by means of studies which focus explicitly on unique situational context, our understanding of stable relationships must necessarily be a shallow one. Research approaches such as that of Kling and Scacchi (1982), who propose a 'web model' of study in which situational context is thickly described, are therefore particularly welcome.

In the case of individual, organizational, and markets contexts, we might focus further on including variables from at least two of these levels in our causal maps. Thus, for example, we might model individual information system use so as to be explainable in part in terms of organizational level differences. Similarly, we might model organizational information use so as to be explainable in part in terms of differences in market context.

Finally, we might carry our causal maps to practice, and seek to understand too those maps of practitioners, whose interpretations are constructed fundamentally out of their necessary enactments. (See, for example, Boland, 1985). In these and other ways, we might therefore build useful bridges among our various work.

ACKNOWLEDGEMENTS

The comments and suggestions of Cynthia Beath, Richard Boland, Mary Culnan, Rob Kling, James McKenney, and Lynne Markus contributed substantially to the development of this chapter, and are gratefully acknowledged.

REFERENCES

Allen, T. J., and Cohen, S. I. (1969) 'Information Flow in Research and Development Laboratories', *Administrative Science Quarterly*, **14**, 12–20.

Argyris, C. (1971) 'Management Information Systems: The Challenge to Rationality and Emotionality', *Management Science*, **17**, 6, B-275–292.

Argyris, C. (1977) 'Organizational Learning and Management Information Systems', *Accounting, Organizations and Society*, **2**, 2, 113–123.

Attewell, P., and Rule, J. (1984) 'Computing and Organizations: What We Know and What We Don't Know', *Communications of the ACM*, **27**, 12, 1184–1192.

Bailey, J. E., and Pearson, S. W. (1983) 'Development of a Tool for Measuring and Analyzing Computer User Satisfaction', *Management Science*, **29**, 5, 530–545.

Banbury, J., and Nahapiet, J. E. (1979) 'Towards a Framework for the Study of the Antecedents and Consequences of Information Systems in Organizations', *Accounting, Organizations and Society*, **4**, 3, 163–177.

Bariff, M. L., and Galbraith, J. R. (1978) 'Intraorganizational Power Considerations for Designing Information Systems', *Accounting, Organizations and Society*, **3**, 1, 15–27.

Barney, J. B., and Ouchi, W. G. (1983) 'Information Cost and the Organization of Transaction Governance', Unpublished working paper, November.

Barrett, S., and Konsynski, B. R. (1982) 'Inter-organizational Information Sharing Systems', *MIS Quarterly*, Special Issue, December, 93–105.

Beath, C. M. (1983) 'Strategies for Managing MIS Projects: A Transaction Cost Approach', *Proceedings of the Fourth International Conference on Information Systems*, Houston, December 15–17, 1983, pp. 133–147.

Beath, C. M., and Ives, B. (1986) 'Competitive Information Systems in Support of Pricing', *MIS Quarterly* (in press).

Bikson, T. K., Stasz, C., and Mankin, D. A. (1985) *Computer-mediated Work: Individual and Organizational Impact in One Corporate Headquarters*, The Rand Corporation, Santa Monica, California.

Bjorn-Andersen, N., and Pedersen, P. H. (1980) 'Computer-facilitated Changes in the Management Power Structure', *Accounting, Organizations and Society*, **5**, 2, 203–216.

Blau, P. M., McHugh Falbe, C., McKinley, W., and Tracy, P. (1976) 'Technology and Organization in Manufacturing', *Administrative Science Quarterly*, **21**, 1, 20–40.

Boland, R. J. (1985) 'Accounting and the Reproduction of Culture: Budgets and the Process of Structuration', Working Paper No. 1168, College of Commerce and Business Administration, University of Illinois, Urbana-Champaign.

Cash, J. I., and Konsynski, B. R. (1985) 'IS Redraws Competitive Boundaries', *Harvard Business Review*, March–April, 134–142.

Chervany, N. L., and Dickson, G. W. (1974) 'An Experimental Evaluation of Information Overload in a Production Environment', *Management Science*, **20**, 10, 1335–1344.

Christensen, G. E. (1982) 'Information Technology and Organizational Characteristics: A Review of Macro Organizational Issues', Working Paper No. A-82.002, Institute for Information Systems Research, Norwegian School of Economics and Business Administration, Bergen, Norway.

Ciborra, C. U. (1984) 'Management Information Systems: A Contractual View', in T. M. A. Bemelmans, (Ed.), *Beyond Productivity: Information Systems Development for Organizational Effectiveness*, North-Holland, Amsterdam, pp. 135–145.

Ciborra, C. U. (1985) 'Reframing the Role of Computers in Organizations: the Transaction Costs Approach', *Proceedings of the Sixth International Conference on Information Systems*, Indianapolis, December 16–18, 1985, pp. 57–69.

Culnan, M. J. (1983) 'Environmental Scanning: The Effects of Task Complexity and Source Accessibility on Information Gathering Behavior', *Decision Sciences*, **14**, 2, 194–206.

Daft, R. L., and Lengel, R. H. (1985) 'A Proposed Integration among Information Requirements, Media Richness and Organization Design', Unpublished working paper.

Daft, R. L., and Macintosh, N. B. (1978) 'A New Approach to Design and Use of Management Information', *California Management Review*, **21**, 1, 82–92.

Daft, R. L., and Macintosh, N. B (1981) 'A Tentative Exploration into the Amount and Equivocality of Information Processing in Organizational Work Units', *Administrative Science Quarterly*, **26**, 207–224.

Daft, R. L., and Weick, K. E. (1984) 'Toward a Model of Organizations as Interpretation Systems', *Academy of Management Review*, **9**, 2, 284–295.

Danziger, J. N., Dutton, W. H., Kling, R., and Kraemer, K. L. (1982) *Computers and Politics: High Technology in American Local Governments*, Columbia University Press, New York.

Davis, G. B., and Everest, G. C., (Eds.) (1976) *Readings in Management Information Systems*, McGraw-Hill, New York.

DeBrabander, B., Deschoolmeester, D., Leyder, R., and Vanlommel, E. (1972) 'The Effects of Task Volume and Complexity upon Computer Use', *Journal of Business*, **45**, 1, 56–84.

Dery, D. (1981) 'The Bureacratic Side of Computers: Memory, Evocation and Management Information', *Omega*, **9**, 1, 25–32.

Galbraith, J. (1973) *Designing Complex Organizations*, Addison-Wesley, Reading, MA.

Galbraith, J. (1977) *Organization Design*, Addison-Wesley, Reading, MA.

Grochla, E., and Szyperski, N. (Eds.) (1975) *Information Systems and Organizational Structure*, de Gruyter, New York.

Guetzkow, H. (1965) 'Communications in Organizations', in *Handbook of Organizations*, J. March (Ed.), Rand-McNally, Chicago, pp. 534–573.

Hannan, M. T., and Freeman, J. H. (1977) 'The Population Ecology of Organizations', *American Journal of Sociology*, **82**, 929–964.

Hedberg, B., and Jonsson, S. (1978) 'Designing Semi-confusing Information Systems for Organizations in Changing Environments', *Accounting, Organizations, and Society*, **3**, 1, 47–64.

Hedberg, B., Nystrom, P. C., and Starbuck, W. H. (1976) 'Camping on Seesaws: Prescriptions for a Self-designing Organization', *Administrative Science Quarterly*, **21**, 41–65.

Huber, G. P. (1982) 'Organizational Information Systems: Determinants of their Performance and Behavior', *Management Science*, **28**, 2, 135–155.

Huber, G. P. (1983) 'Cognitive Style as a Basis for MIS and DSS Designs: Much Ado about Nothing?', *Management Science*, **29**, 5, 567–579.

Huber, G. P. (1984) 'The Nature and Design of the Post-industrial Organization', *Management Science*, **30**, 8, 928–951.

Hunt, J. G., and Newell, P. F. (1971) 'Management in the 1980's Revisited', *Personnel Journal*, **50**, 35–43. Reprinted in Davis and Everest (1976).

Ives, B., and Learmonth, G. P. (1984) 'The Information System as a Competitive Weapon', *Communications of the ACM*, **27**, 12, 1193–1201.

Ives, B., and Olson, M. H., (1984) 'User Involvement and MIS Success: A Review of Research', *Management Science*, **30**, 5, 586–603.

Ives, B., Olson, M. H., and Baroudi, J. J. (1983) 'The Measurement of User Information Satisfaction', *Communications of the ACM*, **26**, 10, 785–793.

Kling, R. (1978) 'The Impacts of Computing on the Work of Managers, Data Analysts and Clerks', Unpublished working paper.

Kling, R. (1980) 'Social Analyses of Computing: Theoretical Perspectives in Recent Empirical Research', *Computing Surveys*, **12**, 1, 61–110.

Kling, R., and Scacchi, W. (1980) 'Computing as Social Action: The Social Dynamics of Computing in Complex Organizations', *Advances in Computers*, Vol. 19, Academic Press, New York, pp. 249–327.

Kling, R., and Scacchi, W. (1982) 'The Web Model of Computing: Computer Technology as Social Organization', *Advances in Computers*, Vol. 21, Academic Press, New York, pp. 1–90.

Leavitt, H., and Whisler, T. (1958) 'Managing in the 1980s' *Harvard Business Review*, **36**, 6, 41–48. Reprinted in Davis and Everest (1976).

Leblebici, H., and Salancik, G. R. (1981) 'Effects of Environmental Uncertainty on Information and Decision Processes in Banks', *Administrative Science Quarterly*, **26**, 578–596.

Lee, R. M. (1986) 'Knowledge and Communication Technologies: Application to Electronic Contracting', *Computers and Information Systems Colloquium*, Graduate School of Management, University of California, Los Angeles, February 6, 1986.

Lucas, H. C. Jr. (1978) 'Empirical Evidence for a Descriptive Model of Implementation', *MIS Quarterly*, **2**, 2, 27–52.

Malone, T. W., and Smith, S. A. (1984) 'Trade-offs in Designing Organizations: Implications for New Forms of Human Organizations and Computer Systems', Working Paper 112, Center for Information Systems Research, Sloan School of Management, Massachusetts Institute of Technology.

March, J. G., and Simon, H. A. (1958) *Organization*, Wiley, New York.

March, J. G., and Feldman, M. S. (1981) 'Information in Organizations as Signal and Symbol', *Administrative Science Quarterly*, **26**, 2, 171–186.

Markus, M. L. (1983) 'Power, Politics and MIS Implementation', *Communications of the ACM*, **26**, 6, 430–444.

Markus, M. L. (1984) *Systems in Organization: Bugs and Features*, Pitman, Marshfield, MA.

Markus, M. L., and Robey, D. (1985) 'Computers and Causality: Information Systems and Organizations', Unpublished working paper, October.

Mason, R. O., and Mitroff, I. I. (1973) 'A Program for Research on Management Information Systems', *Management Science*, **19**, 5, 475–487.

McFarlan, F. W. (1984) 'Information Technology Changes the Way You Compete', *Harvard Business Review*, May–June, 98–103.

McFarlan, F. W., McKenney, J. L., and Pyburn, P. (1983) 'The Information Archipelago: Plotting the Course', *Harvard Business Review*, **61**, 1, 145–156.

McKenney, J. L. (1985) 'The Influence of Computer Based Communication on the Organization', Unpublished working paper, Harvard Business School, February.

Meyer, J. W., and Rowan, B. (1977) 'Institutionalized Organizations: Formal Structure as Myth and Ceremony', *American Journal of Sociology*, **83**, 340–363.

Mintzberg, H. (1973) *The Nature of Managerial Work*, Harper & Row, New York.

Mumford, E. (1971) *Systems Design for People*, National Computing Centre, Manchester.

Mumford, E., Hirschheim, R., Fitzgerald, G., and Wood-Harper, A. T. (Eds.) (1985) *Research Methods in Information Systems*, North-Holland, Amsterdam.

O'Reilly, C. (1980) 'Individuals and Information Overload in Organizations: Is More Necessarily Better?', *Academy of Management Journal*, **23**, 4, 684–696.

O'Reilly, C. (1983) 'The Use of Information in Organizational Decision Making: A Model and Some Propositions', in *Research in Organizational Behavior*, Vol. 5, B. Staw and L. Cummings (Eds.), JAI Press, Greenwich, pp. 103–139.

O'Reilly, C., and Pondy, L., (1980) 'Organizational Communication', in *Organizational Behavior*, S. Kerr (Ed.), Grid, Columbus, Ohio.

Ouchi, W. G. (1980) 'Markets, Bureaucracies, and Clans', *Administrative Science Quarterly*, **25**, 129–141.

Parsons, G. L. (1983) 'Information Technology: A New Competitive Weapon', *Sloan Management Review*, **25**, 1, 3–14.

Pettigrew, A. M. (1972) 'Information Control as a Power Resource', *Sociology*, **6**, 2, 187–204.

Pfeffer, J. (1978) *Organizational Design*, AHM Publishing, Arlington Heights, IL.

Pfeffer, J. (1982) *Organizations and Organization Theory*, Pitman, Marshfield, MA.

Pfeffer, J., and Leblebici, H. (1977) 'Information Technology and Organizational Structure', *Pacific Sociological Review*, **20**, 2, 241–261.

Porter, M. E. (1980) *Competitive Strategy*, The Free Press, New York.

Porter, M. E. (1985) *Competitive Advantage*, The Free Press, New York.

Porter, M. E., and Millar, V. E. (1985) 'How Information Gives You Competitive Advantage', *Harvard Business Review*, July–August, 149–160.

Porter, L. W., and Roberts, K. (1976) 'Organizational Communication', in *Handbook of Industrial and Organizational Psychology*, M. Dunnette (Ed.), Rand-McNally, Chicago, pp. 1553–1589.

Roberts, K. H., and O'Reilly, C. A. (1974) 'Failures in Upward Communication in Organizations: Three Possible Culprits', *Academy of Management Journal*, **17**, 2, 205–215.

Roberts, K. H., and O'Reilly, C. A. (1979) 'Some Correlates of Communication Roles in Organizations', *Academy of Management Journal*, **22**, 42–57.

Robey, D. (1977) 'Computers and Management Structure: Some Empirical Findings Re-examined', *Human Relations*, **30**, 963–976.

Robey, D. (1981) 'Computer Information Systems and Organizational Structure', *Communications of the ACM*, **24**, 10, 679–687.

Schultz, R. L., Ginzberg, M. J., and Lucas, H. C. Jr. (1984) 'A Structural Model of Implementation', in *Applications of Management Science: Supplement 1: Management Science Implementation*, R. L. Schultz and M. J. Ginzberg (Eds.), JAI Press, Greenwich, Conn.

Stabell, C. B. (1976) 'The Organization as an Information Processor: A Note on the Determinants of Information Processing Capacity', Unpublished working paper, Graduate School of Business, Stanford University, August.

Starbuck, W. H. (1975) 'Information Systems for Organizations of the Future', in Grochla and Szyperski (1975, pp. 217–229).

Swanson, E. B. (1974) 'Management Information Systems: Appreciation and Involvement' *Management Science*, **21**, 178–188.

Swanson, E. B. (1978) 'The Two Faces of Organizational Information', *Accounting, Organizations and Society*, **3**, 3/4, 237–246.'

Treacy, M. E. (1985) 'Toward a Cumulative Tradition of Research on Information Technology as a Strategic Business Factor', Center for Information Systems Research, Sloan School of Management, Massachusetts Institute of Technology, April.

Tushman, M. L. (1977) 'Communication across Organizational Boundaries: Special Boundary Roles in the Innovation Process', *Administrative Science Quarterly*, **22**, 587–605.

Tushman, M. L., and Nadler, D. (1978) 'Information Processing as an Integrating Concept in Organizational Design', *Academy of Management Review*, **3**, 613–624.

Tushman, M. L., and Scanlan, T. J. (1981) 'Characteristics and External Orientations of Boundary Spanning Individuals', *Academy of Management Journal*, **24**, 1, 83–98.

Tushman, M. L., and Scanlan, T. J. (1981) 'Boundary Spanning Individuals: Their Role in Information Transfer and Their Antecedents', *Academy of Management Journal*, **24**, 2, 289–305.

Ungson, G. R., Braunstein, D. N., and Hall, P. D. (1981) 'Managerial Information Processing: A Research Review', *Administrative Science Quarterly*, **26**, 1, 116–134.

Weick, K. E. (1979) *The Social Psychology of Organizing*, 2nd Edn., Addison-Wesley, Reading, MA.

Whisler, T. (1970) *The Impact of Computers on Organizations*, Praeger, New York.

Wildavsky, A. (1983) 'Information as an Organizational Problem', *Journal of Management Studies*, **20**, 1, 29–40.

Williamson, O. E. (1975), *Markets and Hierarchies: Analyses and Antitrust Implications*, Free Press, New York.

Williamson, O. E., and Ouchi, W. G. (1981) 'The Markets and Hierarchies and Visible Hand Perspectives', in *Perspectives on Organization Design and Behavior*, A. Van de Ven and W. F. Joyce (Eds.), Wiley, New York.

Zucker, L. G. (1984) 'Micro-computing as Institution Building', *Computers and Information Systems Colloquium, Graduate School of Management, University of California, Los Angeles, May 31, 1984.*

Critical Issues in Information Systems Research
Edited by R. J. Boland Jr. and R. A. Hirschheim
©1987 John Wiley & Sons Ltd.

Chapter 9

STRATEGIES FOR RESEARCH ON INFORMATION SYSTEMS IN ORGANIZATIONS: A CRITICAL ANALYSIS OF RESEARCH PURPOSE AND TIME FRAME

Charles R. Franz and Daniel Robey

ABSTRACT

Reviews of research on information systems in their organizational context show disappointing results. This is in part because the methods most often used fail to allow for the reality of organizational process. This chapter explores the kinds of research strategies that are necessary if we are to achieve an understanding of the dynamic nature of information systems in organizations. The chapter first reviews some ways in which the models currently used in organizational research are often mis-specified because of a failure to clarify their intended purpose or their assumptions about time. It then proposes a typology of research strategies based on whether the purpose is discovery or testing, and whether the time frame is single or multiple period. Eight empirical studies are located within the typology, and evaluated to illustrate methodological strengths and weaknesses. Becoming more aware of the research strategies required by the purpose and time frame implicit in our research questions will contribute to the maturity of our field and the significance of its findings.

1. INTRODUCTION

One sign of a maturing discipline is an increase in the number of review papers and critiques of work done previously. In information systems (IS), there has always been an abundance of frameworks and conceptual models to help clarify our thinking about various issues and problems. Only recently, however, have we begun to examine critically the accumulated research findings in information systems. In most cases, the results are disappointing, especially in areas involving organizational realities (e.g. Attewell and Rule, 1984; DeSanctis, 1984; Ives and Olson, 1984; King and Kraemer, 1984; Robey and Markus, 1986; Zmud, 1979). These reviews typically call for more careful selection of research methods so that accumulated findings can answer the basic research questions posed about IS in organizations, and reduce the confusion in the IS literature.

Many of the interesting research questions about IS in organizations deal directly with processes, that is, streams of activities that occur over time. For example, change over time is presumed in all models of implementation (e.g. Schultz *et al.*, 1984), Nolan's (1982) stage model of growth in the data resource function, the organizational learning model of technology assimilation (Cash *et al.*, 1983),

Markus's (1984) model of IS impacts on organization, and Zmud's (1982) model of IS diffusion and innovation. However, the most common practice in IS research is to conduct a cross-sectional survey at a single point in time. We suspect that mixed or weak findings typically found in IS studies are caused by a failure to use appropriate methodologies for developing and testing ideas about processes. In this chapter our objective is to recommend research strategies to support the construction and testing of more valid theories about information systems in organizations.

While several research areas in IS are subject to this criticism, we choose to focus on studies of IS implementation. The implementation literature contains many studies that examine factors believed to be relevant to system success, such as the characteristics of users, MIS personnel, and organizations. Many researchers have proposed and tested hypotheses about the association of these factors with each other. However, IS implementation is not a discrete event or activity that can be studied with simple research approaches at one point in time. It is a 'package' that contains technology and people who have conflicting interests (Kling, 1980), and whose attitudes and beliefs may change over various stages of the implementation process (Ginzberg, 1981). Studies that treat implementation as a discrete event, or as a classic experimental treatment, convey an inaccurate picture about the effects of such complex phenomena in organizations.

In this chapter, we encourage researchers to consider two fundamental issues before conducting their research, namely to be explicit on both the *purpose* and *time frame* for their efforts. Purpose can emphasize *discovery* of theory, or it can be directed toward *testing* of established theoretical relationships. Time frame may be either *single* or *multiple*, depending on the nature of the phenomena being studied. With a basic research strategy in mind, investigators can then choose methods capable of meeting the needs of a growing discipline.

In our view, the IS discipline requires that greater attention be directed toward understanding processes related to information systems in organizations. Consequently, one of the aims of this chapter will be to emphasize research strategies capable of building dynamic theories of these processes.

We begin by defining what we mean by process and explaining how process research contrasts with 'factor' research. Model mis-specification is then discussed as a problem originating from inappropriate use of factor theories and static research methods to explore process issues. To clarify thinking about research strategy, we then develop a typology for describing research purpose and time frame. This typology enables us to evaluate critically the appropriateness of researchers' methodological choices based on their beliefs about the state of theoretical development of a given research area. Several previous studies, including our own, are examined in detail to demonstrate both appropriate and inappropriate methods. Our goal is to increase conscious awareness of these basic choices so that accumulated IS research in the future will contribute to more valid theories of IS implementation.

2. MIS-SPECIFICATION OF MODELS IN
IMPLEMENTATION RESEARCH FACTOR AND PROCESS

The importance of studying the *process* of implementation was initially identified by Ginzberg (1979), and Lucas (1981) further refined the distinction between factor and process studies. *Factor research* empirically examines user and situational attributes to see how they relate to the outcome (success) of system implementation (e.g. Edstrom, 1977; Lucas, 1978; Franz and Robey, 1986). *Process research* focuses on the relationship between the designer and user, and emphasizes managing the organizational change that takes place during the development of the system (Ginzberg, 1981; Robey and Markus, 1986). The distinction between factor and process research reflects the more general distinction between two goals of science discussed by Dubin (1969). Two goals of science are *understanding* and *prediction*. We *understand* when we know how and why the elements of a theory interact over time. This level of understanding requires an analysis of process. *Prediction* emphasizes a functional relationship among elements, with no explanation as to why or how the relationship occurs. In some areas of science, especially where relationships are relatively deterministic, prediction is a sufficient level of aspiration. In others, characterized more by stochastic relationships, prediction must give way to a greater emphasis placed on understanding (Sutherland, 1973; Taylor, 1971).

Research on the implementation of information technology in complex organizations apparently qualifies as an area of science seeking greater understanding through process models. Schultz and Ginzberg (1984) note that research on implementation has slackened since the mid-1970s because of the inability of models to provide insight into the implementation problem. Further progress, they state, 'will require more complex, realistic models and the development of alternative perspectives for viewing implementation' (p. xi). The proliferation of process models in the IS literature is apparently a response to past frustrations about the limitations of simpler, factor models in guiding IS research.

Process modeling demands attention to the occurrence of events over time. The basic premise is that time affects the relationships among variables and that the value of any given variable changes over time. Many IS researchers appear uncertain about how to conduct empirical research using such process models and continue to rely upon methods more appropriate to factor research or prediction. There is, however, considerable objection to developing and testing process models with static research paradigms (Monge *et al*, 1984; Miller and Friesen, 1982; Heller *et al.*, 1977). Research that tests process models should be longitudinal and use analytical methods capable of increasing our understanding of the social dynamics involved in systems implementation. Using factor research methods to explore or test process issues results in the serious problem of model mis-specification.

3. MIS-SPECIFICATION OF THEORETICAL MODELS

Mis-specification occurs when a complex process is not adequately modeled. The modeling process takes place when the researcher builds relationships among elements that he or she believes offer potential for explaining a complex phenomenon. But when these choices of the modeler are not well substantiated, problems can arise that interfere with valid model construction. Problems can occur in model building and testing either by incorrectly specifying the number of elements in the model, or improperly testing dynamic relationships with static methods. Four different situations can occur.

First, the researcher may propose too few variables and relationships with the result that tests of hypotheses oversimplify the phenomena being investigated. Most typically this underspecification error results in low R-values, and strongly suggests that other unmeasured variables may account for the unexplained variance. Second, too many variables may be included to be tested, but they may not be justified from a thorough review of other empirical studies or derived from the researcher's own empirical discoveries. This may result in operationalizing too many overly simplistic variables that lack empirical grounding. Overspecified models can also result in weak statistical associations and uninterpretable results. Third, the researcher may erroneously specify a static test of predicted relationships among variables when the research objective requires a dynamic test. Improper testing of causal relationships can produce low associations between variables, due in part to a cyclic relationship between two variables (e.g. attitudes and behavior). Fourth, the researcher may intend to test changes in variables over time, but may mis-specify the process model by allowing only simultaneously measured factors to be tested.

Models are mis-specified when a researcher's beliefs about a concept are not sufficiently 'grounded' in observed phenomena (Glaser and Strauss, 1967). For a valid model to be developed, these beliefs must be grounded in additional observing and recording of data. Through investigation, the researcher may observe that certain outcomes occur after particular events or that certain variables do not maintain a constant value over time. The researcher may utilize an iterative data collection method to successively refine the measurement or understanding of a concept (e.g. a specific satisfaction or attitude). In some cases, statistical variance analysis may be appropriate if the researcher wants to build a model to describe and understand a specific process being examined. In other cases, a process analysis consisting of simple recorded observations over time may be most appropriate to explain and understand specific phenomena as they unfold. A sample of one entity may be adequate for such discovery, or a cross-section of many representative entities may be selected depending upon the depth of meaning the researcher wants to pursue to achieve the necessary empirical grounding.

Mis-specification probably accounts for the failure of researchers to produce many convincing results on the issue of user involvement in IS development.

Models used in such research are oversimplified, and other variables which have not been identified probably account for most of the unexplained variance (Ives and Olson, 1984). When R-values are low or non-existent, other factors are most likely responsible for the unexplained variance. Without specifying these factors in advance, the researcher is in a poor position to explain findings based on factor relationships [1].

The problem of mis-specification suggests the need for a fundamental reassessment of research purposes rather than more factor studies of underspecified models. In other words, more attention should be paid to theory development than is currently paid. Longitudinal studies in which data are collected over multiple time periods or on a continuous basis are appropriate to this aim of grounding more complex process theories.

In our 'rush for scientific respectability' in IS research, we have too often pursued factor research and forgotten the value of discovery. The same problems have beset the fields of organizational behavior and organizational theory, which have recently experienced a rethinking of research strategies. One result of this self-evaluation has been the placement of greater attention and value upon intensive, longitudinal, discovery research (Luthans and Davis, 1982). Among the benefits to be gained is development of new models which are more fully specified and thus better able to account for the phenomena being tested.

In the next section we develop a typology that separates research purpose into discovery and testing, and classifies the time frame for conducting observations and data collection as either single or multiple. By understanding where one's research might be placed on the resulting 2 × 2 table, one can reduce the problem of mis-specification by adopting methods appropriate for addressing either factor or process research questions.

4. TYPOLOGY FOR RESEARCH PURPOSE AND TIME FRAME

Early attempts to classify IS research depended upon conventional descriptions of research strategies. For example, Van Horn (1973) classified empirical MIS research as case studies, field studies, field tests, and laboratory studies. This assessment was useful for sorting through the scattered empirical results of the day, but it did not aid researchers in determining which of the four research approaches would be most relevant for their purpose. More recently, Weick (1984) and Benbasat (1984) have provided more helpful assessments. Weick describes Douglas's (1976) 17-tier hierarchy of methodological options, which ranges from simple observation of social experience in everyday life to extensive testing of hypotheses in controlled situations. Benbasat recommends a match between the research focus and the research methodology, recognizing that some areas of IS are more developed than others. He also makes the distinction between factor and process referred to earlier.

TABLE 1 A typology for research strategies

| | | Time frame | |
		single period	multiple period
Purpose	discovery	Observe current state (generate ideas for factor theories	Observe on-going processes (generate ideas for process theories
		Foster and Flynn (1984) Adams (1975)	Gibson (1975) Franz and Robey (1984)
	testing	Test static associations (correlational analyses)	Test dynamic changes (cause and effect)
		Robey (1979) Boland (1978)	Ginzberg (1981) Franz, Robey and Koeblitz (1986)

Our purpose is even more fundamental. In Table 1 we construct a simple typology for classifying research strategy in terms of purpose and time frame. The purpose dimension includes discovery and testing; the time frame dimension includes single time period or multiple time periods for data collection. Considering research purpose and time frame will enable researchers to articulate their assumptions and beliefs about the phenomena chosen for study and to guide the selection of an appropriate research methodology.

The choice between discovery and testing emanates from the researcher's beliefs about how well existing theories are grounded empirically. The researcher may believe that certain issues or concepts require more discovery before sufficient grounding for a theory is obtained. Alternatively, the researcher may believe that sufficient exploratory studies have been conducted to yield meaningful variables and relationships among variables to suggest testing hypotheses.

The distinction between discovery and testing is never completely clear. Our distinction is intended to be a pragmatic way to orient research activity rather than a way to separate intuitive exploration from real science. Taylor (1971) cautions that the social sciences are necessarily interpretive. Thus, organizational reality is an intersubjectively shared interpretation, full of many meanings, not something that can be absolutely verified by collecting data. Furthermore, social reality can be modified by research that alters the language used to define the reality. Thus, 'user involvement' studies may change the way managers and system designers think about the organizational reality of implementation. The consequence for researchers who intend only to test theories about implementation is that their tests may cause the object being studied to change. Thus, testing must not preclude new discoveries because the organizational realities being studied are self-interpretations and subject to continuous revision. The interpretive quality of the objects we study, in Taylor's opinion, distinguishes the hard sciences from the sciences of man.

Researchers also exercise a belief about the conduct of intended research over time. If the research intention is to discover or test simple factor associations, a single time period study will be sufficient. However, if the research intention is to examine time-dependent processes, then a longitudinal study over multiple time periods is more appropriate. Again, the distinction between single and multiple periods is intended to be a useful guide to establishing research strategies. In absolute terms, nothing is static: everything occurs over time as a process. However, our shared perceptions of time shape our research conventions, leading us to consider some events as occurring at the same time while others are separated in time.

The remainder of this chapter evaluates eight published empirical studies, identified in Table 1, to illustrate methodological strengths and weaknesses. We first evaluate the studies in the left half of the table, which deal with single time periods, and then proceed to discussion of the longitudinal research studies. This critical analysis demonstrates the value of choosing a research strategy capable of addressing important questions about the implementation of information systems in organizations. The approach we take can also be applied to other areas of IS research.

4.1 Single Data Collection Periods

By focusing on a single time period, researchers reveal the belief that data collection during a single time period is adequate either to discover new factors or to test previously established relationships. Unfortunately, researchers often address process issues with static research and fail to acknowledge the mismatch between research question and research time frame. Despite their use of rigorous data analysis, the most that single period data collection can demonstrate is a static relationship among variables, so the use of this approach appears *a priori* to be inadequate for research questions that involve processes. However, results from static research can be useful to researchers who use them to reframe process questions and who later choose longitudinal methods to investigate these questions.

In this section we review four studies in detail that are conducted in a single time period. Two studies illustrate discovery as the primary belief of the researcher, and the second two studies illustrate the researcher's belief that relationships among variables were sufficiently grounded and developed in the literature that hypotheses should be tested.

4.1.1 Discovery, Single Time Period

In this cell, the researcher believes that concepts relevant to the research question have not been investigated sufficiently to devise hypothesis tests about variable relationships. The researcher believes that by using various ethnographic data collection methods (such as direct observation, interviews, and collecting documents), concepts can be discovered or further clarified. The research may be conducted as an intensive case study of a single subject, or as a field study surveying many subjects. The researcher also believes that a single time period of data collection will be adequate to reveal insights about new variables or relationships.

The first research study we review was conducted by Foster and Flynn (1984) and involves the implementation of office automation for General Motors' Environmental Activities Staff. Foster and Flynn's purpose in their case description was clearly discovery: 'Its purpose is to give future system designers, organizational designers, and researchers of organizational form and job design the benefit of one experience' (p. 229). Foster and Flynn report changes in each of three areas of organizational design: communication, use of hierarchy, and task structure.

Communication networks expanded and communication became more task-focused as a result of automation, but surprisingly the number of personal contacts also increased. Hierarchy based on formal authority was replaced by a hierarchy of competence, as the system allowed greater visibility of performance. With the wider communication network of the system, users bypassed the traditional hierarchy and initiated 'spontaneous, task-directed, vertical interactions'. As for task structure, the effect of automation was to increase the amount of time available for professional work by eliminating some of the more routine aspects of, for example, document preparation. Other jobs became more fluid, and greater sharing of tasks between hierarchical levels was observed. Foster and Flynn attribute all of these changes to the use of new technologies.

It is difficult to judge the appropriateness of Foster and Flynn's research methodology because virtually none of it is reported in their paper. One of the authors is listed as affiliated with General Motors, and the other with a university in Michigan. But none of the methods used for gathering data are explained, although oblique reference is made to an 'accepted quasi-experimental methodology' in their introduction (p. 229). We must assume that all data were the impressions of one of the authors as a participant in the organization during the time of implementation.

If that is the case, this study should perhaps be considered as a multiple time period study and included in the upper right-hand cell of Table 1. However, we consider this research to be single time period because no method for collecting data (or gathering impressions) over time was specified. The participant reporter probably used retrospection to compare the post-implementation situation with the situation that existed before implementation. We are told that the system was developed between 1981 and 1982, and that changes in the organization occurred within the first year of operation (p. 230). However, this does not describe the time periods at which data were collected. Therefore, we classify this study as a single time period study.

Discovery research has as its objective the uncovering of new relationships or the development of new concepts for further testing. Foster and Flynn do report findings that may prove to be of some value to future investigators. However, they do very little to formalize what they have found or to relate it to other discovery research in the existing literature. Only one reference is used, and that is a *Wall Street Journal* interview with a bank executive. The burden of discovery research, whether undertaken in a single or multiple time frame, is to build concepts and theory for future testing. The reporting of a single case study can only be justified (in an academic sense) if it forges the connection to other work. Foster and Flynn neither review this work nor add to it, and their case study becomes little more than an interesting story. We know little more about the organizational impacts of information technology as a result of their work.

The field survey by Adams (1975) provides a much better illustration of how a researcher can clarify an issue in the IS literature (managers' attitudes toward computers) and contributes an additional insight into a process (involvement in systems development). Adams wanted to discover the attitudes of managers toward the use of information systems, and their perceptions of management's role in systems development. He conducted a cross-sectional survey of 75 upper and middle level managers from ten organizations on their attitudes toward information systems and computers. The managers that participated were equally balanced between upper and middle management and represented various functional areas in their companies. Data collection was restricted to a single time period using direct questions and in-depth structured interview methods.

Adams presented results on managers' views of planning and types of desired changes in information, using a format consisting of percentages and a classification table. He analyzed qualitative differences in manager responses by grouping respondents by function, organizational level, type of activity, and type of environment. Adams's findings revealed that users want control over resources during systems development. This led him to propose that user influence plays an important role for user involvement.

This study clarified some points about management attitudes and contributed an insight into the user involvement process. By probing a manager's perceptions in a structured interview, a researcher can uncover much meaning and provide a richer interpretation of the data than would be possible with simple questionnaire methods. Adams could have substantiated his findings and conclusions more strongly by cross-validating his impressions with other data such as archival records of usage. Rivard and Huff (1984) illustrate appropriate use of multiple measures in a single time period to clarify the importance of organizational and user factors in evaluating user-developed applications.

Both studies (Adams, 1975; Foster and Flynn, 1984) reflect researchers' beliefs that more discovery is necessary before hypotheses are tested. In both areas of inquiry, organizational impacts and managerial attitudes toward IS, we believe they are correct. Adams's conclusions about the role of user-control during systems development contributed to later theoretical and empirical work on user-involvement and user-influence during system design. Foster and Flynn make it difficult for future researchers to learn from their findings because of the lack of attention to theory and the lack of detail in describing their methodology. Their results provide evidence of a single case, at a single point in time, but the contribution to the field is minimized by the failure to frame the discoveries in terms that other researchers would find useful.

4.1.2 Testing, Single Time Period

In this cell, the researcher believes that there is adequate justification to propose a relationship that should be hypothesized and tested. The testing may proceed by setting up control groups and studying the effects of an intervention or by analyzing the relationships between variables without experimental control. The researcher believes that a single time period for data collection is sufficient to test the hypotheses. Even though the ideas for this type of research may originate from process theories, studies in this cell are unable to test process theories. Rather, the methods used can only test hypotheses about factors. The research may be conducted by various means: a field study, employing a survey of multiple subjects (e.g. Zand and Sorenson, 1975); a field test, comparing two different methods of implementing the same system (Robey and Zeller, 1978); or a laboratory experiment in which hypotheses about experimental manipulations are tested (Boland, 1978).

The study by Boland (1978) illustrates a researcher's belief that the IS literature contains sufficient justification for hypotheses on a specific research question, that is, the use of different protocols for information requirements analysis. Boland set up two design groups to test the effect of different protocols on the quality of IS design. His purpose was to test ideas about how users should be involved during systems development. The justification for the research was derived solidly out of many previous empirical studies. Yet the previous research had not actually tested alternative protocols.

Boland designed an experiment that enabled comparison of two protocols for user–designer interaction. The control group used a traditional protocol consisting of the designer interacting with the user by asking questions and collecting data to 'learn, analyze and suggest' problem solutions. The experimental group used an alternative protocol characterized by the designer and user 'teaching, suggesting and critiquing' each other.

Experienced system designers from local firms and registered nurses (users) were selected for the experiment. Boland created pairs of designer/nurse teams by randomly assigning two designers from each organization to either a control group or an experimental group and by randomly assigning nurses to designers. The designers had no previous health care experience and no background information about the design problem. The experimental protocols were administered by means of a worksheet containing step-by-step procedures telling the team how to progress through a design meeting.

All teams worked on the same problem scenario for two hours with the objective of identifying problems and proposing solutions. A panel of seven graduate students evaluated the solutions proposed by the teams to produce a list of idea units. Three expert nurses scored the idea units on a nine-point scale, with each starting at different points in a randomized idea list. Inter-rater reliability ranged from 0.60 to 0.70, and Boland averaged the three-person panel scores to obtain a learning and understanding score assigned by both panels to each team.

Boland's study is a good example of research conducted within the single-time period. It shows good independence of measures and demonstrates how qualitative data can be collected and analyzed quantitatively. Narrative and text data were processed by content analysis to yield scores for later quantitative analysis (Chi-square test). Boland describes completely how he checked for possible errors in the analysis of the text data by reconvening the designers and reviewing the summaries and the write-ups for discrepancies.

Although Boland's stated intentions were to examine the process of design, in execution his study constitutes factor research because he did not measure changes in variables. Rather, he compared two different groups on the same variable at one point in time. He speaks in process terms (involvement, design process, interaction), but the psychological dynamics and interactions of the traditional and alternative protocols are not actually investigated. Therefore many questions pertaining to the process of how users are involved remain after the experiment. This research question could have been investigated longitudinally with other methods such as charting group interactions, collecting notes from the design team, or recording groups on audio or video tape. By collecting data over time on the interactions that occur between designer and user, the researcher could test hypotheses on designer–user social dynamics that took place during the design.

The second study in this category was conducted by Robey (1979). This research studied the correlation of actual usage of an information system with user attitudes toward the system. A sample of 66 salespersons from one organization completed an attitude questionnaire developed by Schultz and Slevin (1975). This measure assesses seven dimensions of users' attitudes toward a system or model, including the effect of the system on user performance, interpersonal relations, organizational changes, goals, and so on. All of the attitude dimensions vary from unfavorable to favorable, and are measured along a five-point Likert scale. Only five of the dimensions (those exhibiting acceptable reliability) were used in the study. Robey operationalized system use by examining records of sales personnel and ranking users on two aspects of actual use: number of customer records maintained on the system, and percentage of customer records that required updating annually. The rank correlations between attitudes and use ranged from 0.42 to 0.79, and all were significant.

Robey's study is considered to be testing rather than discovery because the literature clearly indicated that positive attitudes should be correlated with actual use, although not very much empirical support for that relationship had been reported at the time. The results were even more convincing because attitudes and use were obtained independently, using very different types of measures. The problem of common method variance was thus overcome.

Robey designed his research as a single time period study to test a static proposition about the relationship between attitudes and actual use. However, the choice of this research strategy may be questioned in light of models of user behavior he and others propose. Robey proposed an expectancy model of user behavior in which attitudes are conceived as causes of behavior. Specifically, expectations about the instrumental value of a system in helping a user to attain desired outcomes motivates a user to exert effort toward actual use. However, Robey is unclear about the timing of data collection and is therefore unable to support any statements about cause and effect. In fact, the archival performance data he used were collected for the period *preceding* the collection of attitude data via questionnaire. Insensitivity to the timing of data collection can lead researchers to make such unfounded claims about cause and effect, when other possible models of behavior might be more descriptive. For example, Robey's data could be used to support a model which treats use as the causal variable affecting user attitudes. Such an explanation would be more congruent with theories of cognitive consistency than with expectancy theory.

These two studies (Boland, 1978; Robey, 1979) both illustrate single time period measurements, but different types of theory testing. Robey conducted a static correlational test whereas Boland performed an experiment by manipulating a treatment variable to test differences in a dependent variable. Both believed that the IS literature contained enough discussion and conceptual development to warrant empirical tests. Both studies used multiple methods and measures in data collection. Because of the greater degree of control in the experimental setting, Boland was able to avoid the problems Robey experienced in timing his data collection.

All four of the static research studies reviewed so far appear to be testing theories that would be better formulated as process theories. Foster and Flynn (1984) speak about changes over time, but only report the consequences of implementation rather than the process of change. Adams (1975) really seems interested in the process of user-involvement in system development. Boland (1978) has researched one short phase of the development process with his analysis of group protocols. Finally, Robey (1979) seems most interested in the dynamic relationship between use and attitudes rather than their static relationship. In other words, each of these researchers has chosen a strategy that falls short of being able to address the process issues which appear to be of real interest. While the results of all these studies can be accepted at face value for what they do show, all can be criticized for not going far enough. In the next section, we review four more studies that try to address process issues more directly by choosing multiple data collection periods.

4.2 Multiple Data Collection Periods

In this type of research, investigators hold the belief that better understanding of the dynamics of process requires multiple time periods for collecting data. Whether the objective is discovery or testing, the dynamic nature of the research question demands that proposed causal relationships be examined longitudinally. Longitudinal data collection permits time-dependent relationships to be observed, analyzed, and refined, leading to the development of process theory. These concepts provide the grounding for theories which can then be tested in future research. Testing process theories also requires multiple period data collection, which permits examining predicted relationships among variables from one time period to another and changes in variables across multiple time periods.

In this section we review four studies in detail, two illustrating discovery as the primary belief of the researcher and two where the researcher believed that testing of some hypothesized relationships was necessary and relevant. The first two studies illustrate two fundamental differences about the researcher's role in longitudinal discovery research, namely that of action-research participation and non-participant observation. The last two studies illustrate predictive testing and analyzing variable changes over time.

4.2.1 Discovery, Multiple Time Period

The case study by Gibson (1975) involved data collection on the implementation of a bank model over two years. Gibson and a doctoral student served as participant observers and consultants for the model implementation. This methodology has the advantage of being 'congruent' with the process of implementation itself. Gibson describes the researchers' roles as interpreting, conceptualizing, and developing working hypotheses.

> we sought to observe, record, and interpret behavior and events longitudinally on a case-by-case, exploratory basis. Our aim here was to develop concepts and relationships and to test working hypotheses toward the building of a theory that would be closely grounded in the data and that would yield immediately useful findings for practitioners concerned with the implementation of models. (Gibson, 1975, p. 55)

The researchers developed a comprehensive history of social relationships in the bank over the past twenty years by using interviews, documents, and previously published research on the bank. Gibson contends that two significant insights resulted from their time-consuming data collection that would have had little chance of being discovered with questionnaire methods. First, qualitative data revealed actual decision-making processes that differed from the rational norm that was described by a marketing staff officer of the bank. Second, they discovered two distinct informal coalitions within the bank's officer group that influenced the decision-making process. This discovery led the researchers to administer questionnaires to assess bank officer attitudes, which resulted in clear identification of the two 'social camps of ''bankers'' and ''marketers'' ' (1975, p. 61). Overall, Gibson concludes that the implementation effort was a complex series of events.

Gibson also comments on the weakness of the action research methodology. As action researchers, Gibson and the student unintentionally aroused bank officer expectations of model implementation that interfered with the objective of observation and research. This weakness is reduced if the researcher plays the role of passive observer, but the intensiveness and depth of understanding of the phenomenon may be sacrificed.

Gibson's research represents a broadly focused study of a single organization in which some quantitative data were collected and statistically analyzed to enable exploring and explaining differences in bank officers' attitudes and reactions to a proposed model. This type of research permits insights to be discovered that may be tested in future research.

The second study in this category was conducted by Franz and Robey (1984) in which they tracked a system design team for two years to obtain a description of the process of system design when led by a user. Their motivation was thus discovery because they attempted not to bring preconceived ideas into their observations. The methodology called for multiple methods of data collection, including interaction process recording of project meetings, attitude questionnaires, critical incident files, examination of company documents, and tape-recorded interviews. Twenty-two members of the organization provided varying amounts of data through these methods.

These data were used in the following way. First, evidence from the various sources was compiled to produce a process description. Second, a variety of subjective interpretations from the actors about these events were obtained from the data. From these, Franz and Robey were able to detect two predominant interpretive themes about the events in the process, the rational and political themes. Franz and Robey claim that these dual interpretations reflect the meanings provided by the actors rather than by the researchers' preconceived notions (1984, p. 1204). They argue that, because the themes are just interpretations of the events themselves, different stories may be told about the same sequence of events. By collecting an objective description of the events as they occurred, and by recording the interpretations at the same times, Franz and Robey discovered the rational and political sides of system development.

One weakness of longitudinal discovery research, and of the Franz and Robey study in particular, is the subjective nature of the researchers' use of data. With no hypotheses to test, all data become relevant, and, though they might claim objectivity, looseness of method almost guarantees that the researchers' preconceptions will influence what they see. It would have been useful for Franz and Robey to have their process description interpreted by a third party simply to provide alternative discoveries (Taylor, 1971, p. 29). Thus, nothing is purely objective, although steps can and should be taken to make discovery research as carefully methodical as possible.

These two studies (Franz and Robey, 1984; Gibson, 1975) show how different longitudinal case studies can provide convergence on theoretical constructs. Gibson concludes that influence is one of the important elements in the implementation of the bank's model. Franz and Robey report how political influence of a user can explain why a 'rational' process developed as it did. These studies contribute additional understanding to the concept of influence as an explanatory variable in the implementation process. This understanding could not be obtained without conducting the research longitudinally by means of intensive continuous data collection. Gibson points out that a disadvantage of longitudinal case research is replication of results. Many longitudinal case studies must be conducted before consistent patterns are revealed because observational and even quantitative measures will necessarily be context-specific.

4.2.2 Testing, Multiple Time Period

In this cell the researcher believes that adequate hypotheses can be derived from the literature on a specific research question, and that they require testing across multiple time periods. Viewing process as a series of continuously developing changes requires hypotheses about changes in variables over time (e.g. attitudes before, during, and after system implementation). A researcher may also study predictive relationships, which test a hypothesized relationship between variables over two or more time periods. A further extension of this idea would be to test whether the strength of a relationship grows weaker or stronger in successive time periods.

The study by Ginzberg (1981) illustrates examination of such a predictive relationship. He conducted a longitudinal field study in a large bank to test the ability of users' pre-implementation expectations to predict post-implementation system success or failure. The study was conducted as part of an existing implementation effort by management, systems personnel in the bank, and an external consulting firm, to develop and install an on-line portfolio management (OLPM) system. Users were portfolio managers in the bank's trust department.

The independent variable was 'realism of user expectations', determined by computing the difference between user expectation scores and an average expert opinion group score (consisting of other users and system personnel). Ginzberg conducted interviews with a sample of portfolio managers, system developers, and users to determine specific pre-implementation expectations. From the interviews he developed a questionnaire to examine specific expectations about OLPM and factors suggested by bank experts as important to implementation success (i.e. user participation, management support, user attitudes toward OLPM, scientific approach to management). The instrument was pretested with two portfolio managers and the head of the user department to determine whether the questions were clear and understandable, and if the respondents would interpret them as the researcher had intended. Ginzberg noted that questions were rather specific to the bank's OLPM system and not generalizable to other organizations. The pre-implementation questionnaire was distributed in December 1977 to OLPM user managers, just two months before actual system usage began.

The dependent success measures were post-implementation attitudes and behaviors. Attitudes were measured by questionnaire five months after implementation (February 1978). Ginzberg collected three behavioral measures (connect time, number of sessions, and frequency of function usage) and averaged them over five months from July to November 1978. Ginzberg also used an instrument to measure users' satisfaction and perceived use. He performed a manipulation test on the realism construct by comparing expert group results to randomly selected project participant results. He did not provide any details about the construction of the satisfaction or attitude scales.

Ginzberg's study raises the issue of when to measure pre-implementation expectations. Measures of user expectations were obtained at the last possible moment, just before use of the system, whereas considerable time had elapsed between the project definition stage and implementation of the system. The definition stage was described as completed in Spring 1974, with physical design taking place up through September 1976. Requests for design changes delayed actual use of the system until February 1978. During the two years from 1976 to 1978, the users '. . . had essentially no contact with either OLPM or the external consultant' (p. 465). Two questions raised by Ginzberg's description can only be resolved by further empirical research. Does the realism of user expectations change over time; and how does time affect the ability of user expectations to predict system success?

Overall, Ginzberg's study represents the successful use of longitudinal research to predict the outcome of system implementation. He developed a hypothesis from an extensive review of the empirical literature. The conduct of the research was congruent with the research objective, i.e. to test the ability of pre-implementation expectations to predict post-implementation attitudes and usage. Ginzberg also used more than one method to measure the dependent variable, which permitted alternative confirmation of his predictive tests.

The second study in this category was conducted by Franz *et al.* (1986) on the change in attitudes and perceptions of job characteristics of nurses who used an on-line system in a large hospital. Attitudes and job perceptions were measured using reliable instruments developed in earlier research (Schultz and Slevin, 1975; Sims *et al.*, 1976). Using a quasi-experimental design in a field setting, Franz *et al.* controlled for the effects of pretesting by randomly assigning nurses to pretest groups and no-pretest groups, and showed statistically that the pretest had no effect on post-test scores.

Franz *et al.* hypothesized that implementation of the IS would affect nurses' attitudes and job perceptions, although they did not indicate the direction of change. Their results showed that post-test responses, collected after implementation of the system, were not significantly different from the pretest scores, except for one job characteristic—opportunity for friendship on the job—which had a significantly lower post-test score. Thus, the hypotheses were not supported.

Several features of this study illustrate valuable lessons for the conduct of longitudinal tests of hypotheses. First, measures that exhibited acceptable reliability in previous research were used. In the case of the job characteristics measure, special consideration was given to its prior use in health care settings, and it was judged to be more appropriate than more popular measures. Second, subjects were assigned to experimental groups on a random basis. The importance of random assignment should never be overlooked in experiments because it is the most general-purpose method to control for systematic sources of variance in dependent measures. Field experiments that compare one department with another (e.g. Robey and Zeller, 1978) are vulnerable to the influence of unmeasured and uncontrolled variables that covary with departmental affiliation. Third, the study directly tested the effects of pretesting on post-test results. Only when these were found to be non-significant were the researchers able to test their hypotheses, confident that the pretesting did not affect post-test scores.

This study also raises a concern about the time period between pre- and post-test administration. In any longitudinal research, variable changes are believed to be linked to the passage of time, but researchers seldom have clear notions about how long a time is necessary for the effects to be seen. Franz *et al.* allowed eleven months between pre- and post-test, during which the system was implemented and the users trained. Would the empirical test have provided the same results if measures had been obtained at different pre- and post-implementation times? If not, the conclusions would differ drastically from those drawn from results across the time periods actually used.

The collection of data at only two points in time limits researchers' ability to explain why hypotheses are not supported, even though there are few technical flaws in the design. The importance of post-experimental explanation was illustrated in the Franz *et al.* study because only one of the hypotheses was supported. In trying to explain the non-findings, the authors found themselves unequipped to offer much more than general speculation on the inadequacy of the theory that guided the hypotheses in the first place. Had the researchers systematically collected data on processes that occurred during the implementation period, in addition to questionnaire data at two discrete points in time, they would have been better able to explain what happened.

This shortcoming underscores even more the importance of developing sound process theories before they are tested. Franz *et al.* concluded that they had little real theoretical reason for predicting changes in nurses' perceptions and attitudes, other than a vague faith in the fact that technological change often produces social change. However, vague faith is not theory. Studies that prematurely try to test simplistic notions about cause and effect should be prepared for non-significant or inconsistent findings. Such tests are best conducted cautiously in areas where theory provides a strong basis for hypotheses rather than weak notion. Researchers are also advised to collect additional incidental data which might be useful in explaining unexpected findings in a more exploratory mode if hypotheses are not supported.

These two research studies (Ginzberg, 1981; Franz *et al.*, 1986) both represent longitudinal research at a single site and with a single system to test theoretical propositions that are derived from the IS literature. They both used data collected in multiple time periods to test time-dependent propositions. While the intent of the researchers was to test predictions generated in other research and theory, both also contribute to theoretical understanding by pointing out discrepancies between expected and actual findings. Each study has a very limited research scope, and each is limited in its ability to explain complex dynamics of system implementation. Nonetheless, both are examples of well-conceived and -executed research on IS implementation.

5. CONCLUSIONS

This chapter has taken the position that the researcher's beliefs and intentions play an important role in the conduct of research. We have described two areas where such beliefs exert a basic influence in research on IS in organizations: research purpose and time frame. We feel that researchers are often unclear, in their own minds as well as for their readers, as to the purpose of their efforts. Acknowledging the relationship between discovery and testing should allow researchers to judge whether sufficient grounding exists for testing, or whether additional discovery and exploration are necessary. Because both testing and discovery are interpretive activities in the social sciences (Taylor, 1971), researchers should also guard against making too strong a distinction between the two. To claim that testing is 'real science' and that discovery is 'mere interpretation' is to miss the point that both involve interpretation and that relatively few verifiable facts are available for study.

Further, researchers must become more aware of the implicit assumptions made about time in the research questions that they explore or test. We feel that many of the interesting research issues involving IS in organizations are really questions about process rather than questions about factors. Implementation is certainly one of the important processes in IS theory, but many others can be identified. Adopting a factors approach to building or testing such process theories is a prime example of mis-specification and promises to retard research on IS in organizations rather than to contribute findings of value.

Once the researcher appropriately recognizes the purpose and time frame of his or her research focus, then choices on more specific methodological issues can be made. This chapter has addressed some of these choices in our review of the eight studies in Table 1. However, a more systematic examination is necessary, and it is clear that IS researchers need a broader exposure to research methods in other disciplines. It can be argued easily that IS has no research methodology of its own and that informed research can only be conducted by applying methods used in more basic disciplines.

For longitudinal research in particular, there is much to learn about both the art and technique of performing meaningful research. Some of the lessons in careful observation, collection, and interpretation of data cannot be codified easily. Appreciation of these research arts can be gained by modeling excellent past research (e.g. Mann and Williams, 1960). One reason for the use of research examples in this chapter is to provide models of both sound and unsound practices of the research art. In other areas of process research, IS researchers have new techniques to learn. For example, Miller and Friesen (1982) provide a detailed discussion of the problem of assuming that the effects of change remain linear over time. More likely, measures taken immediately before and after installation of a system will capture 'unstable' data. The transitory nature of assimilating a system into an organization raises many questions about the timing of data collection. By using multiple time periods, the researcher can distinguish such transitory effects from the effects of the implementation.

As IS continues to grow as a discipline, researchers and theory builders will need to recognize the complementary nature of discovery and testing, and make connections between factor and process issues. Theory should guide intelligent questions about the dynamic interactions among various theoretical units. As more observations from discovery research become available, theory can be enriched and better-grounded. Enhanced theoretical models are needed which incorporate newly discovered variables that explain why a relationship exists or why a variable changes from one time period to another. When these new theories are tested carefully, with particular attention to longitudinal methods, we can say more confidently that our knowledge about IS in organizations has matured.

NOTE

[1] The literature on path analysis emphasizes the importance of working with zero-correlated residuals to rule out the possibility of spuriousness (Billings and Wroten, 1978). In process research, greater emphasis is placed on being alert to variables that may unexpectedly explain variance. Price (1968) discusses the problem of spuriousness and how longitudinal measures sequenced over time can serve as a more rigorous means of dealing with spuriousness.

REFERENCES

Adams, C. R. (1975) 'How Management Users View Information Systems', *Decision Sciences*, **6**, 337–345.

Attewell, P., and Rule, J. (1984) 'Computing and Organizations: What We Know and What We Don't Know', *Communications of the ACM*, **27**, 1184–1192.

Benbasat, I. (1984) 'An Analysis of Research Methodologies', in *The Information Systems Research Challenge*, F. W. McFarlan (Ed.), Boston: Harvard Business School Press, Boston, pp. 47–85.

Billings, R. S., and Wroten, S. P. (1978) 'Use of Path Analysis in Industrial/Organizational Psychology: Criticisms and Suggestions', *Journal of Applied Psychology*, **63**, 677–688.

Boland, R. J. (1978) 'The Process and Product of System Design', *Management Science*, **24**, 887–898.

Cash, J. I., Jr., McFarlan, F. W., and McKenney, J. L. (1983) *Corporate Information Systems Management*, Irwin, Homewood, Il.

DeSanctis, G. (1984) 'Computer Graphics as Decision Aids: Directions for Research', *Decision Sciences*, **15**, 463–487.

Douglas, J. D. (1976) *Investigative Social Research*, Sage, Beverly Hills.

Dubin, R. (1969) *Theory Building*, The Free Press, New York.

Edstrom, A. (1977) 'User Influence and the Success of MIS Projects: A Contingency Approach', *Human Relations*, **30**, 589–607.

Foster, L. W., and Flynn, D. M. (1984) 'Management Information Technology: Its Effects on Organizational Form and Function', *MIS Quarterly*, **8**, 229–236.

Franz, C. R., and Robey, D. (1984) 'An Investigation of User-led System Design: Rational and Political Perspectives', *Communications of the ACM*, **27**, 1202–1209.

Franz, C. R., and Robey, D. (1986) 'Organizational Context, User Involvement and the Usefulness of Information Systems', *Decision Sciences*, **17** (in press).

Franz, C. R., Robey, D., and Koeblitz, R. R. (1986) 'User Response to an On-line Information System: A Field Experiment', *MIS Quarterly*, **10**, 29–42.

Gibson, C. F. (1975) 'A Methodology for Implementation Research', in *Implementation Operations Research/Management Science*, R. L. Schultz and D. P. Slevin (Eds.), American Elsevier, New York.

Ginzberg, M. J. (1979) 'A Study of the Implementation Process', *TIMS Studies in the Management Sciences*, **13**, 85–102.

Ginzberg, M. J. (1981) 'Early Diagnosis of MIS Implementation Failure: Promising Results and Unanswered Questions', *Management Science*, **27**, 459–478.

Glaser, B. G., and Strauss, A. L. (1967) *The Discovery of Grounded Theory*, Aldine, Chicago.

Heller, F. A., Drenth, P. J. D., Koopman, P., and Rus, V. (1977) 'A Longitudinal Study in Participative Decision-making', *Human Relations*, **30**, 567–587.

Ives, B., and Olson, M. H. (1984) 'User Involvement and MIS Success: A Review of Research', *Management Science*, **30**, 586–603.

King, J. L., and Kraemer, K. L. (1984) 'Evolution and Organizational Information Systems: An Assessment of Nolan's Stage Model', *Communications of the ACM*, **27**, 466–475.

Kling, R. (1980) 'Social Analyses of Computing: Theoretical Perspectives in Recent Empirical Research', *Computing Surveys*, **12**, 61–110.

Lucas, H. C., Jr. (1978) 'Empirical Evidence for a Descriptive Model of Implementation', *MIS Quarterly*, **2**, 27–42.

Lucas, H. C., Jr. (1981) *Implementation: The Key to Successful Information Systems*, Columbia University Press, New York.

Luthans, F., and Davis, T. R. V. (1982) 'An Idiographic Approach to Organizational Behavior Research: The Use of Single Case Experimental Designs and Direct Measures', *Academy of Management Journal*, **7**, 380–391.

Mann, F. C., and Williams, L. K. (1960) 'Observations on the Dynamics of a Change to Electronic Data-processing Equipment', *Administrative Science Quarterly*, **5**, 217–256.

Markus, M. L. (1984) *Systems in Organizations: Bugs and Features*, Pitman, Marshfield, MA.

Miller, D., and Friesen, P. H. (1982) 'The Longitudinal Analysis of Organizations: A Methodological Perspective', *Management Science*, **28**, 1013–1034.

Monge, P. R., Farace, R. V., Eisenberg, E. M., Miller, K. I., and White, L. L. (1984) 'The Process of Studying Process in Organizational Communication', *Journal of Communication*, **34**, 22–43.

Nolan, R. L. (1982) *Managing the Data Resource Function*, 2nd edn, West Publishing Co., St. Paul.

Price, J. L. (1968) 'Design of Proof in Organizational Research', *Administrative Science Quarterly*, **13**, 121–134.

Rivard, S., and Huff, S. L. (1984) 'User Developed Applications: Evaluation of Success from the DP Department Perspective', *MIS Quarterly*, **8**, 39–50.

Robey, D. (1979) 'User Attitudes and Management Information System Use', *Academy of Management Journal*, **22**, 527–538.

Robey, D., and Markus, M. L. (1986) 'The Organizational Impacts of Information Systems: Models and Research Directions', paper presented at the national meeting of ORSA/TIMS, Los Angeles, 1986.

Robey, D., and Zeller, R. L. (1978) 'Factors Affecting the Success and Failure of an Information System for Product Quality', *Interfaces*, **8**, 70–75.

Schultz, R. L., and Slevin, D. P. (Eds.) (1975) *Implementing Operations Research/Management Science*, American Elsevier, New York.

Schultz, R. L., and Ginzberg, M. J. (Eds.) (1984) *Applications of Management Science: Management Science Implementation*, JAI Press, Norwich, CT.

Schultz, R. L., Ginzberg, M. J., and Lucas, H. C. (1984) 'A Structural Model of Implementation', in *Applications of Management Science: Management Science Implementation*, R. L. Schultz and M. J. Ginzberg (Eds.), JAI Press, Norwich, CT, pp. 55–88.

Sims, H. P., Szilagyi, A. D., and Keller, R. T. (1976) 'The Measurement of Job Characteristics', *Academy of Management Journal*, **19**, 195–212.

Sutherland, J. W. (1973) *A General Systems Philosophy for the Social and Behavioral Sciences*, George Braziller, New York.

Taylor, C. (1971) 'Interpretation and the Sciences of Man', *Review of Metaphysics*, **25**, 3–51.

Van Horn, R. D. (1973) 'Empirical Studies of Management Information Systems', in *Proceedings of the Wharton Conference on Research on Computers in Organizations*, H. L. Morgan (Ed.), pp. 172–182.

Weick, K. E. (1984) 'Theoretical Assumptions and Research Methodology Selection', in *The Information Systems Research Challenge*, F. W. McFarlan (Ed.), Harvard Business School Press, Boston, pp. 111–132.

Zand, D. E., and Sorenson, R. E. (1975) 'Theory of Change and the Effective Use of Management Science', *Administrative Science Quarterly*, **20**, 532–545.

Zmud, R. W. (1979) 'Individual Differences and MIS Success: A Review of the Empirical Literature', *Management Science*, **25**, 966–979.

Zmud, R. W. (1982) 'Diffusion of Modern Software Practices: Influence of Centralization and Formalization', *Management Science*, **28**, 1421–1431.

Critical Issues in Information Systems Research
Edited by R. J. Boland Jr. and R. A. Hirschheim
© 1987 John Wiley & Sons Ltd.

Chapter 10

UNIFYING THE FRAGMENTED MODELS
OF INFORMATION SYSTEMS IMPLEMENTATION

Tae H. Kwon and Robert W. Zmud

ABSTRACT

Information systems implementation is a research area that has received much attention in the last two decades. Yet, little of a unified, coherent body of knowledge has resulted from the effort. This chapter first reviews the research on information systems implementation, characterizing it as having four major research streams. The image of implementation as a technological innovation is then introduced, and a broader perspective on the process of implementation than that provided by the current research streams is discussed. The chapter then reviews the existing research in the diffusion of innovation as well as the research on implementation with respect to this broader perspective. Finally, some directions for future research are suggested.

1. INTRODUCTION

Information systems (IS) implementation is a relatively young field of scholarly inquiry. While the organizational use of computer-based information systems began in the mid-1950s, it was not until the mid-1960s that serious attention began to be directed at better understanding the reasons behind IS successes and failures. At this time, scholars also became concerned with better understanding the reasons behind the successful or unsuccessful application of management science and operations research (MS/OR) models in organizations. While many MS/OR models find their roots in research dating from the mid-1940s, their dependence on the computational power of electronic computers resulted in their large-scale implementation paralleling that of computer-based information systems in general. As a consequence, the IS and MS/OR implementation literatures have evolved together and are often viewed as a single body of literature (Doktor *et al.*, 1979; Schultz and Ginzberg, 1984; Schultz and Slevin, 1975).

Even though IS implementation is a young academic field, one might reasonably expect that considerable progress would have been made over this twenty-year period of time. While important findings have occurred, our understanding of IS implementation is surprisingly incomplete. For the most part, Keen's criticisms of a decade ago still holds (Apple and Zmud, 1984; Schultz and Ginzberg, 1984; Keen, 1977):

(1) no consistent definition of IS implementation has taken root;
(2) the IS implementation literature remains fragmented with most studies following quite narrow research perspectives and few studies conceived as a well-defined research program;
(3) the lack of a dominant paradigm with which to frame IS implementation research efforts.

This chapter suggests an IS implementation perspective which, if accepted, may enable scholars to develop strong theory and to position their studies within the growing body of literature on IS (as well as that of other technologies) implementation.

The chapter begins with a brief review of the IS implementation literature. The aim of this section is to summarize what we do and do not know about IS implementation. Then, IS implementation is viewed from the context of the organizational introduction of a technological innovation. We then critically assess both the IS implementation literature and the diffusion of innovation literature relative to this perspective. Finally, fruitful research directions are suggested.

2. THE IS IMPLEMENTATION LITERATURE

Four rather narrow research streams account for a majority of the research undertaken to date: a factors research stream, a mutual understanding research stream, a process research stream, and a political research stream. A fifth, a prescriptive research stream, has tended to adopt a broader perspective on IS implementation. It focuses on implementation risk factors and prescribes strategies for overcoming these risks.

2.1 Factors Research Stream

Many IS implementation studies try to identify those 'factors' most related to IS implementation success and failure. These studies, in fact, represent the largest research stream in the IS implementation literature.

A variety of individual, organizational, and technological variables have been examined as being potentially important to IS implementation effectiveness, where effectiveness is invariably defined in terms of IS use or satisfaction with such use. The results from these studies have been relatively consistent in that a small set of factors regularly reappear as being significantly related to IS implementation success and failure (Fuerst and Cheney, 1982; Schultz, 1984; Sanders and Courtney, 1985): top management support of the implementation effort; a relevant, high quality IS design; sufficient designer–user interactions during the implementation; and a motivated and capable user. These findings essentially indicate that successful IS implementation occurs when sufficient organizational resources (sufficient developer and user time, sufficient funding, sufficient technical skills, etc.) are directed toward, first, motivating and, then, sustaining an implementation effort.

2.2 Mutual Understanding Research Stream

The quality of designer–user interactions, one of the 'factors' found important in IS implementation, has itself been the focus of a sizeable body of research (Churchman and Schainblatt, 1965; Boland, 1978; Ginzberg, 1981b; Ives and Olson, 1984). Many of the activities that surround IS implementation efforts involve information exchanges among designers and users, exchanges involving issues such as purpose, objectives, design, use, impacts, and evaluation. Following the findings from the factors research stream, the higher the quality of these exchanges the more likely is IS implementation success.

Two topics have tended to monopolize this research stream: the desirability of designer–user interaction, and the cognitive functioning of designers and users. Both of these research areas have been plagued by theoretical and methodological problems (Huber, 1983; Ives and Olson, 1984). Still, agreement does exist that more, rather than less, designer–user interaction is generally preferred (though the extent of desired interaction depends on both the nature of an IS and the implementation task being performed) and that the quality of this interaction does depend on achieving a sense of empathy, or 'mutual understanding', among the designers and users participating in an IS implementation effort.

2.3 Process Research Stream

A relatively recent, and promising, IS implementation research stream views all implementation efforts as consisting of a sequence of generic stages, each of which must be attended to if implementation success is to occur. These 'implementation stages' are distinct from, though not independent of, those traditionally associated with the IS life cycle. Rather than focusing on technical activities, the process research stream focuses on social change activities (Lewin, 1952; Kolb and Frohman, 1970; Schein, 1961).

The major findings from the process stream suggest that implementation success occurs when (Ginzberg, 1979; 1981a): commitment to change exists, commitment to the implementation efforts exists, and extensive project definition and planning takes place. Interestingly, these behaviors arise when the early implementation stages are handled well.

Such findings are not inconsistent with those from the factors and mutual understanding research streams. In fact, they begin to suggest a more complete, though still quite sparse, view of IS implementation. In order to develop and sustain the motivation for appropriate implementation behaviors by management, designers, trainers and users, all must understand and become committed to an implementation effort.

2.4 Political Research Stream

Many motives can induce individuals to promote, engage in, or resist IS implementation efforts. These motives represent the diverse interests sought by the multiple stakeholders associated with IS implementation. The political research stream is concerned with understanding how these vested interests are effected by an IS and how, in turn, these stakeholders act to influence the direction of implementation efforts (Kramer, 1981; Markus, 1983; Pettigrew, 1972). The principal findings of this research stream are that many seemingly irrational or inconsistent implementation behaviors and outcomes can be understood when all of the consequences of IS implementations on all stakeholders are considered.

2.5 Prescriptive Research Stream

This final research stream has examined the findings from the prior research streams in order to identify generic implementation risk factors (Alter and Ginzberg, 1978; Keen, 1981; McFarlan, 1981). These risk factors generally include attributes of the individuals participating in an implementation effort, of the organization contexts with which implementation takes places, and of the implementation project itself. Then, prescriptive strategies (primarily found inductively from experience or observation) for overcoming specific risks are provided.

While this prescriptive research stream does reference the other research streams, it does not represent an integrated treatment of IS implementation. Research findings are not interrelated. Instead, they are dissected and treated, for the most part, as independent events.

2.6 An Overall Critique of the Existing Literature

It would be foolhardy, given the above review, to claim that the existing literature has not developed a better understanding of IS implementation. Progress has been made. This progress, however, has been quite limited. Consider, for example, what we do not know:

— Why have these findings been observed?
— What are the cause and effect relations that induce observed behaviors and outcomes and that tie together related behaviors and outcomes?
— When do specific findings increase or decrease in importance?
— How can the different levels of analysis represented in these findings be related?

Without answers to questions such as these, it will be impossible to guide the proactive, rather than the reactive, management of IS implementation efforts.

We believe that a major reason for the limited success achieved to date regarding IS implementation research is the lack of a common perspective among IS implementation researchers. No core set of constructs exists. Most studies focus on small pieces of the MIS implementation puzzle, without considering larger issues. And, most studies are couched in one, or at most two, of the research streams described above. As a result, it becomes very difficult to position individual studies within the fuller body of IS implementation research activities. In the following section, descriptions of the IS implementation context and process are offered which, we believe, provide an overarching perspective of IS implementation research.

3. IS IMPLEMENTATION AS A TECHNOLOGICAL INNOVATION

Much modern organizational change over the last decade has been technology-driven. Today, as seen in both the popular press and the practitioner literature, information technology has become a major technological force influencing business success. This rapid and rampant movement of information technologies into business organizations has raised managerial concern regarding the capability of today's organizations to manage the organizational introduction of information technology. IS implementation, therefore, has become an important managerial concern focusing on the effective diffusion of information technologies into organizations, business units, and work groups.

The functional parallels between IS implementation and diffusion of technological innovation are clear, as has been suggested by Duncan (1974), Keen and Scott Morton (1978), and McFarlan and McKenney (1982). More recently, Zmud (1984) proposed that two new sets of information systems activities would come to dominate throughout the 1980s and 1990s: first, recognizing and assessing information technology innovations; and, second, facilitating the diffusion of appropriate technologies into an organization's work units.

Here, IS implementation is defined as an organizational effort to diffuse an appropriate information technology within a user community. The reasoning of borrowing a perspective from another discipline is well addressed by McKelvey and Aldrich (1983), as they adopt the population perspective from biology. They state:

> The population perspective is borrowed from biologists, who have developed it into an extensive, conceptually rich theory and method. The advantage of borrowing from another discipline is that much of the theoretical and methodological work has already been done. The disadvantage is that the perspective might not fit. Our view is that it has several clear advantages: 1. it offers a way to break the mental set of the existing model, as its theory and concepts sensitize us to see the organizational world in a new way, 2. it already has in place many essential concepts, and 3. the theoretical and methodological issues are already identified, so we have a map showing where all of the difficulties and points of interest are likely to be. Of course, while

organizations in changing environments have many functional parallels to organisms in changing environments, there are differences. We are fully aware that alterations and new theoretical and conceptual inventions might have to be made for the perspective to be of use in the study of organizations. Our view is that the functional parallels are strong and that the approach has much of promise and ought not to be discarded until it has been thoroughly tried. (McKelvey and Aldrich, 1983, p. 108)

4. A BROADER PERSPECTIVE OF THE IS IMPLEMENTATION PROCESS

Organizational innovation is most often viewed as a three-stage process: initiation, adoption, and implementation (Thompson, 1969; Pierce and Delbecq, 1977). This model of the innovation process is both representative of the literature and conceptually economic (Zmud, 1982a). With initiation, pressure to change can evolve from either need-pull or technology-push forces. In each case, needs and appropriate technologies come together via idea and information exchanges. The next stage, adoption, involves a decision to invest resources necessary to accommodate the change effort. Implementation, the last stage in the model, refers to development, installation and maintenance activities. It is in this stage that resources are expended to promote novel behaviors to diminish opposing forces, and to otherwise insure that expected benefits from investments in new technologies are realized.

The organizational innovation model just described focuses on facilitating innovation, assuming that innovations are inherently good. Thus, it excludes any post-adoption or post-innovation evaluation process. Kimberly (1981) notes that most studies seek to predict adoption and ignore what happens after adoption. Misuse or resistance to use can occur with the introduction of many technological innovations. This may arise from the adoption of an inappropriate innovation or because of faulty implementation processes.

Four assessments, which together establish a base for implementation success, can be incorporated into the innovation process model: acceptance, usage, performance and satisfaction. These four assessments play a critical role within the model as they determine whether an innovation was appropriate or inappropriate. And, these assessments are consistent with those associated with OR/MS/MIS implementation research (Zmud, 1979; Welsh, 1981; Schultz et al., 1984).

While no clear precedence relationship exists among use, performance, and satisfaction, it seems reasonable to suggest that they all are preceded by acceptance in at least two cases: when use is voluntary, and when performance is dependent on committed, rather than vapid, use. This precedence leads to the two post-adoption assessment processes of, first, acceptance and, then, use-performance-satisfaction.

An innovation will tend to be retained until a new pressure for change emerges. Even so, complete diffusion throughout an organization's tasks, people, and structure will not necessarily occur unless a variety of other technical, motivational, social, and political issues are resolved (Yin, 1979). Thus, incorporation can be included as a final 'implementation' process (Rogers, 1983; Zmud and Apple, 1986). Here, incorporation occurs when the innovation becomes embedded within an organization's routine and when the innovation is being applied to its full potential within an organization.

Three stages have, thus, been identified beyond the prototypical terminal IS implementation, i.e. adaptation (development/installation), stage. This results in a six-phase implementation process model. Each stage can be linked to a particular stage in Lewin's (1952) change model (see Figure 1). Also contained in the structure are feedback loops, which may act in positive or negative manners. In extreme cases, positive feedback would be expected to result in the full incorporation of an information technology, while negative feedback would be expected to result in 'exnovation', i.e. the disappearance of an implemented information technology.

5. WHAT WE KNOW ABOUT THE IS IMPLEMENTATION PROCESS

Both empirical and non-empirical studies regarding organizational innovation and IS implementation were reviewed to identify the key forces contributing to successful efforts to introduce technological innovations into organizations. This review identifies five major forces, which represent the constituent elements of Leavitt's (1965) organizational model as well as environmental considerations (Price, 1968; Duncan, 1974).

5.1 Individual Factors

While many innovation studies have considered individual factors, they have generally focused on adoption behaviors. Kimberly and Evanisko (1981) reviewed the innovation literature and found the four most frequently used individual variables to be job tenure, cosmopolitan, educational background and organizational role involvement. Attitude, or receptivity, toward change is highly correlated with these variables and with related change behaviors often invoked

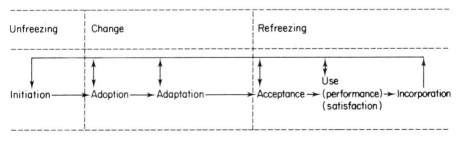

FIGURE 1 A six-phase view of the IS implementation process

in an innovation project. Most OR/MS/MIS researchers have limited their investigations of individual factors to relationships involving IS use-performance-satisfaction.

5.1.1 Job Tenure

Job tenure is generally related to institutional legitimacy. A positive relationship is usually expected through increased functional or political knowledge, while a negative relationship could be argued through an individual's bounded capacity. Consistently positive relationships with adoption have been found in innovation research (Rogers and Shoemaker, 1971; Kimberly and Evanisko, 1981; Paolillo and Brown, 1979). In the IS literature, however, negative associations have been reported with usage and satisfaction (Lucas, 1975, 1976, 1978). Mixed results have been found with performance (Lucas, 1975).

5.1.2 Cosmopolitanism

Cosmopolitanism is generally associated with receptivity to change. Generally, positive associations have been proposed or found due to increased outside contacts and holding broader perspectives (Becker, 1970; Kimberly and Evanisko, 1981; Rogers and Shoemaker, 1971). But, some negative (Counte and Kimberly, 1976; Kimberly and Evanisko, 1981) associations have been also found with adoption. Positive associations have been proposed or found between professionalism, a closely related construct, and adoption (Aiken and Hage, 1971; Pierce and Delbecq, 1977; Thompson, 1969) and incorporation (DiMaggio and Powell, 1983; Galbraith and Edstrom, 1976; Hawley, 1968; Rogers and Shoemaker, 1971).

5.1.3 Education

Education is also related to receptivity toward change. Consistently positive associations have been found with initiation and/or adoption (Becker, 1970; Kaplan, 1967; Kimberly and Evanisko, 1981; Mytinger, 1968; Rogers and Shoemaker, 1971). The study of normative isomorphism suggests a positive association with incorporation (Hawley, 1968; DiMaggio and Powell, 1983) due to internalized norms and dominant models. In the IS literature, negative associations have been found with usage and satisfaction (Lucas, 1975, 1976, 1978). Mixed results have been found with performance (Lucas, 1975; Taylor, 1975).

5.1.4 Role Involvement

Role involvement is another factor associated with receptivity toward change. Broader involvement in managerial activities has been proposed or reported to be positively related to adoption (Cyert and March, 1963; Kimberly and Evanisko, 1981; March and Simon, 1958).

Other closely related constructs such as elite (top management) values and user participation are associated with attitude toward change. In the innovation literature, positive associations have been proposed or found with adoption (Baldridge and Burnham, 1975; Cox, 1967; Hall, 1977; Hage and Dewar, 1973) and with acceptance (R. H. Davis, 1965). OR/MS/MIS research has found positive associations with adaptation and usage (Gorry and Scott Morton, 1971; Neal and Radnor, 1973; Mason and Mitroff, 1973; Radnor and Bean, 1973; Robey and Zeller, 1978) and with satisfaction (Zmud, 1979). But, inconsistent results have been observed between user participation and usage (Zmud, 1979).

5.2 Structural Factors

Both formal and informal structural arrangements exist in organizations. Not surprisingly, both types of structures influence the introduction of technological innovations (G. B. Davis, 1974; Tichy, 1981; Weick, 1969).

Much research has investigated the effects of formal structural factors on innovation, especially regarding initiation and adoption behaviors. Organizational theorists have identified specialization (complexity and functional specialization), centralization (concentration of decision making) and formalization (functional differentiation) as key factors for successful organizational change (Steers, 1977). Many researchers have also used 'size' as a surrogate for complexity. However, there has been a debate on its role as a direct contributor to successful organizational innovation processes (Aiken and Hage, 1971; Baldridge and Burnham, 1975; Kimberly, 1981). Therefore, size has not been included in this analysis.

5.2.1 Specialization

Specialization refers to the diversity of specialists within the organization. Technical rationality are used to explain the positive effects of specialization. However, the potential for increasing social and political conflict has also been raised. Although there have been some negative associations with adoption (Wilson, 1966; Sapolsky, 1967; Zaltman et al., 1973) and with usage (Robey and Zeller, 1978). Specialization has generally been proposed or found to be positively associated with both initiation and adoption (Aiken and Hage, 1968 and 1971; Kimberly and Evanisko, 1981; Moch and Morse, 1977; Pierce and Delbecq, 1977; Thompson, 1969; Sapolsky, 1967; Wilson, 1966; Zaltman et al., 1973) and with performance (Dalton et al., 1980).

5.2.2 Centralization

Centralization reflects the degree of concentration of decision-making activity. A bounded perspective and decreased autonomy are often described as negative aspects of centralization, while increased efficiency is given as a positive aspect. Generally negative associations have been proposed or found with initiation (Clark, 1968; Hage and Aiken, 1967; Kaluzny et al., 1970; Moch and Morse, 1977; Thompson, 1969; Zaltman et al., 1973), with adoption and adaptation (Pierce and Delbecq, 1977), and with performance (Dalton et al., 1980). However, some positive associations have been proposed or found with adoption (Corwin, 1970; Kimberly and Evanisko, 1981; Rowe and Boise, 1974; Zaltman et al., 1973; Zmud, 1982a) and with usage (Robey and Zeller, 1978; Zmud, 1982a).

5.2.3 Formalization

Formalization reflects the degree of functional differentiation. Functional differentiation is believed to develop clear work definition and procedure, but less autonomy. Although there have been a few exceptions (Pierce and Delbecq, 1977; Thompson, 1967), many researchers in innovation have proposed or found negative associations with initiation (Duncan, 1974; Evan and Black, 1967; Hage, 1965; Hage and Aikin, 1967, 1970; Kaluzny et al., 1972; Organ and Greene, 1981; Palumbo, 1969: Rosner, 1968; Rowe and Boise, 1974; Zaltman et al., 1973; Zmud 1982a). Also, consistently positive associations have been proposed or found with adoption (Kimberly and Evanisko, 1981; Moch and Morse, 1977; Pierce and Delbecq, 1977; Rowe and Boise, 1974; Zmud, 1982a), with adaptation (Pierce and Delbecq, 1977), with usage (Neal and Radnor, 1973; Radnor and Bean, 1973; Robey and Zeller, 1978; Zmud, 1982a), and with performance (Dalton et al., 1980).

5.2.4 Informal Network

In the study of innovation, another stream of research exists that focuses on informal structures or emergent networks. Here, research views innovation as a communication and information transfer process, in which interpersonal, informal communications among adopters are a key contributing factor to technological diffusion (Granovetter, 1973; Katz et al., 1963; Rogers, 1983). Consistent research findings stress the importance of multiple, valuable sources of relevant information for reasons of access, reliability and legitimization. In general, these communication network studies have focused on adoption behaviors.

The most widely used communication network variables focus on the social location and social contacts of an organization's members. Some research also examines information search effort, source value, or search frequency (Becker, 1970; Ebadi and Utterback, 1984). Positive associations have been proposed or reported between communication links and initiation behaviors (Allen, 1967; Tushman, 1977), adoption behaviors (Becker, 1970; Menzel, 1966), adaptation behaviors (Ebadi and Utterback, 1984), and the diffusion of technological information (Festinger et al., 1950; Katz and Lazarsfeld, 1955; Katz et al., 1963; Rogers, 1983). In the IS literature, however, only a single related study is known to exist (Zmud, 1983b).

5.3 Technological Factors

The influence of characteristics of innovations on the innovation process has been examined by a number of researchers, as summarized by Tornatzky and Klein (1982). In their meta-analysis of this literature, Tornatzky and Klein identify three innovation characteristics that possess consistent associations with innovation behaviors: compatibility, relative advantage, and complexity. While this research stream has focused its attention on adoption, a few studies have examined both adoption and adaptation behaviors. However, it has been suggested that incorporation could be affected by these innovation characteristics (Kimberly, 1981). In the IS implementation literature, only the political research stream has examined, and here only indirectly, the influence of technological factors.

5.3.1 Compatibility

The importance of an innovation's compatibility to an adopting organization is a frequently cited factor explaining the success of innovation efforts. This factor is related to an innovation's organizational 'fit' as well as its impact on individuals' attitudes regarding change, convenience of change, power shifts, etc. Generally, positive associations (Barnett, 1953; Ettlie and Vellenga, 1979) with adoption and adaptation have been found, with a few exceptions (Fliegel and Kivlin, 1966; Carlson, 1965). However, other research does indicate that the influence of compatibility may primarily reflect an interaction effect (Rogers, 1983) or act as a moderating factor (Zmud, 1982a, 1982b).

5.3.2 Relative Advantage

Relative advantage reflects the degree to which an innovation is perceived as providing greater organizational benefits than either other innovations or the status quo. These cost and benefits may reflect economic legitimacy and/or social or political legitimacy. In general, positive associations (Ettlie and Vellenga, 1979; Petrini, 1966; Mansfield, 1961, 1968; Singh, 1966) with adoption and adaptation have been found. A few studies, however, have exhibited weak negative associations, possibly due to the strong 'publicity values' involved (Carlson, 1965; Fliegel and Kivlin, 1966).

5.3.3 Complexity

Complexity is related to the degree of difficulty users experience in understanding and using an innovation. Lack of skill and knowledge is believed to be a primary factor behind efforts to resist organizational innovations. Thus, unless adopters and users have high needs for growth and achievement, complexity is likely to be associated negatively to the innovation. Negative associations (Graham, 1956;

Fliegel and Kivlin, 1966; Singh, 1966) have been found with adoption and adaptation. Positive associations, however, have also been found (Carlson, 1965).

5.4 Task-Related Factors

Innovation research has paid little attention to task-related factors, particularly those which stimulate change as well as provide a challenge and meaning to work. Tasks can be examined in at least two different ways. One perspective views task uncertainty as a major factor underlying organizational behaviors (March and Simon, 1958; Tushman and Nadler, 1978; Van de Ven, 1980). The other perspective focuses on five key task-related attributes (Hackman and Oldham, 1976, 1980), which are used as work design principles, e.g. the socio-technical systems approach (Bostrom and Heinen, 1977; Cherns, 1976; Mumford and Weir, 1979). The five attributes are: task autonomy, responsibility (significance), variety, identity, and feedback.

5.4.1 Task Uncertainty

Task uncertainty is a multi-facet construct reflecting the degree of routinization, programmability and exceptions in accomplishing organizational tasks. As its positive influence, task difficulty is likely to motivate initiation and usage behaviors, e.g. information search (Blandin and Brown, 1977; Culan, 1983; Ricketts, 1982). As its negative influence, it is also likely to act as an implementation constraint (Thompson, 1967).

5.4.2 Autonomy

Autonomy is concerned with the degree to which individuals exercise personal control over their assigned tasks. A higher degree of autonomy is likely to increase worker motivation, idea generation, satisfaction and performance. Griffin *et al.* (1981) reviewed the organizational literature and noted inconclusive findings for performance. These inconclusive findings were attributed to the moderating effect of individual growth need strength and satisfaction level with the work environment. Generally, a positive association has been found with satisfaction (Hackman and Oldham, 1976; Umstot *et al.*, 1976).

5.4.3 Responsibility

Responsibility is related to the degree of authority invested in an individual to oversee the completion of a task and to improve existing task behaviors. Tasks with low responsibility are expected to create less worker motivation to accept and to seek work system changes (Mumford, 1969). Generally, positive associations have been proposed or found with satisfaction (Hackman and Oldham, 1976; Umstot *et al.*, 1976) and performance (Griffin *et al.*, 1981).

5.4.4 Variety

It is commonly believed that simplified and routinized tasks are not likely to lead to higher performance and satisfaction, particularly with tasks requiring 'value-added' contributions by the task-incumbent. Positive associations have been proposed or found with satisfaction (Hackman and Oldham, 1976; Umstot *et al.*, 1976) and performance (Griffin *et al.*, 1981). In addition, Mumford (1969) argues that when the tasks become routinized, employees are divorced from change and tend to resist change. Quinn (1973) found task variety to be positively associated with adoption, adaptation, and usage.

5.4.5 Identity

Task identity ultimately refers to an individual 'internalizing' an assigned task. Increased identification with and belief in assigned work is likely to increase an individual's task involvement and, hence, lead to the potential for more innovative behaviors. Generally, a positive association has been proposed or found with satisfaction (Hackman and Oldham, 1976; Umstot *et al.*, 1976), while inconclusive results arise with performance (Griffin *et al.*, 1981).

5.4.6 Feedback

Feedback refers to the existence of a mechanism for informing individuals of their task performance levels. Based on reinforcement and learning theory, positive associations are expected between the frequency of feedback and the level of innovation displayed in behavior. As with other task factors, the association with satisfaction has been generally positive (Hackman and Oldham, 1976; Umstot *et al.*, 1976) but inconclusive with performance (Griffin *et al.*, 1981).

5.5 Environmental Factors

Studies of the influence of organizational environments on innovation processes are relatively rare, although assertions regarding its influence frequently appear.

Two different perspectives on environment exist (Aldrich, 1979; Scott, 1981). One views the environment as a source of information. Accordingly, heterogeneity and uncertainty are major attributes of this perspective. The second perspective views environments as a stock of resources. Thus, competition and resource concentration/dispersion represent other factors to be considered. The inter-organizational interdependence construct accommodates both perspectives.

Most innovation research that addresses these environmental issues has focused on initiation and adoption behaviors. A stream of research on isomorphism by sociologists (Hawley, 1968; DiMaggio and Powell, 1983) suggests that positive associations should exist between all of these environmental attributes and incorporation, through coercive, mimetic, or normative processes. Coercive isomorphism is concerned with environmental contingencies, mimetic isomorphism with imitating behaviors of successful cases, and normative isomorphism with informal and formal learnings.

5.5.1 Heterogeneity

Heterogeneity refers to the similarity of environmental entities, e.g. customer diversity, with which an organization must interact. Positive associations with innovativeness have been proposed or found (Baldridge and Burnham, 1975; DiMaggio and Powell, 1983; Hawley, 1968; Heydebrand, 1973). Such findings support a view that increased environmental contingencies foster, rather than inhibit, innovation as the environmental space creates a set of diverse niches. However, rational selection advocates do not agree on this argument (Thompson, 1967) as they tend to view environmental contingencies as organizational constraints.

5.5.2 Uncertainty

Uncertainty is related to the variability of organizational environments. This definition encompasses both instability and turbulence. In general, positive associations have been proposed or found (Cyert and March, 1963; DiMaggio and Powell, 1983; Hawley, 1968; Mohr, 1969; Palumbo, 1969; Pierce and Delbecq, 1977; Schroeder and Benbasat, 1975; Van de Ven and Ferry, 1980) as uncertainty is believed to stimulate innovation through an organization's effort to survive and grow. Others, however, predict a negative association with adoption due to the imposition of constraints on the amount and scope of adaptation available to an organization (Lawrence and Lorsch, 1967; Thompson, 1967).

5.5.3 Competition

Competition is related to environmental capacity (scarcity of resources) and population density. Economists have believed that competition increases the likelihood of innovative activities (Utterback, 1974). Kimberly and Evanisko (1981) have found positive associations between competition and adoption.

5.5.4 Concentration/Dispersion

Concentration/dispersion represents the extent to which resources are evenly spread throughout the environment. Resource concentration is likely to facilitate organizational learning, and hence innovation, in efforts to compete for limited resources (Aldrich, 1979). Positive associations have been proposed or found with adoption (Pfeffer and Salancik, 1978) and with incorporation due to coercive learning pressures (Thompson, 1967).

5.5.5 Inter-organizational Dependence

Inter-organizational dependence is related to the degree to which an organization has a program of sharing resources or exchanging ideas with other organizations. Studies in communication (Fischer, 1980) and networks (Aldrich and Whetten, 1981) provide a rationale of opportunity recognition and collective rationality for a positive association with organizational innovation. Positive associations have been proposed or found with initiation (Pierce and Delbecq, 1977), with adoption (Aiken and Hage, 1968, 1971; Pugh *et al.*, 1968, 1969; Becker, 1970); with adaptation (Pierce and Delbecq, 1977), and with diffusion at a population level (Clark, 1965; DiMaggio and Powell, 1983; Hawley, 1968).

6. ANALYSIS OF THE EXISTING RESEARCH BASE

The findings from this review of relevant literatures examining the influence of various factors on the IS implementation process are summarized in Table 1. This summary indicates that neither the organizational innovation research literature nor the IS implementation research literature has adopted a sufficiently broad perspective regarding the manner in which new technologies are introduced into organizations. Most innovation research has examined individual, structural and/or technological factors and has focused on adoption behaviors. Most IS implementation research has investigated individual factors and has focused on use (performance; satisfaction).

This analysis supports an argument that both organizational innovation and IS implementation research literatures have possessed limited perspectives, even when the introduction of a new technology is viewed as a change process. Assuming that the scope of these studies reflects not only the past and current paradigms of researchers but also their future research directions, we are not optimistic about the future productivity of either of these research streams if their current perspectives are maintained. On the other hand, if the perspectives and research agenda of both fields broaden to accommodate the contributions of each other, then the potential exists for achieving an improved understanding of the process underlying technological innovation in organizations.

7. DISCUSSION AND FUTURE RESEARCH

An IS is a formal, deliberately planned technological innovation composed of man, machine, and procedures that is introduced into an organization in response to a perceived need on the part of one or more organizational members. Not only

TABLE 1 Influential factors and their general association with each stage in innovation process, from both empirical and non-empirical studies

		Unfreezing	Change			Refreezing	
Entity	Attribute	1. Initiation	2. Adoption	3. Adaptation	4. Acceptance	5. a. Use b. Performance c. Satisfaction	6. Incorporation
Individual	job tenure		+			a. ⊖ b. ⊕/⊖ c. ⊖	
	cosmopolitanism	+	+/–				+/⊞
	education	+	+			a. – b. +/– c. –	⊞
	role envolvement		+				
	attitude toward change		+	⊕	+	a. ⊕/⊖ b. ⊕ c. ⊕	
Structure	Formal						
	specialization	+	+	+		a. ⊖ b. ⊞ c. ☐	
	centralization	–	+	–		a. ⊕ b. ☐ c. ☐	
	formalization	–	+	⊕/–		a. ⊖ b. ⊞ c. ☐	
	Informal						
	network	+	+	+			+
Technology	compatibility		+	+			+/⊞
	relative advantage		+	+			+/⊞
	complexity		+/–	+/–			–/☐

continued

TABLE 1 (continued)

Task	task uncertainty	⊞	□		a. ⊕
	autonomy	⊞			b. ⊕ c. ⊞
	responsibility	⊕			b. ⊞ c. ⊞
	variety	⊞	+	+	a. + b. ⊞ c. □
	identity				b. ⊞ c. ⊞
	feedback				b. ⊞ c. ⊞
Environment	heterogeneity		+		⊞
	uncertainty	+	+ / □	+	a. ⊕ b. ⊕ ⊞
	competition		+		⊞
	concentration		+		⊞
	organizational		+		
	dependence	+	+	+	+ / ⊞

Note:
1. + or −: Positive or negative association from studies in the innovation literature.
2. ⊕ or ⊙: Positive or negative association from studies in the OR/MS/MIS literature.
3. ⊞ or ⊟: Positive or negative association from studies in other fields such as organization, sociology, etc.
4. +/−: Very mixed association.
5. The blanks in the table indicate that there exist no appropriate studies in each corresponding area.

do these members represent various segments of the organization, but the 'needs' precipitating an MIS implementation effort also span a broad range of individual and organizational motives. As a result, the difficulty in successfully implementing an IS lies in the complexities of the organization's internal and external environments. Accepting these complexities as well as multi-staged view of IS implementation, the necessity of expanding the currently limited perspective of IS implementation seems apparent.

In this chapter, the perspectives of two research streams, e.g. the organizational innovation and the IS implementation research literatures, have been merged to arrive at a more comprehensive model of the IS implementation process. We believe such a foundation, once validated, will contribute to a better understanding of IS implementation for both researchers and practitioners. IS researchers can draw on and extend the existing base of knowledge on organizational innovation; and, practitioners can draw on both literatures in devising strategies for managing the introduction of information technologies into their organizations.

Our review of the existing literature suggests two major directions for future research. First, the empty cells shown in Table 1 directly indicate fruitful, and needed, research areas. Similarly, the findings and assertions from the organizational innovation studies should be validated within an IS context.

Second, investigations of the dynamics of this more comprehensive model of the IS implementation process is another promising area for future research. It seems likely that the factors influencing IS implementation process possess divergent impacts on the various implementation stages. These differences may be explained, as Zmud (1982a, 1982b) has argued, through interactions among factors and/or relations among stages. Accordingly, research investigating (1) interactions of factors within a stage and (2) relations among the stages (see Figure 1 for possible relations) is also advocated. Studies such as Zmud (1982a) (technology–structure), Zmud *et al.*, (1984) (people–task), and Macintosh (1981) (task–technology–structure–people) are representative of the first research direction, while studies such as Apple and Zmud (1984), Ginzberg (1979), and Zand and Sorenson (1975) are related to the latter effort.

Throughout this paper, it has been stressed that the IS implementation process is as important for IS implementation success as is the IS itself. Adopting the proposed model for IS implementation, managers might begin to view IS implementation as a set of tasks involving unfreezing and refreezing behaviors as well as change behaviors. Working with this perspective, they should be more aware of the need to introduce organizational mechanisms that promote innovative behaviors through all the IS implementation stages. Finally, research findings flowing from this model should enable managers to better understand the many forces influencing implementation success, resulting in their being more able to develop effective strategies for introducing information technologies within their organization.

REFERENCES

Ackoff, R. L. (1967) 'Management Misinformation Systems', *Management Science,* **14** 147–156.

Aiken, M., and Hage, J. (1968) 'Organizational Interdependence and an Interorganizational Structure', *American Sociological Review,* **33**, 912–930.

Aiken, M., and Hage, J. (1971) 'The Organic Organization and Innovation', *Sociology,* **5**, 63–82.

Aldrich, H. (1979) *Organizations and Environments,* Prentice-Hall, NJ.

Aldrich, H., and Whetten, D. A. (1981) 'Organization-sets, Action-sets, and Networks: Making the Most of Simplicity, in *Handbook of Organizational Design,* P. C. Nystrom and W. H. Starbuck (Eds.), Oxford University Press, London, Vol. 1, pp. 385–408.

Allen, T. J. (1967) 'Communications in the Research and Development Laboratory', *Technology Review,* **70**, October–November, 1–8.

Alter, S., and Ginzberg, M. J. (1978) 'Managing Uncertainty in MIS Implementation', *Sloan Management Review,* **20**, 1, 23–31.

Apple, L. E., and Zmud, E. W. (1984) 'A Pharmacokinetics Approach to Technology Transfer: Implications for OR/MS/MIS Implementation', in *Management Science Implementation,* R. L., Schultz and M. J., Ginzberg (Eds.), JAI Press, Norwich, CT.

Baldridge, J. V., and Burnham, R. A. (1975) 'Organizational Innovation: Individual, Organizational and Environmental Impacts', *ASQ,* **20**, 165–176.

Barnett, H. (1953) *Innovation,* McGraw-Hill, New York.

Becker, M. H. (1970) 'Sociometric Location and Innovativeness: Reformulation and Extension of the Diffusion Model', *American Sociological Review,* **35**, 267–282.

Blandin, J. S., and Brown, W. B. (1977) 'Uncertainty and Management's Search for Information', *IEEE Transactions on Engineering Management,* **24**, 4, 114–119.

Boland, R. J. (1978) 'The Process and Product of System Design', *Management Science,* **24**, 9, 887–898.

Bostrom, R. P., and Heinen, J. S. (1977) 'MIS Problems and Failures: A socio-technical perspective — Part 1: The Causes', *MIS Quarterly,* **1**, 17–32.

Business Week (1981) 'The Speedup in Automation: Changing 45 mil. Jobs', 3 August.

Carlson, R. O. (1965) 'Adoption of Educational Innovations', University of Oregon, Center for the Advanced Study of Educational Administration, Eugene, OR.

Cherns, A. B. (1976) 'The Principles of Socio-Technical System Design', *Human Relations,* **29**, 8, 783–792.

Churchman, C., and Schainblatt, A. (1965) 'The Researcher and Manager: A Dialectic of Implementation', *Management Science,* **11**, B69–B87.

Clark, B. (1965) 'Interorganizational Patterns in Education', *ASQ,* **10**, 224–237.

Clark, T. (1968) 'Institutionalization of Innovations in Higher Education', *ASQ,* **13**, 1–25.

Corwin, R. G. (1970) 'Strategies for Organizational Innovation', in 'An Organizational Development Approach to Consulting', D. A. Kolb and A. L. Frohman (Eds.), *Sloan Management Review,* **12**, 51–65.

Counte, M. A., and Kimberly, J. R. (1976) 'Change in Physician Attitudes toward Reform in Medical Education: The Results of a Field Experiment', *Social Science and Medicine,* **10**, 547–552.

Couger, J. D., and Zawacki, R. A. (1980) 'Motivating People at Work', taken from *Motivating and Managing Computer Personnel,* John Wiley, New York, pp. 67–93.

Cox, D. F. (1967) in 'Risk Taking and Information Handling in Consumer Behavior', in D. F. Cox (Ed.), *Risk Taking and Information Handling in Consumer Behavior,* Graduate School of Business Administration, Harvard University, Boston, pp. 604–639.

Culan, M. J. (1983) 'Chauffeured versus End User Access to Commercial Databases: The Effects of Task and Individual Differences', *MIS Quarterly,* **7**, 1, 55–67.

Cyert, R., and March, J. G. (1963) *A Behavioral Theory of the Firm*, Prentice-Hall, Englewood Cliffs.

Dalton, D. R., Todor, W. D. Spendolini, M. J., Fielding, G. J., and Porter, L. W. (1980) 'Organization Structure and Performance: A Critical Review', *Academy of Management Review*, **5**, 49–64.

Davis, G. B. (1974) *Management Information Systems: Conceptual Foundations Structure, and Development*, McGraw-Hill, New York.

Davis, R. H. (1965) 'Personal and Organizational Variables Related to the Adoption of Educational Innovations in a Liberal Arts College', Ph.D. thesis, University of Chicago.

DiMaggio, P., and Powell, W. (1983) 'The Iron Cage Revisited: Industrial Isomorphism and Collective Rationality in Organizational Fields', *American Sociological Review*, **48**, 147–160.

Doktor, R., Schultz, R. L., and Slevin, D. P. (Eds.) (1979) *The Implementation of Management Science*, North-Holland, Amsterdam.

Downs, G. W., and Mohr, L. B. (1976) 'Conceptual Issues in the Study of Innovation', *ASQ*, **21**, 700–714.

Duncan, R. B. (1974) 'Multiple Decision Making Structures in Adapting to the Environment: Some Implications for Organizational Learning', *Decision Sciences*, **5**, 705–725.

Ebadi, Y. M., and Utterback, J. M. (1984) 'The Effects of Communication on Technological Innovation', *Management Science*, **30**, 5, 572–585.

Ettlie, J. E. (1973) 'Technology Transfer—from Innovators to Users', *IE*, 16–23.

Ettlie, J. E., and Vellenga, D. B. (1979) 'The Adoption Time Period for Some Transportation Innovation', *Management Science*, **25**, 429–443.

Evan, W. M., and Black, G. (1967) 'Innovation in Business Organizations: Some Factors Associated with Success or Failure of Staff Proposals', *Journal of Business*, **40**, 519–530.

Festinger, L., Schachter, S., and Back, K. (1950) *Social Pressures in Informal Groups*, Harper and Brothers, New York.

Fischer, W. A. (1980) 'Scientific and Technical Information and the Performance of R&D Groups', *TIMS Studies in the Management Sciences*, **15**, 67–89.

Fliegel, F. C., and Kivlin, J. E. (1966) 'Attributes of Innovations as Factors in Diffusion', *American Journal of Sociology*, **72**, 235–248.

Fuerst, W. L., and Cheney, P. H. 'Factors Affecting the Perceived Utilization of Computer-based Decision Support Systems in the Oil Industry', *Decision Sciences*, **13**, 4, 554–569.

Galbraith, J. R., and Edstrom, A. (1976) 'Creating Decentralization through Informal Networks: The Role of Transfers', in *The Management of Organization Design*, Vol. 2, R. H. Kilmann, L. R. Pondy, and D. P. Slevin (Eds.), Elsevier North-Holland, New York, pp. 289–310.

Gibson, C. F. (1981) 'Managing Organizational Change to Achieve Full Systems Results', *Proceedings of the 14th annual conference of SIM*.

Ginzberg, M. J. (1979) 'A Study of the Implementation Process', *TIMS Studies in the Management Sciences*, **13**, 85–102.

Ginzberg, M. J. (1981a) 'Early Diagnosis of MIS Implementation Failure: Promising Results and Unanswered Questions', *Management Science*, **27**, 4, 459–478.

Ginzberg, M. J. (1981b) 'Key Recurrent Issues in the MIS Implementation Process', *MIS Quarterly*, **5**, 47–59.

Gorry, G. A., and Scott Morton, M. S. (1971) 'A Framework for Management Information Systems', *Sloan Management Review*, **13**, 55–70.

Graham, L. X. (1956) 'Class and Conservatism in the Adoption of Innovations', *Human Relations*, **9**, 91–100.

Granovetter, M. S. (1973) 'The Strengths of Weak Ties', *American Journal of Sociology*, **78**, 1360–1380.

Griffin, R. W., Welsh, A., and Moorhead, G. (1981) 'Perceived Task Characteristics and Employee Performance: A Literature Review', *Academy of Management Review*, **6**, 655–664.

Hackman, J. R., and Oldham, G. R. (1976) 'Motivation through the Design of Work: Test of a Theory', *Organizational Behavior and Human Performance*, **16**, 250–279.

Hackman, J. R., and Oldham, G. R. (1980) *Work Redesign*, Addison-Wesley, MA.

Hage, J. (1965) 'An Axiomatic Theory of Organizations', *ASQ*, **10**, 289–320.

Hage, J., and Aiken, M. (1967) 'Program Change and Organizational properties: A Comparative Analysis', *American Journal of Sociology*, **72**, 503–519.

Hage, J., and Dewar, R. (1973) 'Elite Values Versus Organizational Structure in Predicting Innovation', *ASQ*, **18**, 279–290.

Hall, R. (1977) *Organizations: Structure and Process*, Prentice-Hall, Englewood Cliffs, NJ.

Hawley, A. (1968) 'Human Ecology', in *International Encyclopedia of the Social Sciences*, David L. Sills (Ed.), Macmillan, New York.

Hayworld, G., Allen, D. H., and Masterson, J. (1976) 'Characteristics and Diffusion of Technological Innovations', *R&D Management*, **7**, 15–24.

Heydebrand, W. V. (1973) *Hospital Bureaucracy*, Dunellen, New York.

Hoffman, L. R., and Maier, N. R. (1961) 'Quality and Acceptance of Problem Solutions by Members and Heterogeneous Groups', *Journal of Abnormal and Social Psychology*, **62**, 401–407.

Ives, B., and Olson, M. H. (1984) 'User Involvement and MIS Success: A Review of Research', *Management Science*, 586–603.

Kaluzny, A. D., Glasser, J. H., Gentry, J. T., and Sprague, J. (1970) 'Diffusion of Innovative Health Care Services in the United States: A Study of Hospitals', *Medical Care*, **8**, 474–487.

Kaluzny, A. D., Veney, J. D., and Gentry, J. T. (1974) 'Innovation of Health Services: A Comparative Study of Hospitals and Health Departments', in *Innovation in Health Care Organizations*, A. D. Kaluzny, J. T. Gentry, and J. E. Veney, Health Administration, University of North Carolina, Chapel Hill, NC.

Kaplan, H. B. (1967) 'Implementation of Program Change in Community Agencies', *Milbank Memorial Fund Quarterly*, **45**, 321–332.

Kast, F. E., and Rosenzweig, J. E. (1974) 'Organization and Management: A Systems Approach (2nd Edn.), McGraw-Hill, New York.

Katz, E., and Lazarsfeld, P. E. (1955) *Personal Influence: The Part Played by People in the Flow of Mass Communication*, Free Press, New York.

Katz, E., Levin, M. L., and Hamilton, H. (1963) 'Traditions of Research on the Diffusion of Innovation', *American Sociological Review*, **28**, 237–252.

Kenn, P. G. W. (1975) 'Computer-based Decision Aids: The Evaluation Problem', *Sloan Management Review*, Spring, 12–31.

Keen, P. G. W. (1977) 'Implementation Research in OR/MS and MIS: Description versus Prescription', Research paper no. 390, Graduate School of Business, Stanford University.

Keen, P. G. W. (1981) 'Information Systems and Organizational Change', *Communications of the ACM*, **24**, 24–33.

Keen, P. G. W., and Scott Morton, S. (1978) *Decision Support Systems: An Organizational Perspective*, Addison-Wesley, Reading, MA.

Kimberly, J. R. (1981) 'Managerial Innovation', in *Handbook of Organizational Design*, P. Nystrom and W. H. Starbuck (Eds.), Oxford University Press, London, Vol. 1, pp. 84–104.

Kimberly, J. R., and Evanisko, M. J. (1981) 'Organizational Innovation: The Influence of Individual, Organizational, and Contextual Factors on Hospital Adoption of Technological and Administrative Innovations', *Academy of Management Journal*, **24**, 4, 689–713.

Kivlin, J. F., and Fliegel, F. C. (1967) 'Differential Perceptions of Innovations and Rate of Adoption', *Rural Society*, **32**, 78–91.

Kolb, D. A., and Frohman, A. L. (1970) 'An Organization Development Approach to Consulting', *Sloan Management Review*, **12**, 1, 51–65.

Kramer, K. L. (1981) 'The Politics of Model Implementation', *Systems, Objectives, Solutions*, **1**, 4, 161–178.

Lawless, M. W. (1976) 'Implementation Issues in Criminal Justice Modeling', Paper #p-5508, The Rand Corporation, Santa Monica, California.

Lawrence, P. R., and Lorsch, J. W. (1967) *Organization and Environment*, Graduate School of Business Administration, Harvard University.

Leavitt, H. J. (1965) 'Applied Organizational Change in Industry: Structural, Technological, and Humanistic Approach', in *Handbook of Organizations*, March, J. (Ed.), Rand McNally, Chicago, pp. 1144–1170.

Lewin, K. (1947) 'Frontiers in Group Dynamics', *Human Relations*, **1**, 5–42.

Lewin, K. (1952) 'Group Decision and Social Change', in *Readings in Social Psychology*, Newcombe and Hartley (Eds.), Henry Holt, New York, pp. 459–473.

Lientz, B. P. (1981) *An Introduction of Distributed Systems*, Addison-Wesley, Reading, MA.

Lucas, H. C. (1975) *Why Information Systems Fail*, Columbia University Press, New York.

Lucas, H. C. (1976) *The Implementation of Computer-based Models*, National Association of Accountants, New York.

Lucas, H. C. (1978) 'The Use of an Interactive Information Storage and Retrieval Systems in Medical Research', *Communications of ACM*, **21**, 197–205.

McFarlan, F. W. (1981) 'Portfolio Approach to Information Systems', *Harvard Business Review*, **59**, 5, 142–150.

McFarlan, F. W., and McKenney, J. L. (1982) *Information Systems Management: A Senior Management Perspective*, Irwin, Homewood, IL.

Macintosh, N. B. (1981) 'A Contextual Model of Information Systems', *Accounting, Organizations and Society*, **6**, 1, 39–53.

McKelvey, B., and Aldrich, H. (1983) 'Applied Population Science', *ASQ*, **28**, 101–128.

Mansfield, E. (1961) 'Technical Change and the Rate of Imitation', *Econometrica*, **29**, 741–766.

Mansfield, E. (1963) 'Size of Firm, Market Structure, and Innovation', *Journal of Political Economics*, **71**, 556–576.

Mansfield, E. (1968) *Industrial Research and Technical Innovation: An Econometric Analysis*, Norton and Co., New York.

March, J. G., and Simon, H. A. (1958) *Organizations*, John Wiley, New York.

Markus, M. L. (1983) 'Power Politics and MIS Implementation', *Communications of the ACM*, **26**, 6, 430–444.

Mason, R. O., and Mitroff, I. I. (1973) 'A Program for Research on Management Information Systems', *Management Science*, **19**, 475–487.

Menzel, H. (1966) 'Scientific Communication: Five Themes From Social Science Research', *American Psychologist*, **21**, 999–1004.

MIS Week, (1986) 'What Financial Services Executives Worry About: Computer Security, Technology as a Strategic Advantage Top List', March, 58.

Moch, M. K., and Morse, E. V. (1977) 'Size, Centralization and Organizational Adoption of Innovations', *American Sociological Review*, **42**, 716–725.

Mohr, L. B. (1969) 'Determinants of Innovation in Organizations', *American Political Science Review*, **63**, 111–126.

Mumford, E. (1969) 'Systems Implementation and Post-implementation Review', *The Computer Bulletin (U.K.)*, January 10–13.

Mumford, E., and Weir, M. (1979) *Computer Systems in Work Design: the ETHICS Method*, John Wiley, New York.

Mytinger, R. E. (1968) *Innovation in Local Health Services*, Government Printing Office, Washington D. C.

Neal, R. D., and Radnor, M. (1973) 'The Relation between Formal Procedures for Pursuing OR/MS Activities and OR/MS Group Success', *Operations Research*, **21**, 451–474.

Nelson, R. D., and Sieber, S. D. (1976) 'Innovations in Urban Secondary Schools', *School Review*, **84**, 213–231.

Nolan, R. L. (1978) 'Organizational Response and Information Technology', *Proceedings of National Computer Conference, 1978*, pp. 517–524.

Organ, D. W., and Greene, C. N. (1981) 'The Effects of Formalization on Professional Involvement: A Compensatory Process Approach', *Administrative Science Quarterly*, **26**, 237–252.

Palumbo, D. J. (1969) 'Power and Role Specificity in Organization Theory', *Public Administration Review*, **29**, 237–248.

Paolillo, J., and Brown, W. (1979) 'A Multivariate Approach to Perceived Innovation in R&D Subsystems', *IEEE Transactions on Engineering Management*, **26**, 2.

Petrini, F. (1966) 'The Rate of Adoption of Selected Agricultural Innovations', Series A. Rep. 53, Agricultural College of Sweden, Uppsala.

Pettigrew, A. (1972) 'Information Control as a Power Resource', *Sociology*, **6**, 187–204.

Pfeffer, J., and Salancik, G. (1978) *The External Control of Organizations: A Resource Dependency Perspective*, Harper and Row, New York.

Pierce, J. L., and Delbecq, A. L. (1977) 'Organization Structure, Individual Attributes and Innovation', *Academy of Management Review*, **2**, 27–37.

Pugh, D. S., Hickson, D. J., Hinings, C. R., and Turner, C. 'Dimensions of Organization Structure', *Administrative Science Quarterly*, **13**, 65–91.

Pugh, D. S., Hickson, D. J., Hinings, C. R., and Turner, C. (1969) 'The Context of Organizational Structures', *Administrative Science Quarterly*, **14**, 91–114.

Quinn, J. V. (1973) 'What To Do until the (EDP) Doctors Come!', *Management Advisor*, **10**, 25–29.

Radnor, M., and Bean, A. S. (1973) 'Top Management Support for Management Science', *Omega*, **2**, 63–75.

Ricketts, J. A. (1982) 'An Investigation of Some Effects of Environmental Complexity and Systematic Bias on the MIS User-System Interface: A Simulation Experiment', Unpublished doctoral dissertation, Graduate School of Business, Indiana University, Bloomington, Indiana.

Robey, D., and Zeller, R. L. (1978) 'Factors Affecting the Success and Failure of an Information System for Product Quality', *Interfaces*, **8**, 70–75.

Rogers, E. M. (1983) *Diffusion of Innovations*, Free Press, New York.

Rogers, E. M., and Shoemaker, F. F. (1971) *Communication of Innovations*, Free Press, New York.

Rosner, M. M. (1968) 'Administrative Controls and Innovations', *Behavioral Science*, **13**, 36–43.

Rowe, L. A., and Boise, W. B. (1974) 'Organizational Innovation: Current Research and Evolving Concepts', *Public Administration Review*, **34**, 284–293.

Sanders, G. L., and Courtney, J. F. (1985) 'A Field Study of Organizational Factors Influencing DSS Success', *MIS Quarterly*, **9**, 1, 77–93.

Sapolsky, H. (1967) 'Organizational Structure and Innovation', *Journal of Business*, **40**, 497–510.

Schein, E. H. (1961) 'Management Development as a Process of Influence', *Industrial Management Review*, **2**, 2.

Schroeder, R. G., and Benbasat, I. (1975) 'An Experimental Evaluation of the Relationship of Uncertainty in the Environment to Information Used by Decision Makers', *Decision Sciences*, **6**, 3, 556–567.

Schultz, R. L. (1984) 'The Implementation of Forecasting Models', *Journal of Forecasting*, **3**, 43–55.

Schultz, R. L., Ginzberg, M. J., and Lucas, H. C. (1984) 'A Structural Model of Implementation' in *Management Science Implementation*, Schultz, R. L., and Ginzberg, M. J. (Eds.) JAI Press, Greenwich, 55–87.

Schultz, R. L., and Ginzberg, M. J. (Eds.) (1984) *Management Science Implementation*, JAI Press, Greenwich, CT.

Schultz, R. L., and Slevin, D. P. (1975) 'Implementation and Organizational Validity: An Empirical Investigation', in *Implementing Operations Research/Management Science*, R. L. Schultz and D. P. Slevin (Eds.), American Elsevier, New York, pp. 253–270.

Schultz, R. L., Ginsberg, M. J., and Lucas, H. C. (1984) 'A Structural Model of Implementation', in *Management Science Implementation*, R. L. Schultz and M. J. Ginzberg (Eds.), JAI Press, Norwich, CT, pp. 55–87.

Scott, W. R. (1981) *Organizations: Rational, Natural, and Open Systems*, Prentice-Hall, NJ.

Singh, R. M. (1966) 'Characteristics of Farm Innovations Associated with the Rate of Adoption', Agricultural Extension Education Report 14, Guelph, Ontario.

Steers, R. M. (1977) *Organizational effectiveness*, Goodyear, Santa Monica, California.

Taylor, R. N. (1975) 'Age and Experience as Determinants of Managerial Information Prcessing and Decision Making Performance', *Academy Management Journal*, **18**, 74–81.

Thompson, J. D. (1967) *Organizations in Action*, McGraw-Hill, New York.

Thompson, V. A. (1969) *Bureaucracy and Innovation*, University of Alabama Press, Huntsville.

Tichy, N. M. (1981) 'Networks in Organizations', in *Handbook of Organizational Design*, P. C. Nystrom and W. H. Starbuck (Eds.), Oxford University Press, London, Vol. 2, pp. 225–249.

Time (1980) 'Now the Office of Tomorrow: Technology's Dazzling Breakthroughs Shake up the White-collar World', 17 November.'

Tornatzky, L. G., and Klein, L. (1982) 'Innovation Characteristics and Innovation-implementation: A Meta-analysis of Findings', *IEEE Transactions on Engineering Management*, **29**, 1.

Tushman, M. L. (1977) 'Communicating Across Organizational Boundaries: Special Boundary Roles in the Innovative Process', *Administrative Science Quarterly*, **22**, 581–606.

Tushman, M. L., and Nadler, D. A. (1978) 'Information Processing as an Integrating Concept in Organizational Design', *Academy of Management Review*, **3**, 613–624.

Umstot, D. D., Bell, D. H., and Mitchel, T. R. (1976) 'Effects of Job Enrichment and Task Goals on Satisfaction and Productivity, Implications for Job Design', *Journal of Applied Psychology*, **61**, 379–394.

Utterback, J. M. (1974) 'Innovation in Industry and the Diffusion of Technology', *Science*, **183**, 620–626.

Van de Ven, A. H., and Ferry, D., (1980) *Organizational Assessment*, Wiley Interscience, New York.

Weick, K. E. (1969) *The Social Psychology of Organizing*, Addison-Wesley, Reading, MA.

Wilson, J. Q. (1966) 'Innovation in Organization: Notes towards a Theory', in *Approaches to Organization Design*, J. D. Thompson (Ed.), University of Pittsburgh Press, Pittsburgh, pp. 193–218.

Wolek, F. W. (1975) 'Implementation and Process of Adopting Managerial Technology', *Interfaces*, **5**, 38–46.

Yin, R. K. (1979) *Changing Urban Bureaucracies*, Rand Corp., Lexington Books, Lexington, MA.

Zaltman, D. E., Duncan, R. B., and Holbeck, J. (1973) *Innovations and Organizations*, John Wiley, New York.

Zand, D. E., and Sorenson, R. E. (1975) 'Theory of Change and the Effective Use of Management Science', *Administrative Science Quarterly*, **20**, 530–545.

Zmud, R. W. (1979) 'Individual Difference and MIS Success: A Review of the Empirical Literature', *Management Science*, **25**, 966–979.

Zmud, R. W. (1982a) 'Diffusion of Modern Software Practices: Influence of Centralization and Formalization', *Management Science*, **28**, 12, 1421–1431.

Zmud, R. W. (1982b) 'System Implementation Success — Behavioral/Organizational Influence and Strategies for Effecting Change', in *Teaching Informatics Courses*, Jackson, H. L. W. (Ed.), North-Holland, New York, pp. 125–142.

Zmud, R. W. (1983a) *Information Systems in Organizations*, Scott Foresman, Glenview, IL.

Zmud, R. W. (1983b) 'The Effectiveness of External Information Channels in Facilitating Innovation Within Software Development Groups', *MIS Quarterly*, **7**, 2, 43–58.

Zmud, R. W. (1984) 'Design Alternatives for Organizing Information Systems Activities', *MIS Quarterly*, **8**, 2, 79–93.

Zmud, R. W. (1984a) 'An Examination of "Push–Pull" Theory Applied to Process Innovation in Knowledge Work', *Management Science*, **30**, 6, 727–738.

Zmud, R. W., and Apple, L. E. (1986) 'Measuring the Institutionalization of a Multibusiness Unit Innovation', Working paper.

Zmud, R. W., McLaughlin, C. P., and Might, R. L. (1984) 'An Empirical Analysis of Project Management Technique Implementation Success', in *Management Science Implementation*, R. L. Schultz and M. J. Ginzberg (Eds.), JAI Press, Norwich, CT.

Critical Issues in Information Systems Research
Edited by R. J. Boland Jr. and R. A. Hirschheim
©1987 John Wiley & Sons Ltd.

Chapter 11

RESEARCH AGENDA FOR A TRANSACTION COSTS APPROACH TO INFORMATION SYSTEMS

Claudio U. Ciborra

ABSTRACT

The traditional role of computer-based information systems is to provide support for individual decision making. According to this model, information is to be seen as a valuable resource for the decision maker faced with a complex task. Such a view of information systems in organizations does, however, fail to include such phenomena as the daily use of information for misrepresentation purposes. The conventional systems analysis methods, whether they be data- or decision-oriented, do not help in understanding the nature of organizations and their ways of processing information. This paper proposes what appears to be a more realistic approach to the analysis and design of information systems. Organizations are seen as networks of contracts which govern exchange transactions between members having only partially overlapping goals. Conflict of interests is explicitly admitted to be a factor affecting information and exchange costs. Information technology is seen as a means to streamline exchange transactions, thus enabling economic organizations to operate more efficiently. This paper deals specifically with a variety of research projects and issues which stem from this new and promising approach.

1. INTRODUCTION

The transaction costs perspective on the role of computers in organizations (Ciborra, 1985) challenges the existing conventional wisdom by throwing a different light on such basic issues as:

— Why and how is information processed and communicated within and between organizations?
— What impact does information technology have on organizational processes and structures?
— what organizational models can guarantee that systems analysis and design are sound and effective?

Present-day designers turn to two theories when addressing the above issues: they either tend to a 'data view' of organizations, or, in the case of those most influenced by business needs, to a decision-making view. These two ways of looking at the problems of computerization are so widely accepted and have been so much taken for granted that they can be said to form the conventional wisdom of today. The origins of the former can be traced directly back to the EDP field, while the latter stem from the influential work of Herbert A. Simon (1976a).

It is somewhat surprising that although information technology has gone through an almost revolutionary process of miniaturization, sophistication and diffusion, the design models and criteria concerning its application in organizations are still based on the concepts of the early 1960s. This appears still more puzzling when we examine the fields of sociology, political science, organization theory, economics of information and organizations, which have also undergone a sharp innovative process. But none of the new developments in these disciplines seems to have filtered through to the field of MIS, apart from such aspects, as the political view of system development (Keen, 1981; Kling, 1980; Markus, 1983).

The aim of this chapter is to introduce the reader to the transaction costs approach, which is based on recent developments in the social sciences and economics. The approach can provide a new framework and a new language to better understand and design computer-based information systems.

To anticipate, it is argued that a new *organizational* understanding of information processing must go beyond the individual decision-making paradigm, which at present lies at the core of the conventional wisdom. The concepts of 'exchange' (transaction) [1] and 'contract' between at least *two* individuals or organizational units become the new center of attention. This alternative tact enables us to use the results of the transaction costs paradigm (Williamson, 1975, 1981), which links the notions of information, uncertainty and organization in an original way. Phenomena such as resistance to change and retention of information are not seen any more as irrational, unexpected flaws in a structured system design, but as factors and behaviors which can be rationally understood and carefully anticipated; and issues such as centralization versus decentralization can be viewed in a different light. The presentation of the argument starts in Section 2 with a critique of the received tradition and its implicit, but widespread assumptions: it is shown that the data- and decision-making views are inadequate and unrealistic, because they are based on a view of organizations as perfectly cooperative systems. The need for an alternative framework based on the new institutional economics is addressed in Section 3: it is shown that by considering organizations as networks of exchanges and contracts between members, both cooperation and conflict can be taken into account together with the various usages of information that individuals employ when cooperating and conflicting. Also, the specific role of information technology is illustrated as a means to lower transaction costs. In Section 4 the research paths opened up by the new framework are discussed.

2. A CRITIQUE OF THE CONVENTIONAL WISDOM

2.1 Two Current Views

In order to reframe our understanding of computer-based information systems in organizations, an essential, preliminary step is to discuss two approaches which are at present in good currency: the *data approach* and the *decision approach*. According to the data approach, in applying a computer to an organization it is only necessary to consider (i.e. analyze and design) the data flows and files in that organization. The analyst ascertains management information requirements by examining all reports, files and other information sources currently used by managers. The set of data thus obtained is considered to be the information which management needs to computerize (Davis and Munro, 1977). Unfortunately, the data approach ignores the economic and social nature of organizations and is exposed to the hazards of those economic and social processes which characterize the daily life of organizations and which we, as members of organizations, all know.

The second tradition is more sophisticated from an organizational point of view. It can be traced back to Simon (1977) and was further developed by scholars such as Galbraith (1977), Keen and Scott Morton (1978) etc. According to this approach information technology is support to *decision making*. Managers facing complex tasks and environments use information in order to reduce the uncertainty associated with decision making: 'the greater the task uncertainty, the greater the amount of information that must be processed among decision makers during task execution in order to achieve a given level of performance', states Galbraith (1977). Simon writes in a similar vein about programmable and unprogrammable decisions (Simon, 1977) (see also, for applications, Ackoff (1967); Keen and Scott Morton (1978); Sprague (1980); Pava (1982); Huber (1984)).

It could be argued that the diffusion of communications and data processing technology poses some limits to the scope of the decision-making view, which emphasizes control and feedback rather than communication processes. But, of greater interest here are some puzzling organizational phenomena which challenge that view and invite the suspicion that it is incomplete. Consider the following evidence by scholars in the field of organizations:

— information is gathered and taken into account only after the decision has been already made, that is to say, as an *a posteriori* rationalization (many computer print-outs are used as high-tech cosmetics to already-made resolutions),
— much of the information gathered in response to requests is not considered in the making of those decisions for which the information is requested (Feldman and March, 1981),
— most of the information generated and processed in organizations is open to misrepresentation, since it is gathered and communicated in a context where the various interests conflict,

— when, on the other hand, organizations are informationally transparent, as many DP specialists wish, it has been shown that the decision makers in two different departments, say Production and Sales, could be playing never-ending information games which lead to overall suboptimality (Ackoff, 1967),

— information is not just an input for the individual decision maker, but is also used to persuade and induce the receiver to action. It could indeed be argued that this use of communication is the essence of authority and management (Flores and Ludlow, 1981).

Thus information is not simply interpreted data, rather it is an argument to convince other decision makers; to be effective it must have attributes other than exactness, clarity, etc.: rather than being purely objective, it must be convincing and adequate to the situation at hand.

2.2 Flaws in the Decision-Making View

We now turn to an analysis of the reasons why the conventional decision-making view cannot explain phenomena such as those just described:

— Firstly, the decision-making approach tends to be *individualistic*. Decision-oriented design strategies focus on the information needs and cognitive styles of the individual decision maker facing a complex and uncertain task. Take, for example, Rockart's design method based on the analysis of the Critical Success Factors, which stresses 'the investigation of current information needs of *individual* managers' (Rockart, 1979). While it is worth investigating the role that computers play in individual problem solving, a manager in a particular organization cannot be seen as a solo chess player whose only opponents are the 'technology', a 'random environment', or 'nature'. In organizations the key issue is *collective, coordinative* problem solving (Schelling, 1980; Turoff and Hiltz, 1982). Though this obvious consideration is beginning to make its way in the recent DDS literature (Huber, 1985), few practical suggestions are provided regarding its implications in systems analysis and design (Sprague, 1980; De Sanctis and Gallupe, 1985).

— Secondly, the decision-making control model ignores the fact that organizations are mixtures of cooperation and conflict between participants; its implicit reference is in fact to man–machine systems (Simon, 1977). When dealing with collective problem solving, the model assumes that all the participants share common goals (i.e. a team), (Marshchak and Radner, 1972): information problems related to task execution and coordination are once again considered to be caused by environmental or technological uncertainty only. It is, however, more realistic to say that all coordinative problem solving and the relevant information processing take place in a *mixed-interest* context. A minimal respect for the well-known conflictual processes existing in organizations would indicate that there are other incentives to gather and use information, apart from task uncertainty: information can be misrepresented, promises and commitments can be false, data incomplete, tracks covered etc., all in order to induce others to make decisions most benefiting us in the first place. Or, another possibility is that information can be selectively disclosed to persuade and bias; what this in fact means is that it can be used as an instrument of power to win or gain a better position in the daily organizational games.

The upshot is that in collective coordination and action there is a distinct form of uncertainty besides that characterizing the task, the technology or the environment: it is an uncertainty of behavioral, strategic nature, which has its origins in the conflict of interests between organization members. The information which the decision maker receives or gathers both within and outside the organization, may well be 'unreliable' with the result that he has to perform a surplus of information processing in order to evaluate its reliability. The fact that it is obtained from human sources means that it cannot be trusted *a priori*. It can therefore be stated that in an organization at least half of the on-going information processing is dedicated to the solution of tasks and problems by cooperative means, while the other half is concerned with solving problems of cooperation among members who behave opportunistically.

To analyze information requirements and design a system without considering the inevitable opportunistic information processing which takes place in organizations appears to be risky. System implementation can lead to conflict, resistance, and other negative attitudes which, far from being irrational, represent the members' response to the attempt of changing the way of producing and using information in a mixed-interest organizational setting (Markus, 1983).

— Thirdly, the conventional wisdom is *one-dimensional*: it takes hierarchical organizations for granted, thus ignoring many important facets of the economics of organizing. For example, it must be remembered that the boundary and structure of an organization are not indefinitely fixed: they change every time a manager implements a make-or-buy decision, or he/she decides to integrate or disintegrate a stage of the production process, an office or a department. Moreover, it is insufficient to consider large pyramidal corporations only, since regional networks of small firms, which are even more diffuse, operate in a manner more like a peer group, or family, than a formal bureaucracy (Piore and Sabel, 1984). And even within large corporations changes take place at shop-floor level, where work groups are being introduced at the expense of formal hierarchies. All these developments, which stem from the effort of organizations to respond to the turbulence of the environment, challenge the approach which identifies management and information systems with hierarchies (Simon, 1981; Arrow, 1974). It is in fact time to acknowledge that many systems, including airline reservation, EFT, remote office work, etc. have little to do with the workings of organizations conceived as pyramids of strategic, managerial and operational control systems. They must rather be seen as exchange or market support systems, in that they support market transactions and not procedures of a hierarchy.

— Finally, even recent amendments to the conventional wisdom leave contradictions unresolved. Consider the introduction of computers in organizations. At present this process tends to be regarded as a bargaining process between conflicting parties; the decision making taking place during system implementation is looked at from a political perspective (Keen, 1981; Markus, 1983). However, even these very authors, when considering a specific managerial decision for automation (for example a DSS for budgeting), switch the analysis framework back to the conventional wisdom: the decision maker is seen as a component of a control system, where the system is uncertain and complex, and factual information is needed to keep it under control (Keen and Scott Morton, 1978). How can one agree with such a contradictory treatment of two organizational processes, the implementation of a system and the use of information for managerial decision making? If the former is a bundle of political decisions, why should the latter represent a neutral, purely algorithmic exception? The political view of system implementation has had the merit of breaking the ice and showing that, in certain areas at least, organizations cannot be analyzed and changed by using frameworks exclusively derived from systems theory and computer science, but what they in fact require are investigation and design methods which consider political, economic and sociological phenomena. This particular point of view has not, however, succeeded in providing a complete and coherent reframing of the entire field of MIS.

3. A TRANSACTIONAL VIEW OF ORGANIZATIONS AND THEIR INFORMATION SYSTEMS

3.1 Economic Organizations: Markets, Hierarchies and Groups

It is a tenet of this paper that the processes involved in socio-economic organizations cannot be analyzed correctly unless formal systems analysis methodologies, such as HIPO, BSP, SADT, or other structured analysis techniques (see Couger *et al.*, 1982), are grounded on an understanding of the nature of organizations and of the way computers can be fitted to support their effectiveness. The transaction costs framework and its application to the MIS field stem from the classic answer provided by Coase (1937) to the fundamental question, 'Why are there firms and markets?'.

A *market* is an assemblage of persons desirous of exchanging property, with prices serving both as incentives and coordinating guides to producers in so far as they affect what and how much is produced and demanded. At an equilibrium free-market price the amount produced equals the amount demanded — *with no necessity for a central all-knowing authority.* Individual self-interest, an incentive to obtain greater gains together with lower costs, is what permits resources to be efficiently allocated. Note that the market system requires very *little knowledge* of the participants, i.e. their own needs and the prices (Alchian and Allen 1977). The same problems of economic organization, i.e. the control and coordination of diverse, specialized activities, is solved differently in a *hierarchy* or the firm. In a firm, market transactions are eliminated and in their place we find an entrepreneur–coordinator who is *the authority* who directs production (Coase, 1937). Markets and firms are thus substitutes and the replacement of one by the other is a common event. Think again of any make-or-buy decision. A market contract displaces a bureaucratic contract when a travel agency replaces its ticket delivery person with a messenger service. A hierarchy supplants a market when a firm begins photocopying its own circulars rather than paying for the services of a printer (Hess, 1983).

Given the ease with which an economic system, with its essential functions of coordination and control, can flow from market to hierarchical organization and back, it should be clear that there is a need for a framework for defining the special role of computer-based information systems in such a diverse organizational context. If systems do in fact support organizational control and coordination mechanisms, what mechanism should they specifically support, the price or the authority relation? In what circumstances should they switch from one to the other, and what criteria are there to tell whether systems are supporting the 'right', i.e. more efficient, mechanism? A temptative answer to these questions is the following (Williamson, 1975):

— when transactions are fairly well patterned, the services or products to be exchanged are fairly standardized and all participants possess the relevant information, i.e. the price, then the perfect *market* is the most efficient resource-saving way of organizing the division of labor, with each person producing a service or product and selling it on a market, where he/she can also buy the necessary inputs: the 'invisible hand' (Smith, 1776) coordinates the individual decisions of producing, buying and selling among a large number of independent agents.

— in some contingencies, however, the use of the price mechanism involves costs: prices must be discussed; transactions encounter difficulties due to the complex search for partners; the contract model specifying the terms of exchange is difficult to develop; and it is costly to control *ex post* the execution of the contract. In these contingencies the product/service exchanged is complex and the transaction uncertain due to a conflict of inter-completion of the transaction. Thus it can be better, or rather more efficient to take advantage of organizing agents with the *firm* to mediate economic transactions, rather than to trust entirely to the market mechanism. In this case the 'invisible hand' of the market is replaced by the 'visible hand' of management (Chandler, 1977) [2].

— Finally, there are situations where coordination can take place neither through a market nor through a hierarchically organized firm: products and services are so complex, transactions so ambiguous that the parties involved in the exchanges have to trust each other and give up any attempt at a short-sighted calculation of the reciprocal costs and benefits accruing from the exchange. The 'invisible' and 'visible' hands are replaced by the 'invisible handshaking' (Okun, 1981). The organizational arrangement whereby networks of exchanges are governed in a stable manner by informal relationships of trust has been called a *group* or *clan* (Ouchi, 1980).

Remember that, in general, the obstacles to transacting, justifying the use of the three alternative arrangements, stem from two distinct sources: one is *natural uncertainty* (the product/service is complex and unique, difficult to evaluate and price; there are barriers to communication during the exchange, etc.); the other is *behavioral* or *strategic uncertainty*, which originates from the joint effect of informational asymmetries and lack of trust between the parties. To sum up, if the world was certain to evolve according to one pattern only, the coordination of activities could easily be streamlined. If people could fully agree, cooperation would be smoothly achieved even in an uncertain and complex world. But when uncertainty, complexity, information asymmetries and lack of trust cannot be ruled out *a priori*, then the multitude of contingencies which affect work in organizations may require the negotiation of complicated contractual plans to arrange cooperation. Depending upon the degrees of ambiguity in the service or product object of exchange and the goal congruence among the parties, the three arrangements, the market, the hierarchical firm and the clan or group, are the most efficient organizational mechanisms for solving the fundamental problems of organizing (Figure 1).

3.2 Information Systems

Galbraith's (1977) hypothesis can be now enlarged, if it is to totally comprehend what goes on in organizations. The more complex cooperation and bargaining

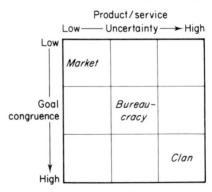

FIGURE 1   Three organizational forms.

are, not only because of the uncertainty of the product/service to be produced and exchanged, but also because of the hazards of opportunism, the more difficult it is to achieve a contract to regulate cooperation and exchange, and the more information has to be processed in order to set up and maintain the organizational relationships between contracting members.

Having thus linked the notion of information within organizations to those of uncertainty and opportunism (lack of trust among cooperators), we are now able to reframe the concept of 'information system'. If we look at organizations as networks of exchanges, *information systems*, whether they be computer-based or not, *are made up of the networks of information flows and files needed to create, set up, control and maintain the organization's network of exchanges and relevant contracts.* Obviously, an information system will prove contingent upon the nature of the organization to which it belongs.

In a *perfect market* where coordination and control are achieved through the price mechanism and spot contracting, the information system is highly standardized, formalized, a-procedural, responsive and extremely simple: the *price* is the only input needed to support members of the market who make basic decisions, such as buying or selling.

In the *hierarchical firm*, or *bureaucracy*, where open, longer-term contracts regulate the exchange of products and services through the employment relation and the authority relationship (Simon, 1957), the information system is represented by the *rules*, norms and plans which convey, mostly in a procedural fashion (Simon, 1976b), the information concerning what should be done under what circumstances, and how it should be controlled.

Finally, business in a *clan* is carried out by parole contract, and partners bind themselves by word or handshake to a complex web of mutual, stable and long-term obligations. Its information system consists of the *rituals*, stories and ceremonies which convey the values and beliefs of the organization. It is highly informal and idiosyncratic: an outsider cannot gain quick access to the decision rules of a clan; on the other hand its information system, which is anything but transparent, has no need for an army of accountants, computer experts and managers: it is just there as a by-product of well-knit social relations (Ouchi, 1979; Wilkins and Ouchi, 1983; Schein, 1984).

It goes without saying that real organizations include a mixture of the three coordination and control mechanisms outlined thus far, and consequently they avail themselves of a variety of information systems. It is, however, possible to distinguish the prevailing one locally. For example, in a multi-divisional company, one can identify an overall bureaucratic, hierarchical structure which links through authority relations the various divisions with the central office, and a corresponding information system, say for budgeting, planning and control. Internal markets regulate the exchange of products and services between the divisions, the relative computer-based information system is a database containing all the transfer prices. Finally, both within the division departments and in the central office, clans exist among managers, among workers in production work groups, among the employees of an office, with each subculture having its own peculiar jargon, set of symbols, rituals, etc. Present MIS theory has focused on bureaucratic organization to the exclusion of all else. By considering the plurality of organizations and information systems we should however realize that there are *multiple strategies for computerization*, all of which are contingent upon the nature of information processing taking place in a specific organization or part of it. Our framework, then, enables us to overcome the problem of one-dimensionality discussed above.

3.3 The Role of Information Technology

If organizations are seen as networks of exchanges, then the organizational use of information technology concerns not only 'data' or 'individual decision making' but also *interdependent decision making and communication related to exchanging*. Information technology belongs to those technologies, like the telephone and money itself, which reduce the cost of organizing by making exchanges more efficient: it is thus a *mediating technology*, i.e. a technology which links several individual through the standardization and extension of the linkages (Thompson, 1967). The costs of organizing, i.e. costs of coordination and control, are decreased by information technology which can streamline all or part of the information processing required in carrying out an exchange: information to search for partners, to develop a contract; to control the behavior of the parties during contract execution and so on. The functions of a computer-based information system can thus be reframed as an 'exchange support system'. And in analogy to Simon's typology of decision making (Simon, 1977), a classification of exchanges and the contracts regulating them can be developed:

— *Structured contracts*, i.e. spot contracts which govern transactions such as those occurring in an ideal market.
— *Semistructured contracts*, i.e. longer-term, open contracts, such as the employment relation, where adaptation, sequential modifications at low renegotiation costs are permissible.
— *Unstructured contracts*, related to those exchanges which cannot be modelled or 'written down' in an explicit contract form, either because communication between the parties is difficult or because they cannot be satisfactorily spelled out and formalized.

Data processing can support all these types of exchanges and related contracts. Consider first the *structured* contracts. Many of the structured market exchanges have already been automated, from airline reservation systems to EFT in banking, to data banks selling pieces of information. Note that the recasting of data processing as a mediating technology indicates that information technology is a means for creating/expanding markets, by lowering search, contracting and control costs. It would be interesting to carry out a census of the running DP applications in the commercial sector today: it is the author's conviction that market transactions rather than bureaucratic firms are at present the main field of application of DP technology, since the structured and standardized nature of those transactions make them more suitable to automation [3]. In what way then can computers support *semistructured* and *unstructured* exchanges? Systems can be dispatchers of heuristics, commitments and promises which streamline the negotiation process embedded in any exchange. And this can take place not only on markets. The organization of work, in an office for example, can be seen in terms of coordinative problem solving which is achieved by the exchange, storage, control and retrieval of commitments between the various employees working in that office. In particular, the computer system together with the local network, could enable the parties required for the execution of a given job to be identified, their mutual interests communicated, their previous/pending commitments recorded and their discretion noted. In this way a personal and collective agenda is built up (Flores and Ludlow, 1981; Fikes and Henderson, 1980), which could support office work conceived as a complex group problem solving (Suchman and Wynn, 1984). Operating systems, such as UNIX, through commands such as 'make', and other OA facilities act as a mediating technology which supports software development performed by various programmers linked to the system (Ritchie and Thompson, 1974).

4. A RESEARCH AGENDA

As it has been recently advocated, the information systems discipline requires more applied multidisciplinary research (McFarlan, 1985); but problems stand in the way. For example, it is difficult effectively to combine contributions from different disciplines, avoiding the forced coexistence of various approaches or just another fragmented view of the topic.

The new institutional economics, which stresses the importance of transaction costs (TC) for economic organizations, is multidisciplinary by origin and vocation: it draws heavily from microeconomics, law and organization theory to begin with (Williamson, 1985), but also sociology and theory of games are germane to it (Williamson and Ouchi, 1981). The application of the transaction costs approach to the information systems (IS) field has the potential to create a new and coherent understanding of a variety of topics, from the analysis and design of IS to the study of computer impacts on organizations, to project management: The approach can thus give rise to a rich research agenda. In fact, many research projects in this area are under way in European and US universities (UCLA, Sloan School and the University of Arizona are those known to the author). In the following some applications of the TC approach are presented, noting on-going research projects and further research issues to be investigated in the realms of methodology and theory. Inevitably, research will confront issues and dilemmas which might point to *limitations* of the TC approach and require the modification of some of its assumptions; that is the challenge for an approach where the surface has been barely scratched so far.

4.1 Applications

That computer-based IS are applied to decrease TC is being recognized and demonstrated in many fields, such as marketing, distribution (Buzzell, 1985), pricing (Beath and Ives, 1985) and, more generally, strategic applications (Wiseman, 1985).

Consider, for example, the impact of information and communications technology (computerized data links) on *industrial distribution*, and more generally on *interorganizational relationships* (Stern and Kaufman, 1985). Corey (1985) convincingly shows that successful strategies of US distributors, such as American Hospital Supply, McKesson Drug and General Electric Supply Company, depend crucially 'on data processing and communication systems that facilitate ordering and delivering and provide a steady flow of information internally as well as between distributors and customers, which is useful for accounting, pricing and inventory control'. In other words, 'internal computerized information systems are applied to reduce transaction costs, with the overall result of a shift in the balance between market-mediated and firm-mediated transactions in favor of the former'.

The same conclusions have been drawn in studying the impact of electronic data interchange in *retailing* and other industries in Norway (Fjalestad, 1982).

More specifically, the whole reshuffling of the boundaries between firms, markets and groups as a consequence of the diffusion of new information technology has been observed and analyzed in a number of industries (clothing, steel, car manufacturing, chemical) in Italy (Ciborra, 1983a). By extrapolating the existing evidence one can apply the TC framework to draw scenarios of *the organizations of the future* (Huber, 1984) and of the future population mix of organizations (Ciborra, 1983a).

It follows that a promising field for empirical research is given by the re-examination of the whole debate about *the impacts of new technology on organizations* (Whisler, 1970). For example, the traditional issue concerning the centralizing versus decentralizing effects of the new technology may be seen in a different light, thanks to the TC framework: the dilemma is not between increased control at the top versus loss of control and more autonomy at the periphery, as scholars focusing on decision making thought; rather, one should think in terms of the *substitution of different control mechanisms*, e.g. the market (a decentralized control system) with the hierarchy (a centralized control mechanism). Thus, decentralization would not simply mean giving up control to the periphery, but also setting up a different incentive scheme to coordinate and control performances through a price mechanism instead of the authority relationship (Ciborra, 1984a).

In addition, the blending of computers and telecommunications in the emergent technology of *telematics* will compel the focusing of attention more and more on *interdependent* decision making between organizations and organization units, thus making the TC framework the best suited for studying the organizational impacts of such a technology.

Today, information technology is heavily used in *public administration* (Kraemer, 1980). Can the TC approach be of any use in explaining the dynamics of computerization in such a typical non-market, apparently non-economic environment? Aren't we in a field where 'politics' is the key factor, while economic forces lie somehow in the background? That politics has been regarded as the key factor explains the fact that studies on the impacts of new technologies on local and central governments, and on the relationship between government and the citizens have dealt almost exclusively with *power games* both within and without administration. However, there are hints that the TC approach could be usefully employed to give new insights. Consider first the present debate and policy programs concerning *deregulation*: these tend to emphasize the trade-off between politics/bureaucracy and markets. The state and the market appear to be alternative mechanisms for governing economic processes and transactions. Information and communications technology should be evaluated as a factor which may contribute to shifting the balance between the two mechanisms. For example, if the new technology dramatically improves the functioning of markets, why rely on government as a substitute for the formerly existing failures of the market?

Still, it remains difficult to apply the TC framework in an organization which is there to suppress economic transactions. It may be necessary to introduce the notion of 'social exchange' besides the one of economic transaction. In social exchanges, goods such as 'votes', 'consensus', and 'laws and regulations' are the object of exchange between social partners (the citizens, lobbies, unions, state bureaucrats, political parties etc.). These goods interfere heavily with the normal economic activity: and the question of whether it is power which is the ultimate factor to regulate the economy or efficiency emerges naturally. Thus, it is clear that empirical research on the impacts of new technology will be confronted with methodological and theoretical problems such as the power versus efficiency, or the politics versus markets (Lindblom, 1977) dilemmas (see below).

The design of *new software systems* can benefit from the idea that computers are a mediating technology aimed at decreasing costs of transacting and coordinating (applications in this vein can be found in Lee (1980), Turoff and Hiltz (1982).

A number of researchers in the USA, Canada, Scandinavia and Italy are exploring the possibility of building new software based on information modelling through illocutionary logic (Searle, 1969; Cohen and Perrault, 1979; Airenti *et al.*, 1984; Humphreys and Lee, 1986).

The essence of management would consist of the communication of *speech acts*, such as promises, commitments, requests, etc. (Flores and Ludlow, 1981). The automation or at least the support of the production of speech acts through various forms of modelling (Lyytinen, Lehtinen, 1984; De Cindio *et al.*, 1983; Cohen and Perrault, 1981) become the object of interest. These efforts are congruent with the concept of the computer as a mediating technology: the various phases of a transaction, i.e. search, contracting, control and maintenance, could be analyzed as ordered sequences of speech acts. Software designed to automate the production and communication of speech acts could become the core of the exchange support systems mentioned above.

There are difficulties, however, in the pursuit of this line of research: speech acts are felicitous (Searle, 1969), i.e. effective, if, among other things, they are candid: a promise is an act if it is a true promise on which one can rely. The TC approach instead looks at organizations and their information systems as continuously coping with the problems generated by opportunistic information processing and communication. How can 'mediating systems' cope with the problems generated by opportunism — the fact that many speech acts circulating in the organization are not felicitous, are not 'acts' at all?

At a broader level, one could think of the *institutional redesign* of the whole infrastructure of our society by using the TC economizing properties of the new technology. Stone (1987) is investigating systematically many implications of introducing information technology to support 'negotiated coordination' occurring in markets, the office, and the political arenas, in transportation and urban settings.

4.2 Methodologies

It is clear that any empirical research program will have to face the task of *dimensionalizing and measuring* transaction costs. Accounting systems in place in organizations do not provide data directly usable for this purpose and one will have to rely on indirect measures and proxies at best. In any event, internal (to the hierarchy) transaction costs seem to be much more difficult to identify and measure than the more visible and clear-cut market costs. Some even argue that trying to quantify transaction costs might destroy the approach, which has only an interpretative power. Needless to say that this point of view must be verified.

Still, even if the measurement problem is not solved, the framework opens up the possibility of constructing a new set of *systems analysis and design methods*. The new methods could focus on the analysis of information flows and stocks surrounding organizational exchanges. Haendlykken (1984) has compared, on a conceptual level, different analysis methods, including one based on TC. At the University of Aarhus concrete applications of transaction analysis have been carried out in the design of the Danish *forests information system* and in a *bank*. (Christiansen and Etzerodt, 1983. Munkholm and Steffen, 1985). In Italy, a *government database for entertainment* is being designed by looking at the entertainment industry as a network of exchanges between artists, performers, the studios, the broadcasting services, government agencies, theaters, etc. Data to be included in the database is the by-product of the main exchanges taking place in the network, and the role of the database itself will be to facilitate such exchanges.

A structured systems analysis method based on TC has yet to come, but so far one thing is emerging consistently: when applied, the TC analysis method has always brought a fresh view on the problem at hand, where other, more structured conventional methods failed or were not capable of leading to creative solutions. Among the existing methodologies, the one which seems to better incorporate the spirit of the TC analysis is BIAIT (Burnstine, 1980).

The development of a more structured methodology would also benefit from any *phenomenological study of transactions* occurring in everyday life of organizations (markets, bureaucracies and groups) (Boland, 1979). For example, Wynn's (1979) ethnomethodological analysis of office conversations can be re-examined focusing on transactions: each turn of the conversations she examined can be attributed to different functions of transacting in an office — search, contracting, controlling and maintaining exchanges as social, organizational and economic relationships (Ciborra, 1984b).

MIS strategic planning is another area where the TC framework may improve current methodologies. These have suffered from being either too 'political', i.e. focusing on the goals of various stakeholders in the organization, thus disregarding more structural considerations, or too data processing-oriented, disregarding the inter-action between EDP and organizational structures. MIS strategic planning methods based on TC could help the joint, strategic design of the architecture of the organization transactions and the application of computers (Ciborra, 1981; Wiseman, 1985).

Finally, *the management of system development* can be an object for a TC based methodology. Beath (1983) describes various project management strategies contingent upon the degree of uncertainty of the project: arm's length (market-type), matrix (bureaucratic-type) and clan. In such a contingency model, adopting one of the three strategies permits the project to reach its goals with a minimum of transaction costs. Thus a set of testable hypotheses can be put forward for empirical investigation.

A different tack to applying the TC framework to systems development is to focus on the *bargaining process* (and their costs) which surround the introduction of any technological innovation. Economics suggests that bargaining is related to the re-allocation of the social, and private, costs and benefits arising from the productivity changes resulted from the new technology. Using TC considerations it is possible to compare on efficiency grounds alternative schemes for bargaining available to management, users, specialists, unions, etc. in planning the introduction of the new technology. This approach has proved to be useful in providing a hard-nosed economic explanation of 'technology agreements' in Europe and, more generally, user participation strategies currently implemented in many companies (Ciborra, 1983).

However, there are still problems ahead. Namely, to what extent can the TC framework be straightforwardly applied to project management? Firstly, in Beath's model, the multiple dimensions of uncertainty which account for the existence of transaction costs are collapsed into one. Most probably, however, uncertainty stemming from strategic behavior cannot be simply 'added' to that stemming from the environment or the technology, i.e. project management organization will be different whether technology is unknown, but high trust exists among interested parties, or whether the technology is known but goal congruence is low. And there may be a more severe limitation concerning the overall ability of the TC framework to explain *organizational change*. This is a matter for theoretical research, to which we now turn.

4.3 Theory

Three areas of theoretical development for the TC framework are worth pursuing in order to establish it as a new paradigm in the information systems field: formal economic modeling, the power versus efficiency dilemma, and the organizational change challenge.

The TC concepts can be applied to build *models of economic processes* which explicitly take into account information. Following and integrating the work of Marschack and Radner (1972), models of information and organization can be developed so as to ascertain by simulation and laboratory experiment the impacts of information technology on the structure of organizations and the design efficient organizations (Baligh and Burton, 1981; Hess, 1983; Burton and Øbel, 1984; Malone, 1985). A whole new theory of economic organization could be put forward to include, in addition to production functions, an information function (Jonscher, 1982).

TC reasoning in the case of public administration has shown the relevance of the *power issue*. But even in economics, some contend that the TC explanation is limited by the power factor (Francis *et al.*, 1983). For example, in the case examined above of industrial distribution, the TC framework does not seem to adequately recognize the complex interdependencies between producers and wholesalers.

Corey (1985) suggests that one 'must turn from economics to political science to understand how power relationships do in fact significantly affect which transactions the firm chooses to internalize within hierarchical organization and which it leave to market mechanisms'. This recommendation is at odds with what Williamson and Ouchi (1981) claim, namely 'that the power approach to the study of organizations is bankrupt': the TC approach tenet is that efficiency in controlling TC costs matters, while power considerations follow. A more discriminating outcome of this debate could help us in addressing issues such as: can information technology improve industrial democracy; can it deliver more democratic forms of decision making (Ciborra, 1984a)? What are the real forces behind the drive to centralization or decentralization brought about by the new technology?

The third arena for theoretical investigation is *the change of economic organization* due to the introduction of new technology. Managers, users and specialists all know that computerization often means a complex and even dramatic change

Issues / Applications	Methodological issues	Theoretical issues
Marketing and distribution, retailing etc.	How to measure transaction costs	**Power vs efficiency role of information in economic organization**
Public administration	Measure transaction costs in non-market contexts	**Power vs efficiency the notion of 'social exchange'**
Software systems	Analysis of speech acts	**Opportunistic information processing**
Systems analysis and design	Measure transaction costs	**Economic modelling of economic organizations**
Strategic planning of IS	Measure transaction costs	**Power vs efficiency**
Project management	What are transactions in organization change ?	**Organizational change**

FIGURE 2 Research topics in application methods and theory.

process. Such 'friction' experienced on a daily basis by members of the organization is almost never admitted in any economic analysis of the firm. Economics simply states that either a firm succeeds in internalizing the innovation or it will be wiped out by competitors smarter at innovating. The TC framework can predict (and recommend accordingly) that an organization using a new computer-based information and communication system should adopt a specific contractual arrangement to govern its set of relevant transactions, but it is mute on the success of the change process itself: it only says 'better do it quickly, or find yourself out of business'. From this point of view the TC framework seems to share the same limitations of any 'structural' approach, being of no practical help in solving the problem of *changing* a corporate culture, a way of doing things, or the legitimate resistance to change and the cognitive difficulties that actors facing change encounter (Argyris and Schoen, 1978).

It may be that looking at project management organization as a set of transactions as Beath (1983) does, stretches the approach too far. An alternative tack would be to enlarge the TC framework so as to include other characteristics of human agents, besides bounded rationality and opportunism, such as *limited learning* (Argyris, 1982), to accommodate the specific problems of organizational change.

In Figure 2 the main applications of the TC framework are listed with the intention of pointing out the methodological and theoretical research areas which need exploration.

5. CONCLUDING REMARKS

An understanding of the nature of economic organizations is an essential prerequisite, not only in governing the development of computer-based information systems, but also in analyzing and designing them in an effective way. The transaction costs perspective can help design information systems appropriate to the functioning of institutions such as markets, bureaucracies and groups. The foregoing analysis can be summarized as follows:

— *Exchange transactions* represent the fundamental organizational relationships between human agents.
— The organization of exchange transactions depends upon contingencies which are both *environmental* (uncertainty and complexity) and *behavioral* (bounded rationality and opportunism).
— Organizations can be regarded as *stable networks of contracts* which govern transactions enabling coordination and control.
— Transacting requires *information processing* to identify partners, define a contract, control its enforcement, etc.
— Information technology acting as a *mediating technology* can, by lowering transaction costs, improve information handling needed in transacting.
— The application of information technology should not contradict *the nature of the organizational transactions* supported.
— Information technology can, in the interests of efficiency, influence the shift from one organizational form to another. The possibility of lowering transaction costs should be considered in any attempt at *joint design*.

Note that this new framework does not render obsolete the standard systems analysis methods, be they data- or decision-making oriented. On the contrary, it augments them with a new organizational and economic background, so that when an analyst goes into an organization with his/her toolbox, he/she has a theory with which to select the relevant organizational phenomena, identify the information requirements and make a forecast of the organizational implications of any redesign put forward.

NOTES

[1] The terms transaction and transaction costs are used here in an economic and organizational sense. Traditionally, for the dp profession, transactions refer to the computer operations triggered by a user message and satisfied by the corresponding computer response, i.e. an *exchange of data* between parts of the machine, and between the machine and the user (Bucci and Streeter, 1979). Economic transactions refer instead to the transfer of a good or service between individuals or departments of organizations (Williamson, 1981). It is a *social relationship* which results where 'parties in the course of their interactions systematically try to assume that the value gained for them is greater or equal to the value lost' (Barth, 1981). However, it should not be excluded that the two concepts might be linked in the case of computer-mediated economic transactons (Ciborra, 1981).

[2] More precisely, the firm supersedes the market when the service 'labor' is the object of exchange: spot contracts regarding the use of labor are in fact exposed to various hazards, since it is difficult to fully specify in advance the precise services required during the execution of a complex/uncertain task; and to control the real effort provided by the worker, especially in the case of teamwork (Alchian and Demsetz, 1972). Under the contingencies determined by environmental and human factors (uncertainty and opportunism, respectively), market contracts are replaced, for the sake of efficiency, by a longer-term, open contract, *the employment relation*, whereby the worker accepts, within certain limits (the indifference zone (Barnard, 1938)), that someone, the authority, specifies in a procedural way what should be done during the unfolding of events.

[3] This conviction is easily justified: in most advanced countries, banks are the main users of data processing. But it is not so much their internal bureaucracy that is automated, it is rather their function as intermediary agents on market transactions (Switzerland has the highest percentage of computers per inhabitant . . .). Consequently, applications in the credit sector should be looked on as market transactions support systems.

REFERENCES

Ackoff, R. L. (1967) 'Management Misinformation Systems'. *Management Science*, **14**, 4, 147–156.
Airenti, G., Bara, B. G., and Colombetti M. (1984) 'Planning and Understanding Speech Acts by Interpersonal Games' in *Computational Models of Natural Language Processing*, B. G. Bara, and M. Guida (Eds.), North Holland, Amsterdam.
Alchian, A. A., and Allen, W. R. (1977) *Exchange and Production: Competition, Coordination and Control* (2nd edn) Wadsworth, Bolton.
Alchian, A. A., and Demsetz, H. (1972) 'Production, Information Costs and Organization'. *American Economic Review*, **62**, 5, 777–795.
Argyris, C. (1978) *Reasoning, Learning and Action*, Jossey-Bass, San Francisco.
Argyris, C., and Schoen, D. (1978) *Organizational Learning*, Addison-Wesley, Reading, MA.
Arrow, K. L. (1974) *The Limits of Organization*, W. W. Norton, New York.
Baligh, H. H., and Burton, R. M. (1981) Describing and Designing Organization Structures and Processes'. *Int. Journal of Policy Analysis and Information Systems*, **5**, 4, 251–266.
Barnard, C. I. (1938) *The Functions of the Executive*, Harvard University Press, Cambridge, MA.
Barth, F. (1981) *Process and Form in Social Life*, Routledge & Kegan Paul, London.
Beath, C. M. (1983) 'Strategies for Managing MIS Projects: a Transaction Cost Approach'. *Proc. Fourth ICIS Conf. Houston, Texas, December 1983.*
Beath, C. M., and Ives, B. (1985) 'Competitive Information Systems in Support of Pricing'. *Proc. Sixth ICIS, Indianapolis, Indiana, December, 1985.*
Boland, R. Jr. (1979) 'Control, Causality and Information Systems Requirements'. *Accounting, Organizations and Society*, **4**, 4, 259–272.
Bucci, G., and Streeter, D. N. (1979) 'A Methodology for the Design of Distributed Information Systems'. *Communications of the ACM*, **22**, 233–245.
Burnstine, D. C. (1980) *BIAIT: An Emerging Management Engineering Discipline*, BIAIT Int. Inc., Petersburg, New York.
Burton, R. M., and Øbel, B. (1984) 'Designing Efficient Organizations: Modelling and Experimentation'. North Holland, Amsterdam.
Buzzell, R. D. (Ed.) (1985) *Marketing in an Electronic Age*, Harvard Business School Press, Boston, MA.

Chandler, D. A. Jr. (1977) *The Visible Hand — The Managerial Revolution in American Business*. Harvard University Press, Cambridge, MA.

Christiansen, E., and Etzerodt, P. (1983) 'EDB Inden for Skovbruget', DAIMI report Aarhus University (in Danish).

Ciborra, C. U. (1981) 'Information Systems and Transactions Architecture', *Inter. Journal of Policy Analysis and Information Systems*, **5**, 4, 305–324.

Ciborra, C. U. (1983a) 'Markets, Bureaucracies and Groups in the Information Society', *Journal of Information Economics and Policy*, **21**, 145–160.

Ciborra, C. U. (1983b) 'The Social Costs of Information Technology and Participation in Systems Design', in *Systems Design for, with and by the Users*, U. Briefs, C. U. Ciborra and L. Schneider (Eds.), North Holland, Amsterdam.

Ciborra, C. U. (1984a) 'Scambio, Potere e Coordinamento', *Annali di Storia dell'Impresa*, **1**, 1, 13–57 (in Italian).

Ciborra, C. U. (1984b) 'Aspetti socio-organizzativi dell'automazione d'ufficio: problemi, modelli e metodi', in *L'automazione del Lavoro d'Ufficio*, G. Bracchio (Ed.), Etas Libri, Milan (in Italian).

Ciborra, C. U. (1985) 'Reframing the Role of Computers in Organizations: the Transaction Costs Approach', *Proc. 6th ICIS, Indianapolis, Indiana, December 1985*.

Coase, R. (1937) 'The Nature of the Firm', *Economica*, November, 387–405.

Cohen, P. R., and Perrault, C. R. (1979) 'Elements of a Plan-based Theory of Speech Acts'. *Cognitive Science*, **3**, 177–212.

Cohen, P. R., Perrault, C. R., and Allen, J. F. (1981) 'Beyond Question-answering', in *Strategies for Natural Language Processing*, W. Lehnert and M. Ringle (Eds.), Lawrence Eribaum, New York.

Corey, E. R. (1985) 'The Role of Information and Communications Technology in Industrial Distribution', in Buzzell (1985).

Couger, J. D., Colter, M. A., and Knapp, R. W. (1982) *Advanced System Development/Feasibility Techniques*, John Wiley, New York.

Davis, G. B., and Munro, M. C. (1977) 'Determining Management Information Needs: A Comparison of Methods. *MIS Quarterly*, June, 55–66.

De Cindio, F., De Michelis, G., Pomello, L., and Simone, C. (1983) 'Conditions and tools for an effective negotiation during the organization/information systems design process', in *Systems design for, with and by the Users*, U. Briefs, C. Ciborra and L. Schneider, North-Holland, Amsterdam.

De Sanctis, G., and Gallupe, B. (1985) 'Group Decision Support Systems: A New Frontier', *Data Base*, Winter, 3–10.

Emery, J. C. (1969) *Organizational Planning and Control Systems — Theory and Technology*, Macmillan, New York.

Feldman, M. S., and March, J. G. (1981) 'Information in Organizations as Signal and Symbol', *Administrative Science Quarterly*, **26** 171–186.

Fikes, R. E., and Austin Henderson, D. Jr. (1980) 'On supporting the Use of Procedures in Office Work', Research report, Xerox PARC, Palo Alto.

Fjalestad, J. (1982) 'Datakommunikasjon og Markedsutvikling', Norwegian Computing Center Report, Oslo (in Norwegian).

Flores, F., and Ludlow, J. J. (1981) 'Doing and Speaking in the Office', in *DSS: Issues and Challenges*, G. Fick and R. Sprague (Eds.), Pergamon, Oxford.

Francis, A., Turk, J., and Willman, P. (1983) *Power Efficiency & Institutions, A Critical Appraisal of the Markets and Hierarchies Paradigm*, Heinemann, London.

Galbraith, J. R. (1977) *Organization Design*, Addison-Wesley, Reading, MA.

Grandori, A. (1984) 'A Prescriptive Contingency View of Organizational Decision Making', *Administrative Science Quarterly*, **29**, 192–209.

Haendlykken, P. (1984) 'Organisasjonsmodeller', Norwegian Computing Center Report, Oslo (in Norwegian).

Hess, J. D. (1983) *The Economics of Organization*, North-Holland, Amsterdam.

Huber, G. P. (1984) 'The Nature and Design of Post-industrial Organizations', *Management Science*, **30**, 8, 928–951.

Huber, G. P. (1985) 'Issues in the Design of Group Decision Support Systems', *MIS Quarterly*.

Humphreys, P. and Lee, R. (Eds.) (1986) *Knowledge Representation and Organizational Theory*, Oxford University Press, London.

Jonscher, C. (1982) 'Models of Economic Organizations', Ph.D. thesis, Dept. of Economics, Harvard University, Cambridge, MA.

Keen, P. G. W. (1981) 'Information Systems and Organizational Change', *Communications of the ACM*, **24**, 1, 24–33.

Keen, P. G. W., and Scott Morton, M. S. (1978) *Decision Support Systems: An Organizational Perspective*, Addison-Wesley, Reading, MA.

Kling, R. (1980) 'Social Analyses of Computing: Theoretical Perspectives in Recent Empirical Research', *Computing Surveys*, **12**, 1, 61–110.

Kraemer, K. L. (1980) 'Computers, Information and Power in Local Governments: a Stage Theory', in *Human Choice and Computers*, A. Mowshowitz (Ed.), North-Holland, Amsterdam.

Lee, R. M. (1980) 'CANDID: A Logical Calculus for Describing Financial Contracts', Ph.D. Dissertation, Dept. of Decision Sciences, The Wharton School, University of Pennsylvania, Philadelphia, PA.

Lindblom, C. E. (1977) *Politics and Markets*, Basic Books, New York.

Lyytinen, K., and Lehtinen, E. (1984) 'On information Modelling Through Illocutionary Logic', *Proc. Third Scandinavian Research Seminar on Information Modelling and Data Base Management, Tampere, January 1984.*

Malone, T. (1985) 'Organizational Structure and Information Technology — Elements of a Formal Theory, CISR working paper, no. 130, MIT.

Markus, M. L. (1983) 'Power, Politics and MIS Implementation', *Communications of the ACM*, **26**, 6, 430–444.

Marschak, J., and Radner, R. (1972) *Economic Theory of Teams*, Yale University Press, New Haven, CT.

McFarlan, W. F. (Ed.) (1985) *The Information Systems Research Challenge*, Harvard Business School Press, Boston, MA.

Munkholm, B., and Steffen, K. (1985) 'KANDIS, Kontor Analyse og Design i Systemudvikling', DAIMI report, University of Aarhus (in Danish).

Okun, A. (1981) *Prices and Quantities*, Basil Blackwell, Oxford.

Olson, M. H. (1983) 'Remote Office Work: Changing Work Patterns in Space and Time', *Communications of the ACM*, **26**, 3, 182–187.

Ouchi, W. G. (1979) 'A Conceptual Framework for the Design of Organizational Control Mechanisms', *Management Science*, **25**, 9, 838–848.

Ouchi, W. G. (1980) 'Markets, Bureaucracies, and Clans', *Administrative Science Quarterly*, **25**, 129–141.

Pava, C. (1982) 'Microelectronics and the Design of Organization', Working paper, Division of Research, Graduate School of Business Administration, Harvard University.

Piore, M. J., and Sabel, C. F. (1984) *The Second Industrial Divide*, Basic Books, New York.

Rockart, J. F. (1979) 'Chief Executives Define their Own Data Needs', *Harvard Business Review*, **57**, 2, 81–93.

Schein, E. H. (1984) 'Coming to a New Awareness of Organizational Culture', *Sloan Management Review*, **26**, 2, 3–16.

Schelling, T. C. (1980) *The Strategy of Conflict* (2nd edn), Harvard University Press, Cambridge, MA.

Searle, J. R. (1969) *Speech Acts, an Essay in the Philosophy of Language*, Cambridge University Press, London.

Simon, H. A. (1957) 'A Formal Theory of the Employment Relation', in *Models of Man*, H. A. Simon (Ed.), Wiley, New York, pp. 183–185.

Simon, H. A. (1973) 'Applying Information Technology to Organization Design', *Public Administration Review*, May–June, 268–278.

Simon, H. A. (1976a) *Administrative Behavior*, Free Press, New York.

Simon, H. A. (1976b) 'From Substantive to Procedural Rationality', in *Method and Appraisal in Economics*, S. J. Letsis (Ed.), Cambridge University Press, Cambridge.

Simon, H. A. (1977) *The New Science of Management Decision*, Prentice-Hall, Englewood Cliffs NJ.

Simon, H. A. (1981) *The Sciences of the Artificial* (2nd ed.) MIT Press, Cambridge.

Smith, A. (1776) *The Wealth of Nations*.

Sprague, E. H. (1980) 'A Framework for the Development of Decision Support Systems', *MIS Quarterly*, **4**, 4, 1–24.

Stern, L. W., and Kaufmann, P. J. (1985) 'Electronic Data Interchange in Selected Consumer Goods Industries: an Interorganizational Perspective', in Buzzell (1985).

Stone, P. J. (1980) 'Social Evolution and a Computer Science Challenge', *Scientia*, **25**, 125–146.

Stone, P. J. (1987) 'Negotiated Coordination', manuscript, Harvard University.

Strassman, P. A. (1980) 'The Office of the Future', *Technology Review*, January, 56–64.

Strauss, A. (1978) *Negotiations — Varities, Contexts, Processes and Social Order*. Jossey-Bass, San Francisco.

Suchmann, L. A., and Wynn, E. (1984) 'Procedures and Problems in the Office', *Office Technology and People*, **2**, 2, 133–154.

Thompson, J. D. (1967) *Organizations in Action*, Sage, New York.

Toffler, A. (1980) *The Third Wave*, Morrow, New York.

Turoff, M., and Hiltz, S. R. (1982) 'Computer Support for Group Versus Individual Decisions', *IEEE Transactions on Communication*, **30**, 2, 82–91.

Whistler, T. L. (1970) *Information Technology and Organizational Change*, Wadsworth, Belmont, CA.

Wildavsky, A. (1983) 'Information as an Organizational Problem', *Journal of Management Studies*, **20**, 1, 29–40.

Wilkins, A. L., and Ouchi, W. G. (1983) 'Efficient Cultures: Exploring the Relationship between Culture and Organizational Performance', *Administrative Science Quarterly*, **28**, 468–481.

Williamson, O. E. (1975) *Markets and Hierarchies: Analysis and Antitrust Implications*, Free Press, New York.

Williamson, O. E. (1981) 'The Economics of Organization: The Transaction Costs Approach', *American Journal of Sociology*, **87**, 3, 548–577.

Williamson, O. E., and Ouchi, W. G. (1981) 'The Markets and Hierarchies Programme of Research: Origins Implications and Prospects, in *Perspectives on Organisation Design and Behaviour*, A. Van de Ven and W. Joyce (Eds.), John Wiley, New York.

Williamson, O. E. (1985) *The Economic Institutions of Capitalism*, MacMillan, New York.

Wiseman, C. (1985) *Strategy and Computers, Information Systems as Competitive Weapons*, Dow Jones-Irwin, Homewood, IL.

Wynn, E. (1979) 'Office Conversation as an Information Medium', Ph.D thesis, Department of Anthropology, University of California, Berkely.

Critical Issues in Information Systems Research
Edited by R. J. Boland Jr. and R. A. Hirschheim
©*1987 John Wiley & Sons Ltd.*

Chapter 12

SOCIAL CHANGE AND THE FUTURE
OF INFORMATION SYSTEMS DEVELOPMENT

Heinz K. Klein and Rudy Hirschheim

ABSTRACT

Whereas it is widely recognized that information systems development (ISD) is one of the factors influencing social change, the reverse has received little attention. The principal purpose of this chapter is to explore the recent research literature with the intent of testing the conjecture that social change will affect the future of ISD by influencing research directions, professional orientations, methods, and tools. In order to analyze pending large-scale societal changes which are difficult to perceive, the notion of an image is introduced. Examples of classical works which influenced the image of society are Plato's *Republic* and Hobbes's *Leviathan*. On the basis of analyzing recent image changing books, major social changes are examined under six categories: (1) societal attitudes, (2) organizational incentives, (3) peer orientations of information systems professionals, (4) the accepted research paradism, (5) values and norms (design ideals) for ISD and (6) accepted methods and tools. Recent research publications seem to suggest that broad social change is on the way and is likely to fundamentally affect which approaches to ISD are acceptable in the future. If this is so, then there are important ramifications for the IS community. Three possibilities for the future are outlined. IS research could: (a) aim at emulating the standards of 'hard' science by adopting the proven methods of the natural sciences, (b) aim at becoming more practical and applied by better conforming to demands of societal interest groups, or (c) aim at becoming an institution of fundamental criticism. Whatever the case, it is concluded that rapid social change seems likely to place the individual analyst in an existential dilemma.

1. INTRODUCTION

An area which continues to receive considerable attention in both the popular and academic press, is that of information systems development (ISD). Over the years, numerous books and papers have been written on the subject. This is hardly surprising, given the vital role information systems are thought to play in the survivability of today's organizations. Attention has been focused on the approaches for developing information systems. Although a vast number of approaches have been developed (see Olle *et al.*, 1982, 1983; Maddison *et al.*, 1983; Couger *et al.*, 1982), there is a common underlying philosophy which runs through them — a shared paradigm. It is possible, therefore, to speak of an ISD orthodoxy, one where fundamental tenets are shared and form a general conception of how information systems can and should be developed. Recently, however, it is possible to note the emergence of some radically different approaches to ISD, ones which do not share the same paradigm, which possess an underlying philosophy that is quite different from the orthodoxy, and which challenge the basic assumptions, values and beliefs of the past (see Howard, 1985; Bjerknes and Brattetieg, 1984, 1985; Ehn and Kyng, 1985; Lyytinen 1986).

Whilst it would be interesting to explore in detail both the substance of the alternative paradigms and why they have come about, such a treatment would require much more than could sensibly be done within the space of one chapter or paper. We therefore concentrate on exploring the reasons why radically different approaches to ISD have begun to surface, as well as what their implications are likely to be for the IS community. Elsewhere (Hirschheim and Klein, 1986), an explication of the various ISD paradigms is provided.

We postulate that the divergence of perspectives and methods in recent information systems development research can be explained by the following fundamental conjecture: there exists a link between new research directions in information systems development and social change in society, such that all of the alternatives to the currently accepted ISD orthodoxy are inspired by the same kind of forces or influences that in general drive social change in industrial societies. Social change thus affects which approaches to ISD are socially acceptable and appropriate. The question of how social change actually affects the emergence of new directions in IS and ISD research has not received very much attention by the IS community.

The basic contention, and line of reasoning used to argue its case, is that research interests in general are inextricably bound up with societal norms, values and beliefs. If society changes, so too will its values and beliefs. As such changes are likely to cause dissatisfaction with old beliefs and norms which govern existing practices of ISD, the latter is eventually forced to change in a way which is consistent with societal change, or to justify its current approaches and results in a different way. The early signs of such a relationship between social change and information systems development research interests as reflected in the most recent literature are explored in the following sections of this chapter. Additionally, some conjectures on how societal change might affect IS as an academic and professional discipline are also offered.

The basic approach of this analysis is to look for concepts that promote a better understanding of those factors or 'forces' which are responsible for (i.e. drive) social change. Those which also drive the direction of recent IS research are examined. A further concern is to explore the implications for the future of ISD.

It is important to note that when we speak of 'forces', we merely mean cultural and social factors that channel and guide human behavior. These can be effective at the conscious or subconscious level. In either case it is not appropriate to interpret them as 'hard' causes that determine social changes in some predefined way as is usually implied by the notion of cause–effect relationships [1], but as subtle yet powerful influences which mould human action.

The purpose of this chapter is therefore to perform three tasks: (i) to point out why the perception of social change is a critical research issue not just for ISD but for the whole of the IS research community; (ii) to clarify how social change can be perceived in its early stages; and (iii) to explore the connections which exist between social change and the directions for IS research in the future.

The chapter is organized as follows. Section 2 identifies those social forces which are thought to drive ISD. Included in this discussion is the consideration of not only how they are embraced by ISD but also how the forces of social change are influencing the future of information systems development approaches. Section 3 outlines the implications for ISD in terms of three alternative futures: (a) continuing in the present direction with existing standards derived from the empiricist research traditions, which is shown to lead to a further erosion of the bases of legitimation; (b) responding to changing social forces by becoming more responsive to them without questioning their value basis, which is likely to lead to fashionable conformism; or (c) reflecting on the fundamental reasons for the unresolved practical application problems with the goal of identifying novel alternatives, which could lead to new and interesting possibilities. Section 4 concludes the discussion by reflecting on how social change is likely to pose an uncomfortable dilemma to the individual practicing analyst.

2. ANALYSIS OF SOCIAL CHANGE

The conjecture posed here is that there exists a strong dependency of IS research on the larger societal domain. Because the societal domain is changing, so too must ISD; and with it, research about ISD. Yet social change is very difficult to perceive. It is all around us and it is not clear which changes point to a new pattern and which are simply variations of the old. Before one can analyze the relationship between social change and change in IS research it is necessary to find a way of perceiving social change as it emerges. One needs some sort of early indicators. In order to deal with this difficult issue, we will focus on the concept of the 'image' of social reality and argue that if we can point to significant changes in this image it is a possible indicator of social change. The importance of a public image for shaping society was noted by Boulding (1956). He suggested that the public image not only shapes society, but society continues to re-model the image of itself. Image, therefore, is a key to understanding the dynamics of social change.

It should be noted that it is not claimed that image changes are the cause of social change and can be used to provide unfailing predictions. In other work, we have clearly indicated why causal analysis is inappropriate in social systems (Klein and Hirschheim, 1983, 1985). Rather it is argued that images can foreshadow possible changes. To the extent that they are believed in, they can act as self-fulfilling prophecies. The purpose here is not to predict, but to analyze the way in which IS research is likely to change if image changes were a valid predictor. We use social image changes as quasi-filters for extracting from the vast research literature in IS those projects which deserve more attention on the assumption that the image provides insight about the future of the social environment of IS.

2.1 How to Perceive Social Change: Images

In order to better recognize current image changes related to society and the quality of the human condition, it may help to recall some image changes of historical dimensions. The image of the rational society was first described by Plato in *Republic*. In it, he outlined the design of a 'good state' and suggested that good leadership was a matter of appropriate training. (Before then it was widely held that the qualification for good leadership was primarily a question of birth.) Plato's design of a 'good state' was so comprehensive that it regulated everything from the division of labour, the education of leaders and administrators, the status of women, and the role of the family, to eugenics and state propaganda to achieve patriotism. Much of what was first described in Plato's image, has become reality in the modern state—in particular that education is a public concern, that only those properly qualified by education and experience should be awarded positions of significant responsibility, that administering policies is different from designing new ones, and so forth. Another classical image is that of Hobbes's *Leviathan*. It is divided into four parts. The first part described the image of man and included a discussion of the senses, reason, science, free will, power, justice and dignity, religion and happiness. The second, third and fourth parts described the three commonwealths: mankind and its institutions; Christian origin; and the Kingdom of Darkness. The image of the second part of *Leviathan* was very effective for establishing the sovereignty of the state. The ideas of the first part helped to discredit religion as a source of valid knowledge and to establish empiricist science as the only sanctioned form of knowledge.

The reason why *Republic* and *Leviathan* were selected as exemplars of societal images is not that they were written by recognized and important philosophers, but that they are very comprehensive in scope and were once widely read, not only by philosophers, but by the informed public—the opinion leaders in education, business, public administration, and politics. To find equivalent books which encode the image changes of society after the Second World War, we must not go to current philosophical writings—as they are not widely read—but to books which are now the functional equivalent of the classics. Several come to mind: The works of Peter Drucker on management; Daniel Bell's *The Coming of Post-industrial Society*; E. Schumaker's *Small is Beautiful*, and Fritz Machlup on the *Knowledge Industry*.

Of particular concern here, however, are those recent additions to the list of key image changing books. These will differ for different countries, but the following three have become widely known and have had a dramatic effect on societal trends and image setting: Alvin Toffler's *Third Wave* (1980); John Naisbitt's

Megatrends (1982) and Thomas Peters and Robert Waterman's *In Search of Excellence* (1982). Of course, others could be referenced, but what is remarkable is that it would only serve to reinforce our thesis: the image displayed by these books shows a remarkable degree of consistency and coherence. It is almost as if the authors had been working on different parts of the same picture which was globally conceived by a single author. If consistency among independently conceived works is any indication of validity, then radical change is on the way, because the society implied by these books is very different from the society to which we have become accustomed during the last 20 years. Here we shall draw on some of the available alternative images of society for the purpose of understanding what they imply for changing the following six social 'forces'.

— societal attitudes
— organizational incentives
— peer orientations
— research paradigm
— design ideals
— tools and methods

These six have been chosen because they provide a conceptual link between social change and emerging research directions in ISD. For more information on why these six are considered of primary importance, see Klein and Hirschheim (1986).

2.2 Social Change: Societal Attitudes

Attitudes in general are defined as predispositions to react positively or negatively to ideas, conditions, or events. They are like preprogrammed responses which save mental energy and help us to respond quickly. Of special interest here are common societal attitudes to conditions which are affected by new information technology. Information technology tends to affect a complex of conditions which define a sphere of life in modern society. Examples of life spheres are education, work, government, family, etc. Each of these refer to a set of experiences which are similar for the members of a particular culture — for instance in Finland the family experience includes the regular taking of saunas, whereas in other countries (like England) this experience is not normally shared with children. Together the various life spheres with their associated attitudes define the overall conditions of human existence which are typical for a particular society.

The new image-shaping books point out that future IS will have important effects in many life spheres. It is therefore of interest to note the new attitudes which are propagated and thereby influence the informed public. It is not claimed that the changes to which the following examples point necessarily reflect current social reality; not even that they will become reality. Rather what is being conveyed are changes in images that are widely circulated. It is possible that these images are self-fulfilling prophecies in that they may bring about the kind of reality which they project. Although there is no guarantee that this will indeed happen, there appears sufficient agreement in the literature (see Weisbord, 1985) to suggest that a number of important image changes are increasingly believed in. If the new images take hold they imply a number of significant societal attitude changes which are of particular relevance for IS research. Examples are attitude changes about work and its relationship to family life, about authority, the nature of organization, planning, learning, knowledge, information, science, technology and perception of reality, while it is difficult to present a firm list, these are sufficient to communicate the kind of societal attitudes of interest for IS researchers.

2.2.1 Work

Past work attitudes were largely shaped by the 'Protestant Ethic'. Work has seen as a human duty. The injunction from *Genesis* was that Man had to earn his livelihood by the sweat of his brow and woman was to bear children and guard the home. In both cases, much toil and misery was involved in this world but rewarded in the after-life.

The division of labor implied by this 'duty and toil' vision of work has crumbled under feminist criticism (see Dinnerstein, 1976). Child-rearing is to be shared, work is seen more as a right for man and woman than back-breaking labor. To confine woman to the role of homemakers is to 'throw away half of humankind's talent for the sake of a few years which are necessary for child bearing'. Work is seen more as a right than a burden to be endured, because it is the means for earning important rewards on this world: recognition by peers, challenge, opportunity for personal growth, and so forth. In short, work is the principal means by which the individual becomes a respected member of society — without work the individual loses a part of his identity, and feels like a second-class citizen (see Jenkins and Sherman, 1979).

2.2.2 Family

The changing work attitudes must have a major impact on family life. The family, for thousands of years, was seen as the fundamental and key social group, responsible for satisfying and providing for most higher level human needs: esteem, trust, love, satisfaction, and so on. Families were the source of inspiration and strength; the nucleus of human existence.

Now, however, significant human needs (for both men and women) are frequently met outside the family: the family has become more incidental. For many, it is no longer the primary sphere where emotional and other higher level needs are met. Family activities must compete with attractive occupations away from the home. Alternatively, work could come home to the family. This is advocated by the notions of an 'electronic cottage industry' or 'telecommuting' (see National Academy of Science, 1985). If these ideas become widespread reality they will change the way in which time is allocated to different activities around the home. To some extent this has already happened (see Vitalary *et al.*, 1985). If the nature of home life changes, the concept of family life and the attitudes associated with it will change along the lines indicated to be compatible with the new work attitudes.

2.2.3 Authority and Power

In the past the legitimation of authority was based either on tradition (as conferred by noble birth) or on formal status and position. In either case it was admired, and was the source of respect. The formal symbols of authority invited others to consult the wisdom of those who had been blessed with power. On the other hand, those in power enjoyed the reassurance of authority which was by and large unquestioned unless abused.

In contradistinction, authority is now widely perceived as a necessary evil which stands in the way of participation and democratic forms of decision making. Those in power are not seen to be endowed with special wisdom, and their decisions are examined with scepticism. The legitimation of power is based on expertise and merit, which is continuously challenged by new ideas and discoveries. This puts the power-holder on the defensive, because he cannot fully justify each decision made. Time pressures, the complexity of subject matters and the limits of education and experience prevent this. Existentialist anxiety rather than the pride of achievement is now the typical situation of the power holder.

2.2.4 Organization and Planning

The past attitude towards organization emphasized its instrumental purpose in that organization provided structure and order which would assure that things were done efficiently and effectively. Similar attitudes applied to planning. Past management textbooks characterized planning and organization as extensions of the managerial mind. They were seen as social means to implement efficiency 'from the top down'. Organization and planning centralized intelligence and decision making by allocating it to segregated units, called staff and line respectively.

More recently, the human systems nature of organizations is emphasized. Life in organizations is seen as a valued source of personal satisfaction; joining an organization is seen as a vehicle to expand the peer network. To the extent that organizations supply the individual with resources to pursue valued activities, they become an object for identification and a source of shaping one's own identity. Organizations still define objectives and procedures, but these are to be proposed and supported much more 'from the bottom up'. Organizations are the means of realizing personal growth objectives. The need for planning continues to be recognized in this context, but as the prerogative of everyone (cf. Ackoff's (1970, 1974) motto 'plan or be planned for'). The old staff–line distinction is seen as invalid and dysfunctional. Planning is seen as interactionist and creative, leading to information-sharing and consensus-based implementation.

2.2.5 *Knowledge, Learning and Perception of Reality*

If what has been said so far is seen as contributing to a new context of life, then it has a number of direct implications for attitudes related to information and knowledge. In the past, knowledge was seen to be based on well-established, codified principles of learning. It was acquired by following well-planned courses and passing predefined tests; knowledge was considered relatively certain and stable. Truth was largely seen as invariant — what was true today must have been true in the past and will be true in the future. These attitudes were reinforced by a traditional trust in the institutions of learning: established schools, the Church, and the like. The leaders and masters of these institutions were seen to possess a special kind of expert authority simply by virtue of being in their positions. It also led, as was already pointed out, to their being recognized as legitimate sources of knowledge.

In contrast, learning is now seen to occur by insight and feedback from practical experience. Preplanned curricula are notoriously out of date, tests have little to do with the current state of the art in research or practice, and so on. Knowledge is inherently uncertain. There is widespread scepticism in the effectiveness of the institutions of learning. They are inhabited by bureaucrats and teachers whose thoughts are not only shackled by outmoded curricula, but also by the lack of access to the real sources of knowledge — the research and experiences of the people who 'work in the real world'. Similar kinds of attitudes are clearly expressed in Illich's (1973) call for 'deschooling' society.

One reason why the new scepticism towards knowledge and learning could take hold is that the following beliefs are more widespread than ever before: reality is complex; things are not what they appear to be; immediate, unaided impressions are ambiguous and frequently misleading, common sense cannot be trusted because there is probably more than meets the eye; and so on. Of course, these insights were already known to Plato. They are contained in his famous cave metaphor in which by direct observation humans can only study shadows on the wall which are cast by objects obscured from their sight. Knowledge about the real objects which are concealed from vision must therefore be obtained in other ways. What is new is that the informed public has widely accepted this kind of attitude towards knowledge, because it is aware of the constantly changing nature of knowledge as caused by so-called 'scientific revolutions' (see Kuhn, 1970) or new breakthroughs. This is a major change from the classical empiricist attitude that reality is objectively given and governed by unchangeable laws to be discovered by 'exact' sciences.

2.2.6 Science and Technology

The attitudes inherited from the Renaissance and the period of Enlightenment were that science and technology are the salvation of mankind; by applying the rigor of clear scientific method, the answers to most of mankind's important questions will ultimately be found. This kind of attitude is still expressed in Popper's (1963) *Conjectures and Refutations*.

Now, however, it is widely believed that the powers of science and technology are limited in scope; even if all scientific questions had been answered, the most important problems of human life have not yet been touched (see Wittgenstein's *Tractatus Logico-Philosophicus*, proposition 6.52). This sceptical attitude is sometimes radicalized by making technology a scapegoat for the many problems which have surfaced in recent years. Significant minorities perceive technological innovations as potentially dangerous, because every advance has had its price.

The above changes in societal attitudes have implications for IS development. Most important are those related to knowledge and work. If knowledge is uncertain and continuously changing, IS cannot rely on stable scientific methods for producing information. Instead, ISD might seek to: provide creativity and productivity tools, facilitate human interaction, and support learning. Individuals no longer seem willing to let systems development be the sole domain of the data processing department. People are demanding the right to participate in anything which is likely to affect their jobs. This is in line with the new attitudes towards organizations. If organizations cannot adapt, they are simply left and the stock of special tools to which the user has become accustomed will go with him. To keep the qualified and competent employee, organizations must provide the right kind of incentives.

2.3 Social Change: Organizational Incentives

Incentives are objects, outcomes, and the like, which an organization provides under the assumption they are desired by organizational members and that employees will try to attain them. They are a means by which an organization tries to enforce or reinforce its wishes. Doing what the organization wants, is instrumental for gaining the incentive. The effectiveness of different types of incentives (both monetary and non-monetary) depends on individual preferences which in turn are affected by social change. The images of future society suggest that the reliance on bureaucratic incentives to achieve compliance with predefined policies will decrease. Possible hints of the kind of incentives which will acquire more significance than conventional forms of remuneration are provided by asking what motivates people in the black or underground economy. By black economy we mean that part of activity which benefits the economic welfare of individuals, but is hidden from taxation and other government controls and which is not perceived by society as clearly criminal. Examples are 'moonlighting', performing services for acquaintances in exchange for other services, and the like. The black economy concept should be widened to include organizational activities which are carried on in the 'organizational underground' and hidden from official management controls. The motivators in this type of activity is 'knowing' how to provide a valuable direct service to others as opposed to complying with rules developed by some bureaucracy; close identification with the activity at hand; autonomy with respect to what is being done, for whom; that remuneration is perceived to be freely negotiated among equals; and the feeling of freedom that comes from the option that one can refuse to do something without serious consequences. If the underlying concepts portrayed here are analyzed, it is discovered that these ideas govern a free market economy, but are for whatever reasons out of reach of most people in the official economy. The free market notions of negotiation among equals, individual contracts where both parties win, freedom, rewards for personal ingenuity, search for synergy among different activities, and so forth, have been stymied by the official economy.

The growth of black economy activities can be noted in employees' behavior at the workplace. Peters and Waterman (1982) make the point that successful companies are characterized by an abundance of 'intra-organizational entrepreneurs' who freely bargain and negotiate across bureaucratic rules and territories. This has far-reaching implications for requirements specification. If IS are designed to improve and enforce existing policies and procedures, they will interfere with (if not wipe out) intra-organizational entrepreneurs. Instead they should provide information which facilitates bargaining and free negotiation through private networking. The same concepts which presumably motivate people to use computers at home for the exchange of useful information should govern their design and implementation at the organizational workplace. Similar conclusions have been reached by the transaction cost theory of IS (see Ciborra, 1981, 1983).

2.4 Social Change: Peer Orientations

Peer orientations in the IS profession are basic beliefs and values held by professionals which precede the formation of attitudes. They are evoked in solving those professional problems which cannot be handled through pre-programmed responses (attitudes), because the nature of the problem requires novel responses. While the economizing effect of attitudes also applies to ISD (e.g. 'this is a bad design because it confuses physical and logical aspects'), systems development projects often involve issues which go beyond the scope for which existing attitudes are effective. They must be addressed in a creative fashion by relying on more general conceptions — the concepts and tools learned as part of graduate professional training and initiation into the trade. One could speak of intellectual background knowledge and simplifying constructs which are mastered by the leaders of a trade. There is some evidence that these also are changing to keep in tune with societal values and attitudes.

Floyd (1985), for example, notes a change in peer orientation in the area of software engineering. The basic distinctions on which software engineering builds are the 'prevailing views' of the nature of programs and systems, their quality and integration into the IS environment, and their implications for human communication, learning and the nature of methods. These distinctions appear to indicate the beginning of a shift in prevailing professional orientations. The software engineering changes seem to imply that programs should be viewed as elements whose effectiveness depends on how well they fit with better forms of voluntary cooperation and therefore whose design must meet social criteria of acceptability. Consequently, systems are evolving social forms of sense-making by which different groupings relate to each other and an uncertain environment. From this perspective, quality of programs is to be measured by the degree to which they are socially desirable and support legitimate functions. User-friendliness does not mean that it is easy for the user to do what the program expects of him, but that the program fits what the user expects of a 'good' system in his line of work. As social interactions produce continuous learning by example, counter-example, analogy and leaps of insight, software development cannot be split into development and maintenance, but is embedded in larger social evolution. The process of learning may be more important than the results, because it is through this process that new meanings are created and gain social legitimacy (shared acceptance). Floyd writes:

> today we no longer face the original software crisis, but a different situation. Its characteristics are, that programs are admittedly reasonably well structured, approximately correct and even finished on time, but that when applied, they are not appropriate tools for their users, they destroy the social network of user organization, fail to realize the expected gains of rationalization and cannot be adapted to changing user requirements. (Floyd 1985, p. 2)

2.5 Social Change: Research Paradigm

A research paradigm is an implicit or explicit view by which a group of researchers approaches its field of study (see Morgan, 1980). Research communities share certain basic beliefs which help them to understand each other in the pursuit of their specialized interests (see Kuhn, 1970). At a fundamental level, they share beliefs about the nature of reality (and whatever it is they are studying: literature, ideas, etc.) and how they can improve their knowledge about their objects of study. A set of assumptions about the understanding of 'what there is' is called an ontology and a set of assumptions about the mode of inquiry, that is how to obtain knowledge and demonstrate that it is valid, is called an epistemology (literally logic or order of knowing). These two sets of assumptions can be used to analyze the most fundamental differences among paradigms. Different research traditions conflict along these dimensions. Since the eighteenth century various schools of empiricism embracing realist ontologies and objectivist epistemologies became the fashion. These were preceded by idealist ontologies (first systematically described by Plato) and interpretivist ontologies.

There is clear evidence to suggest a dissatisfaction with the present logical empiricist method as a vehicle for knowledge acquisition in the social sciences (see Van Maanen, 1979; Mumford *et al.*, 1985). The result has been a plethora of alternative research paradigms. The details of a possible paradigm change need not concern us here. Instead we shall concentrate on some of the implications of this for defining the very nature of IS and for ISD. The point to be made is that different research paradigms, whatever they are, will have important implications for the development of IS. They will affect both our fundamental conception of what information systems are and how they should be developed.

Drastically simplified, there are two ontological dimensions to information systems: (1) the nature of IS; and (2) the nature of their consequences. In the former there are two possibilities: they are either technical or social in nature. In the first case, their design is primarily an engineering problem. In the second, IS are conceived as social systems, their design and implementation is viewed in terms of social evolution, role changes, policy making, and planned organizational change. In the second dimension (the nature of their consequences) three conceptions are possible: their consequences are either technical in nature, social in nature, or a combination of both. Of course, many important variations of these basic positions exist in the literature, but the ones offered here appear as archetypes. Table 1 attempts to classify the basic positions on IS as they are portrayed in the literature. It can be seen that five of the six possibilities are directly observable in the literature. A technical interpretation of information systems along with a technical view of their implications is the position likely to be adopted by

TABLE 1 Basic views of IS

| | NATURE OF CONSEQUENCES | | |
	Technical	Social	Both
Technical	'hard' computer science, software engineering	behaviorist, human factors	socio-technical systems
Social	not found	transaction cost theory	critical social theory
		sense-making: phenomenological/ ethnomethodo-logical approaches	language action view of IS

NATURE OF INFORMATION SYSTEMS

'hard' computer scientists and software engineers. Here, an information system is defined, for example, as 'a system that has been developed in order to create, collect, store, process, distribute, and interpret information sets' (Lundeberg *et al.*, 1979, p. 10). Gessford (1980) offers a similar definition, 'an information system is a symbol processing system. It receives symbols, stores them, transforms them, transmits them, and prints alphabetic, numeric, and pictorial symbols' (p. 3).

Other authors propose an alternative to the strictly technical interpretation of information systems. Mader (1979), for example, defines IS in terms of three resources: hardware, software and people. He notes the importance of people, but only as a set of components whose interface follows behavioral as opposed to technical laws. This interpretation suggests that ISD is a technical intervention in an organization which must take into account the behavioral consequences, or in brief: IS are technical systems with social consequences. The elements of technology are hardware, software, models, databases, and manual procedures (Davis and Olson, 1984).

Another variation of this theme is the socio-technical adaptation of a technical view of IS. Here, IS are perceived as so-called socio-technical systems with the emphasis placed on the technical rather than social side. However, little more than lip-service is paid to social aspects other than quality of working life concerns related to job satisfaction needs.

The alternative to the technical ontology of IS is to view them as social systems. An example of such a view defines IS as social transaction architectures. Ciborra (1981) defines an information system as: 'the network of information flows that are needed to create, set up, control, and maintain the organization's constituent contracts' (Ciborra, 1981, p. 309). This view leads to an interpretation of ISD as a social intervention in the organizational transaction architecture which changes the social arrangements of communication and exchange. Its principal effect is to change the economic trade-offs between different forms of social control structures (markets, bureaucracies and clans). These changes can be investigated by an objectivist, economic research framework (see Ouchi, 1979, 1980).

A variation of the social ontology of IS is the language action (LA) view. It defines IS as a special type of language which changes existing modes of communication, understanding and life forms. Information systems are 'formal linguistic systems for communication between people which support their actions' (Goldkuhl and Lyytinen, 1982, p. 14). As all languages can be described by a grammar, informations systems development should be viewed as the specification of a formal grammar which is implemented on top of the existing modes of communication in order to improve the 'rationality' of communication. This implies that physical, linguistic and social barriers and distortions to existing communication should be removed through ISD.

The notion of IS as a grammar is unusual but is explained in the LA view by conceiving of an information system as a special kind of language which facilitates human interaction through exchange of formalized messages. From this perspective, an IS consists of lexical units (data dictionary entries which refer to something) and rules for communication. These rules govern syntactic and semantic aspects. The latter define the propositional content, the basic intents of messages (e.g. to claim or promise something, to warn, to instruct—this is known as illocutionary meaning) and the actual behavioral effects of messages (their perlocutionary meaning or effects). These depend on the social conventions which are highly culturally contingent (life-form dependent).

The language action view of IS (see also section 2.7) assumes that ISD is a deliberate language change which interferes with the socially accepted forms of sense-making and shared conceptions which facilitate understanding and existing ways of organization and work life (so-called 'life forms' — Lyytinen and Lehtinen, 1984). Sense-making refers to the modes by which a group interacts to interpret their environment and arrive at socially shared meanings. These meanings are then taken as legitimating certain types of decisions in routine activities. ISD interferes with legitimacy of existing modes of action, because it questions the rationality of the very medium through which sense-making occurs: human language as shared by a specific group, for example an organizational department or the members of a profession.

2.6 Social Change: Alternative Design Ideals

A design ideal consists of a set of values and norms which guide design. It dictates what is a desirable design and suggests how to achieve it. In practice, design ideals manifest themselves in system objectives. In the light of the value and attitude changes described earlier, it should not be surprising that system objectives are also being called into question. The value standard of classical industrial society is profitability and technical efficiency, i.e. the design ideal of economic–technical rationality. A number of alternatives are increasingly being found in the literature. Table 2 provides a list of possible societal design ideals which are based on the work of Rule (1974) and Kling (1978). It can be noted that there exists some interdependence of design ideals at different levels of human action, e.g. between the values that are seen to govern modes of social control in society and those in the workplace. Table 3 summarizes some of the design ideals that currently motivate systems design and computer applications. The classification is not meant to be closed, but open-ended. In fact, social progress occurs through the construction of new design ideals.

In addition to these, there are some currently emerging design ideals which may play an important role in the future of ISD. Three are of particular interest and are examined below.

2.6.1 The Design Ideal of Maintaining Craftmanship

Ehn and Kyng (1984, 1985) have proposed the ideal of enhancing craftmanship. They speak in terms of 'a tool perspective on design'. It implies that technology

TABLE 2 The Kling/Rule core design ideals

1. *Private enterprise ideal*. The preeminent consideration is with profitability. Systems are designed such that the firms providing or utilizing the systems achieve maximum profitability. Work and organization rationalization is considered fundamental to this ideal. Other social goods such as users' privacy is considered secondary.

2. *Statist ideal*. The strength and efficiency of government institutions is the highest goal. Government needs for access to personal data on citizens and needs for mechanisms to enforce obligations to the state always prevail over other considerations.

3. *Libertarian ideal*. The civil liberties as specified by the US Bill of Rights are to be maximized in any social choice. Other social purposes such as profitability or welfare of the state are to be sacrificed if they conflict with the prerogatives of the individual.

4. *Neopopulist ideal*. The practices of public agencies and private enterprises should be easily intelligible to ordinary citizens and be responsive to their needs. Societal institutions should emphasize serving the common man.

should not displace human skills which have evolved over centuries and resulted in high quality products. No single occupational group should be expelled from the profession by new technology. The exercise of traditional human skills is tied in with a life form which imparts feelings of self-worth and social significance on those who have acquired these skills (examples are most trades such as furniture making, print setting, etc.). To implement the ideal of maintaining craftmanship, alternatives must be suggested which prevent technology from displacing job skills for the sake of a narrow economic market rationality, because this means loss of a quality product to the consumer and loss of a valued tradition to the worker. Rather the design of technology must aim at enhancing this craftmanship by retaining its desirable aspects as they were inherited from the traditional masters of the craft, and using technology to improve upon them. This is best achieved by the workers taking over the research and development of new technological options. The design ideal of craftmanship provides the justification for a union-based strategy of system development.

2.6.2 The Design Ideal of Union-based IS Development

Whereas the traditional reaction of trade unions to technological change was to negotiate protection clauses for workers or to push for social legislation, the trade-union ideal is that the workers should craft technology which furthers their interest — just as company financed R&D is aimed at serving interests of shareholders and management. The ideal presupposes a conflict model of society. It holds that market and profit objectives cannot be reconciled with the social values of the workforce regarding job skill, quality of work, and quality of products unless new technology is developed with a clear and strong commitment to these values. The ideal of realizing social work values is expressed in the acronym UTOPIA which, in Swedish, stands for 'training, technology, and products from a skilled worker's perspective' (Howard, 1985). The ideal is to give the unions an even

TABLE 3 Systems design ideals

1. *Socio-technical ideal*. The principal objective is to optimize the interrelationships between the social and human aspects of the organization and the technology used to achieve organizational goals. *Both* the quality of working life (satisfaction of human needs at work) *and* profitability or system efficiency are to be improved through a high degree of fit between job characteristics (as defined by work design) and a limited set of human needs (as defined by social and psychological profiles) (see Bostrom and Heinen, 1977; Pava, 1983).

2. *Decision support systems ideal*. The final criterion is 'to help improve the effectiveness and productivity of managers and professionals'. A necessary condition for achieving this is to gain user acceptance and actual systems use. In some parts of the literature this is seen as a worthwhile goal in itself. In any case, the emphasis is on tailoring the system design to the user's needs and preferences. Sophisticated techniques for analysis of personality traits or other psychometric variables such as cognitive style, locus of control, motivational type, and attitudes are proposed as design tools. A thorough 'understanding' of the user's problems and a strategy of mutual trust building through highly participative systems development in a series of small, adaptive steps with rapid feedback through demonstrations are seen as the 'right' approach (see Keen and Scott Morton, 1978).

3. *Dialectical inquiry ideal*. Above all information systems must be designed such that they produce maximal motivation to generate 'objective' knowledge through the synthesis of the most opposing points of view — each supported by the best available evidence. Truth and objectivity are of prime importance and can only be found through an adversarial process in which the competing points of view are confronted such as in a court of law. Peace, willingness to compromise, or consensus create dangerous illusions which threaten the objectivity of knowledge and justice (see Churchman, 1970, 1971; Mason, 1969; Klein *et al.*, 1980).

4. *Participatory design ideal*. Emphasizes that the process by which systems are developed may be more important than the features of the final product, because 'people should be able to determine their own destinies'. Hence the ultimate moral value to be achieved through participation is human freedom which then leads to such other goods as motivation to learn, and genuine human relationships based on equality and commitment to what one has freely chosen to accomplish (Mumford, 1983; Land and Hirschheim, 1983).

5. *Systems ideal*. The primary goal is that systems be technically elegant, well-organized, efficient, and reliable (see Jenkins, 1969; Optner, 1965).

hand in the design of new workplace technology before it reaches the shop floor. Otherwise the bias of the private enterprise design ideal (see above) will constrain the features of new technology to such a degree that worker participation in the implementation phase will achieve little or nothing. (See also the DEMOS project — Ehn and Sandberg, 1983.)

2.6.3 The Design Ideal of End-user Computing (EUC)

This shares some concerns with both the participatory and union-based design ideals, yet is different in important ways. Most people think of EUC as users doing their own programming instead of relying on the DP department to respond to requests for new systems or enhancements. The basic ideal is to make the end-user as independent as possible from IS personnel and DP center staff. However, this analysis is too superficial. What is ultimately at stake is the *control* of ISD. The control aspects come into focus where EUC is discussed in relationship to information center (IC) management (see Martin, 1984). The IC is proposed to both encourage and aid EUC (e.g. through training and advice), but also to 'manage' it (e.g. by standards and policies) to maintain some degree of compatibility and consistency with the existing IS architecture and organization goals. The ideal of EUC is to remove controls and thereby emancipate the individual not only from the dependency on classical data processing, but also from the hierarchical controls of management authority. In the struggle between the interests of the community and the interest of the individual, EUC takes the side of the latter. It differs from both the participatory and union-based design ideal in that it distrusts the collectivistic controls inherent in both. Why bother with participation if the individual can do it all by himself if given appropriate tools? Of course, this rugged individualism overlooks the many social constraints that exist to bias and channel an individual's design choices. The most obvious of these is the nature of the tools supplied and the assumptions made when designing EUC applications. Both are heavily influenced by the commercial culture of software vendors and organizational ideology. Another influential constraint is the existence of centrally maintained files or databases [2].

The three design ideals examined above are closely associated with the emergence of alternative methods and tools of systems development. This is particularly obvious in the case of EUC which relies on very high level, 'fourth generation languages' (see Martin, 1982, 1985). In the case of the union-based strategy and the ideal of maintaining craftsmanship, the methods and tools of systems development must be suited to realize the social concerns of these ideals. Hence the emergence of new tools is an important factor which will determine the extent to which these ideals will actually determine the future shape of IS.

2.7 Social Change: Alternative Tools and Methods

A design ideal gives a global direction, a method is a more detailed specification of steps to be taken to achieve a given end. Methods have proliferated since Descartes insisted that in Science we need to rely on a proper method to discover the truth. By method he understood a set of 'certain easy rules such that everyone who observes them exactly will never take anything false to be true and, without any waste of mental effort but by increasing his knowledge step by step, will arrive at a true understanding of all those things which do not surpass his capacity' (Copleston, 1963, p. 83). Since then, methods have been seen as the primary means to achieve technical progress by applying the laws of science. Some methods rely on tools. A tool is an object which has an independent existence of a method — the same tool can be used by different methods in different ways.

Each wave of social change requires its own tools and methods. Without tools, ideas cannot be implemented. As the prevailing design ideals and societal attitudes change, new requirements emerge and the number of users who are dissatisfied tends to grow. Two issues appear to take hold and gain wide recognition: (1) While man first creates tools to better control the products of work, they often end up controlling him, by setting up expectations and pressures beyond individual control (see Cooley, 1980). (2) Inhumane tool technologies, which are often developed for purely economic and/or controlling purposes, threaten human existence. Health, safety, and worker satisfaction are often ignored. This has led to research into the requirements of an alternative 'convivial' technology (Illich, 1973) which enhances the human condition. The following requirements for future tools have been proposed (Hirschheim, 1986). Whereas these requirements may be Utopian in the sense of asking for the impossible (because it is difficult to see how they can be implemented), they, nevertheless, project a new image on how technology should relate to the human condition.

(1) The technology and/or its function should be intelligible to the community as a whole. If not, the community should at least be willing to give tacit acceptance to those experts who do understand it.

(2) It must fulfil a socially useful purpose. The application of technology must address social needs which are recognized as justified by an informed democratic consensus.

(3) It should be under the operational control of the local workforce. If not, the local workforce should at least have a say in its control.

(4) It should not displace more jobs than it creates.

(5) It should, wherever possible, use indigenous resources and skills, and contribute to their growth.

(6) Its production and use should present no undue health hazards or risks.

(7) Wherever possible, it should be non-polluting, ecologically and aesthetically sound.

(8) It should not lead to external cultural domination.

(9) Its use should permit those elements of work which are recognized as being related to high job satisfaction to be improved (e.g. development of new skills, task variety, challenging tasks, and the like).

(10) It should not disturb the existing social order if this is widely accepted as just and fair unless the new social order brought about by the change advances and improves society as a whole and can be defended by Rawls's (1973) *Principles of Justice*.

Although these requirements may be considered by some to be Utopian, there are cases where they have formed the basis of a 'new generation of tools' which were used in IS development. The need for such tools, in fact, underlies several recent research projects. For example, in the MARS project (Lanzara and Mathiassen, 1984), approaches for improving the self-insight of system developers are being sought. The UTOPIA project (Bodker, 1985) emphasizes the need for a better symbiosis between new technology and work traditions. It has been shown for instance that size and resolution capabilities of current technology still lags behind the functionality of conventional, backlit layout tables for typesetters. Another research project, called SAMPO (Lyytinen and Lehtinen, 1984), aimed at developing humanistically inspired tools for supporting the process of ISD itself. Because of its novel conception of IS and IS development, and its potential importance in guiding the future direction of ISD, it is discussed in more detail.

SAMPO (a continuing research project) aims at developing methods and tools which are consistent with the LA view of ISD. It radicalizes the idea that ISD means a change of 'life form', suggesting that it is important to consider three closely interlinked notions when developing information systems: *life form*, *means of communication* (in particular language and symbols), and *understanding* of the world through reinterpretations and creation of new meanings. The three are like three corners of a triangle. If one is changed the others change with it, such as the shape of a triangle if one corner is 'dragged'. (This idea was originally conceived by the later Wittgenstein who noted that there is no fixed correspondence between what we say and what we mean. Rather the meaning of what we say evolves with the social uses of the phrases and other symbols.) The SAMPO researchers built on this idea by viewing ISD as a process of normative linguistics — an IS is a rule system for exchanging prespecified meanings with an artificially contrived language — which requires methods and tools to model organizational discourses. Speech act theory has been used in this context. Tools are considered important because they are part of the life form and can change both language and understanding. Through (human/social) discourse modeling, the IS developer both reconstructs (in analysis) and then purposefully changes (in design) the organizations' communication practices. This requires ISD to focus both on the intentions and social consequences of the form and technical means of communication. Traditional ISD has primarily focused on the objects or events which terms and symbols 'denote' or refer. It thereby abstracts from the intentions and social conventions which govern the use and meanings of language to the participants from their own perspective. The latter is the 'emic' (or within) view of the users' life form as opposed to the 'etic' (outside) view of user interaction by an external observer. An analysis of denotations as practiced in classical data modeling or file design is also important, but speech act modeling makes it clear that this is not complete. It must be supplemented by an analysis of intentions (illocutionary meanings) and the social consequences of communication acts (performative means). The SAMPO researchers believe that by approaching ISD from such a perspective they can overcome many of the existing dysfunctions of ISD and increase the creative potential of ISD as an organizational change process (see Lehtinen and Lyytinen, 1983, 1984; Lyytinen, 1985, 1986; and Lyytinen and Lehtinen, 1984).

2.8 Summary

The purpose of this section was to suggest that broad social change is on the way. Societal change will imply organizational changes and if such changes are to lead to social progress, current methods and tools need to change. The notion of images about the future of society was introduced as a way to perceive societal change. No attempt was made to spell out the details of current image changes, only their general direction. If we assume that change is on the way, then current IS research may need to change. Several research projects, which are currently not considered to be in the mainstream can be looked upon as the forerunners of alternative research paradigms. The SAMPO project was described as an example of such an alternative paradigm.

3. POSSIBLE FUTURES OF INFORMATION SYSTEMS RESEARCH

This chapter has touched on many points that have not been explicitly recognized in the literature as belonging together. The motivation for seeing them in this way has been the desire to contribute to an emerging, new sense-making perspective of ISD, and to explore its implications for IS as a professional discipline and field of academic study.

The previous journey through the rapidly changing scene of IS research suggests to us three possible conclusions. One, there are several options on how IS research might evolve — alternative futures, so to speak, which are not necessarily mutually exclusive. Two, it is unlikely that any of these futures will win the unanimous support of all relevant participants: IS researchers, their potential financial sponsors, the potential 'consumers' of IS research and, of course, the students of ISD who typically see IS as an applied, professional discipline. Third, if IS development and research is indeed evolving away from a commonly accepted core (as suggested above), it is likely to create an existential dilemma for practicing analysts who look towards science for the legitimation of their professional methods and tools. These conclusions have serious consequences and are thus explored in some detail below.

3.1 Possible Futures of IS Research

There are three possible directions or options on how future research in IS might evolve.

(1) The first is to strengthen the received, positivist research program and aim at becoming a 'hard' science of analysis and design.
(2) The second is to become more sensitive to the immediate pressures of surrounding society so that IS research addresses itself more resolutely to the current practical problems and searches for solutions which meet with minimal resistance from the recognized powers, i.e. leaders in management, government, unions, and depending on national differences, trade unions.

(3) Look for a new and broader research approach in order to provide a radical alternative to (1) and (2). The first aim of such a third option could be to study the fundamental reasons for the unresolved practical problems associated with ISD with a view to identifying novel solutions. The second aim could be to serve as an institution of fundamental criticism which exposes the underlying assumptions of IS work, in particular examining the often negative impacts of information technology on people, organizations and society. Fundamental criticism is necessary to balance the professional optimism of vendors and consultants.

No immediate choice among these three options is necessary from a purely research-oriented perspective, because different research groups can pursue different research programs. The previous analysis of the research literature has shown that to some degree, this has already happened. If the trend continues, IS as an applied discipline will be practicing 'methodological pluralism' (Hirschheim, 1985a; Morgan, 1980; Hirschheim and Klein, 1986)—a phenomenon which in the past was typical of a number of disciplines: philosophy, sociology and religion. Unfortunately, if we look at the situation of the practicing analyst, we find that methodological pluralism could create serious existential dilemmas for responsible practitioners. In order to understand these dilemmas more fully, the following issues need to be considered for each option in order to bring out some of their practical consequences:

(a) What are the research strategy implications of each option, given that different research strategies imply differing bases for valid knowledge?
(b) To which interest group in society does each option appeal, and how much support is each option likely to mobilize?
(c) Is there an historical analogy which can help to assess the long-term social desirability of each option?

3.2 Implications of Practicing the Scientific Method

The research strategy of the first option is to study and adopt the research methods and tools from those disciplines which are considered to have been successful, i.e. which are founded on the scientific method. The principal examples which come to mind are operations research and applied mathematics, computer science, engineering, and so forth. A typical example of scientific results produced by such a strategy are the structured programming and design approaches of software engineering.

This option will appeal most to those researchers who come to IS from the relatively 'hard' reference disciplines: engineering, mathematics, and computer science. It is also likely to appeal to managers and users in industry. But this requires a more careful analysis.

To the extent to which the scientific method can produce practicable results, these will play into hands of those who hold power in organizations. For example, engineering is basically a science of control. Control is gained by exploiting knowledge about recurring patterns which in the ideal case are described by causal laws. Factual knowledge of regularities in human behavior can be used to better control people. ISD thus becomes part of the science and art of management control and will find the approval of this interest group. Historical analogies suggest themselves in the evolution of other management disciplines; applied social science in marketing, applied economics and mathematics in managerial finance and accounting, engineering applied to production management, and so forth.

History also suggests that insofar as such an approach finds the support of management, it might meet with the resistance of the non-managerial work force, the result of which could contribute to continued IS failure. IS could be resisted because it would be seen as potentially undermining their socio-economic positions in organizations (see Bjorn-Andersen and Hedberg, 1977; Dutton and Kraemer, 1978; Markus, 1983; Newman and Rosenberg 1985). The most likely long-term social consequence of this option is IS contributing to the existing, alienating divisions in society. To some extent such a perspective is already visible, through the emergence of trade-union strategies in the Scandinavian countries (see the UTOPIA and DEMOS projects). Another example is research on how computers can lessen the plight of the 'unwaged' (those unemployed, underemployed or otherwise economically disadvantaged) in Great Britain (see Darwin et al., 1985). The financial interests behind this kind of work decidedly act to oppose the effects of systems developed with managerial interests.

However, another scenario is also possible. It holds that not all of science is necessarily applied and consistent with managerial interests. Thus option (1) is likely to meet with indifference from both management and trade-union leadership, because the 'hard science' approach to IS does not necessarily address the most urgent problems in the most useful way (see Shrivastava and Mitroff, 1984). The undesirable long-term social consequence of this scenario is that IS research regresses into the proverbial ivory tower, becoming a platonic science whose esoteric jargon will be of interest only to its own cast of academic priests. In conclusion then it may be thought that option (1) will partly cater to vested interests and thereby meet with political resistance from other groupings, and partly it will be irrelevant to most social interests with the exception of those in academic research.

3.3 Implications of Emphasizing Applied Research

The research strategy of the second option requires close attention to current problems and deals with them in a way which emphasizes the practical relevance of results over objectivity of method and/or rigor (reproducibility) of results. Practical relevance in this context implies that IS research should produce tools and methods for the analyst which can help him or her to move along the path of least resistance in implementing 'successful' systems—although again successful as seen in the eyes of management. Widely known examples of such a research strategy are Nolan's (1982) 'Stage Theory of Growth' and Rockart's (1979) 'Critical Success Factors' approach to requirements determination. The stages of growth theory, for example, has been credited by DP managers with helping them to anticipate problems so that an orderly strategy could be found. Critics of such a research will come both from advocates and options (1) and (3). They will be quick to point out that the second option leads to an IS research program that is determined by prevailing computing fashions, and lacks a critical perspective both in methods and objectives.

Nevertheless, the second option will most likely appeal to those whose interests this type of IS research can advance. In principle, IS research can become the partisan of any existing social interest group which has the resources and foresight to draw IS researchers into its camp. IS can be strategic weapons for political parties, churches, government, industry and so forth. It is also interesting to note that students exert a strong pull on their teachers to move towards the second option. They expect their professors to study the practices of 'The real world' and pass on the knowledge so that they can meet the expectations of their future employers.

The second strategy implies that IS research projects would be supported by and aligned with the various social interest groups, which would reinforce the existing societal divisions. This strategy also adopts instrumental and conformist attitudes toward knowledge and learning. The instrumental attitude treats knowledge primarily as a means to achieve career success. The conformist attitude relies on docility: obey rather than challenge existing practices. There are two historical analogies which can help assess the social consequences of such a strategy: the Sophists of ancient Greece and the Mandarins of ancient China.

The Greek Sophists provide an interesting example of an instrumental attitude. The Sophists, whose vanity was eventually exposed by Socrates and Plato, were perhaps the first who claimed to have the knowledge to teach their students how to achieve worldly success. They were, so to speak, the first consultants of the Western world, selling what they knew at a high price. As the Sophists unscrupulously sold their services to anyone who was able and willing to pay, they undermined the morality of Greek democracy and produced unscrupulous careerists, corrupt politicians and Macchiavellian leaders. (A well-known example is Alkibiades, the gifted general who did not hesitate to change fronts several times whenever it suited his interest.)

The Chinese Mandarins, on the other hand, provide an example of a conformist attitude. They were ancient magistrates who believed in abiding by convention. Their beliefs can be traced back to the qualifying exams of public officials in ancient China which were based on an elaborate study of the accepted administrative procedures and royal decrees. These were to be known, not questioned. The first consequence of such an approach applied to IS suggests that a class of modern

'System Mandarins' would become opposed to change and thereby reduce the flexibility to maintain the competitiveness of national industries (unless of course the Mandarin ideal of knowledge becomes a world-wide phenomenon). Conformist IS research would try to compile the knowledge which can turn students into obedient bureaucrats and technocrats who can pursue the goals set by those who pay their salaries. This is different from educating students to be creative and responsible workers who can think ahead and contribute to the long-range vigor and competitiveness of industry which requires the courage to be innovative, and thus the need for critical thought. The requirements for this are almost the opposite from motivating students to absorb current practice. Emphasis on current practice almost invariably depends on a commitment to teach its inherent 'goodness', which leads both researchers and students away from fundamental criticism.

3.4 Implications of an Emancipatory IS Research Program

The research strategy of the third option, is to study the problems and interests of all groups by whatever approach appears most promising. There is no specific preferred reference discipline. Historical analysis, anthropological and ethnomethodological approaches, philosophical analysis and empirical data analysis, etc. can all be useful to broaden our understanding of the issues and to elicit better system requirements. From this perspective, IS research aims to 'transcend' (look beyond and emancipate itself from) the prevailing ideology of whatever interest groups dominate government and industry. By taking a decidedly independent stance, IS research could contribute to improving the understanding and documentation of the interests and goals of different social groupings and forms of social development. The researcher would form an independent judgement of how IS work could contribute to improving the situation and ultimately to a better society. Hence IS research could help others to emancipate themselves from unwarranted constraints. In principle this goal is similar to that pursued by the scientific method, but the means of inquiry are conceived to be much broader by allowing for more interpretivist or subjectivist research approaches. Greater cross-cultural sensitivity and awareness could help to overcome tunnel vision and to uncover new solution approaches (for a pilot study conceived in this spirit see Klein and Alvarez (1985)).

Both the works on 'practical action' (see Suchman, 1983; Suchman and Wynn, 1984) and the Florence project (Bjerknes and Bratteteig, 1984, 1985) build on an anthropological perspective which recognizes that user communities evolve different life forms that are much more complex than any outside analysis usually realizes. Suchman and Wynn show that purchase clerks evolve specific modes of thought which manifest themselves in speech acts by which new situations in office work are diagnosed, interpreted and the participants manipulated until ambiguities are sufficiently cleared up, so that they can be handled with existing policies. Their analysis clearly demonstrates that office conversations are tied to evolving customs and practices that are not easily documented. The Florence project radicalizes this insight by recognizing that IS intervene with the evolution of professional life forms and thereby become a strategic weapon which can strengthen one user community at the expense of another. In their case study it was found that the researchers intervened in the history of the nursing profession and in the struggle between doctors and nurses for patient control. These insights point to the need for system designers to become sensitive to not upsetting the balance among the various subcommunities in the organization. This insight could give a new meaning to the role for IS planning and strategy. They would have to pursue the notion of 'balance' between different user communities, for instance through an approach of participatory planning of IS architecture. In this context IS architecture means the definition of the interrelationships between the components of the IS applications portfolio and the priorities for its evolution as seen from different user communities. IS planning in this sense becomes synonymous with maintaining a rational discourse about the future among different user communities who adhere to conflicting ways of thinking and speaking— which is quite different from the notion of defining a comprehensive enterprise model by better 'reality modeling'. It is also different from a 'plan' in the sense of a structure sanctioned by an authoritative decision; rather IS planning here means constant fundamental criticism of the status quo to counteract bureaucratic rigidities and conformism.

This option is unlikely to find many followers, as its greatest appeal lies with educational idealists. It is likely to remain under-resourced and cannot be easily developed, because it lacks the backing of any strong interest group. Nevertheless it has the chance of attracting some civic-minded supporters in all walks of life.

The historical analogy which suggests itself to this option, is the knowledge ideal of the Age of Enlightenment. In this period it was believed that the knowledge resulting from free inquiry would emancipate mankind from its principal ills. Unfortunately the analogy suggests serious difficulties. With the benefit of hindsight we can see that the Age of Enlightenment produced two antagonistic social consequences. On the one hand, by emphasizing critical analysis it freed human thought from superstition and unwarranted dogmas. On the other hand, the application of the same principles of rational inquiry to seek more efficient forms of organization lost its critical edge. It created rigid techno-structures which forced people into the mold of elaborate bureaucratic rule systems. Hence the Age of Enlightenment has given way to the scientific justification of bureaucratic dogmatism. The result is that:

> Computerized society has become so bureacratically impersonal that it is no longer guided sufficiently by forces that are in the highest sense humane. (p. xv of Ziolokowski's foreword to *The Glass Bead Game* by Hermann Hesse, Bantam Books)

If we accept such an assessment of the state of modern society, the knowledge ideal of the Age of Enlightenment has led to the paradoxical result of new constraints on inquiry. The new dogmatism comes from using the so-called scientific method as a legitimizing ideology in order to justify the inevitable truth and correctness of existing administrative practices and norms. These then serve as filters to exclude alternative proposals for organizational goals and strategies to achieve them (see Klein and Lyytinen, 1985).

In summary, the third option suggests the setting free of IS research by creating a much broader research strategy, by breaking out of the 'mental prison' of the scientific method (Morgan, 1980). IS research would become one of the active forces that help to reshape society in accordance with democratic ideals. The long-term issue of this strategy is whether it will create its own new forms of dogmatism as the historical analogy of the Age of Enlightenment suggests or whether this tendency can be counteracted by broadening the concept of science to include all forms of critical thought as legitimate.

4. CONCLUSIONS: IMPLICATIONS FOR THE INDIVIDUAL ANALYST

The previous analysis suggests that IS research can evolve in radically differing directions. Each has its own difficulties. Whereas most research is likely to proceed along options (1) and (2), none is likely to displace the others. (See, for example, the work of Suchman and Wynn, and the Florence project cited above, which are alternatives to the first two options.) What does the continuing change of IS research and the split in the IS research community mean for the practicing analyst?

Systems development is an emerging profession. It has started to develop model curricula and the discussion of standards and accreditation has begun (see Nunamaker et al., 1982; Buckingham et al., 1986). Professionals are paid to correctly apply a stable core of knowledge—witness the examples of physicians, accountants and lawyers. Moreover, for various psychosocial reasons, professionals need to identify with this knowledge. They need to believe both in the correctness and goodness of what they practice. Professions typically view themselves to be among the pillars of society. The correctness of the stable core of knowledge is sanctioned by a combination of the following: tradition (the legal profession is among the oldest), democratic law (for example taxation and creditor protection in the case of accountants) or the scientific method (in the case of physicians, engineers, etc.). The goodness of the knowledge is judged by the results which it produces: doctors heal, lawyers support the process of justice, and so on. On both counts—correctness and goodness of their practices—systems developers face a problem which is likely to lead them into an existential dilemma.

According to Mowshowitz (1976), over 50 per cent of all information systems are failures. Substantial resources are spent on systems which are not used, used unhappily, or used for only a part of what they were developed for, and so on. A whole line of research has evolved to study the social impacts of information systems. Much of the research suggests that IS often turn out to be socially negative (see Kling, 1980; Hirschheim, 1985b). On the basis of these results, the individual analyst can hardly be proud of his profession. If doctors would kill half their patients and half of the buildings of civil engineers were to collapse, these professions would certainly suffer a legitimation and identity crisis.

The result experienced by the analyst is likely to be one of personal disorientation, stress, and alienation. (It is similar to a situation where practicing doctors could not rely on the medical establishment to approve clinical procedures, but would have to decide whether they prefer to listen to alchemists or faith healers.) One common reaction to disorientation is problem avoidance: see, speak and hear no evil, but follow whatever seems to satisfy the next higher level in the organization. Those who cannot pass the buck upward, face the stress of 'inescapable malpractice', because in the absence of an expert consensus on proper methods and tools of ISD, the correct practice remains undefined. Whatever approach is picked, is likely to be attacked by some group of experts. From the perspective presented in this chapter the above state of affairs is hardly surprising. ISD suffers a chronic expert consensus deficit on accepted principles of good professional practice of system development, because it is undergoing fundamental change.

Another reaction is to seek comfort in numbers. Watch what the industry leaders do and then follow suit. But none of this addresses the root of the problem: the lack of a stable core of knowledge and of inquiring methods that are legitimized by the broad-based consensus of a strong IS research establishment (analogous to clinical research in medicine).

Whatever the reaction adopted by the analyst, the underlying dilemma is not going to go away. It needs to be addressed head on. The result of our analysis suggests that the field of IS must make some hard choices about how it should progress. It is our view that the adoption of the third option (the emancipatory IS research strategy) provides the most fruitful avenue for the future. It is not an easy route, but one which is most likely to realistically deal with the fundamental dilemma which both of the other two strategies avoid: how to be relevant and practical yet not sacrifice the ideal of independent and critical inquiry.

NOTES

[1] The conceptual difficulties of applying cause–effect thinking to social phenomena have been recognized in earlier work (Klein and Hirschheim, 1983, 1985), with the result that the consequentialist perspective was proposed to deal with them. The spirit of the consequentialist approach also applies here in that the epistemological issues of prediction in the social domain also arises in this chapter.

[2] Whilst EUC has become very popular in North America it has not been as successful in Europe. There are a number of reasons why this may be the case: (1) there is a greater degree of participation in Europe already; (2) there exists a more positive attitude towards individual initiative and self-reliance in North America; (3) EUC technology is less expensive and thus a better bargain in the US; (4) there is less peer pressure in terms of keeping up with the latest technological changes in Europe; and (5) there is less technological optimism in Europe.

ACKNOWLEDGEMENTS

This work was in part funded by the Academy of Finland (grant number 03/097). This chapter has benefited from the helpful comments of Paul Jowett.

REFERENCES

Ackoff, R. (1970) *A Concept of Corporate Planning*, Wiley–Interscience, New York.

Ackoff, R. (1974), *Re-designing the Future*, Wiley–Interscience, New York.

Bjerknes, G., and Bratteteig, T. (1984) 'The Application Perspective — Another Way of Conceiving Systems Development and EDP-based Systems', in *The Seventh Scandinavian Research Seminar on Systemeering, Helsinki, August 1984*, M. Saaksjarri (Ed.).

Bjerknes, G., and Bratteteig, T. (1985) 'FLORENCE in Wonderland — Systems Development with Nurses', *Proceedings of the Conference on Development and Use of Computer-based Systems and Tools, Aarhus, August 1985*.

Bjorn-Andersen, N., and Hedberg, B. (1977) 'Designing Information Systems in an Organizational Perspective', in *Prescriptive Models of Organizations, TIMS Studies in the Management Sciences*, Vol. 5, P. Nystrom and W. Starbuck (Eds.).

Bodker, S. (1985) 'UTOPIA and the Design of User Interfaces', *Proceedings of the Conference on Development and Use of Computer-based Systems and Tools, Aarhus, August 1985*.

Bostrom, R., and Heinen, S. (1977) 'MIS Problems and Failures: A Socio-technical Perspective — Parts I and II', *MIS Quarterly*, September and December.

Boulding, K. (1956) 'General Systems Theory–The Skeleton of Science', *General Systems*, Vol. 1.

Buckingham, R., Hirschheim, R., Land, F., and Tully, C. (1986) *Information Systems Education: Recommendations and Implementation*, Cambridge University Press, Cambridge.

Churchman, C. (1970) 'Operations Research as a Profession', *Management Science*, **17**, 2.

Churchman, C. (1971) *The Design of Inquiring Systems*, Basic Books, New York.

Ciborra, C. (1981) 'Information Systems and Transactions Architecture', *Policy Analysis and Information Systems*, **5**.

Ciborra, C. (1983) 'Management Information Systems: A Contractual View', in *Beyond Productivity: Information Systems Development for Organizational Effectiveness*, T. Bemelmans (Ed.), North-Holland, Amsterdam, 1983.

Cooley, M. (1980) *Architect or Bee? The Human/Technology Relationship*, Hand and Brain Publication, Slough.

Copleston, F. (1963) *A History of Philosophy*, Vol. IV, Doubleday Books, Garden City.

Couger, J. D., Colter, M., and Knapp, R. (1982) *Advanced Systems Development/Feasibility Techniques*, John Wiley, New York.

Darwin, J., Fitter, M., Fryer, D., and Smith, L. (1985) 'Developing Information Technology in the Community with Unwaged Groups', *Proceedings of the Conference on Development and Use of Computer-based Systems and Tools, Aarhus, August 1985*.

Davis, G., and Olson, M. (1984) *Management Information Systems: Conceptual Foundations, Structure, and Development*, McGraw-Hill, New York.

Dinnerstein, D. (1976) *The Mermaid and Minotaur: Sexual Arrangements and Human Malaise*, Harper & Row, New York.

Dutton, W., and Kraemer, K. (1978) 'Management Utilization of Computers in American Local Governments', *Communications of the ACM*, **21**, 3.

Ehn, P., and Kyng, M. (1984) 'A Tool Perspective on Design of Interactive Computer Support for Skilled Workers', in *The Seventh Scandinavian Research Seminar on Systemeering, Helsinki, August 1984*, M. Saaksjarvi (Ed.).

Ehn, P., and Kyng, M. (1985) 'STARDUST MEMORIES: Scandinavian Tradition and Research on Development and Use of Systems and Tools', paper presented at the Conference on Development and Use of Computer-based Systems and Tools, Aarhus, August 1985.

Ehn, P., and Sandberg, A. (1983) 'Local Union Influence on Technology and Work Organization: Some Results from the DEMOS Project', in *Systems Design for, with and by the Users*, U. Briefs, C. Ciborra, and L. Schneider (Eds.), North-Holland, Amsterdam.

Floyd, C. (1985) 'Towards a Paradigm Change in Software Engineering', paper presented at the Conference on Development and Use of Computer-based Systems and Tools, Aarhus, August 1985.

Gessford, M. (1980) *Modern Information Systems: Designed for Decision Support*, Addison-Wesley, Reading, MA.

Goldkuhl, G., and Lyytinen, K. (1982) 'A Language Action View on Information Systems', *Proceedings of the Third International Conference on Information Systems*, Ann Arbor, December 1982.

Hirschheim, R. (1985a) 'Information Systems Epistemology: An Historical Perspective', in *Research Methods in Information Systems*, Mumford, E., Hirschheim, R., Fitzgerald, G., and Wood-Harper (Eds.), North-Holland, Amsterdam.

Hirschheim, R. (1985b) *Office Automation: A Social and Organizational Perspective*, John Wiley, Chichester.

Hirschheim, R. (1986) 'The Effect of *a priori* Views on the Social Implications of Computing: The Case of Office Automation', *Computing Surveys*, **18**, 2.

Hirschheim, R., and Klein, H. (1986) 'Pluralism in Information Systems Development: Stories, Consequences and Implications for Legitimation', Oxford Institute of Information Management, RDP 86–14, Templeton College, Oxford.

Howard, R. (1985) 'UTOPIA: Where Workers Craft New Technology', *Technology Review*, **88**, 3.

Illich, I. (1973) *Tools for Conviviality*, Fontana, New York.

Jenkins, G. (1969) 'The Systems Approach', *Journal of Systems Engineering*, **1**, 1.

Jenkins, C., and Sherman, B. (1979) *The Collapse of Work*, Eyre Methuen, London.

Keen, P., and Scott Morton, M. (1978) *Decision Support Systems: An Organizational Perspective*, Addison-Wesley, Reading, MA.

Klein, H., and Alvarez, R. (1985) 'Information Systems in the Hotel Industry: Part of a Problem or Part of a Solution?', *Proceedings of the Conference on Development and Use of Computer-based Systems and Tools, Aarhus, August 1985*.

Klein, H., and Hirschheim, R. (1983) 'Issues and Approaches to Appraising Technological Change in the Office: A Consequentialist Perspective', *Office: Technology & People*, **2**, 1.

Klein, H., and Hirschheim, R. (1985) 'Fundamental Issues of Decision Support Systems: A Consequentialist Perspective', *Decision Support Systems*, **1**, 1.

Klein, H., and Hirschheim, R. (1986) 'Legitimation and Information Systems Development: A New Perspective of Why Information Systems Fail', Working paper.

Klein, H., and Lyytinen, K. (1985) 'The Poverty of Scientism in Information Systems', in *Research Methods in Information Systems*, E. Mumford, R. Hirschheim, G. Fitzgerald, and T. Wood-Harper (Eds.), North-Holland, Amsterdam, pp. 131–161.

Klein, H., Meadows, I., and Welke, R. (1980) 'The Effectiveness of Dialectical Inquiry for Decision Making in Self-organizing Groups', *Proceedings of the International Congress on Applied Systems Research and Cybernetics, Acapulco, 1980*.

Kling, T. (1978) 'Value Conflicts and Social Choice in Electronic Funds Transfer Systems Developments', *Communications of the ACM*, **21**, 8.

Kling, R. (1980) 'Social Analyses of Computing: Theoretical Perspectives in Recent Empirical Research', *Computing Surveys*, **12**.

Kuhn, T. (1970) *The Structure of Scientific Revolutions*, 2nd Edn., University of Chicago Press, Chicago.

Land, F., and Hirschheim, R. (1983) 'Participative Systems Design: Rationale, Tools, and Techniques', *Journal of Applied Systems Analysis*, **10**.

Lanzara, G., and Mathiassen, L. (1984) 'Mapping Situations within a Systems Development Project: An Intervention Perspective on Organizational Change', DAIMI PB-179, Mars Report No. 6, November.

Lehtinen, E., and Lyytinen, K. (1983) 'SAMPO Project: A Speech Act Based IA Methodology with Computer Aided Tools', Department of Computer Science, University of Jyvaskyla, Report WP-2.

Lehtinen, E., and Lyytinen, K. (1984) 'A Model Theoretical Interpretation of Information Systems using Illocutionary Logic', Working paper, Department of Computer Science, University of Jyvaskyla, 1984.

Lundeberg, M., Goldkuhl, G., and Nilsson, A. (1979) *Information Systems Development: A Systematic Approach*, Prentice-Hall, Englewood Cliffs, NJ.

Lyytinen, K. (1985) 'Implications of Theories of Language to Information Systems', *MIS Quarterly*, March.

Lyytinen, K. (1986) 'Critical Social Theory and Information Systems — A Social Action Perspective to Information Systems', Unpublished doctoral thesis, University of Jyvaskyla.

Lyytinen, K., and Lehtinen, E. (1984) 'On Information Modelling through Illocutionary Logic', *Proceedings of the Third Scandinavian Research Seminar on Information Modelling and Data Base Management, Tampere, 1984*.

Maddison, R., Baker, G., Bhabuta, L., Fitzgerald, G., Hindle, K., Song, J., Stokes, N., and Wood, J. (1983) *Information Systems Methodologies*, Wiley–Heyden, Chichester.

Mader, C. (1979) *Information Systems: Technology, Economics, Applications, Management*, 2nd Edn., Science Research Associates, Chicago.

Markus, M. L. (1983) 'Power, Politics and MIS Implementation', *Communications of the ACM*, **26**, 6.

Martin, J. (1982) *Application Development without Programming*, Prentice-Hall, Englewood Cliffs, NJ.

Martin, J. (1984) *An Information Systems Manifesto*, Prentice-Hall, Englewood Cliffs, NJ.

Martin, J. (1985) *Fourth-Generation Languages*, Vol. I: *Principles*, Prentice-Hall, Englewood Cliffs, NJ.

Mason, R. (1969) 'A Dialectical Approach to Strategic Planning', *Management Science*, **15**, 4.

Morgan, G. (1980) 'Paradigms, Metaphors, and Puzzle Solving in Organization Theory', *Administrative Science Quarterly*, December.

Mowshowitz, A. (1976) *The Conquest of Will: Information Processing in Human Affairs*, Addison-Wesley, Reading, MA.

Mumford, E. (1983) *Designing Human Systems*, Manchester Business School Publications, Manchester.

Mumford, E., Hirschheim, R., Fitzgerald, G., and Wood-Harper, T. (Eds.) (1985) *Research Methods in Information Systems*, North-Holland, Amsterdam.

National Academy of Science (1985) *Office Workstations in the Home*, National Academy Press, Washington.

Naisbitt, J. (1982) *Megatrends: Ten New Directions Transforming our Lives*, Futura, London.

Newman, M., and Rosenberg, D. (1985) 'Systems Analysts and the Politics of Organizational Control', *Omega*, **13**, 5.

Nolan, R. (1982) *Managing the Data Resource Function*, 2nd Edn., West Publishing Company, Minneapolis.

Nunamaker, J., Couger, J. D., and Davis, G. (1982) 'Information Systems Curriculum Recommendations for the 80s: Undergraduate and Graduate Programs — A Report of the ACM Curriculum Committee on Information Systems', *Communications of the ACM*, **25**, 11.

Olle, T. W., Sol, H., and Verrign-Stuart, A. (Eds.) (1982) *Information Systems Design Methodologies: A Comparative Review*, North-Holland, Amsterdam.

Olle, T. W., Sol, H., and Tully, C. (Eds.) (1983) *Information Systems Design Methodologies: A Feature Analysis*, North-Holland, Amsterdam.

Optner, S. (1965) *Systems Analysis for Business and Industrial Problem-solving*, Prentice-Hall, Englewood Cliffs, NJ.

Ouchi, W. (1979) 'A Conceptual Framework for the Design of Organizational Control Mechanisms', *Management Science*, **25**, 9.

Ouchi, W. (1980) 'Markets, Bureaucracies and Clans', *Administrative Science Quarterly*, **25**, March.

Pava, C. (1983) *Managing New Office Technology: An Organizational Strategy*, Free Press, New York.

Peters, T., and Waterman, R. (1982) *In Search of Excellence: Lessons from America's Best-run Companies*, Harper & Row, New York.

Popper, K. (1963) *Conjectures and Refutations: The Growth of Scientific Knowledge*, Routledge & Kegan Paul, London.

Rawls, J. (1973) *A Theory of Justice*, Oxford University Press, Oxford.

Rockart, J. (1979) 'Chief Executives Define their own Data Needs', *Harvard Business Review*, March–April.

Rule, J. (1974) *Private Lives and Public Surveillance*, Schocken Books, New York.

Shrivastava, P., and Mitroff, I. (1984) 'Enhancing Organizational Research Utilization: The Role of Decision Makers' Assumptions', *Academy of Management Review*, **9**, 1.

Suchman, L. (1983) 'Office Procedure as Practical Action: Models of Work and System Design', *ACM Transactions on Office Information Systems*, **1**, 4.

Suchman, L., and Wynn, E. (1984) 'Procedures and Problems in the Office', *Office: Technology & People*, **2**.

Toffler, A. (1980) *The Third Wave*, Pan Books, London.

Van Maanen, J. (1979) 'Reclaiming Qualitative Methods for Organizational Research: A Preface', *Administrative Science Quarterly*, **24**, 4.

Vitalari, N., Venkatesh, A., and Gronhaug, K. (1985) 'Computing in the Home: Shifts in the Time Allocation Patterns of Households', *Communications of the ACM*, **28**, 5.

Weisbord, M. (1985) 'Participative Work Design: A Personal Odyssey', *Organizational Dynamics*, Spring.

Critical Issues in Information Systems Research
Edited by R. J. Boland Jr. and R. A. Hirschheim
© 1987 John Wiley & Sons Ltd.

Chapter 13

DEFINING THE BOUNDARIES OF COMPUTING
ACROSS COMPLEX ORGANIZATIONS

Rob Kling

ABSTRACT

All analyses about the adoption, development and use of computer-based technologies draw boundaries to include significant participants. Conventional analyses draw formal, *a priori* boundaries around direct computer-based systems and immediate users, their work groups, or at formal organizational boundaries. These boundaries often fail to capture important social relationships which influence the development and use of computer-based systems. This chapter examines an alternative, behaviorally grounded approach which draws boundaries around groups which influence the adoption or use of computer-based technologies, regardless of their social location. The criteria for drawing boundaries are based on 'web' models, a kind of resource-dependency model.

Within these behaviorally drawn boundaries, web models help explain (1) the social leverage provided by computing arrangements, (2) the co-requisites for smoothly operating systems, and (3) the ways in which the social settings in which computing arrangements are developed and used shape their configurations and consequences.

Web models are contrasted with conventionally rational 'discrete-entity' models which are a-contextual, a-historical, and assume that adequate infrastructure can always be available as needed. Predictions of computing development and use based on discrete entity models usually underestimate the problems of implementation and underestimate the extent to which computer-based systems play important roles other than as direct aids in leveraging information processing capabilities in a work organization.

Computer-based systems increasingly extend beyond the narrow boundaries of a work group or small-scale organizational unit and are increasingly an element in more complex social relations. Consequently, discrete-entity models are becoming less relevant as a basis for guiding information systems research. Web models of computing appear especially appropriate when (1) the production or support of computer-based systems is socially complex or (2) their adoption or operation depends upon social relations that extend far beyond the behavioral setting in which the technology is developed or used. As computer-based systems become more socially complex, web models will become increasingly critical as approaches for explaining the development and use of computing.

1. INTRODUCTION

What influences the adoption of new computer-based technologies? How are particular computer-based technologies ordinarily used? What are the social consequences of using computer-based technologies? These are some of the critical questions about the social dimensions of computerization. During the last 15 years there has been a surge in the number of scholarly studies which have tried to answer these general questions. These studies examine particular kinds of computer-based systems (e.g. information systems, computer assisted instruction), particular kinds of social settings (e.g. offices, classrooms, local governments, Federal agencies), and examine different kinds of social outcomes (e.g. quality of working life, shifts of power, changes in social relations). This chapter does not attempt another summary of this large and growing body of research [1], instead it examines some key assumptions in research about computerization [2].

Any study which answers questions like those above must characterize the computer-based technologies, the social settings where they are used, and the social forces which shape their use. I have found that studies differ in four ways which have a tremendous influence on the design of the research and the character of research findings. Social studies of computerization often differ in:

(1) the scope of the boundaries they draw around a computer-based system and the key actors identified — developers, users, regulators, maintainers, promoters, system saboteurs, etc.;
(2) the extent to which the social relations between key participants, such as the kinds of interdependence, control, cooperation and conflict, are examined;
(3) the extent to which the resources that key participants have to carry out important lines of action are examined; and
(4) the extent to which actual social meanings which participants bring to their encounters with computer-based technologies are examined.

Unfortunately, social analyses of computing developments rarely test on explicit assumptions or models [3]. This chapter examines two explicit models [4] which underlies much of the social research about computerization. These models characterize some of the key choices that researchers often make along the four dimensions we identified above. We contrast how well or poorly these two models account for critical aspects of computing developments: their costs and effectiveness, their speed of planned change, and their integration into organizational life.

One class of models focuses on relatively formal-rational conceptions of the capabilities of information technologies and the social settings in which they are developed and used. These conceptions, which we label *discrete-entity* models, focus on explicit economic, physical, or information processing features of the technology. The social context in which the technology is developed and used, and the history of the participating organizations, are limited to a few formal relationships or are ignored. Systems are assumed to be loosely aggregated collections of equipment, people, procedures, and beliefs, which may easily be broken down into separate elements, and costed and evaluated independently.

Social relations are assumed to be cooperative and resources are available as needed. Discrete-entity analysts also assume that 'good' social actors will value 'better' technologies [5]. These conceptions are most common in professional and academic publications which emphasize positive management [6].

The second class of models, web models, are a form of 'resource dependence' models. They make explicit connections between a focal technology and the social, historical, and political contexts in which it is developed and used (Pfeffer and Salancik, 1978; Pfeffer, 1982; Kling and Scacchi, 1982) [7].

Computer systems, in this conception, are developed, operated, and used by an interdependent network of producers and consumers and cannot be analyzed solely according to their discrete features and components. Web models treat computerized systems as a form of social organization with important information processing, social, and institutional properties: they are not only flexible information processing tools. Their 'shape', the way they are used, the leverage they provide, and the interests they serve depend upon the interplay of stakeholders, resources, and social games within which they are deployed.

Web models of computing expand upon resource dependence conceptions by emphasizing the history of commitments made in the course of computing deployments and the infrastructure that supports the deployments of computer-based technologies. They draw 'larger boundaries' around the focal computing resources than do discrete entity models, by examining how their development and use depends upon a social *context* of complex social actions in which the focal computing resources is developed or used. Web models define a social context for computer-based technologies by taking into account:

(a) the *social relations between a set of participants* who can influence the adoption, development, or use of the focal computing technologies;
(b) the *infrastructure* available for their support;
(c) the *history* of commitments made in developing and operating related computer-based technologies.

In a refined form, these three elements will serve as key organizing concepts later on. In addition, they point to useful methodologies for doing 'web' analyses. We discuss appropriate methods briefly near the end of the chapter.

It is tempting to try to simplify this exposition by simply renaming the models along disciplinary lines. Discrete-entity models would be relabelled as 'psychological' or 'engineering economic' models and web models would simply be labelled 'sociological'. This strategy is attractive at first glance because it might simplify this exposition and help us avoid the use of yet additional special terminology. Unfortunately this strategy doesn't work well. The variety of social science approaches and the boundaries between disciplines blur too much to make terms like 'psychological' or 'sociological' define precise analytical approaches. While many psychologists study tiny behavioral settings and ignore their context, some social psychologists are working hard to include a larger set of behavior settings within the frame of their theories and empirical studies (e.g. Stokols, 1983; Wicker, 1984). Sociologists also vary in the scale of social system they choose for theoretical and empirical purposes. At one extreme, microsociologists like ethnomethodologists and some symbolic interactionists, are as likely as psychologists to focus upon tiny social settings and to ignore historical commitments. At the other extreme, macrosociologists who study computerization often ignore the kinds of infrastructure which makes computing workable or problematic in the behavior settings where people and technologies meet.

Discrete-entity models and web models represent ideal constructs [8]. By making them explicit and sharpening their differences we can contrast the analytic power of each model and ask about the insights each model provides into the sagas of computing in organizational life. This chapter argues that discrete entity models which have dominated research on computerization to date are inadequate, have ignored important questions, and often provide unreliable answers to the questions analysts who use it have asked.

2. MODELS OF COMPUTING: DISCRETE-ENTITY AND WEB

In contrasting discrete-entity and web models, it is first useful to examine their underlying assumptions in more detail, and to identify their implications [9]. Table 1 lists five key assumptions of discrete entity models.

The basic units of analysis of discrete-entity models are computing resources [10] (e.g. an Apple Macintosh computer, a specific computer program) and the formal tasks to which they are applied. Analysts who employ discrete-entity models assume instrumental rationality, and base their predictions and diagnoses on two logics of technical development: piecemeal aggregation and direct substitution. A simple example of these attractive assumptions can be illustrated when participants describe their computing environments by a list of equipment. Suppose that the staff of a university department describe their computing environment by listing this set of equipment:

—*Microcomputers*: 5 IBM PCs, 10 IBM PC/ATs, 5 Apple Macintoshes;
— *Word processors*: Microsoft Word 2, PC-Write 2.6.
— *Dot matrix printers*: 4 Toshiba 1340s, 3 Epson RX 80s, and 2 Epson LQ 1000s.
— *Laser printers*: 1 Apple Laser Writer;
— *Databases*: Dayflo 1.2 and Dbase-III;
— *Spreadsheets*: Multiplan.

The first logic of technical development, piecemeal aggregation, assumes that new components add new capabilities whose *best features are available for all participants*. For example, by aggregation, one could assume that any microcomputer user in this department could use a laser printer. In practice, diverse sets of equipment

TABLE 1   Assumptions of discrete-entity models

D1. A computing resource is best conceptualized as a particular piece of equipment, application, or technique which provides specifiable information processing capabilities.
  a. Each computing resource has costs and skill requirements which are largely identifiable.
  b. Computer-based technologies are tools, and are socially neutral.
D2. Role of infrastructure:
  a. The infrastructure for supporting the focal computing resource and the organizational procedures by which it is organized and sustained are critical elements.
  b. Each computer-based service is provided through a set of structured computing resources and organized infrastructure. Deploying, managing, and setting procedures for these infrastructural resources is separable from deployment of the focal computer-based technology. Infrastructure, either technical or administrative, is a neutral resource.
  c. 'Human factors' must be taken into account to ensure that people are well trained and motivated to do what is required. But 'human factors' are 'organizational problems' which are separable from 'technical problems'.
D3. Control over infrastructure: Organizations have ample resources to support all of their computing developments and uses simultaneously. Elements of infrastructure are necessary for making the equipment or technique available to developers or users, and they can be counted on to be of adequate quality and available as necessary.
D4. The focal computing resource and any element of infrastructure can be analyzed independently of:
  a. its interactions with other computing resources;
  b. the social or organizational arrangements within which computer-based services are developed and provided (infrastructure and macrostructures).
D5. Social action:
  a. Organizational behavior is best described by the formal goals, procedures, and administrative arrangements of the acting units.
  b. The use of a computing resource is best described by its formal purposes and features.

like those on this list are usually organized into several collections that work well together. But the ensembles may not work well together. For example, suppose that the faculty use the IBM PCs and PC/ATs and have the dot matrix printers. Suppose that the departmental secretaries and office staff use the Macs and share the single laser printer. The laser printer may work well with Microsoft Word on the Macs, but not with applications run on IBM PCs. Documents which the office staff prepare may routinely appear around the university with distinctive laser-printed fonts. University administrators might assume that the faculty also can use the LaserWriter. But the PC software may not have drivers which allow the special capabilities of the laser printer to be used. On the other hand, the faculty may be able to have staff support with budgeting on spreadsheets since they all use Multiplan. This department may look computationally richer than one which has no laser printers. But the factoring of the milieu into somewhat distinct computing worlds means that only one subworld is 'rich' in laser printers. Conversely, only the users of the IBM-PCs may be able to use the databases.

TABLE 2   Assumptions of web models

W1. A computer system is best conceptualized as an ensemble of equipment, applications, and techniques with identifiable information-processing capabilities.
- a. Each computing resource has costs and skill requirements which are only partially identifiable.
- b. In addition to its functional capabilities as an information processing tool, computer-based technologies are also social objects which may be highly charged with meaning.

W2. Role of infrastructure:
- a. The infrastructure for supporting the focal computing resource and the organizational procedures by which it is organized and sustained are critical elements.
- b. Each computer-based service is provided through a set of structured computing resources and organized infrastructure. This organization of essential resources makes computer-based systems into a form of social organization. Like any organization or institution, it is not necessarily neutral.
- c. There is no 'human factor' which is specially separable from the delivery of computer-based information services. Much of the development and routine operations of computer-based technologies hinge on many human judgements and actions carried out within complex, organized social settings.

W3. Control over infrastructure:
- a. Organizations have limited resources. Not all necessary infrastructural resources are available (in adequate quality) as needed.'
- b. Computer-using organizations rarely have complete administrative or political control over all their requisite infrastructure. Infrastructural resources may be spread across several organizational units or nominally independent organizations.

W4. The information processing leverage provided by a focal computing resource, and its other costs and benefits, social and economic, are contingent upon:
- a. its interactions with other computing resources;
- b. the social or organizational arrangements within which computer-based services are developed and provided (infrastructure and macrostructures).

W5. Social action:
- a. Political interests, structural constraints, and participants' definition of their situations often influence organizational action. An organizational process model (Allison, 1971; Cyert and March, 1963) or a negotiated order model (Strauss, 1978) of social activities is used to analyze social relations.

The second logic, direct substitution, assumes that the gains realized by replacing one computing device by a more powerful are the same for all participants in all settings — from a testing laboratory to an office. For example, suppose that the department chair considers two proposals:

(a) Replace several of the cheaper dot matrix printers with an equal number of finer quality printers of the same brand.
(b) Replace the five IBM PCs with IBM PC/ATs.

These two proposals illustrate the archetypical case of direct substitution; a better component replaces a lesser quality component and users of the components can exploit the information processing capabilities that the new component offers. A third proposal, to replace several of the cheaper dot matrix printers with another Apple LaserWriter, may also appear as direct substitution. At one level of abstraction this substitution on the department's computer inventory list may make it appear to be computer richer. However, in terms of the day to day work of faculty and staff, this third proposal is redistributive. Some faculty would lose printing capabilities because they would relinquish their dot-matrix printers and have to share the remaining printers while the departmental staff would gain access to a second laser printer. A fourth proposal, to replace the five IBM PCs with more powerful workstations based which run Unix System V would also appear as enriching on paper. But if the faculty who used the PCs lost access to important software (like DBase III and a strong word processor) in the shift from the PCs to the workstations, they could end up computationally poorer.

These technological illustrations suggest the difficulties of examining the value of computing resources as isolated entities. In the case of this hypothetical university department, we have examined the interplay of technical features. However, in most situations we need to examine the interplay of both technical and social features. This leads us to web models.

Five critical assumptions of a web model are listed in Table 2 [11]. Web analysts are concerned with the array of activities that people actually engage in while pursuing some task, rather than examining isolated components of a computer-based system and assuming that they will be smoothly grafted into a formal task system. Thus, a web analyst would not start by asking 'what kind of equipment is being used?' or 'what are the formal goals of this organization?', but 'who are the key actors, what kinds of things do they do here, what incentives influence their activities, and what organizational routines constrain their actions and choices?'. The web analyst identifies the local ecology of games (Long, 1958) and local behavioral constraints to examine how they influence the computerization. Assumptions W2 and W3 bear directly on the complexity of social arrangements into which computing is embedded and the extent to which different participants control key resources. These analyses are *explicit* rather than implicit [12]. The logical framework of web analyses rests on the assumption that a computing resource is being used by an interdependent network of producers and consumers. We call this network a production lattice [13]. The production lattice for a particular computer-based system or service is a social organization which is embedded in a larger matrix of social and economic relations and is dependent on a local infrastructure. According to web models, broader social relations and the local infrastructure shape the kind of computer-based service made available at each node of the production lattice. Those 'broader social relations' specially include (1) the interdependencies between different groups who develop and use a computing resource and (2) other social agents who most depend upon the computing resource or upon whom the resources' users most depend.

Workable computing arrangements depend upon the infrastructural resources available. Some of these infrastructural resources, such as equipment and staff with specialized technical skills are difficult to replace instantly. They evolve over time. Computing developments are shaped by a set of local commitments to technologies and social arrangements to support them which develop over time. In short, web models view computer-based systems as complex social objects whose architecture and use are shaped by the social relations between influential participants, the infrastructure that supports them, and the history of commitments. Web analyses focus explicitly on each of these influences.

This chapter emphasizes the logical structure of these two models, but each has a connotative aspect as well. Analysts who use discrete-entity models can argue that computer-based systems are powerful media — for good or bad. Analysts who use a discrete-entity model can emphasize *new capabilities* and *new opportunities* by focusing on the capabilities of computing resources while neglecting the available infrastructure, the context of likely use, or the history of computing commitments which may constrain a computer-using organization. Social boundaries that are drawn tightly around a computer system and a single user can make it appear that the user can gain all the information processing benefits that the system can provide. A boundary drawn tightly around the administrative domain of a manager can make it appear that he is in control of his organizational unit's destiny.

Analysts who argue that computers dehumanize work can also rely upon discrete-entity models. For example Zuboff (1982) argues that computer users are isolated from the meaning of the data they use, from their clients, and other significant social relationships. Their work is 'computer-mediated' and computing insulates users from essential kinds of knowledge and social contact. Some people do work in settings where they are buffered from their clients and others by electronic technologies, such as computer-based systems and telephones. Airline reservationists are an interesting example. The airline reservationists who work full time with telephones have no face contact with their clients. In contrast, the reservationists who work at airport counters or travel agencies deal with some of their clients face to face. These two kinds of reservationist jobs differ in their face contact, tempo, and strategies of supervision. Even when they use the same computer system, the two kinds of jobs differ. The two classes of reservationist jobs differ because the telephone reservationists can be organized in large groups out of their clients' sight and have their work efficiently organized through specialization, repetition, and close monitoring. But their work organization is 'telephone-mediated' as much as it is 'computer-mediated'. Zuboff ignores these contextual elements which weaken the direct connections between computer use and impoverished jobs.

Focusing on the context of computer use, the infrastructure which supports computer use, and on the history of computing developments usually adds constraints and conditions which weaken the direct links between computer use and some social outcome — whether it is socially desirable or troublesome. If new computing resources or organizations which adopt them depend upon the resources or cooperation of others, then it is less certain that participants will experience the most extreme capabilities of computing. Examining the available resources further (e.g. assumption W3a) can also mute enthusiasm or criticism. Moreover, assumption W4b focuses on social practices which can highlight conflict, as well as cooperation. Assumption W4b also points to activities which can stigmatize organizations if they are evaluated in a conventional moral perspective. Overall, these foci make web analyses less intensely exciting or frightening than the hopes of liberation or fears of dehumanization which are often married to new computing developments in discrete-entity analyses.

3. SITUATIONS, CONTEXTS AND PROCESSES OF COMPUTERIZATION

Before embarking on a substantive analysis of computing developments, we need to lay our conceptual groundwork. A major difference between discrete-entity and web models hinges on the concept of 'context'. An operational definition of *context* can help us. We have used the lay definition of 'context' as 'something larger' that gives meaning to the topic in focus. This is a rather vague conception for empirical analysis. Our operational definition will hinge on another common and vague term, 'situation', which we will also sharpen. Last, we will explain how our analysis rests on two different perspectives on social action in organizational life: organizational process (Allison, 1971) and negotiated order (Strauss, 1978) [14].

3.1 Situations of Computing Development and Use

Our primary unit of analysis is the *situation* in which individuals or larger collectivities carry out their going concerns while they engage with computer-based technologies. [15] Situations can vary considerably in:

(1) the *number of participants*;
(2) the *set of artifacts* involved;
(3) the *spatial scale and arrangements* of activity;
(4) the *time periods* of key social activities [16]; and
(5) the *primary social processes* that shape critical behavior.

Particular situations may be located along the first two dimensions based on the number of participants or artifacts within them. Situations may be located along the spatial dimension by the amount of space their equipment occupies and by the amount of space their participants take up when engaging with computing and related activities. Situations may be located on the time scale based on the periods of time over which key events or social relations developed [17]. At the smaller end of these dimensions is the fleeting encounter between a person and

TABLE 3   Situational Dimensions Relevant to Computing

Population scale:			Encounter
			Role
			Organizational subunit
			Production lattice
			Organization
			Social world
			Industry
			Settlement/Community
Equipment			
	Simple	⟨-----⟩	Complex
	Obsolete	⟨-----⟩	State of the art
	Batch	⟨-----⟩	Interactive
	Disconnected	⟨-----⟩	Closely-coupled
	Single-vendor	⟨-----⟩	Multiple vendor
Spatial			
	Local	⟨-----⟩	Distant
	Compact	⟨-----⟩	Geographically dispersed
Temporal			
	Time scale:		
	picoseconds	⟨-----⟩	centuries
	Scheduled	⟨-----⟩	Unscheduled
	Open-ended	⟨-----⟩	Near-deadline

a discrete computing resource, e.g. an airline passenger and a video screen listing flight departure times in an urban airport. Somewhat larger on these dimensions is the use of an automated class assignment and scheduling system to match students, classes, and times in a university. Even larger still is the monthly preparation, dispersal, and reception of 36 million individual payments by the Social Security Administration.

Table 3 identifies some characteristics of the population scale, equipment, spatial features, and temporal dimensions of situations which we find useful in understanding computing developments. Situations are somewhat open-ended, and these structural dimensions and their characteristics are simply useful constructs, rather than eternal verities. It is not sufficient simply to identify a set of participants. Critical social relationships between them must also be identified. At the very least, the bases and kinds of cooperation or conflict between various groups is often critical. Computer systems will usually 'work' more smoothly if all parties cooperate in sharing relevant data, cooperate in providing infrastructural support, etc. When a behavior setting that surrounds computer use is populated by groups who are in conflict, computing resources easily become bound up in the larger conflicts.

The kinds of social relations that bind participants together are particularly critical: their division of labor, relative status and power, etc. Processual elements of a situation will also be important: the beliefs of participants, their resources, common practices and procedures, and the rates of change of key social relationships. We will discuss both social relations and key social processes in a following section.

Any account of computing development or use implicitly defines situations by identifying participants, equipment, location, and time scales. Not all situational definitions are equally useful for understanding the actual consequences of computerization. Situations should be defined by a set of participants, equipment, spatial and temporal relations, and social processes which shape participants' actions. We will develop some examples in the next few sections.

3.2 Context of Computing Development and Use

Discrete-entity and web analysts differ considerably in drawing boundaries which define situations for explaining the payoffs, problems, and dilemmas of computing. This chapter examines ways of drawing social boundaries for web analyses and contrasts them with the strategies of discrete-entity analysts.

Discrete-entity analyses use formal criteria for bounding the development and use of computer-based systems. These formal criteria — such as official jobs and roles typically lead to compactly defined situations. For example, a dominant image in the computing literature emphasizes one person employing a particular piece of equipment as a tool in some well-defined task. Some examples are the programmer working at a terminal developing a new application, the manager using a routine computer-based report to make a specific decision, the bank customer extracting funds from an automated teller machine, and the student using a special instructional computer package. Description of situations that are larger than person and machine are also common:

(a) Larger population scale (e.g. the students and faculty at XYZ University (XYZ-U) have access to a network of 50 powerful workstations and 20 minicomputers for text processing and scientific computations to support scholarship and instruction).
(b) Larger equipment scale (e.g. the computing equipment at XYZ-U supports several text editors (EMACS, vi), formatters (Nroff, Troff, Tex82), programming languages (C, Prolog, Fortran-77, and Ada), a database (Ingress), a statistical package (SPSS-X) and all the machines run Berkeley Unix 4.3).
(c) Larger time scale (e.g. XYZ-U has owned this equipment for two years).

In these situational definitions, groups are usually identified by their formal relationships and behavior is often defined by official roles.

In contrast, web analysts use fundamentally social criteria for defining situations. They ask: how do participants conceptualize their actions, what resources they have available, what are their common practices and procedures, what coalitions they participate in, what options they have, what constraints they face etc.? There is considerable evidence that social elements such as these profoundly influence the kind and quality of computer-based products that organizations produce, adopt, and use (Kling, 1980). Sometimes these social elements are referred to as 'context'. But 'context' is a vague label—it is not behaviorally specific. Resources, relationships between interest groups, social meanings, procedural constraints, are often defined in another situation that is yet 'larger' on some of the four dimensions of population size, equipment, space, and time. Any large organization that employs computer-based technologies is rich in examples of computing developments that are shaped by larger situational definitions that include the purposes, common practices, resources, procedural constraints, options, etc. that shape smaller-scale developments. But one cannot easily and accurately infer these inherited meanings, social relationships, and resources from the smaller definitions.

These social relations in a larger-scale situation are what we mean when we use the term 'context'. We often say that one situation (Sc) provides a context for understanding a second situation (Sf). The term *context* indicates a relationship between the two situations, Sc and Sf: Situation Sc is the level of analysis at which intentions which are observed in Sf are enacted and constraints made that influence other behavior observed in Sf. For example, the computing milieu described above at XYZ University would typically be more attractive to computer scientists than to social or physical scientists. Some faculty, such as economists, sociologists, physicists, etc. are likely to want software developed at other universities and which runs on IBM mainframes or on Vaxes under VMS, but not on the minicomputers at XYZ University under Berkeley Unix. The elements (a,b,c) above define a situation Sf. The relationships between economists at XYZ-U and their colleagues at other universities who expect certain kinds of time series analyses which are not supported by the software described in (b) defines part of a larger situation Sc. Since academic scholarship is evaluated in a national community, often funded by federal agencies, and rewarded by promotions committees on particular campuses, these groups are likely to participate in the situation (Sc) which a scholar, like our economist, uses in defining the appropriateness of the computing equipment at XYZ-U. Sc is the context which makes the attractiveness of the equipment described in (a,b) above to an economist who is a participant in Sf.

It is always possible to enlarge the definition of a situation to larger and larger populations, sets of equipment, space, and time. One could examine computerization at XYZ University in the context of industrial development in late twentieth-century United States or even post-ice-age human developments on the planet Earth. Operational criteria which lead to useful boundaries that are less broad are essential. Below we propose two criteria which restrain any easy expansionist sentiment that aim for the most holistic defining situations; they require the analyst to make explicit causal ties between key elements of the defining situation and variations in the development of use of the focal computing resource.

Where and how should one draw useful boundaries? It is possible to set up boundaries *a priori*? Turner (1981), for example, suggests that the whole organization that develops or uses computing provides useful situational boundaries. This criterion is a useful heuristic and expands the range of participants, equipment, space, resources, and procedures to a larger set than is usually found in most discrete-entity analyses of computing developments. Unfortunately, it does not help explain patterns of computer use that are influenced by social or economic patterns in still larger situations like Sc above (Kling and Gerson, 1977; Kling, 1978a–d; Goodman, 1979; Dutton, 1981; Danziger *et al.*, 1982). In these studies, organizational participants select computing arrangements to leverage their negotiations in a larger social order. They also find that participants are constrained by resources and organizational routines that are defined outside the formal boundaries of their organizations.

Organizations that have critical on-going negotiations with outsiders — clients, auditors, regulators, vendors, competitors — will sometimes develop computing arrangements to enhance their bargaining positions. To understand these choices, a larger situational boundary that includes this expanded organizational set must be drawn. These boundaries cannot be completely defined *a priori*. Nor can they be defined before the participants of these larger negotiating contexts are identified. Also, the choices that organizations can make relative to computing are limited by actions taken by agents outside their boundaries (e.g. clients, equipment vendors, auditors, competitors, labor unions, regulators) or by the ecologies from which they draw resources (e.g. local labor markets, vendor supply practices). These critical exogenous elements will vary from situation to situation, and fixed boundary criteria will be far too rigid for explanatory purposes. Useful boundaries depend upon the behavior being explained and the lines of explanation adopted.

Following Lofland (1976), we propose two criteria for drawing the boundaries of larger-scale situations Sc which serve as useful contexts for a given focal situation Sf:

The *defining situation* Sc is bounded by the populations, equipment, spatial and temporal (PEST) elements that meet either of these criteria:

C1. the actors in Sf take the PEST elements or time of Sc into account when constructing their action in the focal situation Sf; *or*
C2. the PESTs of Sc constrains the action of the actors in the focal situation, Sf. (The focal actors need not be aware of their social relationships with the PEST of Sc and their influence on their behaviors.)

The defining situation Sc also includes those social processes that meet criteria C1 and C2. These two criteria are essentially social. In contrast, discrete entity analysts usually draw formal boundaries and stay within one level of analysis.

TABLE 4   Discrete-entity situation in which to explain CHEMMOD use

Population:	the design engineer
Equipment:	CHEMMOD and an I/O device (e.g. terminal)
Space:	an office physically proximate to the equipment or the engineer's typical workplace
Time:	sufficient to undertake a family of analyses for a design — minutes to several weeks
Social processes:	formal organizational roles define activities; norms of cooperativeness and analytical rationality are assumed
Resources:	ample time to think through designs carefully and ample computing resources so that runs can be made in a timely manner, on demand

Web analysts almost by definition work with multiple units of analysis, both Sf and Sc at minimum. Web analysts choose boundaries for the defining situation Sc depending upon the questions they ask [18]. They take care to draw boundaries for a defining situation Sc that are neither too limited nor so encompassing as to explain nothing. Suppose one wishes to answer the question: how useful will a particular modeling package (CHEMMOD) be in helping a chemical engineer design a chemical processing plant? Table 4 identifies a discrete-entity situation for answering this relatively common question (for example, Streeter, 1974).

Such a situational definition helps focus on the information-processing leverage provided by CHEMMOD relative to manual methods or alternative models. However, many important contingencies are neglected. At the very least, all parties who the engineer knows will review the design (and those colleagues from whom she solicits advice about computers or the model or the design), should be included in the set of participants since there is some evidence that engineers will work differently when they are being audited by outside firms hired by their clients to review their work. The set of equipment should be enlarged to include any ancillary equipment on which the engineer might depend (e.g. pocket calculator, computer configuration, communication lines) and the data sources for the model. If this model is used over a period of years, it will probably be altered to fit (and misfit) new design situations. So the temporal scale should be closer to the life-cycle for the model and its associated software rather than the time frame for the engineer to undertake one analysis.

Criteria C1 and C2 should be applied to develop a suitably 'large' defining situation, while avoiding unworkably 'vast' situations. There would be no explanatory gain in enlarging the defining situation of CHEMMOD to include all human beings living and dead since the Ice Age in continental shelf territories and all artifacts ever built by these people which required the explicit cooperation of seven or more people. Fortunately, criteria C1 and C2 will lead to a focus upon the kinds of participants and social relationships examined in the last paragraph. C1 and C2 will exclude improbably wide situational boundaries like all post-Ice Age communities since people who are long dead are very unlikely to have much direct influence upon an engineer at CHEMMOD (C2) or be taken into account by her (C1).

3.3 Two Key Perspectives about Social Relations and Processes

So far, we have emphasized relatively static dimensions of situations: populations, equipment, space, and time. But to breathe real life into situations that develop in and around computing, we need a model of the social terrain on which people act (with or without computers). Modern complex organizations, have a special kind of terrain: they produce most of their goods or services for some external clientele, and organize their work through a variety of specialized groups and explicit divisions of labor.

We view organizations as work systems in which participants make decisions about their work rather than as decision systems in which work is incidentally done. This apparently academic distinction is of far-reaching importance. While many people make decisions in the course of their work, most jobs result in a set of actions based on whatever decisions are made by the actor or others. In organizational life, the physical work with and around computers influences what is done and what is used. We take seriously the lines of action in which people come to engage with computing, the going concerns of the organizations they inhabit, and the patterns of incentives and constraints which influence them (Kling and Scacchi, 1982).

Organizations differ in a myriad of ways. To focus our attention, we will emphasize relatively large, complex, non-voluntary organizations: medium-sized to large business and public agencies. We will examine social processes in complex organizations through two broad perspectives: organizational process (Cyert and March, 1963; Allison, 1971; Steinbruner, 1974) and negotiated order (Strauss, 1978). In the organizational process perspective, organizations are noisy production systems composed of a network of work groups which exchange and produce goods and services according to a host of relatively standardized procedures, formal and informal (Cyert and March, 1963; Allison, 1971). Information, actions, and material flow imperfectly from node to node along standard channels. The characteristics of channels and nodes are also subject to routinized temporal patterns: staff can change at nodes because of shift work each day, regular vacations, or rotating assignments. Communication and transportation through channels is also subject to temporal regulation — material may be transported on fixed schedules, information passed at regular intervals, etc. Certain key events and resources may occur on regular schedules: systems are often audited, data archived, and budgets renewed on regular cycles. Channels and nodes are imperfect: delays and losses commonly occur.

In this model, organizations and their subunits are characterized by their routine outputs and their average behavior in providing these goods or services. This perspective emphasizes the production of typical outputs and the character of typical inputs [19]. Clients make typical demands and organizational participants develop routines (formal or informal) to get on with their work. Resources come from relatively standardized sources (e.g. standard vendors, standard labor pools, etc.). Outputs go to standard markets, etc.

The organizational process perspective emphasizes the broadly purposive side of organizations. It departs from formal-rational approaches in many critical matters: 'organizational goals' are redefined by subunits that enact them, organizational participants have limited capacities to process information; participants' pursuit of their interests is tempered by their propensity to avoid uncertainty; participants have limited capacities to process information; behavior is characterized by many common routines and procedures, even if these don't match formal or public rules and practices: organizations adapt slowly as a byproduct of solving particular problems (Cyert and March, 1963). Groups neither share common values nor do they agree on common goals, but jointly cooperative outcomes are common. In the organizational process perspective, larger organizational arrangements, the values of participants, the distribution of rewards and constraints, and the set of procedures which describe ongoing behavior are largely taken for granted. We require a different perspective to ask how these elements of organizational life develop.

The negotiated order perspective views the actions of organizations as the byproducts of *ongoing* negotiations (Strauss, 1978). Analysts who use the negotiated order perspective have often taken the coordination of complex organizations as a central issue, and one which is problematic for participants. Analysts who adopt an organizational process analysis usually assume work is factored into tasks for specialized subunits, and that dominant coalitions play a strong role in assuring that organizational outcomes do not undermine their interests. Negotiated order analysts do not take the influence of a dominant coalition for granted. They pay special attention to who is bargaining over what, and with what options in different negotiating contexts. Both perspectives presume that participants' definitions of situations are influenced by their socialization, training, group allegiances, and the social worlds in which they participate.

The organizational process perspective takes organizational routines for granted and simply assumes that they were the outcome of some bargaining between coalitions; but the bargaining takes place offstage (Cyert and March, 1963). The negotiated order perspective focuses on the creation of procedures and how variations are negotiated (Strauss, 1978). While both perspectives accept conflicts as an ordinary element of the ongoing interplay of groups and organizations, the details and tapestry of conflict are more center stage in the negotiated order perspective. Participants' strategies, the stakes they contend for, their options and relative power, and the bargains they strike in a negotiating context are all central. Moreover, participants in some complex work organizations are viewed as engaging in multiple and overlapping negotiating contexts in which their stakes and option provide cross subsidies and constraints (Becker, 1960). These two perspectives will provide somewhat different and useful insights for drawing boundaries around computer-based technologies and the social systems in which they are adopted, developed, and used.

4. TWO BRIEF CASES OF COMPUTERIZATION

We will describe two brief cases of computerization which provide useful examples for our later analyses.

4.1 World Wide Military Command and Control System

A recent report by the General Accounting Office (GAO) criticizing the current operations and future plans for the World Wide Military Command and Control System (WWMCCS) illustrates discrete entity analyses of complex systems. (Comptroller General, 1981) [20]. The report criticizes the current operational capability as inadequate to meet stated military requirements, a ten-year plan for replacing the system as too slow, undue emphasis placed upon defining system architecture before information requirements are defined. The report comments:

> DOD, despite dozens of large-scale studies, has failed to make meaningful progress toward implementing a responsive, reliable, and survivable (system) . . . rapid improvements are necessary to minimize shortfalls in capability . . . modernization planning is proceeding far too slowly. . . .

The report makes a series of nine recommendations that include replacing equipment, completing information requirements, employing life-cycle management techniques, and 'proven, state-of-the art technology (p. iv.)'.

Of interest here is not the accuracy of GAO's claims, but the kind of analysis performed, the kinds of recommendations proposed, and the location of this document within the career trajectory of WWMCCS. This report is the eighth report written by GAO since 1970 criticizing WWMCCS development.

DoD's official reply criticizes the report as 'drawing few conclusions which have not been covered by previous GAO reports on the subject (Appendix IV)'. GAO authors reply, 'The primary reason for this is DoD's continuing reluctance to take effective, decisive action (Appendix IV)'. In short, the report focuses on what DoD did in contrast with what GAO reviewers expect is 'sensible'. Most significantly, for our purposes, is the way in which the battles over the capabilities and prospects of WWMCCS have continued for over a decade. The GAO report typifies many discrete-entity analyses. Problems are identified, but the ecology of social relationships within which WWMCCS develops is not identified. As a consequence, one can only assume that DoD staff and contractors continually fail to do what they are supposed to do by legislative and administrative mandate because they are incompetent, insubordinate, or otherwise irascible.

The report also hints of broader issues. For example, GAO auditors write,

> The modernization plan describes two (WWMCCS) alternatives. . . . For either alternative to be effective and efficient, standard data elements must be identified and agreed upon by users. . . . Yet, after more than 30 years of effort, commanders still cannot agree on essential items for providing ADP support in the command and control environment. (pp. 13–14)

It appears that defining uniform information requirements for WWMCCS requires that field commanders in all the three services must concur on the kind of data they need. Different tactical battle doctrines held by officers within and across the military services differ in the importance they place on different kinds of data and different priorities on who should receive what information, when [21].

WWMCCS is developing along some trajectory which is bound up with many historically developed commitments and conflicts within DoD. GAO's eighth report does little to identify which constraints are serious, and which are more easily altered. Problems are identified and solutions proposed. Even if GAO auditors accurately diagnosed the major problems of WWMCCS development, they provide little insight into how well DoD can respond. Web analysts would think it likely that GAO auditors will continue to find problems with WWMCCS during the next decade.

4.2 Information Systems and Microcomputers at PRINTCO

PRINTCO is a medium-sized manufacturing firm which designs, produces and markets dot matrix line printers for the mini computer and small business computer marketplace [22]. The President founded the firm in the mid-1970s and positioned it as a low-cost supplier. They started shipping printers in 1975 and during the late 1970s maintained a fairly constant demand of 12–15,000 printers a year despite market fluctuations. During the early 1980s the firm grew rapidly, and became a major producer of dot matrix line printers.

Early in the company's development, the President instituted several critical organizational strategies beyond aiming at low-cost production — meeting shipment schedules on time and providing well above average support for their products in the field. All of the professional staff were made aware of the importance of their contributions to these goals.

Soon after PRINTCO started shipping printers in 1975, the manufacturing staff recognized that they were having problems building up inventory. With their rudimentary inventory and scheduling system, the material controllers couldn't phase the timing of purchased parts properly or reschedule these purchases when manufacturing demands changed. In 1977, all the corporate officers attended a week-long seminar taught by one of the 'gurus' of inventory control systems. They became convinced that a complex computerized inventory control system (called MRP) would solve their problems. They purchased an MRP software package written in RPG-II from a local developer and an IBM System 32 minicomputer on which to run it.

The Manufacturing Division started hiring Material Control staff with MRP experience. The firm sent their managers and supervisors in Material Control, Production Control, Purchasing, Marketing and Accounting to seminars to learn about MRP. By 1978, the effects of the new MRP system were being felt: PRINTCO's staff were able to keep their inventory at acceptable levels and they could make timely adjustments to new forecasts. The material staff at all levels (except the purchasing agents) believed in the MRP system. When they saw problems with the system, they wanted it improved, not discarded and replaced by a fundamentally different kind of inventory control strategy (like re-order points, just-in-time, etc.).

PRINTCO became more competitive in the marketplace by adding customized printer features for their major industrial customers. While they were still manufacturing three basic types of printers, they developed many unique configurations. The careful timing of part purchases became even more critical at this stage of their evolution. As their business expanded, they tracked more parts and moved their MRP package to an IBM System 34 minicomputer which easily ran programs that ran on an IBM System 32.

4.2.1 Creating Discipline in System Usage

Accurate data was critical for creating trustworthy and usable computer-based reports. One of the Senior Material Planners reported that he wouldn't be needed if the data were complete and accurate; a clerk could do his job. He claimed that Senior Material Planners have the experience and skill to identify inaccurate data. Data could be inaccurate for many reasons: reports not updated in a timely manner, production expeditors failing to complete their paperwork, late reports, bad sets of computations, etc. However, since the MRP system works best with completely accurate data, the staff worked specially hard to create data that was acceptably accurate. There were extensive activities 'behind-the-scenes' to help create more accurate data. These included educating the staff in the importance of timely updating of transactions and daily manual inventory counts called 'cycle counting'. To achieve 79 per cent inventory accuracy required consistent training of the stockroom staff for over three years.

Education about the MRP program was fostered through repeated seminars, professional organizations, and inside meetings and discussions. The seminars provided arenas for higher level managers to construct and reinforce a set of meanings about 'what the inventory control program meant for PRINTCO', and also to inculcate values among the lower level staff.

PRINTCO encouraged relevant staff who used MRP reports and their programmers to attend meetings of a national organization for material managers. They also encouraged users to attend classes about inventory control systems and to become 'certified' as computerized inventory specialists. As a result, most users of the inventory reports learned the system's underlying philosophy along with the ways in which their own work was integrated into the overall structure.

Despite the usefulness of seminars for teaching skills and inculcating attitudes, they did not automatically produce new behavior at PRINTCO. For material managers, the major difficulties in using the inventory control program were creating an environment that would support the program and instilling the discipline required to work with it.

At PRINTCO, effective use of the inventory control program required accurate data. However, data were not always accurate. Staff had to be sufficiently skilled in identifying inaccurate data and correcting them before appropriate decisions could be made. Senior planners were retained because they have the experience and the skill to identify inaccurate data — e.g. reports updated late, production expeditors failing to complete their paperwork, reports distributed late or bad computations.

Managers devised ways of producing 'acceptably accurate' data. An accurate stock status report was one essential component. The stockroom manager's supervisor monitored his performance. Material managers also instituted a manual 'cycle' counting scheme whereby stockroom clerks regularly rotated the counting of specific parts in stock.

Another strategy for producing accurate data included the elimination of separate functional roles in the stockroom and the training of all stockroom employees in all functions. Inventory accuracy increased from 79 to 90 per cent after the manager instituted these changes so that the data became acceptably trustworthy. This strategy also enlarged the jobs and increased the skills of stockroom clerks.

Staff recognized that data could never be 100 per cent accurate: certain kinds of mistakes would always be made. The development of accurate data was problematic since inaccuracies could come from so many different sources. Usable data could be imperfect, but had to be sufficiently accurate overall so that staff could rely upon them rather than other sources of information such as manual records or physical inspections. Standards for acceptable accuracy were defined by the staff most active in promoting the inventory control system.

Work also became more disciplined as the inventory control program was woven into the firm's operations. At PRINTCO the new discipline was tied to smarter rather than to harder work. Moreover, work was restructured by increasing knowledge about system usage, expanding jobs, and increasing awareness of the constraints imposed by the interdependent nature of system usage.

Groups, such as the stockroom staff, were under continuous pressure from many other groups at PRINTCO to improve the accuracy of their data. These demands for improved performance led to new work practices and tighter social control. Inventory reports served to broadcast the deviant aspects of their performance to many other users of the system.

The coupling of organizational units through the inventory control system gave PRINTCO staff several options: accept data that were often inaccurate; have those staff responsible for entering or auditing inventory data develop tighter discipline; or abandon this inventory control system. In the short run, most of the managerial staff found the second alternative most attractive. Consequently, staff such as production planners, production coordinators and material planners pressured departments such as stockroom and purchasing department to tighten their practices. However, not every group complied with these pressures [23].

4.2.2 Inventory Control Conversion Project

The Manufacturing administrative staff became troubled with MRP system problems that they had not anticipated. They were most bothered by its inability to track revision levels (the cut-out date of an 'old' part and the cut-in date of the 'new' one). It only picked up the latest revision level for each part and would calculate parts demands so that all printers would be assembled with all parts at the latest revision level. These simultaneous multiple revisions in a product co-existed for various reasons of cost, convenience or reliability. Some revisions might be absolutely necessary to implement for all printers immediately (for example, in the case of a newly discovered unreliable part). Other parts might be phased in only when the old part ran out in stock.

Manual workarounds in the form of documentation and comment lines on reports were instituted in order to handle this situation. This presented problems because it caused extra work and also because it increased the probability of error in purchasing the correct parts and building printers. Parts shortages on the production floor could cause assembly lines to shut down. This increased the possibility that printers might not be shipped on schedule.

PRINTCO's inventory control system also lacked computerized modules to calculate allocation lists, lot-sizing, planned orders, capacity-planning and work in process. A group of six senior officers in manufacturing, finance, and data processing started searching for more sophisticated MRP software. After six months of investigation they found an MRP package that satisfied their preferences. This package was written in a different programming language, Basic, in which the staff had no previous training. Because they wanted the software, they also decided to purchase the required hardware, a Data General S350 Eclipse. The committee justified this decision by arguing that the DG S350 Eclipse had more capacity than their IBM System 34s and that it could support the 30 terminals that they eventually wanted to install around the firm.

The conversion was scheduled to be finished in one year, but it took much longer than was originally anticipated. The informal committee neglected to follow through with a schedule after they made the decision to do the conversion. After 18 months, the conversion had not progressed very far. Morale was low in DP, numerous problems seemed unsolvable: support for their Data General computer system was not locally available and users at PRINTCO were tired of waiting indefinitely to satisfy their needs. The major DP effort was focused on the conversion and there was still no end in sight.

Several senior managers formed a Data Processing Steering Committee to start guiding and directing the DP Manager. The Steering Committee consisted of basically the same group which searched for the new MRP program. They put the DP Manager on schedules and tried to hire programmers who knew both RPG-II and Basic. However, they couldn't find (or attract) programmers with skills in both languages [24]. The conversion project did not progress at a rapid rate. It soon became evident that the conversion project was a failure. They needed someone to carry out the decision to 'dump' the project: they started searching for a new DP Manager.

After six months of searching and interviewing, the Steering Committee finally hired a DP Manager who promptly terminated the conversion project. The members of the DP Steering Committee were resigned to lose their investment in the software and to sell the hardware. They would enhance the MRP system as they could and possibly lease another minicomputer if it was needed. The DP Manager instituted several formal arrangements for DP requests from users and derived priorities for departmental work both for the short and long run from the direction and advice of the committee.

Despite the long and arduous work invested in hiring the new DP Manager, the DP Steering Committee was not satisfied with his progress. He focused his primary energies on purchasing a newer computer, an IBM System 38, and was avoiding starting the MRP system enhancements on their System 34. The Steering Committee wanted to see some improvements with the MRP system on their present equipment since they believed that they had been 'standing still' for too long. Conflict between the DP Manager and the other Steering Committee members heightened over time until he was fired after 10 months.

The Steering Committee members did not want to search for another DP Manager outside the firm. They promoted an internal manager to be the DP Manager. They also decided to buy an IBM 4331 and found new MRP software for it which would satisfy their preferences.

4.2.3 Microcomputing at PRINTCO

The major purpose of the conversion project had been to satisfy the needs of Manufacturing staff. Users in other departments had been instructed that they would have to wait until the new MRP System was 'up and running' before their DP requests for new or more frequent reports or the development of new systems, for example, could be fulfilled. Because the conversion project took longer than was anticipated, staff in other departments began searching for other ways to fulfill their computing needs.

While the computing staff was preoccupied with this major redevelopment, a large number of requests for altering existing programs or developing new ones for other departments were delayed. Several departments obtained microcomputers from test equipment cast off by other departments and upgraded them into usable computing equipment. This was possible because of the availability of skilled staff to perform these tasks. Managers in some of the departments which were poorly served by computing during this long and fruitless effort of new development, persuaded a few top managers to allow them to purchase their own microcomputers and develop their own small applications. PRINTCO's President advanced a policy which limited microcomputer purchases to one family of machines produced by a single vendor (e.g. DEC LSI-11s). Within a year, about 12 different microcomputer systems were deployed throughout PRINTCO. The micro-computers were coordinated by an engineer who was organizationally independent of the data processing department and the finance department within which it was situated.

The DP Steering Committee did not become aware of the extent of the proliferation of decentralized computing arrangements until late in 1981. They began counting the number of LSI-11s currently in use in the organization and were shocked to learn that there was over one million dollar's worth of microcomputing equipment dispersed throughout the organization. This exceeded the book value of the two IBM System 34s which were the focus of their attention. The DP Steering Committee wanted to control this proliferation of microcomputers. They brought the LSI-11 informal 'expert' into their group and created a new LSI-11 Steering Committee under their auspices. They began to make justifications for new LSI-11s more stringent and to require users to share equipment for small applications. In the beginning of PRINTCO's micro-revolution, LSI-11s meant freedom from central control. By 1983 their users were reined back under an umbrella of central oversight and regulation.

We will refer to the practices of computerization at PRINTCO in the following sections. At this point, it is simply important to underline a few of the ways in which PRINTCO's practices of computerization develop through a complex web of social relations that extend far beyond any single workplace. PRINTCO's top managers' strategy of serving as a low-cost printer manufacturer made economizing on material costs attractive, if not essential. An MRP system seemed like an appropriate technology to help manage complex inventories under conditions of varying demand. The use of the system led managers in many different work groups to develop tight work disciplines to support accurate inventory records. Consequently, there is a strong link between business strategies formulated in the boardroom and record-keeping practices in the stock room, the purchasing department, the shop floor, etc.

The business strategy of customizing printers led to a search for a different MRP system. Despite managerial 'will', the technical staff failed to convert their old system to a newer system. Their difficulties were based in their lack of training in large-scale development efforts and their difficulties in hiring staff with appropriate development skills in their local labor markets. These difficulties and the delays in getting service from the DP staff, led professionals and managers in some departments to seek their own microcomputers, the DEC LSI-11s. The DP Steering Committee was willing to approve the purchase of new LSI-11s because of the continual backlogs of programming work. They bought off a set of disgruntled staff while they (and the DP staff) were preoccupied with their MRP conversion. However, the top managers preferred centralized arrangements, and moved to control the LSI-11s when they realized how much book value the equipment represented.

5. COMPUTING IN A SOCIAL WORLD

In this section we examine some key dimensions which are central to web analyses and which discrete-entity analyses ignore: (1) how *the social world in which computing developments are embedded* influence their relative advantages for participants; (2) the *co-requisites of computing developments*; and (3) the constraints placed upon developers and users from *historically accumulated commitments*.

5.1 Social Leverage in a Participant Ecology

For web analysts, explanations of the social leverage to be expected from computerized technologies depends upon the interactions between users of the focal technologies and other parties with whom they negotiate in ways that involve computing resources. Examples of boundaries that extend outside the immediate computer using group which define significant influences are commonplace and varied. For example, in many large organizations, the choice of equipment is not wholly discretionary for computer-using groups. Sometimes they must use central facilities or adopt equipment from one of a few 'approved' vendors, such as buying DEC LSI-11s at PRINTCO. When they have discretion, some computer-using groups will purposely select equipment which is not compatible with other groups so that they can ward off demands to share their data, software, etc. Sometimes decision support systems are employed to help an organizational actor make a decision. Othertimes, these technologies are used as persuasion support systems to help the direct user convince others that they should see things his way by virtue of better data, technology, or analytical tools, independently of their actual quality. Good analyses of social leverage should account for phenomena like these.

Most discrete-entity analyses conceptualize computing leverage based on a view of computerized technologies as information-processing systems. Their utility is linked to social action through cognitive theories of decision making under uncertainty (Simon, 1977) and their extension to organizational activities in which improved information and reducing uncertainty go hand in hand (Galbraith, 1977) [25]. The theoretical links between digital computers and decision making are indirect: the relatively rich analytical and normative theories of decision making are coupled to the equipment through a view of digital computers as general-purpose symbol manipulating devices [26].

Assumption D1 of discrete-entity models usually rides on characterizations of computing leverage which emphasize the information-processing characteristics of computers. This a-contextual conception is insufficient for robust analyses that are behaviorally descriptive or usefully normative.

5.1.1 What are Computers Good For?

The easiest answer to this question would come in the form of a specific list of different computer applications and the interests they serve. Is there a compact way to abstractly characterize those situations in which computerized technologies provide a participant with some clear social leverage in his decisions and actions? In the root metaphor of discrete-entity analysis, computerized technologies are 'tools' which can help organizational participants solve problems in which data manipulation and communication support 'decision-making and organizational control'. The examples of WWMCCS and MRP use at PRINTCO illustrate this theme.

I don't know of any theoretically cogent account of which problems are amenable to computerized solutions which has special empirical bite. An example of Turner's (1981, p. 7) illustrates the issue nicely:

> A designer was asked to build an integrated payroll personnel system for a firm. Including both functions in one system makes good sense since about 60% of the data elements are duplicated. However, in this situation the payroll department reported to one VP while the personnel office reported to another. The two departments were located in different sections of the country, and they had a long history of interdepartmental conflict. The designer pointed out that management was asking the proposed new system to accomplish . . . an administrative action — the combination of the two departments. He suggested that the administrative change be made prior to the design of the system rather than burdening the system with the resolution of conflict, thereby reducing the probability of successful implementation.

This example illustrates the conceptual limits of sensitive discrete-entity analyses. The analyses can suggest questions, but not have the analytical richness to answer them. Someone proposed a computerized system, but to what end? Clues of multiple problems abound in this account. Some manager or coalition is attempting to develop an integrated information system, but his relationship to either the payroll or personnel departments is unclear. Presumably he is trying to foster some cooperation between them, and the overlap in the data they collect may or may not be an additional incentive for him to advance an automated 'solution'. The designer argues that building an integrated information system is not attractive to him (e.g. a solution to his problems) if it may not be well implemented or widely used. He argues that an integrated information system is not currently seen as a solution to problems for key staff in one or both of the departments that are to feed and use the system. Moreover, he proposes a political action to strengthen the administrative integration of the departments before attempting the automation. Turner's analysis is an interesting point of departure since it assesses the kinds of social relations which facilitate implementing cross-departmental computer systems [27]. But it does not go far in examining the web of social relations in which the administrative problems override the naïve introduction of a new computer-based information system.

Web models provide better explanations of the ways that computer systems of different kinds work out under differing kinds of cooperation and conflict between key participants. Cooperation on all matters between developers, resource controllers, users, clients, etc. is neither essential nor likely. But we have little reliable data from which to generalize beyond a few cases of severe conflict (Albrecht, 1979; Dutton, 1983; Kling, 1978a; Markus, 1979; Kling and Iacono, 1984b). Sometimes organizational participants face problems in which improving the kinds of data storage, retrieval, manipulation, and transmission will do much to resolve. Other times, participants are in conflict, and incentives to share data and cooperate are minimal. Under these conditions, computing will not do much to help and can even provide yet another weapon in organizational battles. In general, we know little about the role and shape of computerized systems which are implemented in organizational terrains which are fraught with conflicts, large or small.

5.1.2 Attribution

Good analyses of computerization must be able to attribute leverage to computing and to co-requisite practices. Particular kinds of automation are often accompanied by altered work organization and work arrangements. Some of the net payoffs or problems are more attributable to these associated changes than to the presence or absence of computers, *per se*. For example, when demand-dependent inventory (MRP) systems are installed in manufacturing firms, production administrators have to obtain much more accurate inventory counts than in manual systems. At PRINTCO material managers strove to improve their inventory records from accuracy levels of around 60–70 per cent to well over 90 per cent. Some new and efficient manual inventory counting methods were instituted in parallel (e.g. cycle counting) to improve the accuracy of inventory records. In addition, PRINTCO's managers employed many 'small' strategies to encourage workers to develop workplace disciplines which supported accurate data 'the system required it'.

It is inappropriate to attribute 'more accurate inventory' as a consequence of computerization at firms like PRINTCO if computerized systems are only equipment ensembles. They are also a catalyst by which managers can cajole their staffs to increased vigilance in recording and using inventory data. On the other hand, if computerization denotes the whole package of equipment and procedures that accompany an automated strategy, precise attributions of outcomes to elements of the local computing package are more difficult. They are significant since usually important social practices mediate between the availability of a computer-based information processing resource and some valued outcome such as more accurate inventory. Between computer-assisted instruction systems and learning outcomes lie the skills of teachers, children's access to equipment, etc. Between the availability of urban planning models and better informed land use decisions lie skills in interpreting the meaning of demographic data, economic assumptions, and model runs. Such social links between computer-based technologies and other social outcomes are almost universal.

Moreover, these social links are also influenced by resource dependencies which extend outside the behavioral setting in which the focal computing resource is used. In schools children's access to computer equipment and teacher's skills are influenced by school finances, and the sources of equipment supply. Teachers' willingness to develop good teaching skills with computerized technologies also hinge on other negotiations between them and parties such as the local school board. The social links between urban planning models and interpreted analyses are similarly influenced by relationships that extend outside the immediate behavioral setting of data analysis, even though the detailed relationships differ from those in schools. These mediating social links and the web of social relationships which influence them complicate the relationship between a focal computing resource and some specific outcome. They also complicate attributing an outcome primarily to a focal computing resource.

Discrete-entity analyses of automation rest on a conception of computerization which emphasize equipment and algorithms. In contrast, web analysts take some care in attributing outcomes to equipment, concurrent organizational practices, and broader social patterns.

5.1.3 Work Organization and Organizational Process

New computerized technologies usually differ from older ones in one or more of five dimensions: increases in *speed, reliability,* and *information processing flexibility,* or decreases in *cost* or *size* for given functionality. It is easy enough to provide examples in which faster data processing or data communications yields speedier decisions, and speedier decisions yields faster organizational action. Similarly, greater flexibility in manipulating data allows participants to pursue more options, or to consider new ones in which the cost of information handling was heretofore prohibitive.

These transitive translations of technical computing improvements into speedier, more astute, or more reliable organizational actions are the basis of discrete-entity analyses. But they do not always occur. As we noted above, important social links often couple computer-based technologies to valued outcomes. These links often depend on a wider set of social relationships which extend outside the immediate behavioral setting of computer use. Arbitrarily large improvements in digital computation will rarely show proportionate gains in organizational action. The relative gains from computing are limited by the abilities of organizational units to process information arbitrarily fast, to communicate it with arbitrary speed, and to consider an arbitrarily large number of complex options. In addition, organizations vary considerably in these characteristics and in their ability to alter them. As a consequence, sometimes there are large gains from the introduction of a CBIS and other times there are none.

This abstract account suggests that the appropriate lines of analysis link the information processing capabilities of computing to the work organization of the computer-using organizations. Work organizations, and their resources, in turn are embedded in a larger web of social relations which are central, not incidental.

When changes in information processing capability increase the slack in some resource, the profits may be captured by leveraging that slack into a different style of action [28]. Possible slack might occur in speedier decision making, greater reliability in organizational information handling or more rapid action. If these gains are not captured directly, they may be taken in at least three other ways: (a) increasing the volume of work done, while retaining a fixed product; (b) decreasing the labor invested in each product, while retaining a fixed product; (c) attempting to improve the product's quality. These individualized and rationalized lines of action are simply points of departure. Discrete-entity models are so weak that predicting which of these lines will dominate in a particular organizational ecology is highly speculative. Sharp predictions are difficult when some participants have substantial discretion over their actions, and they can select alternatives (a), (b) or (c) [29]. Levin and Abend (1971, p. 141) note:

> Perhaps the greatest effect of the modern (digital) high speed computer on the Penn-Jersey study was the temptation it offered the staff to embark upon the development of models that . . . were . . . too complicated to manage or too unrealistic. . . . computers were initially utilized in transportation studies to save time, money, and labor; however, as the capacity of the machines increased, the planners began to realize the possibilities of undertaking more detailed analyses that should, presumably, have increased costs only slightly.

While Levin and Abend found the early changes in aspiration levels debilitating for planning projects, they are not necessarily so. One who uses automated text processing to draft documents may opt for speed and volume one day, while spending hours the next day to custom tailor a fancy format. Enhanced computing capabilities opens an array of options.

The example of instructional computing is also useful to illustrate the role of work organization on patterns of computer use and their consequences. To what extent will university faculty and students value a new instructional computing modality as a resource which they will exploit as much as possible? Discrete-entity models which focus upon the additional intellectual capabilities a computing resource provides are most commonly used in answering this question. In this frame, analysts view courseware primarily as a *cognitive resource*. Students and faculty will use (and benefit from) courseware that is intellectually stimulating.

Web analysts examine the role and value of courseware in different terms. Faculty members' lines of work and work orientations are critical ingredients for web explanations (Kling and Scacchi, 1982; Kling and Iacono, 1986b). Faculty and students are likely to bring different orientations to their classes. Each has a complex job that extends beyond any single course. Faculty juggle a mix of teaching, and administration, research and professional service. Each course is one activity in a larger space of events and commitments. Faculty bring different sentiments to their classes — from excitement in teaching to viewing teaching as an inescapable chore. Each professor has his favorite classes to which he devotes more attention. Instructional computing can fit a class from many angles. New courseware takes significant amounts of time to develop. But developed courseware may save time if faculty can and use it without modification.

Students also view courses in a complex economy of effort which mixes courses with part-time jobs, extracurricular activities and social life. They conceptualize courses as interesting or required. They differentiate between those that are worth 6 hours of work each week and those that are worth 15 hours. In the 1980s we have a generation of students who are specially preoccupied making their grades. In this frame of reference, new computing media are not just interesting cognitive resources. They also take time to access, to learn to use, and to use. Some students may find a new instructional computing arrangement so attractive that they will make time for it in addition to other traditional course materials — books, lectures, discussions, written exercises, etc. However, many students evaluate new course activities within a zero-sum economy: each new activity drives something else out.

There is no simple way of predicting how students will redistribute their economies of time. Students won't necessarily use new instructional resources like computer systems, additional readings, or discussion sections when they are optional. They may also reduce their use of other resources (e.g. read less) to make time. Some students will invest more time in particular courses by using additional resources and not reducing the time they spend on other activities. But one can't guarantee this pattern simply by providing interesting instructional resources to students (or faculty). Much depends upon *how faculty computerize* a course — how they embed computer use into the mix of resources and rewards they organize as a course.

Developing, learning and using computing systems all take time. Students and faculty use computing resources in ways that depend upon the structuring of their other work commitments. An answer in these terms is less glamorous than an answer which portrays each new computing application as a high power magnet for academic attention. But it helps explain why we should expect many people to use systems in relatively simple ways. Faculty and students rarely take the time from their other commitments to learn elaborate system features or explore rich systems in depth. It is commonplace for people to learn the rudiments of computer systems so they can get their work done, and little more.

An eye on cross-commitments helps identify the conditions under which faculty can find instructional computing specially attractive — when it provides resources they can use to help leverage other commitments. The professor who gets an Apple Macintosh to use in a course can also utilize it for other applications and as an *entrée* to a computing subworld (the world of graphics, mice, icons and windows and people who love them).

When participants become aware of the slack provided by new information processing resources, they can slowly lay claim to the slack so that activities are readjusted ('ratcheted') and the net slack is not perceived as very large. For example, students and faculty may claim that their computer systems help them get more done in a given day. But they may work as long and hard after computerization as they did before [30]. Students may learn more, but the effort of taking or teaching a particular class may not be reduced. The time may come when students or faculty have to add on additional time to manage the use of and their access to the computing resources.

Web models are more likely than discrete-entity models to examine the dynamic social changes which influence patterns of computing development, adoption, and use under changing conditions of resource availability, costs, and substitutability [31]. These observations lead us to examine the negotiating contexts that open up and close off real options of computerization.

5.1.4 Negotiations

Despite the refinement of analytical theories of decision-making under certainty used by discrete-entity analysts, they describe only a small fraction of the actual ways that people and organizations process information [32]. A simple illustration will help: organizational participants often collect additional data to justify a decision they have already made. This is common enough without computers on the scene; and one can find occasions in which automated data systems are turned to legitimizing decisions made on other grounds (Kling, 1978a). This behavior could be absorbed into an information processing model of people and organizations, but not into models of rational choice in which information is collected to reduce uncertainty before a decision is made.

An actor seeking additional information post hoc only bears unnecessary costs in the received theory which emphasizes the role of information in reducing *a priori* uncertainties in *making* decisions. But he may be improving his chance for realizing his preferences through the actions that *others take* in an action theory that hinges on negotiations. In many situations, one participant has to convince others to concur with his preferences, or at least not to contest them.

If the negotiations are antagonistic, then additional data can strengthen one's bargaining position — data that will snow the opposition, data that will best convince the opposition, data that might even confuse the opposition. There is no necessary relationship between the sorts of data that will help any of the parties reach a private decision, and the kinds of data that will most convince others.

Even when negotiations are not wholly antagonistic, as between the Comptrollers of organizations and staff requesting funds for projects, the Comptrollers and their staffs often seek evidence that the requests they approve are well-founded and that those making them have thought them through. After a project or department manager makes his own decision, he faces a set of negotiations in which he may be asked to demonstrate a more useful and systematic analysis than he needed to convince himself. Moreover, he may face a negotiation context in which the resource controller may prefer to fund the best justified projects rather than those that promise the best payoffs.

In either case, strengthening the case to justify a decision is a plausible element in a negotiating strategy. Computerized data systems may play two roles in situations like these by providing direct information processing leverage or symbolic leverage (Kling, 1978b; Feldman and March, 1981). Participants can directly gain information processing leverage by turning automated data systems to the compilation and manipulation of data that would best persuade *other* parties in the expected negotiations. They can gain symbolic leverage in situations where participants value analytical rationality simply by virtue of using computerized procedures, even if the substantive analysis or data quality is technically poor or even irrelevant [33].

These examples do not exhaust the ways in which computerized technologies have been used and which differ from discrete-entity models [34]. Web analyses more adequately account for the leverage provided by computerized data systems since they include negotiating leverage as a central element.

5.1.5 Summary

Computing developments are attractive to some organizational participants because they provide leverage of several sorts: increasing control, speed, and discretion over work, or in increasing their bargaining capabilities. Even if these gains are realized, they are not Pareto optimal for all participants. Some will lose when others gain. Fear of losing control or bargaining leverage will lead some participants to oppose particular computing arrangements, and to propose alternatives that better serve their interests (Danziger *et al.*, 1982). Web models emphasize purposive rationality on a larger, social terrain which is partly structured.

Computerized technologies or new arrangements for organizing them, do not always yield the leverage which advocates seek or their competitors fear. When gains are realized they are not always byproducts of increased information-processing capabilities. Sometimes leverage accrues from the negotiating edge provided by symbols of rationality, innovation, or special analytical procedures. In any of these cases, the leverage provided by computing technologies cannot be directly inferred from characteristics of the technology alone; its integration into particular work organization or social order explains important variations in the actual leverage provided by similar technologies. (Thus, the extent to which supermarket scanners and labor reductions are coupled may hinge on local laws that regulate unit-pricing.) Accurate analyses computing leverage hinge on careful examinations of work organization and social action. Discrete-entity models lose their predictive power since they ignore work organization or treat it in highly stereotypical terms.

On the other hand, expected leverage may be hard for protagonists of computing developments to realize. While causes vary, we will examine two kinds of constraints in the next two sections: (a) the scale of co-requisite commitments upon which smooth computing depends, and (b) the extent to which historical commitments in overlapping negotiating contexts constrain the ways in which the focal computing resource may be developed and deployed.

5.2 Infrastructure of Computing Development and Use

When automated information systems are operated 'routinely', the array of supporting resources strongly influences the quality of computer-based service which is actually available to users. A large fraction of the studies of computing in organizations focus on relatively exciting, early stages in the development of technologies: adoption, innovation, design, implementation [35]. It is easier for these approaches to ignore infrastructure, even when they identify political processes influencing the adoption of computing, design strategies, etc.

While discrete-entity analyses oversimplify or ignore the social context which influence the adoption of systems, even some web-like analyses ignore infrastructure. After the developers turn over a computer-based technology to their clients, the local saga of computing continues, as in the cases of WWMCCS and PRINTCO. Since the ways that computing is integrated into organizational life depends upon many events and arrangements that take place after a system is 'signed off', we will devote some special attention to the infrastructural resources for computing.

The infrastructural resources for a given activity refers to those adjunct resources which help carry out the activity smoothly. Urban planners refer to such physical basics as roads, sewers, and utilities, which support social and business activities as the 'urban infrastructure'. Infrastructural resources for using reports from a computer-based information system include skilled staff, accurate and complete documents, sharp operations procedures, and enforceable equipment contracts. For software developers, infrastructure includes programming skills, information about systems, working hardware, etc. For computer hardware, critical infrastructural resources also include physical systems such as reliable 'clean' electrical energy and low-noise communication lines. The PRINTCO case illustrates how critical infrastructure can be developing workable information systems. We attribute the failure of PRINTCO's first MRP conversion effort to higher level managers' tacit assumption that their infrastructure for computing development was complete as soon as they acquired the hardware and software they preferred. They ignored their programmers' skills, the form of support for their new minicomputer, etc.

5.2.1 Identifying Infrastructural Resources

Discrete-entity analysts can ignore infrastructural resources, but web analysts need a way to identify them. We identify key infrastructural resources by following the chain of resources, equipment, consumers and providers which support a given computing resource. This network is called the 'production lattice' for the focal computing resource in Kling and Scacchi (1982) and Scacchi (1981). Those resources that each consumer/provider depends upon constitutes an element in the infrastructure for the focal computing resource. We have found three ways to identify the production lattice for a particular computing resource:

PL1. Trace the chain of social and technical interactions from the focal computing resource outward to various suppliers of basic resources and skills which enable it. These basic inputs include data, supporting equipment, energy, communications, etc. They also include participants who provide expert assistance, ensure that basic inputs of adequate quality are provided by negotiating with suppliers, training resource producers, auditing the quality of inputs, etc.

PL2. Include those inputs or resources whose alterations yield (large) improvements in the quality of output provided by the focal computing resource.

PL3. Include those inputs or resources whose failures reduce the quality of the focal computing resource [36].

Criterion C2 guides how far outward from the focal computing resource one should follow the chain of dependencies indicated by criterion PL1. Narrow boundaries drawn close to the computer room miss the dependencies of computerized information systems on other organizational resources such as inter-office mail and telephone lines. Narrow boundaries miss relations with equipment vendors or outside consultants which may also be critical.

Goodman (1979) provides a useful example which draws the chain of dependencies rather widely when he analyzes the capabilities of the Soviet computing community to develop and use sophisticated computer systems. He argues that the kinds of skills learned by Soviet computer specialists, and the ability of the Soviet military to appropriate critical resources on demand limit the practical

TABLE 5   *Selected infrastructural resources for TRACKER*

Information system: TRACKER
    System information (e.g. documents, consultants)
    System alterations (e.g. maintenance procedures, skilled application
      programmers)
    Organizing data
    Accurate Data (e.g. data auditing and error correcting procedures)
    Skilled data feeders
    Training staff
    Data integrity — (procedures for compensating for crashes)
    Information paths (e.g. inter-office mail)

Programming language: RPG-II
    System information (e.g. documents, consultants)
    Vendor support for revisions and bug patches
    Programmers' skills

Operating system: for IBM System 34
    System information (e.g. documents, consultants)
    System programmers
    Programmers' skills

Hardware: IBM System 34 mini + (disk, tape drives, printers, key-tape machines, terminals)
    Skilled operators
    Operations procedures
    Electrical power
    Physical space
    Performance-oriented vendor contracts
    Policies, procedures, and practices for allocating computer time, terminals

abilities of Soviet civilian-oriented ventures to develop very sophisticated machines. He uses criterion C2 in drawing a relatively wide boundary. In contrast, discrete-entity analysts who draw a narrow boundary around the laboratories examine technical contingencies which link one stage of technical sophistication to the next. They argue that certain missing technologies (e.g. DBMS) make a critical difference in Soviet computing developments. In contrast, Goodman argues that overall institutional weaknesses, particularly a two-tier economy, are most debilitating and specific technical capabilities are less central to the Soviet's capabilities (Goodman, 1979). Since Goodman's analysis has been used to frame official technical trade policies for the United States, alternative interpretations which hinge on boundary definitions are not merely academic.

Table 5 lists some typical infrastructural resources for an automated inventory control system like that used at PRINTCO, called TRACKER. This list is suggestive, rather than exhaustive. TRACKER is composed of applications programs, reports, data sets, operations procedures, etc. The infrastructural resources are those things which help various actors use TRACKER and which support production lattices defined by criteria PL1, PL2, and PL3. The elements of Table 5 are primarily static, and we will examine three static characteristics first:

(a) Infrastructural resources are layered. TRACKER is written in RPG-II which runs under a simple operating system on an IBM System 34 minicomputer. The focal computing resource for one participant (e.g. the operating system as seen by a systems programmer) is infrastructure for participants further up the (production) chain. (Infrastructure is a *relationship* between a focal resource and a supporting resource.)

(b) Infrastructural resources for computing may be coextensive with or part of other organizational procedures and resources. At various points, the mail room which disseminates reports, the electrical system which provides AC current, procedures for hiring and firing staff, or for procuring equipment, can be bound up in the support of a focal computer system (e.g. TRACKER).

(c) Some of the resources are relatively concrete objects (e.g. a document, contract), or people (e.g. skilled programmers). Others are capabilities for reproducing these more concrete resources on demand (e.g. the ability to hire or train skilled programmers, the ability to purchase, or write new documents).

Computer-based systems are often tightly coupled through the various elements of infrastructure, both horizontally (through a particular production lattice) and 'vertically' through various layers. In the case of complex information systems, such as TRACKER, each of these layers is itself a relatively complex work organization. When PRINTCO's managers tried to convert from their MRP system like TRACKER to a new system which ran on the Data General Eclipse, they were changing several layers of infrastructure simultaneously. But they provided little special support for this complex transformation.

Computer-based technologies and arrangements for using them vary considerably in the scale and complexity of the production lattices which support them. The production lattices supporting a programmable calculator used by an engineer may be very small (e.g. sources of design data in the firm and vendor support for repairs). On the other hand, information systems which cut across many organizational subunits (e.g. accounting systems, inventory control systems) or which cut across many organizations (e.g. WWMCCS) are markedly more complicated [37].

Most of this chapter is devoted to these computer-based systems of larger social scope. Any user of a complex computer-based system used to support some instrumental lines of work, stands at the intersection of two work organizations. One work organization is framed around the instrumental tasks enacted by the computer user (e.g. production planning in a manufacturing firm, actuarial analyses in an insurance firm, land use analyses in an urban planning department, or processing various transactions—payroll checks, work orders, purchase orders, travel vouchers). The second work organization is visible as he faces the computer and other core resources (e.g. data sources) which support his computational universe: the production lattices which provide any of the computer-based productions in use.

This production lattice slices through several of the distinct layers of the infrastructure for computing support. The user of several different computer-based systems stands at the intersection of several different work organizations: his own instrumental activities and a production lattice for each computer-based system. These lattices may overlap, to the extent that the computer-based systems ride on shared resources, or they may be quite distinct. Discrete-entity analyses view the smooth coordination of these multiple work organizations to be as difficult as straightforward. For web analysts they are problematic and will be the focus of our attention in the next few paragraphs.

5.2.2 Negotiations around Production Lattices

It would be analytically attractive if we could apply discrete entity models to help understand the kinds of infrastructural resources which are available to participants who develop and use computer-based systems. However, the way that production lattices are layered and often cut across organizations usually makes discrete-entity analyses too weak. The negotiated order perspective helps explain variations in the kinds of resources which are (or could be) available to different parties. The organizational process perspective, as well as discrete-entity models, lacks the conceptual richness to easily explain phenomena such as these:

(a) When some computing resources are shared by several participants (e.g. individuals, organizational subunits, coalitions), service will often be differentially provided, and more powerful participants will often receive better levels of service where the provider has discretion. Thus, for example, the material control staff at PRINTCO received better computing support than did departments like Test Engineering. (Ultimately, less advantaged departments at PRINTCO acquired their own DEC LSI-11 microcomputers.)

(b) Computing resources may be selected so as to improve the negotiating posture of service providers in conflicts over control which are defined at larger scales of action than a particular bundle of computer services [38].

(c) Resources may be selected in line with social meanings defined in larger social worlds in which some key actors participate. For example, systems programmers and facility managers may have special preferences for equipment defined in vendor-specific worlds (e.g. IBM, DEC). When performance criteria are ambiguous, social definitions may dominate decisions about adoption. At PRINTCO, the second DP manager sought to upgrade to a new computer which his vendor was advocating as a high status alternative to his current equipment, while his clientele wanted improvements made on their existing equipment.

(d) Sometimes there are conflicts between the kinds of computer-based service a consumer desires and what a provider sees as his line of work or the going concern of his organization. A common, relatively individualistic example is the difficulty many managers and users find in having programmers adequately document their software. Programmers receive many rewards—both psychological and in their careers—for writing programs. Documentation is not their line of work, and does little to advance a programmer's career on the job market.

In each of these four kinds of situations computing resources and the services provided are probably 'sub-optimal' based on narrow considerations of task. The resources selected are based in part on negotiations which take place in social settings defined by boundaries that extend well beyond the focal computing resource and its immediate users.

Negotiations matter in practice. Structural analyses only explain a fraction of the kinds of choices organizational participants make when selecting or providing computer-based resources. Moreover, today's structural arrangements (e.g. routines for allocating computing resources) are often the byproduct of battles or negotiations worked out previously [39].

5.3 History of Commitments in and around Computing

Over time, key actors developed an array of infrastructural resources to support their computer applications. Discrete-entity analysts usually take these resources for granted. Web analysts view existing arrangements as embodying a complex set of commitments made earlier. Some of these commitments are particular to computing (e.g. the kind of equipment in use). Others are defined in larger settings within and without the organization (e.g. hiring procedures, procurement procedures).

There are few published studies of computing arrangements which carefully trace the way that commitments made over long time periods influence the use of a computer application, how its constituencies shape and adapt it, etc. The studies that examine historically derived commitments usually focus on periods of a few years (Kling, 1978b; Markus, 1979, 1981; Dutton, 1981) although longer periods are sometimes examined to provide 'context' (Laudon, 1974) [40].

Organizations develop infrastructures for computing support over months and years—the routines, the equipment selected, the expertise developed in different subunits, the meanings and ideologies developed to justify them, etc. These are not easily altered when troubles arise. In general, infrastructures are developed incrementally, rather than by large and swift changes. Discrete-entity analysts try to identify the problems of computer use by focusing on specific procedures or equipment. If one views infrastructure as a product of short-term organization building, then it should be easy to change when needed. Web analysts are usually

344   DEFINING THE BOUNDARIES OF COMPUTING

less sanguine that infrastructures can be rapidly created or altered by simple administrative will.

Any analyst of computing developments tacitly selects a temporal frame in which to situate his account. Discrete entity analysts rarely begin their accounts before the initiation of the focal computing resource. Such historical frames are often too limited to help explain the kinds of constraints faced by key actors in the local saga of computing. In the cases of WWMCCS and PRINTCO, we have illustrated how our criteria C1 and C2 provide more useful guidelines for selecting historical envelopes.

5.3.1 WWMCCS in Historical Perspective

The case of WWMCCS is particularly instructive. Web analysts would view the continuing development in a quite different way than the GAO's auditors who used discrete-entity models. First, web analysts would use criteria C1 and C2, to define the situation which should be examined. The relevant time scale would be defined by the history of social relations or practices which constrain the choices for WWMCCS, rather than the WWMCCS birthdate of 1966 [41].

In a structural analysis, web analysts would pay special attention to the routines which shape the relevant action by various DoD staff. In this case, there are two different kinds of routines: (a) those that field commanders expect when they are in situations for which WWMCCS use might provide key information and (b) those which influence the ability of DoD staff and commercial vendors to design and develop WWMCCS. Those routines which enable projects to be developed across military services are of critical importance. Unfortunately, there is substantial evidence that cross-service collaboration is problematic — particularly in the procurement of weapons systems and battle support systems to meet common requirements (Coulam, 1977). Strong inter-service rivalries have debilitated common actions (in peacetime) and go back at least until the 1960s when Secretary of Defense McNamara unsuccessfully pushed for common weapons systems such as the TFX fighter-bomber to be shared by the Air Force and Navy (Coulam, 1977). The structural analyst would surmise that joint service ventures would require special efforts [42]. Unfortunately, no reference is made in GAO's report to any special efforts. Its authors assume that officers in all services will cooperate as much as necessary, if only WWMCCS were 'well managed'.

The negotiated order analyst would share the structural analysts' concern that a central unresolved issue in WWMCCS development is the difficulty of officers in the military services sharing ideologies, procedures, and resources which enable them to be distinctive: own battle doctrines, own communication protocols, own resources. The set of participants in a negotiated order analysis would be identified by asking: whose cooperation is required here and who are the parties to the critical negotiation? The analyst identifies a set of negotiation contexts [43]. There is a vast set of negotiation contexts in the case of WWMCCS. Negotiating contexts are defined by issues, participants, options, etc. (Strauss, 1978). A list of some participant pairings is suggestive:

— Each of three Services–Defense Communications Agency (DCA) [44].
— Each of three services pairwise (Army, Navy, Air Force)
— DCA–equipment vendors (e.g. IBM, Honeywell, Mitre)
— DCA–Office of the Secretary of Defense (OSD)
— DoD–Congress
— Vendors–Vendors

A complete list would be vast. Since it draws participants from different social worlds, WWMCCS development is best examined as a large social arena rather than as a simple technology to develop and manage — like a large dam. Within the larger negotiation contexts which give shape to the arena are many smaller contexts. For example in Congress, the House Armed Services Committee, House Committee on Appropriations, and the GAO are but a few of the relevant actors who negotiate with different parts of DoD and also each other. In this light, there have been continuous negotiations between Congress and the DoD about the development of WWMCCS, and the GAO has been a continual participant in many of those negotiations since 1970. Different negotiation contexts have different relevant histories. The inter-service rivalries may go back decades and make development of detailed WWMCCS requirements practically infeasible. But the negotiations between the DCA and major computer vendors such as IBM and Honeywell may only extend back until the 1960s.

Gestures make sense primarily in terms of ongoing negotiations. Thus, GAO's reports on WWMCCS should be viewed as an instrument in the negotiations between Congressional actors and DoD rather than as a searching scientific analysis of the prospects and potential problems of WWMCCS. It should be viewed as an attempt by some Congressional actors to stimulate certain DoD actors to improve WWMCCS [45].

Negotiation contexts are the situations in which criteria C1 or C2 are invoked to select appropriate temporal scales. There are many histories to WWMCCS — of tri-service systems acquisitions, of computing development in DoD, of GAO–DoD relations, of battle doctrines held by field commanders, of training field commanders in WWMCCS use, of relations between the DCA and the Office of the Secretary of Defense, etc. Useful histories are developed within a sufficiently large social envelope that social relationships which constrain current choices are sharply laid out. These include shifting balances of power, developing commitments, perceived options, etc. This is a complex inquiry for a system like WWMCCS.

A web analysis of WWMCCS actual capabilities may appear to be hopelessly complex and consequently infeasible. Web analyses become attractive only because the simple discrete-entity analyses don't have the predictive value we need. Any reasonable and coherent argument that WWMCCS can be designed and administered so that it meets the military goals set for it will be a web analysis. If such an analysis proves to be too complex, then no one could reasonably predict WWMCCS's feasibility and utility. Then no one would be able to make a convincing substantive case that WWMCCS should be built and trusted.

The case of WWMCCS is unusually complex, but nevertheless instructive. Complex computing developments, even those of substantially smaller scale, are initiated, designed, altered, used, expanded, decommissioned, revised, and superseded by participants acting within constrained negotiation contexts (Markus, 1981). The structuring of incentives faced by different participants and the choices they face are not completely open-ended. They develop over time. As particular arrangements are negotiated, they develop into organizational routines, structures, equipment configurations, precedents, etc. History here denotes the temporal frame in which these arrangements have been negotiated such that they still bear on the present through criteria C1 and C2. This conception is quite different from that of the historian, who is often interested in a larger set of these smaller histories, and is concerned with the shaping of many different presents during the career trajectory of a particular technical development [46].

The strategy for selecting time periods and relevant participants, social relations, etc. emphasizes constraints upon possible lines of current action, as well as possible opportunities. This is not a form of determinism. Rather, organizational actors cannot rapidly design new social relationships in and around computing developments simply because they want to, 'ought to', etc.

5.3.2 PRINTCO's Computing Histories

Work arrangements with computing do not necessarily develop unilinearly; sharp discontinuities are possible. The case of CBIS developments at PRINTCO illustrates historical discontinuities. Since PRINTCO's managers had succeeded in rapidly building a profitable business and had developed a good complex inventory control system, one might assume that the firm would have a routine experience in extending their CBIS in the next decade. However, when PRINTCO's DP staff began to convert from their first MRP system to a second system, they faced substantial technical problems. These problems were local and specialized: the programming staff were changing between operating environments (e.g. IBM System 34 to a Data General Eclipse 350), between programming languages (RPG-II to Basic), and between specific MRP packages. They simply didn't have the experience to move along all these dimensions simultaneously.

PRINTCO's managers tried to hire a new DP manager. After a laborious search, they found a person who clarified some of their software practices. But he was most interested in a move along yet another frontier — to acquire a System 38 which IBM had then positioned as its prime business-oriented minicomputer. The DP Steering Committee wanted to stay with their smaller IBM System 34 and enhance their existing software. Finally, the DP steering committee fired their new DP manager and decided to buy a still larger IBM computer, a model 4341, and a new MRP package.

Any of these changes could be rationalized in the common discrete-entity terms of 'meeting a business need' or 'solving an operational problem'. However, PRINTCO's staff continually searched for new technological solutions along a path which cannot be genuinely understood without reference to their previous steps along the path. The PRINTCO case also illustrates the way in which a web analysis provides insights when discrete-entity analyses fall short.

6. DRAWING BOUNDARIES: DISCRETE ENTITY AND WEB MODELS

Discrete-entity analysts easily draw defining boundaries. They can focus on a computer-based systems and a single user, a work group or some formally defined unit, like a public agency or a business firm. In contrast, web analysts have a more difficult time in defining boundaries since they use social criteria which lead to different boundaries in different settings.

There are no methods handbooks for carrying out web analyses [47]. However, we can sketch the elements of a web method for defining analytically useful boundaries [48].

The analyst begins with a set of questions about the value, adoption, development, or use of a computer-based technology. She identifies social settings where these technologies are deployed [49]. Analysts are usually concerned with the conditions under which a *class* of technologies are valued or troublesome. They select particular technologies which represent a suitable exemplar of a class: a typical array of the technologies, especially sophisticated versions, etc. Or they examine computer-based technologies which are deployed under special social arrangements: a consortium of users, complex and flexible fee-for-service arrangements, used by organizations of varying wealth, social complexity, etc.

In a particular setting, the web analyst:

(1) maps the social and technical architectures of the computer-based technologies;
(2) characterizes the social contexts in which the technologies are developed and used, and choices of social architecture framed;
(3) maps the infrastructures which support the deployment of the computer-based technology for various users [50];
(4) characterizes the history of key social relationships as we have described above.

Useful units of analysis are lines of work or the set of social relationships which shape the behavior of participants who develop, support, and use computer-based systems based on criteria C1 and C2.

The starting questions focus upon the social relations people and organizations are playing out as well as the information processing tasks they use computing for. The analyst identifies the key stakeholders who are linked to the computer-based technology: providers, promoters, vendors, data users, suppliers of ancillary services, regulators, resource controllers, etc. Also, the analyst identifies key groups with whom these groups interact and which involve the computer-based resource: clients of data users, competitors of users and service providers, etc. may be significant. The analyst draws boundaries within organization which include these groups. Boundaries also extend across diverse organizations to include actors, such as professional associations, auditors or funders, who are located outside the computer-using organization.

These larger boundaries which include groups which seem a bit remote from the immediate setting of computer use sometimes puzzles discrete-entity analysts who see them as 'irrelevant'. It is easiest to argue that distant groups are irrelevant when the causal connection between computing and behavior is simple and direct. The reasons for including a group which may seem socially remote, like vendors, professional associations, auditors, regulators, etc. is that it has influenced the shape of computerization in the focal setting. Narrow boundaries which are set *a priori* by formal criteria simply miss many important causal connections and mislead.

After web analysts draw boundaries, they link the use of computer-based technologies to:

(1) negotiations between these parties;
(2) routines in communications, resources, etc. that regulate key social relationships between these parties. These include temporal regularities as well as channels.

These relationships supplement the examination of information processing capabilities of the computer-based technology. Gathering data about wide-ranging negotiating contexts requires sampling widely within and across organizations: direct users or service providers alone are an incomplete set of informants. Informants should be selected who have different relationships to the computing resources being examined: direct and indirect users, casual and frequent users, service providers, resource controllers, regulators, educators, clients of the computer-using units who deal with computer-based data, computing support staff, computer operations staff, etc.

A chronology of computing-related events should be compiled to identify (1) key participants, (2) the history of commitments, (3) organizational styles, (4) routines, and (5) other behavior which drive and constrain organizational actions which strongly influence patterns of computing development and use. Events should be characterized by the key actors who participate, the technical or social changes they valued, what happened, and how. Also, the distribution of computing resources and support systems among departments should be mapped, and important episodes and patterns should be examined.

These strategies for collecting and organizing data help the web analyst answer his driving questions, but they are not an algorithm. These procedures help draw rather large boundaries across organizations and through time. However, certain relationships will be much more central than others — thus reducing the number of possible relationships. The driving question which helps reduce the boundaries to manageable size is a paraphrase of criteria C1 and C2: which social relationships and technological capabilities most explains the behavior in question? The data reported in our cases of WWMCCS and PRINTCO and our analysis of them for specific examples in which we applied these strategies.

If one conducts a comparative study of some form of computerization (e.g. desktop computing, large-scale CBIS, expert systems, or instructional computing) it is likely that a different set of participants will be important in different settings. For example, in one school district funds for instructional computing may have come from a Federal grant while in a second district a parents' group may have raised the funds, and in a third district the equipment may have been donated by a computer vendor. In one school district, a board of teachers may have oversight over instructional computing. In another district, teachers may be left on their own. These different patterns of funding and oversight, may well lead to different configurations of instructional computing, different expectations by participants, different infrastructure, different forms of accountability, and different patterns integration into classes. It would be a mistake to ignore different funding patterns and bodies which govern computing (if any) *a priori* in a study of the ways that schools integrate instructional computing into their programs. This illustration suggests that standardized sampling — the heart of survey research — is problematic for developing strong causal models about the shape of computerization: its antecedents and its consequences for participants.

In a standard survey, the researcher could inquire about funding sources or any other discrete item. *Once the researcher knows what to ask*, she might develop appropriate questions in a standard survey and proceed as usual. This line of argument skirts two fundamental issues. First, the researcher must know what small set of relatively standard questions are worth asking in a survey. Good surveys may follow *after a researcher has already done a web analysis of computerization*. Second, the traditional survey is administered to a standard set of informants. However, any single class of informants may not know about the character of key contextual variables. For example, classroom teachers may not be able to provide good information about the conditions under which their school received funding for instructional computing. This problem can be resolved, in part, by surveying a variety of participants in each setting and identifying reliable informants for different classes of issues. For example, a school principal may be a superb informant for information about the funding of computing, but she may know very little about the dilemmas a teacher faces in organizing classes which use the equipment in a meaningful way. Teachers may be superb informants about classroom practices, etc.

There are important theoretical and methodological conclusions from these observations. When traditional surveys to one kind of participant are the only form of systematic data collected in a study, then discrete-entity explanations are most likely to follow. They will follow not because they are better than web kinds of explanations but because of the impoverished set of data the researcher has collected. Second, if web analysts conduct surveys, they must do so in conjunction with other forms of data collection which examine social and technical relations outside of the immediate behavior setting of computer use.

7. CONCLUSIONS

Analysts who rely upon discrete-entity and web models interpret the opportunities and constraints of computing developments very differently. Discrete-entity models offer the advantage of analytic simplicity: 'systems' are systematic and meet their design goals; costs can be well known and benefits can be sharply defined. This apparent clarity comes at some cost. First, predictions based on these models tend to overestimate the leverage that will be realized from some computational resource or technique, and also to underestimate the requisite time and costs. Second, these models offer an impoverished conceptual vocabulary for understanding the conditions of moderate leverage and do little to explain how success for some is failure for others.

Discrete-entity models clearly fail to account for the conditions under which computer-based technologies are exploited as symbols of legitimacy in inter-group negotiations. But discrete-entity analyses also provide little help in explaining or predicting the occurrence of commonplace difficulties such as mis-specified systems, delays, maldistributions of services, cost overruns, or rigid systems. Often problems occur because of social relations and resource dependencies between direct users, resource controllers and other actors who appear outside the boundaries of the task groups most closely connected to the focal computing resources. If these relationships are ignored, one is left with peculiar explanations for troubles: (stupid) people used the wrong technology (Ackoff, 1967), developers and users did not plan properly, or participants mismanaged their resources. Individualistic explanations like these provide little insight into the difficulties of developing very large scale computerized systems such as WWMCCS. Nor do they explain why members of the public might have systematic difficulties in correcting errors in computerized information systems (Sterling, 1979, 1980).

Web models reverse the balance of virtues and difficulties. Their primary virtue is their empirical fidelity, while they are analytically more complex, and somewhat cumbersome. They are organized to better account for the major social relations which influence the development and use of computerized technologies in complex organizations.

We have emphasized three critical elements of a theory to account for the embedding of computing in organizational life: (a) the social leverage provided by computerized technologies; (b) the co-requisites for smooth computing developments and operations (infrastructure); and (c) the historically developed constraints and opportunities that participants face when they are engaged with computing in organizational life. Useful definitions of the situation of computing development and use include larger populations, sets of equipment, spatial arrangements, and temporal periods than those which are proximate to the behavioral setting in which the focal computing resource is developed and used.

These elements are relatively abstract. They take on special meaning within particular organizations for understanding the social relationships that develop around particular computer-based technologies. Our examination of WWMCCS entailed very different social groups and time periods from our study of PRINTCO which was different in detail from our study of instructional computing in universities (Iaconco and Kling, in press). Web models provide a useful approach for studying social behavior in and around such different computer-based technologies in different institutional settings because they indicate how to identify relevant social groups and units of analysis.

The work organization in which computing is embedded often plays a critical role: work organizations often define the situation in which organizational participants and their clients gain negotiating leverage through the information processing capabilities or symbolic connotations of digital computation; production lattices which compose the infrastructure for a computing resource are a form of work organization; and historical commitments which limit their degrees of freedom often develop within the work organizations pertinent to computing developments.

In line with criteria C1 and C2, boundaries which extend beyond a work group (or even a single organization) are usually critical:

(1) Kling's (1978b) analysis of the persistence of an automated welfare information and referral system which helped the staff of a Southern city impress Federal auditors;
(2) Goodman's (1979) analysis of Soviet computing capabilities shows that their ability to develop high performance computer systems is hindered by a two-tier economic system which impedes software development even though it supports modest advances in component hardware technologies [51];
(3) Dutton's (1981) analysis of the way in which the utility of fiscal impact models by urban planners in Tulsa, Oklahoma, hinged on alterations in the local political climate;
(4) King's (1983) examination of the success of a company, Data Resources Incorporated (DRI), which sells a widely used large-scale econometric model. King argues that DRI does not succeed because its model helps economists develop exceptionally accurate forecasts of economic indicators in the US economy. The model is not technically superior to DRI's competitors' models. King attributes part of DRI's success to the way it provides its clients with a rich infrastructure for helping them use its model and data.

(5) Kling and Iacono's (1984a) detailed examination of patterns of social control at PRINTCO. They found that many workers who used the computerized inventory control system worked in a highly disciplined work organization. However, poor behavior and social pressure was not simply a product of supervisors monitoring their subordinates. Rather, users of the systems were embedded in a web of social relations that cut across many work groups within the firm. This tight pattern would not be very apparent by examining any single work group in isolation.

(6) McHenry's (1985) examination of the difficulties that Soviet managers have in using a major set of management information systems. McHenry argues that the difficulties come, in part, from the way in which central ministries develop information systems software and ship it out to manufacturing firms to be used with little local customization.

In each of these studies, critical negotiating contexts extended well outside the immediate work organization in which computer use was embedded. Such critical negotiations are difficult, if not impossible, to reconstruct if analysts do not open their data nets widely enough to report them (Strauss, 1978). Without such accounts, we cannot understand the real social choices, consequences and dilemmas of computerization.

ACKNOWLEDGEMENTS

I wrote the original manuscript for this chapter in the winter of 1982. Since that time I have circulated the progressively refined drafts of the manuscript to many colleagues and presented portions of it in seminars at the Claremont Graduate School, Harvard University, and New York University. Many people helped me sharpen the ideas developed here through conversation and critique. I am particularly appreciative of conversations with Kurt Borchardt, Frank Cancian, Les Gasser, Eli Gerson, Sara Kiesler, John King, Ken Kraemer, Kenneth Laudon, Lynne Markus, Robert Pepper, Charles Perrow, Walt Scacchi, Jaqueline Shriber, Lee Sproull, Anselm Strauss, and Alan Wicker. Janet Asteroff, Richard Boland, Sy Goodman, Kathleen Huddleston, Bill McHenry, and Karen Wieckert made some very helpful editorial suggestions. I specially appreciate my discussions and debates with Suzanne Iacono who has helped me to think through some of the more puzzling social dilemmas of computerization. This research was supported under NSF Grants 81-17719 and CSD 85-08484.

NOTES

[1] For recent reviews of the substantive findings of many social studies of computerization, see Kling (1980), Attewell and Rule (1984), and Hirschheim (1985).

[2] Analysts can cluster along many kinds of dimensions: particular topics studied, research methods, theoretical orientations of researchers (Kling, 1980), *a priori* biases of researchers (Hirschheim 1986), etc. This chapter is not aimed at classifying social studies of computerization. Rather, it sets some useful guidelines for those who are designing social studies of computerization.

[3] Unusual exceptions include Scacchi (1981), OTA (1982), Koch (1984), and Kling and Iacono (1984b).

[4] For simplicity, we will talk about models, rather than continually distinguishing between underlying perspectives and models which are more sharply drawn within a particular perspective.

[5] The conceptions of 'better' vary across analyses. Usually better means newer, but in detail newer technologies may have more capabilities than older ones. Regardless of the metric of 'better' used, analysts of this persuasion usually assume that *all* participants will prefer technologies which are improved along their preferred metric. These metrics characterize the technology, not any relationship between technology and setting which varies across settings.

[6] See Kling and Scacchi [1982] for more fine-grained exposition of these two models. Exemplary discrete-entity analyses may be found in research monographs (Inbar, 1979, Hiltz and Turoff, 1978), publications for computing practitioners and working managers (Simon, 1973; Kochar, 1979; Wise *et al.*, 1980; Poppel, 1982; Strassman, 1985; Zuboff, 1982), and recent MIS textbooks (Burch *et al.*, 1979, Part IV; Gessford, 1980; Kanter, 1977, Chapter 8; Hussain and Hussain, 1981, Chapter 17; Taggart, 1980, Chapter 8). Discrete entity models are not straw men.

[7] Exemplary resource dependence analyses of computing may be found in research publications such as (Kling and Scacchi, 1979a; King and Kraemer, 1981a; Markus, 1979; Dery, 1981; King, 1983; Kling and Iacono, 1984b, Witt, 1985; Laudon, 1986) and books aimed at computing practitioners and managers (Keen and Scott-Morton, 1978; Mumford and Pettigrew, 1976; Withington, 1979). We are not aware of any textbooks that are developed primarily from a perspective that emphasizes resource dependence models. The distinction between web models and discrete entity models parallels the differences between open systems and closed systems models. But web models differ significantly from open systems models and general systems theory by not assuming an overall level of system 'function' or 'quality', coherent controllers, system stability, etc.

[8] Between these two theoretical extremes is a third 'partial-web' model. These models are a-historical and treat computer technologies as relatively isolable entities. However, they examine developments in a context of close-in, intergroup and intra-group relations. These models emphasize human relations school themes such as status, quality of worklife, and workplace control, but are largely apolitical (Kling, 1980). (See Note 11 below.)

[9] See Kling and Scacchi [1982] for more fine-grained exposition of these two models. These models are my syntheses. Authors identified in this and the previous section as employing these models do not make the assumptions identified in this section explicit. Nor do they use the labels 'discrete-entity' or 'resource dependence' models.

[10] The 'boxes' also may be managerial techniques such as cost–benefit analyses or project scheduling disciplines.

[11] Table 2 characterizes an 'extended web' or 'web' model. The 'partial web' model mentioned in a previous footnote can be constructed from the following assumptions: D1a&b; D2a&b, W3a&b; W4a and W4b. Boundaries are drawn around 'small groups' close to the focal computing resource; Assumption 5, the model of social action, is that adopted by Human Relations analysts (Kling, 1980; Lucas, 1981). Partial web analyses are common, but will not be examined in this chapter.

[12] While discrete-entity and web models are ideal types, it is instructive to examine the extent to which particular analyses of computing hang more strongly on assumptions closer to one model or the other. Cortada's (1980, pp. 96–100) example of defining the costs of a new computer application is instructive. While his example is presented with little rationale for what is included, both direct computing costs and some infrastructural costs (e.g. site preparation and staff training) are included. The costs borne by the staff of computer-using departments are also included. However, costs are assumed to be estimable to the nearest hundred dollars. The assumption that there are no uncertainties in time or costs makes more sense for budgeting than for estimating expected costs. Many infrastructure costs are implicit rather than explicit. Programming times are estimated (e.g. 55 man-months), with no indication about the assumptions made about the relative skill levels of the programmers who will actually do the work. In a discussion of internal rate of return, Cortada mentions that some organizations set a threshold for a minimal rate of return for acceptable projects. That managers might juggle costs to make projects look more or less attractive isn't mentioned (p. 107). Cortada later suggests that such 'hidden influences can be taken into account' with 'matrices of probability (p. 108)'. This book is a contemporary text for practicing managers. But managers who have substantial experience in computerized environments may make less explicit analyses that depend more on the assumptions of web models.

[13] See some of the following sections and Appendix A2 of Kling and Scacchi (1982) for a detailed discussion of production lattices in computing.

[14] These concepts will support the substantive analyses of computing which occupy our attention in a later section. Readers who are anxious for substantive analyses of computing might skim this section on a first reading, but should be sure to note criteria C1 and C2 described below for drawing boundaries around defining situations.

[15] These forms of involvement extend beyond designing, programming, and using computer-based reports. They include a variety of other activities: learning about computing developments, training, consulting, selling, budgeting, creating space for equipment, etc.

[16] This formulation follows Lofland (1976, p. 26).

[17] Identifying the critical social processes is a separate matter which we will examine below.

[18] It is useful to expand and contract the definition of the focal situation and contexts to see whether one has adequate explanatory power at a sufficiently small level of analysis.

[19] Since some managers manage by exception, their typical efforts are not spent dealing with routine events; rather they husband their time to focus on the non-routine. Thus, their typical behavior is not well covered by this conception of organizations.

[20] WWMCCS is pronounced 'wimmix'. In 1966 WWMCCS was a loose federation of over 150 computers in dozens of military commands. By 1979 it was running with an explicit budget of over $150 million annually, and a total cost of over $1 billion (Comptroller General, 1979). In the early 1980s, the system was renamed WWMCCS Information System (WIS). Since we are examining events prior to 1980, we will use the original WWMCCS designation.

[21] For example, the Air Force maintains a command and control system for assigning planes to sorties worldwide. Planes are assigned by tail number (a unique identifier) from a centralized command center in the USA. In contrast, the Navy has developed a tactical command and control system, NTDS, that gives substantial control over weapons assignments to fleet commanders and even to fire control officers aboard ship. While these systems are not directly comparable (they deploy different levels of resources), they suggest that prevailing Air Force doctrines probably emphasize more centralized control over battle operations than does current Navy doctrine.

[22] PRINTCO is a pseudonym. The firm employed about 800 people at the time of our study. Les Gasser, Suzanne Iacono, and Rob Rittenhouse and I conducted over 50 interviews with a wide variety of PRINTCO's manufacturing staff at different levels in the hierarchy and in different departments between 1980 and 1982. This case description is excerpted from Kling and Iacono (1984a), Kling and Iacono (1984b), Kling and Iacono (1986a), and Kling and Iacono (1986b). See these articles for further details about this case and theoretical analyses of the data.

[23] See Kling and Iacono (1984a) for a discussion of resistance by the purchasing staff.

[24] The firm was also unlikely to pay a sufficiently good salary to attract people with good development skills to work in a data processing 'back water' — defined by equipment, languages, and little interest in sustaining new development efforts.

[25] The conventional information processing perspective is incomplete since computerized technologies are sometimes harnessed to drive machinery and manipulate it flexibly. Thus, the printing of airline tickets at reservation desks by computer-driven printers, the directional control of missiles in flight by on-board computers with navigational procedures and motor drivers, the use of robots that weld on automobile assembly lines exemplify applications where physical work, rather than simply automated cognition, provides much of the useful leverage. Most discrete-entity analyses that link computerization to social action focus on the cognitive elements of information processing; the production side of computing is easily integrated, but points away from cognition and to a world of energetic action and broader defining situations.

[26] The perspective rides on several disparate anchors. Theorems that Turing machines are universal computers and simple mappings from any useful programming language onto Turing machine manipulations serve as a formal anchor. On the other hand, of a wide array of applications from mailing list sorting through story-generation by computers (Meehan, 1979) in which flexible and general symbol manipulation is a central element added by software serve as a practical anchor. The perspective also gains weight through theories of individuals (Newell and Simon, 1972) and organizations (Galbraith, 1977) as task-oriented information-processing systems.

[27] However, shared information is a weak integrating mechanism (Kling, 1978b); information systems may be impossible to implement when they are bound up in fierce intra-organizational conflicts (Albrecht, 1979).

[28] As theoretical terms, 'effectiveness' and 'efficiency' are too abstract; useful categories should help specify particular lines of action.

[29] A second complication comes in predicting whether any of these options will be *systematically* selected so that the wide open world of computing can be seen to have a general drift (Kling and Kraemer, 1982; Kling and Iacono, 1984b). Analyses of social action and work organization must link gains in information processing capabilities to organizational outcomes, since *actual* outcomes matter. In the organizational process models, as in many individualistic models of social action, behavior is driven by unbounded self-aggrandizement. In these models, lines of action are constrained by (1) the limited rationality of participants, (2) underlying conflicts between coalitions with conflicting interests that require satisficing rather than optimizing, and (3) acquiescence to various organizational routines which further constrain likely lines of action. Within such a model, collective behavior would be predicted from the structuring of incentives and organizational routines or by extrapolating from recent history.

[30] An analogy with urban freeways is most graphic: new lanes in downtown arteries don't reduce commuter congestion for long periods of time: if tolerance for a given level of congestion is relatively widespread, many people will increase their travel during times that were otherwise prohibitively congested. The net volume of traffic may increase, while net transit times in the urban core may return to their original levels.

[31] Despite the economic terms, it is not an economic analysis, since substantive social preferences and the range of options participants can actually exercise are critical elements.
[32] This has not been problematic for information-processing psychologists. It is important that much human behavior be captured in information-processing terms, not necessarily reflected in the kinds of information handling recommended by analytical decision theorists (see, for example, Colby (1975) and Feldman and March (1981)).
[33] Certain negotiating contexts will specially reward symbolic action. When one party evaluates the product of another party — as in negotiations between buyers and sellers, auditors and audited — and the quality of the product is difficult to easily ascertain, the evaluator will be encouraged to seek behavioral clues from the producer that are surrogates for product quality. Good records, advanced technical procedures, etc. may be specially salient in industrial or Western bureaucratic settings. (Kinship or local religious affiliation may play a similar role under different cultural conditions.)
[34] An important kind of leverage is that in which computerized technologies are adopted and shaped by management and workers in their contests for control over work (Braverman, 1976; Gregory and Nussbaum, 1982).
[35] See Lucas (1981) for a review.
[36] Thus, the extent to which a.c. power failures lead a computer to be down when it is otherwise expected to be up and running would be evidence for adding the a.c. power system as an infrastructural element.
[37] The larger-scope systems are not necessarily more reliable on a day-to-day basis. The practical reason is that actors who purchase simpler systems may have fewer expert resources to employ in repairing difficulties and may simply have purchased less redundancy. One reason why private purchasers of inexpensive microcomputer systems have difficulty is that they purchase systems with minimal resources and have less margin of error to compensate for failures of hardware or software, and also less substantial vendor support, than do adopters of more expensive systems.
[38] Thus, for example, in 1978 we studied one multi-national engineering firm in which two major divisions maintained their own computer systems, one based on IBM equipment and the other on CDC. The staff in each division developed their own applications and used arguments about hardware incompatibility as a justification to prevent the centralization of computing into one, larger corporate-wide center.
[39] It would be useful to know how much behavior the structural and negotiated perspective orders each account for. Unfortunately, few comparative studies are organized to compare the explanatory power of alternative perspectives. The best studies which examine several competing perspectives simultaneously have begun to ask what kind of behavior does each emphasize and best explain (Allison, 1971; Markus, 1979; Kling, 1980; Kling and Scacchi, 1980, 1982; Scacchi, 1981; Kling and Iacono, 1984b; Koch, 1984).
[40] One exception is a study of the computerization of records systems by the US FBI (Marchand, 1980).
[41] GAO auditors suggest that DoD use modern software development management strategies and set up a life-cycle management system for WWMCCS. While such strategies might be useful for short-term project control, they do not provide an adequately long history for understanding the constraints on WWMCCS development. Software life cycles or stages of implementation define a temporal period which starts with the initiation of a computer-based system. See below for the reasons why this starting point is too recent for developing workable requirements for WWMCCS, or evaluating whether WWMCCS is feasible at all.
[42] This need not always be the case, since several services have cooperated in setting requirements for a new common programming language tailored for military applications (Ada). However, Ada is just becoming operational, and may be used differently by the three military services when it is deployed. Also see Fallows's report of the bizarre case

of a simple flashlight developed in the US Air Force which was expanded to a multipurpose, unwieldy, and unworkable tri-services flashlight (Fallows, 1981, pp. 50–51).

[43] Negotiation contexts are different situations defined by relatively stable participants and issues (Strauss, 1978)

[44] The DCA administers WWMCCS developments and operations.

[45] This claim is speculative. The Congressional actors are also engaged in many other negotiation contexts (e.g. with the President, OMB, various constituents). Their encouraging GAO to report on WWMCCS, and to report in a certain way, may be bound up by strategies and constraints that are defined in these other negotiation contexts. To the extent that Congressional action is part of WWMCCS development, and GAO's nudging reports are part of the Congressional outputs, their character and role is part of the analysis. Constraint C2 returns with a vengeance.

[46] See, for example, Sapolsky's (1972) history of the Polaris missile project.

[47] Standard social research methods texts leave the definition of social and temporal boundaries to the discretion of the analyst: boundaries around social units are to be drawn on theoretical grounds. Thus studies of sampling examine alternative strategies for sampling elements from a socially defined unit, but not strategies for usefully bounding the unit. However, some social scientists have recently become concerned about theoretical strategies for drawing boundaries. Stokols (1983) developed a rationale for defining context similar to our criterion C2. And Wicker (1984) examines the boundaries of behavior settings and social relations within them in ways that parallel this chapter.

[48] These methods are strongly influenced by the qualitative fieldwork strategies developed by symbolic interactionists within American sociology. See especially Glaser and Strauss (1965) and Becker (1960). Studies based on these methods include Kling (1978b), Markus (1979), Scacchi (1981), Gasser (1984), Dutton and Kraemer (forthcoming), and King, Kraemer, Fallows, and Dickhoven (forthcoming).

[49] In these stages, the concerns of scholars and practitioners differ. Practitioners are usually examining the values or problems associated with a particular technology in a particular social setting. Technology and setting are usually selected because the practitioner or his client care about those particular technologies and settings. A school district superintendent who cares about the utility of computer-assisted instruction in high school education will usually care most about the schools in his district and the technologies they now own or can afford to purchase.

[50] The criteria PL1, PL2 and PL3 elaborated earlier provide for an operational strategy for tracing various production lattices.

[51] See Kling and Scacchi (1982, pp. 34–36) for a synopsis.

REFERENCES

Ackoff, Russell (1967) 'Management Misinformation Systems', *Management Science*, **14**, B147-156.

Albrecht, Gary (1979) 'Defusing Technical Change in Juvenile Courts', *Sociology of Work and Occupations*, **6**(3), 259–282.

Allison, Graham (1971) *The Essence of Decision: Explaining the Cuban Missile Crisis*, Little, Brown and Co., Boston, MA.

Alter, Steven (1980) *Decision Support Systems: Current Practice and Continuing Challenges*, Addison-Wesley, Reading, MA.

Attewell, Paul, and Rule, James (1984) 'Computing and Organizations: What We Know and What We Don't Know, *Communications of the ACM*, **27**, 1184–1192.

Becker, Howard S. (1960) 'Notes on the Concept of Commitment', *American Journal of Sociology*, **66**, 32–42.

Becker, Howard S. (1982) *Art Worlds*, University of California Press, Berkeley.

Bikson, Tora K., and Gutek, Barbara (1983) 'Advanced Office Systems: An Empirical Look at Utilization and Satisfaction', Rand Corporation, Santa Monica, CA.

Bikson, Tora, Stasz, Cathleen and Mankin, Donald (1985) *Computer-mediated Work: Individual and Organizational Impact in One Corporate Headquarters* (Report No. R-3308-OTA), Rand Corporation, Santa Monica, CA.

Boland, Richard (1979) 'Control, Causality, and Information Systems Requirements', *Accounting, Organizations, and Society*, **4**(4), 259–272.

Borchardt, Kurt, and LeGates, John (1981) 'Use of Information Resources: The Impact of Change', Program on Information Resources Policy, Harvard University, Cambridge, MA.

Braverman, Harry (1976) *Labor and Monopoly Capital*. Monthly Review Press, New York.

Brewer, Gary (1973) *Politicians, Bureaucrats, and the Consultant: A Critique of Urban Problem-Solving*, Basic Books, New York.

Budnitz, Mark (1983) 'Federal Regulation of Consumer Disputes in Computer Banking Transactions', *Harvard Journal on Legislation*, **20** (1), 31–98.

Burch, John G., Strater, Felix R., and Grudnitski, Gary (1979) *Information Systems: Theory and Practice*, 2nd edn), John Wiley, New York.

Carzo, R., and Yanouzis, J. (1967) *Formal Organization: A Systems Approach*, Irwin-Dorsey Press, Homewood, IL.

Colby, Kenneth (1975) *Artificial Paranoia*.

Colton, Kent (1978) *Police Computer Systems*, Lexington Books, Lexington, MA.

Comptroller General of the United States (1979) 'Database Management Systems — Without Careful Planning There Can be Problems', Report # FGMSD-79-35, US General Accounting Office, Washington, D.C.

Comptroller General of the United States (1980) 'The Navy's Computerized Pay System is Unreliable and Inefficient — What Went Wrong?', Report # FGMSD-80-71, US General Accounting Office, Washington, D.C.

Comptroller General of the United States (1981) 'The World Wide Military Command and Control System — Problems in Information Resource Management', Report # MASAD-82-2, US General Accounting Office, Washington, D.C.

Cortada, James W. (1980) *EDP Costs and Charges: Finance, Budgets, and Cost Control in Data Processing*, Prentice-Hall, Englewood Cliffs, NJ.

Coulam, Robert (1977) *Illusions of Choice: The F-111 and the Problem of Weapons Acquisition*, Princeton University Press, Princeton, NJ.

Cyert, Richard, and March, James (1963) *A Behavioral Theory of the Firm*, Prentice-Hall, Englewood Cliffs, NJ.

Danziger, James (1979) 'The "Skill Bureaucracy" and Intraorganizational Control', *Sociology of Work and Occupations*, **6**, 204–226.

Danziger, James, Dutton, William, Kling, Rob, and Kraemer, Kenneth (1982) *Computers and Politics: High Technology in American Local Governments*, Columbia University Press, New York.

Dery, D. (1981) *Computers in Welfare: The MIS Match*, Sage Publications, Beverly Hills, CA.

Dutton, W. (1981) 'The Rejection of an Innovation: The Political Environment of a Computer-based Model', *Systems, Objectives, Solutions*, **1** (4), 179–202.

Dutton, W. (1983) 'Decision Making in the Information Age: Computer Models and Public Policy', in *Progress in Communication Science*, Vol. 5, Melvin Voight and Brenda Dervin (Eds.), Ablex Publishing Co., Norwood, NJ.

Ein-Dor, Phillip, and Segev, Eli (1978) 'Organizational Context and the Success of Management Information Systems', *Management Science*, **24** (10), 1067–1077.

Elliot, Lance (1981) Personal Communication, U.C. Irvine, March.

Fallows, James (1981) *National Defense*, Random House, New York.

Feldman, Martha, and March, James (1981) 'Information in Organizations as Signal and Symbol', *Admin. Sci. Q.*, **26** (2), 171–186.

Foucault, Michel (1977) *Discipline and Punish: The Birth of the Prison*, Vintage Books, New York.

Galbraith, Jay (1977) *Organization Design*, Addison-Wesley, Reading, MA.

Gasser, Les (1984) Ph.D. dissertation, Department of Information and Computer Science, University of California, Irvine, Irvine, CA.

Gessford, John (1980) *Modern Information Systems*, Addison-Wesley, Reading, MA.

Glaser, Barney, and Strauss, Anselm (1965) *The Discovery of Grounded Theory*, Aldine Publishing Co., Chicago.

Goodman, S. E. (1979) 'Soviet Computing and Technology Transfer: An Overview', *World Politics*, **31**, 539–570.

Gregory, Judith, and Nussbaum, Karen (1982) 'Race against Time: Office Automation of the Office', *Office: Technology and People*, **1** (2 + 3), 197–236.

Hiltz, Roxanne Starr, and Turoff, Murray (1978) *The Network Nation: Human Communication via Computer*, Addison-Wesley, Reading, MA.

Hirschheim, R. A. (1985) *Office Automation: A Social and Organizational Perspective*, John Wiley, New York.

Hirschheim, R. A. (1986) 'The Effect of A-Priori Views on the Social Implications of Computing: The case of Office Automation', *Computing Surveys*, **18**(2).

Hussain, D., and Hussain, K. M. (1981) *Information Processing Systems for Management*, Irwin Dorsey Press, Homewood, IL.

Iacono, S., and Kling, R. (in press) 'Office Technologies and Changes in Clerical Work: A Historical Perspective, in *Technology and the Transformation of White Collar Work*, R. Kraut (Ed.), Lawrence Erlbaum, NJ.

Inbar, M. (1979) *Routine Decision-making: The Future of Bureaucracy*, Sage Publications, Beverly Hills, CA.

Kanter, J. (1977) *Management-oriented Information Systems*, 2nd edn, Prentice-Hall, Englewood Cliffs, NJ.

Keen, Peter, and Scott-Morton, Michael (1978) *Decision-Support Systems: An Organizational Perspective*, Addison-Wesley: Reading, MA.

Kerola, Penti, and Freeman, Peter (1981) 'A Comparison of Life-Cycle Models', *Proc. Fifth International Conference on Software Engineering*, San Diego, CA.

King, John Leslie (1983) 'Successful Implementation of Large-scale Decision Support Systems', *Systems, Objectives, Solutions*, **3** (4), 183–206.

King, John Leslie (1984) 'Ideology and Use of Large-scale Decision Support Systems in National Policymaking', *Systems, Objectives, Solutions*, **4** (2), 81–104.

King, John Leslie, and Kraemer, Kenneth L. (1981a) 'Assessing the Interaction between Computing Policies and Problems', Working paper, University of California, Irvine, Irvine, CA.

King, John Leslie, and Kraemer, Kenneth L. (1981b) 'Cost as a Social Impact of Computing', *Telecommunications and Productivity*, Mitchell Moss (Ed.), Addison-Wesley, Reading, MA.

Kling, Rob (1978a) 'Information Systems and Policymaking: Computer Technology and Organizational Arrangements', *Telecommunications Policy*, **2** 22–32.

Kling, Rob (1978b) 'Automated Welfare Client Tracking and Service Integration: The Political Economy of Computing', *Communications ACM*, **21** (6), 484–493.

Kling, Rob (1978c) 'Value Conflicts and Social Choice in Electronic Fund Transfer System Development', *Communications ACM*, **21**, 642–656.

Kling, Rob (1978d) 'Information Systems as Social Resources in Policy-Making', *Proceedings 1978 National ACM Conf.*, Washington, DC.

Kling, Rob (1980) 'Social Analyses of Computing: Theoretical Perspectives in Recent Empirical Research', *Computing Surveys*, **12** (1), 61–103.

Kling, Rob (1982) 'An Empirical Approach to Studying the Citizen-orientation of Automated Information Systems', *Information Age*, **4** (4), 215–223.

Kling, Rob (in press) 'The New Wave of Academic Computing: Elements of a Social Analysis', *Outlook*.

Kling, Rob, and Dutton, William (1982) 'The Dynamics of the Local Computing Package', in Danziger *et al.*, (1982).

Kling, Rob, and Gerson, Elihu M. (1977) 'The Social Dynamics of Technical Innovation in the Computing World', *Symbolic Interaction*, **1** (1), 132–146.

Kling, Rob, and Gerson, Elihu M. (1978) 'Patterns of Segmentation and Intersection in the Computing World', *Symbolic Interaction*, **1** (2), 24–43.

Kling, Rob, and Iacono, Suzanne (1984a) 'Computing as an Occassion for Social Control, *Journal of Social Issues*, **40** (3), 77–96.

Kling, Rob, and Iaconco, Suzanne (1984b) 'The Control of Information Systems after Implementation', *Communications of the ACM*, **27**, 1218–1226.

Kling, Rob, and Iacono, Suzanne (1986a) 'Printco', in *A Casebook for Management Information Systems*, Henry Lucas (Ed.), McGraw-Hill, New York.

Kling, Rob, and Iacono, Suzanne (1986b) 'Computer Systems as Institutions: Social Dimensions of Computing in Organizations', Working paper, Public Policy Research Organization, University of California, Irvine, CA.

Kling, Rob, and Kraemer, Kenneth (1982) 'Computers and Urban Services', in Danziger *et al.* (1982).

Kling, Rob, and Scacchi, Walt (1979a) 'Recurrent Dilemmas of Computer Use in Complex Organizations', *Proceedings 1979 National Computer Conference*, New York, AFIPS Press, Vol. 48, pp. 107–116.

Kling, Rob, and Scacchi, Walt (1979b) 'The DoD Common High Order Programming Language Effort (DoD-1): What Will the Impacts Be?', *SIGPLAN Notices*, **14** (2), 29–41.

Kling, Rob, and Scacchi, Walt (1980) 'Computing as Social Action: The Social Dynamics of Computing in Complex Organizations', *Advances in Computers*, Vol. 19, Academic Press, New York.

Kling, Rob, and Scacchi, Walt (1982) 'The Web of Computing: Computing Technology as Social Organization', *Advances in Computers*, Vol. 21, Academic Press, New York.

Koch, Susan (1984) 'The Negotiated Order of Computer Implementation Planning', Unpublished Ph.D. thesis, University of Texas, Austin, Texas.

Kochar, A. K. (1979) *Development of Computer-based Production Systems*, Edward Arnold, London.

Kraemer, Kenneth L., and King, John Leslie (1981a) 'Comparative Study of Computing Policies and Impacts in Cities', Unpublished manuscript, PPRO, University of California, Irvine, Irvine, CA.

Kraemer, Kenneth L., and King, John Leslie (1981b) 'Computer Technology in Local Governments in the 1980's: A U.S. Forecast', *International Review of Administrative Sciences*, **XLVII** (2), 155–125.

Laudon, Kenneth (1974) *Computers and Bureaucratic Reform*, Wiley–Interscience, New York.

Laudon, Kenneth (1980) 'Privacy and Federal Data Banks', *Society*, **17** (2), 50–56.

Laudon, Kenneth (1986) *The Dossier Society*, Columbia University Press, New York.

Levin, Melvin, R., and Norman, A. Abend (1971) *Bureaucrats in Transition: Case Studies in Area Transportation Planning*, MIT Press, Cambridge, MA.

Lofland, John (1976) *Doing Social Life*, John Wiley, New York.

Long, Norton (1958) 'The Community as an Econology of Games', *American J. of Sociology*, **LXIV**, November, 251–261.

Lucas, Henry C. (1981) *Implementation: The Key to Successful Information Systems*, Columbia University Press, New York.

Lukes, Stephen (1974) *Power: A Radical View*, Macmillan, London.

McHenry, William (1985) 'The Absorption of Computerized Management Information Systems in Soviet Enterprises', Ph.D. dissertation, School of Business and Public Administration, University of Arizona, Tucson, Arizona.

Mader, C., with Hagin, R. (1974) *Information Systems: Technology, Economics, and Applications*, Science Research Associates, Palo Alto, CA.

March, James G., and Olsen, Johan P. (1979) *Ambiguity and Choice in Organizations* 2nd edn, Universitetsforleget, Bergen, Norway.

Marchand, Donald (1980) *NCIC Chronology*, University of South Carolina, Charleston, SC.

Markus, M. L. (1979) 'Understanding Information System Use in Organizations: A Theoretical Explanation', Ph.D. dissertation, Department of Organizational Behavior, Case Western Reserve University, Cleveland, OH.

Markus, M. L. (1981) 'Implementation Politics: Top Management Support and User Involvement', *Systems, Objectives, Solutions*, **1** (4), 203–215.

Meehan, James (1979) *Talespin*, Greenwood Press, Greenwich, CT.

Mosher, Frederick (1979) *The GAO: The Quest for Accountability in American Government*, Westview Press, Boulder, CO.

Mumford, Enid, and Pettigrew, Andrew M. (1976) *Implementing Strategic Decisions*, Longman, New York.

Newell, Alan, and Simon, Herbert (1972) *Human Problem Solving*, Prentice-Hall, Englewood Cliffs, NJ.

OTA (Office of Technology Assessment) (1982) 'Implications of Electronic Mail and Message Systems for the U.S. Postal Service', US Government Printing Office, Washington, D.C.

Perry, James, and Danziger, James (1980) 'The Adoptability of Innovations', *Administration and Society*, **11** (4), 461–492.

Pettigrew, Andrew (1973) *The Politics of Organizational Decision-making*, Tavistock, London.

Pfeffer, Jeffrey (1982) *Organizations and Organization Theory*, Pitman Publishing Inc., Boston.

Pfeffer, Jeffrey, and Salancik, Gerald (1978) *The External Control of Organizations: A Resource Dependence Perspective*, Harper & Row, New York.

Poppel, Harvey (1982) 'Who Needs the Office of the Future?', *Harvard Business Review*, **60** (6), 146–155.

Poster, Mark (1984) *Foucault, Marxism, and History: Mode of Production versus Mode of Information*, Polity Press, Oxford, England.

Sapolsky, Harvey (1972) *The Polaris System Development*, Harvard University Press, Cambridge, MA.

Scacchi, Walt (1981) 'The Process of Innovation in Computing: A Study of the Social Dynamics of Computing', Ph.D. dissertation, Department of Information and Computer Science, University of California, Irvine, Irvine, CA.

Simon, Herbert A. (1973) 'Applying Information Technology to Organizational Design', *Public Administrative Review*, **33**, 268–278.

Simon, Herbert A. (1977) *The New Science of Management Decision*, Prentice-Hall, Englewood Cliffs, NJ.

Steinbruner, John (1974) *The Cybernetic Theory of Decision: New Dimensions of Political Analysis*, Princeton University Press, Princeton, NJ.

Sterling, Theodore D. (1979) 'Consumer Difficulties with Computerized Transactions: An Empirical Analysis', *Communications ACM*, **22** (5), 283–289.

Sterling, Theodore D. (1980) 'Computer Ombudsman', *Society*, **17** (2), 31–35.

Stokols, Daniel (1983) 'Scientific and Policy Challenges of a Contextually-oriented Psychology', Unpublished manuscript, Program on Social Ecology, University of California, Irvine, Irvine, CA.

Strassman, Paul (1985) *Information Payoff*, The Free Press, New York.

Strauss, Anselm (1978) *Negotiations: Varieties, Contexts, Processes, and Social Order*, Jossey-Bass, San Francisco, CA.

Streeter, Donald (1974) *The Scientific Process and the Computer* (Chapter 2D), John Wiley, New York.

Taggart, William, M., Jr. (1980) *Information Systems: An Introduction to Computers in Organizations*, Allyn & Bacon, Boston, MA.

Taylor, Stephen P. (1983) 'The Use of Decision Support Systems in Complex Organizations', Master's thesis, Department of Information and Computer Science, University of California, Irvine, Irvine, CA.

Turner, Jon (1981) 'The Use of Organizational Models in Information Systems Research and Practice', Working paper GBA-81-21, Graduate School of Business Administration, New York University, New York.

Turner, Jon (1984) 'Computer Mediated Work: The Interplay between Technology and Structured Jobs-claims Representatives in the Social Security Administration', *Communications of the ACM*, **27** (12).

Wicker, Alan (1984) 'Behavior Settings Reconsidered: Temporal Stages, Resources, Internal Dynamics, Context', in *Handbook of Environmental Psychology*, Daniel Stokols and Irwin Altman (Eds.), John Wiley, New York.

Wise, K., Chen, K., and Yokely R. (1980) *Microcomputers: A Technology Forecast and Assessment to the Year 2000*, Wiley–Interscience, New York.

Withington, Frederick G. (1979) *The Environment for Systems Programs*, Addison-Wesley, Reading, MA.

Witt, Richard R. (1985) 'The Politics of Implementing an Advanced Office Automation System', Master's thesis, Department of Information and Computer Science, University of California, Irvine, Irvine, CA.

Zuboff, Shoshannah (1982) 'New Worlds of Computer-mediated Work', *Harvard Business Review*, **60** (5), 142–152.

Critical Issues in Information Systems Research
Edited by R. J. Boland Jr. and R. A. Hirschheim
© 1987 John Wiley & Sons Ltd.

Chapter 14

THE IN-FORMATION OF INFORMATION SYSTEMS

Richard J. Boland, Jr.

ABSTRACT

We all know that information is the meaning or inward-forming of a person that results from an engagement with data. Yet, we consistently avoid the problem of meaning in our information systems research and practice, assuming information to be structured data instead of meaning. This chapter explores the metaphors and images inspired by Herbert Simon that we use to justify this substitution, and five misguided fantasies about information that result from them. In addition to the fantasy that information is structured data, we fantasize that an organization is information, that information is power, that information is intelligence, and that information is perfectable. These fantasies lead us to ignore the fundamental nature of interpersonal dialogue in the achievement of meaning, and reduce our ability to design humanly satisfying systems. The chapter argues for our ethical obligation to reject these fantasies, if the historically bound, sense-making, human subject is to be respected by the research and practice of information systems.

1. INTRODUCTION

This chapter addresses a problem that has plagued research on information systems since the very beginning. The problem is the elusive nature of information itself, and the way we as researchers have failed to address the essence of information in our work. The essence of information is revealed to us in its name. Information is an inward-forming. It is the change in a person from an encounter with data. It is a change in the knowledge, beliefs, values or behavior of that person. The in-forming could be part of a general 'sense-making' process and be found in the distinctive way a person has come to understand the world, or it could be the way a particular situation has come to be defined. In any case, the inward-forming that is the proper and ultimate interest of information systems research is not readily available for observation. Data in the form of reports, graphs, models or inquiry responses, on the other hand, are readily available. But data is not information.

Information systems researchers have known this from the very beginning. Claude Shannon made it clear that he was not talking about meaning in his theory of communication, and Norbert Weiner also reminded us of the limits of his cybernetics when it came to the problem of human meaning. Both made it clear they were talking about data, not information. Yet, despite those initial warnings, we as researchers have consistently confused the two: treating the mere structured data that happens to be so readily available in information systems as if it were information. As a result, the process of inward-forming which is critical to the effectiveness of information systems, has been excluded from our efforts to analyze, design, implement and evaluate them. This is a curious situation. We all know what information is and what it is not, yet we all deal in our research with what it is not, rather than with what it is. This chapter asks why that should be so.

At one level, the question of why can be answered with the rather standard set of excuses used in many information systems text books, including my own (Tricker and Boland, 1982). Those excuses center on the subjective nature of the 'real' phenomenon of interest to us, and the idiosyncratic way that individuals derive meaning from the data available through an information system. Faced with a hidden and personal 'reality' that requires the rather intensive research strategies of symbolic interactionism (Blumer, 1969; Boland, 1979), or other interpretive approaches to understanding the inward-forming process (Bernstein, 1976; Geertz, 1973; Berger and Luckman, 1967; Boland, 1985), researchers have opted to use 'structured data' as a surrogate for their true interest, information. The researcher must then assume that the users of data systems employ a standard and shared set of interpretive structures to gain meaning from the data. Thus, the problem of meaning is sidestepped and relegated to the status of a mediating variable — a filter whose impact on the transformation from data to meaning can be put aside for the moment. In-formation becomes a constant awaiting future research efforts.

What's so wrong with that? It sounds like a perfectly reasonable and practical strategy when confronted by the stumbling block of meaning. What harm can come of it? Most likely there *is* a widely shared set of interpretive structures that users employ to derive information out of data. Of course, the critical theorists might not like that answer, and might argue that the shared, taken-for-granted interpretive structures we use cannot be dismissed that way. They would argue that those interpretive structures are of central importance and reveal much about the forms of legitimation and modes of domination in our society. Only if we are content to be the willing dupes of an oppressive regime could we simply accept the taken-for-granted interpretive structures as a mere given, a harmless constant. But that is not an argument we will pursue here, even though it deserves, and is beginning to receive, careful attention.

Instead, this chapter is concerned with the imagery that is used to justify and sustain the avoidance of in-formation, and the consequences of that imagery for our ability to locate and think about information systems in the larger scheme of human affairs. In fact, this chapter will argue that the images and metaphors we use to think about information without in-formation, distorts our very ability to think about the larger world of human affairs. This is because we have allowed an image of information without in-formation to become the central, defining image of the modern world.

2. *IMAGES OF INFORMATION WITHOUT IN-FORMATION* [1]

Our images of information affect the way we are able to think about the world we live in, because today we define the world in terms of information and information processing. Our place in history, our economy, our political processes, and our hopes for the future are all cast in terms of information. We have named the age in which we live as the *Information Age*, We are reconceiving our ideas on the nature of work to better fit our images of the *Information Economy*. We speak as if computers, telecommunications, and data storage devices hold the promise of the future. They are the basis of our latest thinking on corporate strategy. Information technology is the hope of the professions from medicine to law, and of enterprise from agriculture to manufacturing. This technology will make it possible to heal the sick, feed the hungry, produce the goods, and ensure the future of our freedoms.

Industry, politics, science, education, and the professions are all coming to be understood through an information image. They are all decision-making processes whose quality depends on the data and programs of information systems. We talk about the world as if improvements in the quality of information systems will improve the quality of decision making in each of these sectors of human concern, and therefore improve the quality of our social world. Information systems are the hope of the new social order.

Information technology is seen as an all-purpose technology; information is the common denominator that can bring matter, energy and time into a single, unified framework of analysis. All matter-energy transformations are change of state information and can be represented with a string of bits. Bits of information are thus seen as the primary building blocks of the physical and social world. Through bits, all physical and social processes can be known. The computer is the most powerful processor of bits. Its ability to analyze is bounded only by the speed of light, and its reach is expanding at an accelerating rate. We talk and act as if computers and other information technologies are the defining elements in the type of current and future world that is possible.

This central role for information technology in the images of the modern world is attractive, but insidious. It is attractive because it promises to locate the information systems professional in the highest levels of policy making, management, and control. It is insidious because its images of information without in-formation deny the importance of an intentional human community based on interpersonal dialogue and the search for meaning. Instead, we are fostering an image of the world in which the human meaning of knowledge and action are unproblematic, predefined, and prepackaged. The human being is not a necessary element in the *Information Age*.

Am I just being sentimental and raising the often repeated call to 'put the human being back into human systems'? Not at all. The problem is more fundamental than that. It rests on an understanding of what the social world is, and how far we can go in distorting our images of it for the expediency of 'getting on with the work at hand', before our images fail to make any sense at all, and result in such gross misperceptions of the social world that our ability to think clearly about it is lost. At issue is the nature of language and human communication, and their role in our social construction of the everyday world. The problem that concerns us here is the way our images of information without in-formation lead to an ignorance of language and our human search for meaning which together deny the very possibility of human communication. The process of constructing the social world is a process of language and communication. Our distorted images of information and communication, and their widespread use to understand our everyday world, threaten our ability to construct and reconstruct it in humanly satisfying ways.

Language is symbolic action, through which we search for meaning in the world. There is no simple one-for-one mapping between words in a language and objects or conditions in the world. Words are symbols and meanings are always multiple and ambiguous. Meanings are found through our lived experience of being in the world. In fact, there is no possibility for gaining meaning from words apart from our active involvement in day-to-day living (Wittgenstein, 1974; Stamper, Chapter 2 in this volume). The search for meaning is a continuous search that is never completely or finally realized. Meaning is always in doubt and needs to be reaccomplished. It is always about to slip from our grasp.

It is through dialogue that we accomplish and reaccomplish meaning, and thus bring order to the social world. Through dialogue we name objects and give them significance. Our norms of social interaction and our basis for defining social reality are constituted by language practice. It is through dialogue that the symbolic order of our shared social world is made real. Through dialogue we tell each other what is important and why. We search for the purpose, significance and meaning of our institutions and ourselves that is the social order, through our everyday interpersonal dialogue. Images of information that ignore the problem of meaning and diminish our attention to the quality of dialogue our systems support, negatively affect the possibilities for our social construction of reality.

In the balance of this chapter, I will explore in greater detail the nature of five mistaken images of information without in-formation that structure our serious thinking about the design of information systems. The objective is to challenge information system professionals to be accountable for the logic that guides their system designs and to begin a search for images that better serve the public interest. Images of information that deny the importance of symbolic action, language practice and interpersonal dialogue are a professional disservice. They are misguided fantasies that may inspire allegiance, but they divert our attention from the quality of dialogue and communication that creates our everyday world.

3. *IMAGES AND THE TWO FACES OF FANTASY*

Fantasies are strong, imaginative devices that powerfully shape the images (Boulding, 1956) that are so central to the way we impose order and give meaning to the world. Fantasies do not picture a reality, but suggest a possibility. They suggest another place, another time, another world. Yet, they deal with something important about the world and how we should approach it. Fantasies do not provide an immediate guide to action. Instead, they provide a symbolic image that helps us orient ourselves toward the world and structure our search for meaning in it (Bettelheim, 1975). Fantasies have two faces: a productively imaginative one, and an erroneous, self-deluding one.

One face of fantasy gives us an image that is an inventive, creative leap. It brings coherence to disparate events, makes the world sensible, and provides theories to guide inquiry. This is the side of fantasy we refer to as productive imagination. When Kekulé sat before his fire half-asleep and dreamed of a snake coiling and biting its own tail, his fantasy allowed him to 'see' the benzene ring. Arthur Koestler (1964) called this juxtaposition of incongruous elements to gain new insights into a problem as the essence of creativity, and argued that its structure is the same as that of humor. Koestler saw this form of productive fantasy as the process underlying all creative human thought. From Watson and Crick's image of the double helix, to Picasso's *Guernica*, we see the natural and social sciences as well as the arts being informed by productive fantasies. Even in the day-to-day practice of the sciences and the professions we can see the fundamental importance of fantasy in the creative acts of generating hypotheses, interpreting data and designing experiments.

The other face of fantasy gives us images that are simply mistaken. They are not only unreal but also false and not suited for guiding serious thought. The images produced by this face of fantasy are the works of fools. The creative force that has the structure of humor is absent and the results are mere folly. No useful insights come from this face of fantasy, only delusion, unfounded speculation and error. In the world of commerce, almost all advertising displays this second face of fantasy. The images they present suggest that drinking alcohol and smoking cigarettes is beautiful, sexy, athletic and sophisticated; that everything from automobiles to hair shampoo will make you desirable to the opposite sex, and in general that consuming products makes your life significant.

The first, productive fact of fantasy gives insight by anticipating an understandable pattern that can be applied to the world or to our experience. It is the source of paradigms. The second, purely fanciful face gives us images that may have great appeal but are misguided, unsound and potentially dangerous as a basis for action. Both faces of fantasy yield powerful images that can mobilize others to follow as true believers. Whether a fantasy has a truth value in that it results in productive, humanly satisfying outcomes, or whether a fantasy is false in that it results in destructive, humanly unsatisfying outcomes is always problematic. But this is all the more reason to be relentless in our criticism of the taken-for-granted fantasies that guide information system research and information system design.

4. FANTASY AND METAPHOR IN INFORMATION SYSTEMS

Information technology is involved in some of the most popular fantasies of our time. They are found in the metaphors we use to help us understand the nature of information as well as the way we use information itself as a metaphor for some of the central aspects of the social world. I argue that although the first, productive face of fantasy can be seen in some of these images of information, we are altogether too willing to see them as insightful, profound and paradigmatic when, in fact, they are pretentious and self-deluding.

Overarching all the fantasies of information I will discuss is the work of Herbert A. Simon. His influence on the imagery we use to identify and think seriously about information processing is almost universal. It influences the mode of discourse used within cognitive psychology, computer science and organization studies, among others. Simon's basic line of imagery was established in 1947 by his *Administrative Behavior* and has been elaborated by him and a wide range of others since then. His ideas are rich and important, and I will attempt to summarize his core imagery below.

The major line of Simon's imagery that concerns us derives from a chain of metaphors that runs throughout his work [2]. The chain starts with the metaphor: *organizations are decisions*. This provides an initial orientation toward organizations that allows them to be decomposed into a series of hierarchically structured decisions. To study organizations is to study decisions. Decisions, in turn, are understood as a series of intelligence, design and choice activities. If we want to understand organizations, we must understand these decision processes.

The second metaphor in the chain pictures decision making as the movement through a 'problem space': *decisions are journeys through space*. The image of a journey through space allows us to create an *entity* out of the amorphous notion of a problem. A space can be bounded, as indeed Simon proposes rational decision processes to be. The space Simon gives us is a flat, two-dimensional space. It is a table upon which the problem is displayed. Units of information (be they facts or alternatives) are localized sub-entities in the problem space; nodes in a network that covers the tabletop.

A third metaphor in the chain is: *decisions are rules for moving through a problem space*. Decision makers move from node to node through the problem space using a calculus of algorithms or heuristics. Each node of information is a premise applied to data. Each move is intended to reduce the distance between the solution of the problem (the goal) and the present location in the problem space. This imagery transforms decision making and therefore organizations to a series of procedures and allows organizational discourse to speak at length on the technology of decision-making moves as if they were the essence of organizations.

This chain of metaphors is an important, productive fantasy for thinking about information processing phenomena. It transforms a problem into an object, an entity we can locate in space and time and manipulate in simple, familiar ways. It also proposes an interchangeability among other entified phenomena such as organization, decision, and information.

Over time, the productive fantasy of Simon's metaphorical complex has become our taken-for-granted way of thinking about organizations, decisions and information. Along the way, it has collapsed into the second face of fantasy as his basic vision was extended into the realm of organizational control. He proposes that individual decision makers are 'informed' by data when they conjoin data with a decision premise as a basis for action. Since a decision premise has been metaphorically entified by locating it as a part of each node in a decision space, it can be handled, moved and manipulated like any other object. Organizational control is therefore to be achieved by differentially distributing two objects, data and decision premises, to various organizational members within the organizational space [3]. The organization itself, through the decision making of individual members, is thus transformed into a calculating machine and organization control becomes the science of designing its calculative procedures. By manipulating data and decision premises, we can create information at will.

Though Simon himself adds contradictory images in his later writings [4], his core image of information processing is the root for the five major information fantasies I will discuss below. These five fantasies are part of our everyday working assumptions when thinking about information systems in organizations. I will argue that these five are from the second face of fantasy and that they are false and present a distorted and unfounded view of language, communication and the importance of dialogue in the creation of meaning.

5. FIVE FANTASIES OF INFORMATION

The five fantasies identified below are presented in a sequence that traces the progressive removal of the human actor from our consideration as she struggles to make sense of the world and produce its social reality through dialogue. To preview the argument, we first fantasize that *information is structured data*. This is the basic fantasy on which the others build. It allows us to ignore the universal hermeneutic problem of interpretation and to see information as an object, or as I will argue, an entity. The second fantasy, that *an organization is information* is an extension of Simon's work that allows system designers to believe they can orchestrate organizational life through the manipulation of structured data. It also emphasizes a particularly rationalistic way of characterizing organizational life as goal-driven and purposive which further legitimates ignoring the individual actor's need to interpret and make sense of organizational situations.

A third fantasy, that *information is power* glorifies the role of the designer as an allocator of power, but most importantly, it distorts the idea of power relationships. This fantasy reduces power from an interactive, relational phenomenon to a commodity that operates uni-directionally. Thus, both information and power are transformed into entities to be manipulated by the system designer, and the active role of the individual is further reduced. A fourth fantasy, that *information is intelligence* links the information systems field to a branch of cognitive science in which mind is disembodied. The result is the complete removal of human beings and their problems of action and sense-making from the domain of information systems discourse.

The fifth fantasy, that information *is perfectable*, is the culmination of this progressive sequence. Through the use of an economics of information, we fantasize the existence of a perfect, 'true' future to which system designers have special access and in light of which their systems will be evaluated. Whereas the previous fantasies removed human beings and their problems of action and interpretation from consideration, this final fantasy removes the concrete historical moment of the situation from consideration and defines system design in terms of a timeless, context-free, ideal future.

The result of these fantasies is to effectively remove the human problems of action and meaning from our dialogue on information systems, and to propagate an object-oriented approach to our research. This is doomed to failure, because information is not a thing, it is a skilled human accomplishment (Giddens, 1979). Information is not structured data. It is not an object that can be manipulated to design organizations. It is not an object that possesses intelligence. It neither gives nor brings power, and it is not perfectable. Information is found in the lived experience of the human condition and the fantasies which delude us into looking elsewhere will only lead us to search in vain.

Each of the fantasies and their progressive establishment of a distorted program of research in information systems are further developed below.

5.1 Fantasy # 1: Information is Structured Data

This is perhaps the most pernicious of the information fantasies because it undermines the possibility for taking the problem of language seriously and it makes it possible to begin the study of techniques for managing human communication through the structuring of data. This fantasy is derived from Simon's image of a decision as a predictable outcome of the conjunction of data and premises. Even though our information system texts are willing to acknowledge that information is really the *meaning* of data to a free, intentional human being, they quickly dismiss the possibility of a science of such meanings, and move on to a 'serious' discussion using the substitute assumption that information can be treated 'as if' it were structured data. A typical example of this procedure is provided by Schoderbek *et al.* (1980).

The substitution of 'structured data' for 'meaning' in the discourse on information allows us to legitimize discussion and theory building on organizational processes by imposing stereotypical, rationalistic versions of meaning, values and significance on the actors (Boland, 1979).

Scientism is the fallacy that the methods normally associated with the 'hard', natural sciences are the *only* methods for attaining valid knowledge and that any area of human concern can be approached with these methods. We will see how the five fantasies collectively make scientism possible in organizational analysis and information system design. It will be argued that we have an ethical responsibility to reject these fantasies and the scientism they promote. Scientism requires the fantasy that information is structured data. Without it, we lose the ability to apply the methods of 'hard' science to human affairs. 'Meaning' is not publicly observable or reproducible as 'structured data' purports to be, hence without this fantasy, a science on the model of physics, as popularly conceived, would not be possible. Unfortunately, by fantasizing that information is structured data, we deny the importance of dialogue as the basis for all human understanding. By taking structured data seriously as a substitute for information we deny the universal hermeneutic problem that we all continuously confront: the problem of engaging in dialogue in order to gain understanding and make sense of the world.

Hermeneutics has its origin in the search for reliable methods to interpret religious texts, especially the Bible. In biblical interpretation, we are presented with a text whose author, culture and language are alien to us, yet we believe the text has important meaning and we are willing to work hard to understand it. Gadamer (1976, 1984) helps us see that the problem of hermeneutics in biblical interpretation is one that applies to our everyday life. The world we confront everyday is an alien world; it was written, spoken and structured in an historical process no less distant from us, by authors no less unfamiliar, with a meaning no less important to understand. The world-as-a-text speaks to us through tradition. Our tradition is a prejudice, certainly, but it is also necessary as the way we are able to be open to the world and able to gain meaning from it. The prejudice of tradition is necessary if we are to begin the hermeneutic process of interpreting the world-as-a-text and our place in it.

Our tradition and our language and hence the understanding we are able to have of the world-as-a-text is fundamentally historical. Tradition, language and our ability to interpret and gain meaning in the world are always specific to a concrete moment in time. There is no single, stable, immutable meaning, as the fantasy of structured data would suggest. Meanings are always multiple and ambiguous, and understanding must continuously by struggled for, and must always be won anew. The universal hermeneutic problem of interpreting the world we confront as well as create is a continuous achievement; a perpetual challenge.

5.2 Fantasy # 2: An Organization is Information

This fantasy is directly derived from Simon's image of organization control as the differential distribution of information and decision premises. It extends the fantasy that information is structured data and applies it to the entire organization. It turns the organization as a whole into structured data. In so doing, the pretense of substituting 'structured data' for 'meaning' at the level of the individual person is carried to the level of interpersonal relations. As a result, the very ground for dialogue in the social setting of an organization is negated.

Jay Galbraith's *Organization Design* (1977), which draws on Simon's core imagery, was perhaps the first full treatise based on this fantasy, though it is now widely adopted in organization theory and management information systems. With this imagery, the process of interpersonal dialogue and historically situated language use, as a medium for making sense of organizational actions, events and objects, is replaced with a network of probabilistically determinate relations. The very real and continuous human problem of accomplishing meaning is replaced by a technology of packaging data.

Together, the first two fantasies allow the fallacy of scientism to guide a discourse on the way management scientists, and especially information system designers, can orchestrate organizational life through intervention in the formal structuring of data. These two fantasies join to allow management scientists to develop elaborate and subtle theories that penetrate to the individual psyche and incorporate details of motivation, cognitive style and utility preferences into their schemes of organization design and control.

This second fantasy perpetuates a fundamental confusion in the relation of order and action that is associated with scientism and compulsive rationalist imagery in general. This is the misconception that order in the form of theory, knowledge or coherent intention necessarily precedes action. This sequence of ordered knowledge followed by action is essential for the official accounts of natural science. Unless a theory has yielded an hypothesis for testing, and unless an experiment has been designed to disconfirm the null hypothesis, you do not have a 'science'. Karl Weick (1979) drawing especially on Alfred Schutz (1967) has discredited this notion of the priority of an ordered purpose, and argued persuasively for the priority of action and the retrospective nature of almost all understanding of action as purpose (Boland, 1984). Yet, this confusion persists.

I suggest that its persistence is tied to the scientistic perspective of management scientists and information system consultants. Acceptance of the retrospective, interpretive nature of knowledge in the social world would allow too much control in the hands of the actors themselves. It would give the actors a freedom that would reduce a system designer's ability to claim the special expertise of a science of structured data. That expertise, that knowledge of social process, is important to what they sell as a consulting service.

5.3 Fantasy # 3: Information is Power

This fantasy has a long heritage, especially in political writings and a classic summary of the insights to be gained from it is provided by Machiavelli's *The*

Prince. More recently, the work of Pettigrew (1973) and Pfeffer and Salancik (1978) explore this imagery with respect to organizations and information systems. The error with this fantasy comes as it goes beyond the awareness of a relationship between information and power, and joins with the first two fantasies to further inflate the scientistic promise of order by the information system designer. The fantasy that information is power puts the management scientist as system designer in the special position of designing a system of power, not just a system of data. It inflates the role of the system designer to include the creation and reallocation of power. Thus, this fantasy is a flattery to the designers of information systems.

It is also an important element in expanding the scope of effect promised by systems design. Elaborating the reach, functions and level of detail of an information system is not so much a risk of failure through excessive and unmanageable complexity as it is claim to importance through an increased grasp of power. The more information that is formalized, captured and processed, the more power that is possessed. The more hierarchically structured the information system, the greater the power commanded by the top of the hierarchy which has hired the information system designers.

The fallacy with this fantasy of equating information as 'structured data' with power is its further assault on our ability to take seriously the way that language and dialogue constitute organizational process. This is because the image of information as power is a one-sided image of a one-way relationship. The control of structured data by superiors erroneously denies the duality of power relationships that follows from the necessity of dialogue by organizational actors, as they interpret and try to understand their organizational world. Anthony Giddens (1979) helps us to see this duality of power in which each party to a relationship, be they superior, subordinate or lateral, has access to power over the relationship. Crossier's classic study of bureaucracy in a French factory, especially the control exercised by machine maintenance, is testimony to Gidden's discussion of the duality of power.

Just as the fantasy that information is structured data allowed information to be entified, so the fantasy that information is power allows power to be entified. Power now has a location. It can be molded, shaped, redistributed and possessed as if it were a three-dimensional object. But power is not an entity. Properly understood, power is a relationship, not an object. The dynamics of power are dialectic and found in human interaction. Power does not emanate from some location, but like meaning, is produced and reproduced through action and sense-making dialogue. Thus, this fantasy supports a further separation of information systems from the responsible, hermeneutically involved actor.

5.4 Fantasy # 4: Information is Intelligence

This fantasy is the major image that has been pursued by Simon since the publication of *Administrative Behavior*. In successive editions of *The Sciences of the*

Artificial (1981) and especially *The New Science of Management Decision* (1977) Simon has explored the promise that information as structured data and the computer as a technology for moving through a problem space equals intelligence. Each edition promises the almost complete duplication of human intelligence 'within a decade'. The moving horizon of promised results keeps the image forever young.

The issue is not whether Simon's unbridled optimism is in some sense justified, nor to what extent 'machine intelligence' can be achieved. The issue is the scientistically inspired position that human intelligence is represented by the DONALD + ROBERT = GERALD puzzle solving procedures of Simon's journey through a problem space. The error, again, is the entification of intelligence, localizing and transforming intelligence into an object, making intelligence into a 'thing' subject to the creation of the designer. Intelligence is a relationship of sense-making between an entity and the world. In the Turing test, intelligence is not an object contained or localized in a machine, it is the behavior of the machine in dialogue.

If there were an adequate machine intelligence, it would be recognized when the machine engaged in dialogue with human beings. If the machine had some 'thing' of intelligence to share, it would be found in dialogue, through language, as but one historical moment in the universal hermeneutic problem of mankind. Machine intelligence, like man's understanding of himself, would forever have to be reaccomplished through the human community that defines it to be so. The fantasy that information is intelligence, like the first three, continues to expand the fallacy of scientism. Now we reach beyond communication, beyond control and beyond power into the realm of the organization as designable mind. The fallacy that intelligence is an object, a refined example of structured data, is especially insidious because it provides the further and now complete separation of information from the human agent. In the previous three fantasies, the human being, docile and determined, was at least present. This fantasy allows the organization to be totally disembodied.

There is no need to even consider the relation of human action to knowledge, as the actor is no longer an element in the discourse. Whether knowledge precedes action or action precedes knowledge becomes an irrelevant distinction. Intelligence just is. Like a book or a chair, it can be designed, manipulated, presented, or taken away. That the social world is constituted by language and dialogue, and that the hermeneutic problem is universal and continuous are no longer even possible to discuss. The scientistic claim of the system designer is nearly complete. All that is required is fantasy number five.

5.5 Fantasy # 5: Information is Perfectable

This fantasy is the basis for uniting economics with information system design and transforming the problem of design itself into an economic choice activity. Demski's *Information Analysis* (1980) is a popular exposition of the way the information system choice problem has been developed as an information economics. Briefly put, the information value of any data is measured in relation to its maximum possible value for the decision maker. The maximum possible value is the location in the decision space that would be reached with perfect information. Thus, the value of any information system is calculated as how close it comes in the decision space to where perfect information would lead.

The fallacy we are concerned with here does not have to do with the numerous conceptual problems of information economics. The fallacy of interest is the concept of perfectability itself. As summarized by Demski, perfect information is knowledge of a future 'state' in the problem space that is complete and error-free. The future state and our knowledge of it holds true regardless of our subsequent action. Perfect information thus allows us to choose optimal actions, and serves as a standard against which any particular information system can be judged in cost-effectiveness terms.

What is necessary in order for perfect information to be possible? For one thing, it requires that we *can* have 'complete and error-free' knowledge of a situation (be it in the present, future or past). If this were possible, the hermeneutic problem is dispensed with. The essential ambiguity of any situation and the need to interpret meaning is no longer a fundamental, universal problem. It is a closed issue. In order to accomplish this, the world of 'perfect information' must be outside of history. Any situation is located in the flow of time with webs of connection to myriad past and future events, and that makes the meaning of any specific situation an interpretive problem that cannot be ignored by assuming the possibility of 'perfect information'.

It is now over two decades since the assassination of John F. Kennedy and we are still in the process of making new interpretations of it. It is now over one decade since the 'oil crisis' and our understanding of what it was and what it means is still unclear. These are but two examples. The point is that any situation, because it is located in an historic matrix, will always be open to interpretation and reinterpretation. Like a good book or poem, the world has no single, immutable meaning, which the possibility of perfect information requires.

The question is, what kind of world must we be talking about to take the idea of perfect information seriously? What does the notion of perfectability require us to believe about the world? I can only assume that Demski and others must, deep down, be harboring images of a platonic form behind the notion of a 'state of nature'. Perfect information is a description of the 'true form' of nature — an unattainable, transcendental ideal against which all real 'states of nature' are imperfect realizations — much like the notion of an ideal oak tree of which all existing oaks are flawed copies!

I have no quarrel with neoplatonism as such, but I do object to the way the fantasy of the perfectability of information further glorifies the use of scientism in information system design. Through this fantasy, system designers base their expertise on their knowledge of these perfect forms, which transcend human interaction and exist apart from any specific historical moment.

With fantasy number four, the human actor was removed from the stage, and with the perfectability of information, time itself is removed from consideration. Not only can we ignore the presence of actors whose dialogue is necessary for developing an interpretation of the world, but we can also ignore the historical nature of the social world — ignore the fact that social life takes place in concrete historical moments of space and time.

The scientism used to approach the question of designing information systems is now complete. Knowledge of the social world has been totally transformed into an object and allowed to float free under the complete command of the information system designer. Information as an entified object is now purified and homogenized into a commodity, a familiar resource, or as Demski puts it, '. . . a factor of production' (1980, p. 35). The human community which alone, through dialogue, can create the socially relative images of perfection or imperfection has been totally denied. As opposed to the hermeneutic problem of continually accomplishing and reaccomplishing meaning, we are given a single, immutable meaning — without an actor, without a history, without a future.

6. SUMMARY AND IMPLICATIONS

Of what consequence are these fantasies for information systems research? What difference does it make if they are in some sense inaccurate? We all use metaphors and images to bring order to our perceptions and actions, and these particular images of information seem to have worked. We are designing and installing computer-based information systems in all sorts of organizations all over the world. Granted, they seldom deliver the economic benefits we promise when we sell them, but they don't create an obvious harm in organizations, and most importantly, managements pay for them — if what we did was so bad, they wouldn't spend good money on it.

These types of arguments are used by systems professionals and others in the management consulting 'game' to legitimize their activity. They push responsibility onto the client and point to crude measures of success as justification for adopting the information fantasies of scientism. But they are faulty arguments. They are faulty because they engage in the further fantasy that action can be amoral and specifically that designing an information system can be amoral. Collectively, the scientistic fantasies of information picture the design of an information system as a purely technical act. Clearly, this is not the case.

Designing an information system is a moral problem because it puts one party, the system designer, in the position of imposing an order on the world of another. No matter who pays for it or how the decision is made, the designer's responsibility for imposing an order on the world cannot be escaped. The modern world is yearning for a technologically based order. The promise of a perfectly controlled information order is the overarching fantasy of the information age. But this does not free us as professionals from an ethical responsibility for critically analysing the societal fantasies in which we are enmeshed. The fact that managements yearn for the services of the technocrats which system designers have become is beside the point.

I argue that as professionals, it is our ethical responsibility to reject the scientism of these information fantasies. These fantasies should be rejected not simply because they are erroneous, as we have shown them to be. Nor should they be rejected because they result in organizations that are monotonous, unchallenging, white-collar sweat shops, which they do. They should not even be rejected simply because they fail to respect the dignity of the individual worker. They should be rejected because they destroy the possibility of the type of human community that information system professionals are responsible for upholding. They should be rejected because they deny the fundamental importance of interpersonal dialogue and the search for meaning through language in a human community.

In casting aside these fantasies the systems professional must discard the entified images they legitimize. In the social world, problems do not exist as objects, decisions do not exist as objects, problem spaces do not exist as objects, power does not exist as an object, perfect information does not exist as an object, and intelligence does not exist, except as it is embodied in a human being. Information is not a resource to be stockpiled as one more factor of production. It is meaning, and can only be achieved through dialogue in a human community. Information is not a commodity. It is a skilled human accomplishment (Giddens, 1979).

What exists in the social world and what must be taken seriously by information systems professionals is the face-to-face interaction of human beings. An organization is face-to-face interaction. Problems in organizations are found in face-to-face interaction. Solutions, intelligence, power and the only possibilities for perfection in organizations are all found in the face-to-face interaction of organizational actors. The only information system designs which are morally acceptable are those which put a primary emphasis on improving the possibilities for face-to-face interaction within the organization — those which take dialogue, interpretation and an individual's search for meaning as sacred.

The logic of an organization is a lived logic. The contradictions of an organization are lived contradictions. Any fantasies which present disembodied, ahistoric images of information divert us from a search for the lived experience of organizational members and must be rejected. Each information system design must have the quality of organizational dialogue and the quality of each individual's hermeneutic search for meaning as its ethical standard of success.

NOTES

[1] The argument presented here is developed from an earlier version that was first presented as 'Fantasies of Information', Boland (1986).
[2] The brief metaphorical analysis offered here is a small effort to follow a program of understanding metaphorical structuring proposed by Lakoff and Johnson (1980).

[3] I use the term entify, even though it is rare, to emphasize the way we metaphorically turn decisions and information into a three-dimensional object. We go beyond reification, which is treating an abstraction as a real thing, and we metaphorically locate, move and reconfigure decisons and information as entities in a 'problem space'. We then create a technology for observing, touching, shaping and designing these entities.

[4] See in particular his discussion of the Marshall Plan and the important role that naming it as a type of situation plays in defining the type of decision problem it could become (Simon, 1981, pp. 164–166).

REFERENCES

Berger, P. L., and Luckman, T. (1967) *The Social Construction of Reality: A Treatise in the Sociology of Knowledge*, Anchor, Garden City, NJ.

Bernstein, R. J. (1976) *The Restructuring of Social and Political Theory*, University of Pennsylvania Press, Philadelphia.

Bettelheim, B. (1977) *The Uses of Enchantment*, Random House, New York.

Blumer, H. (1969) *Symbolic Interactionism, Perspective and Methods*, Prentice-Hall, Englewood Cliffs NJ.

Boland, R. J. (1979) 'Control, Causality and Information System Requirements', *Accounting Organization and Society*, **4**, 259–272.

Boland, R. J. (1984) Sense-making of Accounting Data as a Technique of Organizational Diagnosis', *Management Science*, **30**, July, 868–882.

Boland, R. J. (1985) 'Phenomenology: A Preferred Approach to Research on Information Systems', in *Research Methods in Information Systems*, E. Mumford *et al.* (Ed.), North Holland, Amsterdam.

Boland, R. J. (1986) 'Fantasies of Information', in *Advances in Public Interest Accounting*, Vol. 1, N. Neimark, B. Merino, and A. Tinker (Eds.), JAI Press, Greenwich, pp. 49–65.

Boulding, K. E. (1956) *The Image*, University of Michigan Press, Ann Arbor.

Demski, J. (1980) *Information Analysis*, 2nd Edn., Addison-Wesley, Reading, MA.

Gadamer, H. G. (1976) *Philosophical Hermeneutics*, University of California, Berkely, CA.

Gadamer, H. G. (1984) *Truth and Method*, Crossroads, New York.

Galbraith, J. (1977) *Organization Design*, Addison-Wesley, Reading, MA.

Geertz, C. (1973) *The Interpretation of Cultures*, Basic Books, New York.

Giddens, A. (1979) *Central Problems in Social Theory*, University of California Press, Berkely, CA.

Koestler, A. (1964) *The Act of Creation*, Macmillan, New York.

Lakoff, G. and Johnson, M. (1980) *Metaphors We Live By*, University of Chicago Press, Chicago.

Machiavelli, N. (1984) *The Prince*, P. E. Bondanells and M. Musa (trans.), Oxford University Press, London.

Pettigrew, A. (1973) *The Politics of Organizational Decision Making*, Tavistock, London.

Pfeffer, J., and Salancik, G. R. (1978) *The External Control of Organizations*, Harper & Row, New York.

Schoderbek, C. G., Schoderbek, P. P., and Kefalas, A. G. (1980) *Management Systems*, BPI, Dallas, Texas.

Schutz, A. (1967) *The Phenomenology of the Social World*, Northwestern University Press, Evanston, IL.

Simon, H. A. (1977) *Administrative Behavior*, Macmillan, New York.

Simon, H. A. (1977) *The New Science of Management Decision*, Prentice-Hall, Englewood Cliffs, NJ.

Simon, H. A. (1981) *The Sciences of the Artificial*, 2nd Edn., MIT Press, Cambridge, MA.

Tricker, R. I., and Boland, R. J. (1982) *Management Information and Control Systems*, John Wiley, Chichester.

Weick, K. (1979) *The Social Psychology of Organizing*, 2nd Edn., Addison-Wesley, Reading, MA.

Wittgenstein, L. (1974) *Philosophical Investigations*, Basil Blackwell, Oxford.

AUTHOR INDEX

Abend, N. A. 334
Ackoff, R. 99, 147, 282, 350
Ackoff, R. A. 94, 96
Ackoff, R. L. 16, 255, 256
Adams, C. R. 210, 213, 216
Addis, T. R. 95
Aiken, M. 234, 235, 236, 240, 241
Airenti, G. 265
Albrecht, G. 332, 355
Alchian, A. A. 259, 271
Aldrich, H. 231, 232, 239, 241
Alexander, C. 82, 95, 98
Allen, T. J. 186, 236
Allen, W. R. 259
Allison, G. 312, 315, 319, 356
Alloway, R. M. 113
Alter, S. 230
Alvarez, R. 298
Anderson, J. 137, 155
ANSI-X3-SPARC 49
Anthony, R. N. 162
Apple, L. E. 227, 233, 244
Archer, L. B. 94, 102, 103
Argyris, C. 175, 185, 194, 269, 270
Arrow, K. L. 257
Astley, W. G. 18
Attewell, P. 24, 193, 194, 205, 352
Austin Henderson, D., Jr. 263

Bailey, J. W. 117, 122
Baldridge, J. V. 235, 240
Baligh, H. H. 268
Banbury, J. 94, 190
Bar-Hillel, Y. 75
Bariff, M. 16, 23
Bariff, M. L. 193
Barnard, C. I. 271
Barnett, H. 237
Barney, J. B. 197

Barrett, S. 197
Barth, F. 271
Bartol, K. M. 123, 125
Basili, V. R. 117, 118, 122, 123, 124
Bazjanac, V. 94
Bean, A. S. 235, 236
Beane, J. 118
Beath, C. M. 196, 197, 264, 267, 269
Becker, H. S. 322, 357
Becker, M. H. 234, 236, 241
Behrens, C. A. 127
Bell, D. 278
Bemelmans, T. H. 27
Benbasat, I. 122, 170, 209, 240
Benjamin, R. I. 57, 159
Berger, P. L. 7, 364
Bernstein, R. J. 364
Bettelheim, B. 365
Bikson, T. K. 187
Billings, R. S. 223
Bjerknes, G. 286, 298
Bjorn-Andersen, N. 193, 296
Black, G. 237
Blandin, J. S. 238
Blau, P. M. 191
Blumer, H. 364
Blumethal, S. C. 21
Bodker, S. 292
Boehm, B. W. 12, 113, 116, 117, 120, 121, 126, 127
Boise, W. B. 236
Boland, R. J., Jr. 4, 14, 16, 18, 20, 22, 27, 31, 35, 36, 76, 200, 210, 214, 215, 216, 229, 267, 364, 371, 372, 377
Bostrom, R. P. 238, 290
Boulding, K. 277
Boulding, K. E. 367
Boynton, A. C. 167
Bracchi, G. 34

381

L.-Brault